Collection «Do & Understand»
Graziel Press

CREATE YOUR OWN 3D GAMES LIKE PROS

With Blender Game Engine

I dedicate this book to my father, Ernest, who has taught me that you must now enjoy life and never postpone your dreams, otherwise they'll never happen. I remember those long nights where we copied program lines together, without really understanding their meaning. Then the day came when I realized I could create. He was a good man, hardworking, inquisitive and clever with his hands. *You wanted to travel and explore the world... I hope that wherever you are, you can paint the world with the largest color palette.*

And I would also like to dedicate this book to you, readers, with the secret hope that this book inspires you beyond theory. Everyone has a story to tell. I rely on you for telling yours through a game and giving your family, friends and, why not, whole world through the Internet, a chance to play it. This potential is in you. The game is probably the best way to transmit knowledge, employ it wisely.

And never forget that *«Nothing great in the world has ever been accomplished without passion»* (Hegel)

Greg G.d.B.

Copyright Graziel Press – Legal depot: december 2015
ISBN: 979-10-93846-01-9

Graziel Press
9, chemin des Barroutiers
81300 Graulhet
France
Phone: 33 952 054 015
Fax: 33 957 054 015
RCS: Castres B 801 370 800

email: infos@graziel.com
website: www.graziel.com

Author: Gregory GOSSELLIN DE BENICOURT
Collection «Do & Understand»

For the first edition of this book

Press :

«More than a book, the author developed a method based on martial arts: to understand, you should repeat a gesture until it was perfect.» (AFJV, Association Française pour le Jeu Vidéo)

«It'll be your reference book on the Blender game Engine thanks to its recipes step by step» (Web site developpez.com)

«The author has developed a new approach to educate children and young peoples to video-game creation. By teaching them the necessary techniques for this job, players can see differently their games, giving way to a creative approach. » (Programmez)

Feedback from readers :

«Perfect for beginners like me. I was first surprised by the quality of the content, the text was written in a smart and effective way […]. A book that I further recommend to Blender users to learn some subtleties» (Jeremy H.)

«I am really pleased to have this book. Computer graphics designer by profession, I use 3DSMax for many years and I had listen good things about Blender. But I did not known that we could create some games or interactive demonstrations with it! I did not want to program, but the visual editor is pleasant. I learned plenty about video games creation, I recommend it to beginners and also to passionate» (Aurélie P.)

«It's very empowering. You can't imagine how much I dreamt about this book in my childhood» (Pierre A.)

«I have always been intrigued by the way the games are made until this book, I thought it takes a real genius to produce a game. Actually, it's not the case – I don't understand why it has taken so long for an author to write a book where we can find everything I need to create a game. Thanks for this wonderful book, a revelation and a Bible for video game creation!» (Sébastien R.)

«A book with a content which cover the subject beyond my expectations, far beyond. Saying that it's excellent is a euphemism... it's a must-reading! Thanks to the author for this jewel which proposes turnkey functionalities and a pragmatic approach.» (Christian B.)

Thanks to the others whose we don't reproduce the feedback but we was been enormously touched.

Table of contents

I - FOREWORD

Reserved, for a long time, to a small circle of enthusiast developers, 3D is not yet commonly used by independent video games development studios (the Indies). And it's for a good reason: **the entrance ticket is relatively high**. Create a 3D game requires a lot of knowledge because it's a multidisciplinary domain. In addition, software are mostly overpriced and development times are much longer than for 2D games.

With this book, we want you to discover this vast field, with an introduction to the creation of several types of games, arcade games such as "platform" for FPS (First-Person Shooter), through adventure games or racing cars. We realize that it's difficult for a newbie to make his first game, but we hope we'll give him the motivation to increase one's knowledge with many tutorials and videos web-based. Before being a book on Blender, this is primarily a book about video games creation.

Ultimately, what better use of a computer can we expect that the creation of his own universe and the possibility to see it live and grow? Limited only by imagination...

Game is entertainment, but it's also a great tool for learning. The "Serious Games" and edutainment games have a great future ahead of them.

The author discovered the computer through the Amstrad CPC 464 and a book "Adventure Game Writers Handbook for CPC" written by Jörg Walkowiak. For that reason, his first book is dedicated to this topic. Passionate about game development and player, he wanted to pay tribute to all those games that have revolutionized the field. With this book, the author hoped that young people can find more enjoyment in creating games than playing them. Computer engineer by training, he has created two video games that have been published in France, Germany and the United States. He hosts a **blog** on video game creation, with a particular attention to game engines and 3D graphics: www.benicourt.com.

All scripts offered in this book can be freely used in your projects whether educational or commercial respecting licenses when limitations are indicated. A mention of the author and this book would be **greatly appreciated**.

Acknowledgments

Firstly, many thanks to Ton Roosendaal for creating the finest tool for modeling and 3D animation, and offering it to the community.

Thanks to **Alexandre Laurent**, in charge of the «2D/3D/Games» section of «developpez.com», for its corrections and suggestions.

Thank you to Jörg Walkowiak for enchanted my childhood with the book "Adventure Game Writers Handbook for CPC" published by Data Becker / Micro Application.

Thank you to the community of **BlenderArtists.org** (Monster, Agoose77, Mobious, HG1, BluePrintRandom, Kheetor, Solarlune, Raco, and all others) for their help, their imagination and passion shared on these forums. And to the Francophone community **Blenderclan**.

Thank you to artists who have generously shared their creations on **BlendSwap.com** and without whom this book would not been able to go so far in creating different projects.

Also thank you to **Clark Thames** and his excellent **tutorialsforblender3d.com** site that has served me as a basis for racing cars project.

Thank you to **Dorian** and **Usul** for their chronic "Merci Dorian" on **jeuxvideo.com**

Thank you Marc Lacombe, aka **Marcus** for his show «Retro Game One». I always look with much happiness.

And finally, I would particularly like to thank my wife, without whom this book would never have been possible, for her support, her patience, proofreading, and for accepting my need to write about a subject where the passion is stronger than economic interest.

Collection «Do & Understand»

Today, information travels at the speed of light in all directions. The Internet has opened a new path to knowledge transfer. Will books become one day obsolete? Yes, probably, in their "paper" form that makes them static, unlike e-books. However, it's always essential to find information focused on a support with a didactic approach. So, whatever its form, the book still has a bright future ahead of him.

We love books and technologies, that's why we have created this collection, **a wealth of information**. Books of this collection are organized in this way: projects, recipes to supplement these, and a set of summary sheets for beginners and those wishing to improve their knowledge.

The updates of these books will be regular so that you can find information always updated. We count on your participation to improve our work, edition after edition, while respecting the principle that "*perfection is reached, not when there's nothing more to add, but when there's nothing more to remove*».

You'll find on the website www.graziel.com all the books of the collection, but also additional resources to improve your reading. You can also contact us to suggest improvements for the next edition of this book.

The editor, Graziella Haution

WHAT IS THE BLENDER GAME ENGINE ?

Blender is a **free** and **open source** software for modeling, animation and 3D rendering. It's available in many languages and on many platforms including Microsoft **Windows**, **Linux** and **OSX**.

Thanks to "Blender Game Engine" (BGE), Blender can be used as a game engine. It manages the game logic, i.e. the ability to program the interactions between entities in the game, and without having to align a single line of code.

All the game logic can thus be "programmed" graphically without having to go through lines of code. The graphical bricks system is the heart of BGE, but it's also possible to extend its functions by using python scripts.

With the Bullet physics engine, BGE handles collisions between objects, gravity and other forces.

It also includes the management of sounds in a 3D environment. BGE is not exclusively for the video game world. It allows technical demonstrations (Tech Demos), realtime applications such as simulations, interactive drawings, virtual reality, robotics, etc..

A few figures: Blender, it's more than 4 million downloads per year. The larger community, "BlenderArtists", has more than 2.7 million posts about 300,000 discussions. There are regularly more than 1,100 users connected to the forum (with a max of 6650) and the number of users exceeds 200,000.
Blender clan is the largest Francophone community: it's more than 13,000 members, nearly 500,000 posts in 40,000 subjects. There are regularly more than 50 users online. On Facebook, nearly 100,000 people like this software.

Little story: In 1988, Ton Roosendaal co-founded the Dutch animation studio NeoGeo, it quickly becomes one of the leading animation companies in Europe. It's under NeoGeo that Blender development begins, first as a tool used internally and distributed free through the company NaN (Not a Number), while other tools cost a fortune. In late 2002, the "Blender Foundation" (nonprofit organization) bought the software from NaN and distributed it under the General Public License (GNU GPL). Acquisition is done through a call to donate 100 K€ was obtained from Blender users in only 7 weeks. Which goes to show crowd funding is not a novelty*!*

WHY NOT DEVELOP DIRECTLY?

Because you need to develop your own game engine before devoting to the development of the game.

To "code" your own 3D Game Engine, you must:
1. **Develop a 3D renderer**: choose between **OpenGL** (or Vulkan) and **DirectX** to take advantage of hardware accelerated graphics cards. In all cases, It would be best to use the shaders, which increase the process but allows some beautiful effects and better optimizations. This requires a good knowledge of mathematics, matrix calculus, quaternions. After a few months, the engine will be able to **load meshes** (modeled with a modeler like Blender, Maya or 3DS Max) and it remains to develop space partitioning routines and animation
2. **Develop the user interface** (like keyboard, mouse and joystick), the display of widgets (graphical elements such as buttons, check-boxes, etc)
3. Develop or interface with a **physics engine** to handle at least the gravity and collisions. A **particle**

system would be interesting too (effect of fire, explosion, water, etc...)

4. Develop or interface with a **sound library**, which can handle sounds in 3D Space
5. Develop some **Artificial Intelligence functions** ("Path Finding" to move a character from one point to another, etc...)

After all these efforts, you'll still be far from being able to match the **Blender Game Engine**!

WHAT ARE THE ALTERNATIVES TO BGE?

Game engines can be classified into two categories:

- Those who don't present a game editor or particular tools and are more close to libraries (set of functions) of programming with useful functions for game development (engines like Panda 3D, Irrlicht, Crystal Space or a 3D rendering engine such as Ogre 3D). Irrlicht is equipped with Copper-Cube, a game editor very promising because he exports to WebGL / javascript and Flash.

- Those who present a game editor and possibly an integrated modeler as **Blender**. The Game Development Conference 2015 has announced great changes in the licenses of many professional Game Engines. Unity 5 is free (personal version) but not open source. **Unreal Engine** (Epic Games) is now free and open source since 4.7 («when you love something, make it free»). **Source 2** (Valve) will also be free for developers.

- And those, standard but not available for all studios (indies) because of the costs: **Id Tech** (Id Software), **CryEngine** (Crytech). However, in the end of march 2014, Crytech announced they open their kits to indies and other people with little subscription.

In any case, you can make a prototype of your game with BGE and make your choice later to deploy it with another game engine. **90% of work will be re-useable**.

Illustration 1: Yo Frankie ! Game produced by the Blender Institute in 2008. It takes more than 8 months of work to 10 graphic designer and Software engineer.

WHAT ARE THE BENEFITS OF BGE?

You can make a commercially viable game from resource modeling to final product, with or without programming. Thereupon, it's better to know Python to develop a game with BGE, but it's not indispensable. It's sufficient to use scripts in this book or another downloaded from the internet.

BGE is a good choice to learn programming a 3D game, to make a prototype or to make a game.

BGE is free, Open Source and in a constantly evolving. Using it's a challenge for the future: with the open source community, it could be more used and better than other game engines.

Games like «Yo Frankie !» (www.yofrankie.org) and «Sintel the Game» (www.sintelgame.org) are examples given by the Blender foundation about BGE capacities and reliability.

Illustration 2: Sintel The Game, Game produced by the Blender Institute in 2010

Some students of the Queensland University of Technology won a set of prices by creating the game «Primitives». Here is what the project manager said: «My name is Daniel Feltwellet, I am part of the Team Ugly Stick, an independent studio with students of the Queensland University of Technology. The beta version of the game Primitives is recently released, all the assets are made with Blender. Our animation team is a fervent follower of Blender and now, our university is moving all its projects from Maya to Blender!».

Primitives is a third person strategy game type «survival». It's based on an extraterrestrial world with various fauna and flora. The player manages a primitive tribe.

For further information http://bit.ly/1Nvl0Hy

COMPUTING PLATFORM FOR GAMES

With BGE, it's possible to create an executable file for platforms PC, Mac and Linux. However, it's not possible to make directly a game for Android, iOS or a hand-held gaming system (PS4, Xbox One).

Web:
Export to Web can be do by a Plug-in (**Burster**) only under Windows or Linux. For using it, go to (sheet #9).
Official Web Site: http://geta3d.com

Blend4web: (Illustration 3). It's a new open source framework which enables to display the Blender 3D scenes in interactive way on a web navigator, supporting sounds and Physique. The purpose is to display interactive presentation such as games on the Internet. The display is done directly in HTML5/WebGL, so it's not useful to download a plugging like Burster. It works on any platform with WebGL like mobile platforms (iPhone, Android, etc).
Blend4Web is not a porting from Blender Game Engine to WebGL – it has a different API in JavaScript. However, the team is working on its integration to BGE «Logic Editor».
Official website: http://blend4web.com

Illustration 3: Game made with Blend4web – tutorials available on: http://bit.ly/1yzlnqL

IPhone and Android: OpenGL ES

To port a software is to modify the source code to allow the operating software on other platforms. The source code is the program's root.
BlenderPlayer for OpenGL ES 2.0 represents an initial response to port BGE on Android and iOS.

For more information: http://tinyurl.com/n4n9okp

iOS and Android: GameKit

An exciting project: the GameKit (Illustration 4). It's an alternative game engine to Blender's internal game engine (BGE). GameKit can be added to Blender as an Addon and so, you can alternatively use DirectX (only on Windows) and OpenGL.

Gamekit enables logic bricks. 3D Rendering engine **Ogre** (previously Crystal Space), Bullet and OpenAL are used for sound. Scripts in **pythons are not yet supported**, it's then necessary to perform a conversion to Lua language. It's a good project to follow if you want to develop for mobile devices.

Site: https://code.google.com/p/gamekit/ - Download the file matching the corresponding environment, decompress the contents and then, move files which are in the directory «BlenderAddon» in the directory «scripts/addons» of Blender. In user's preferences (Ctrl+Alt+U), Tab «Addons»: activate «Game Engine: GameKit Engine».

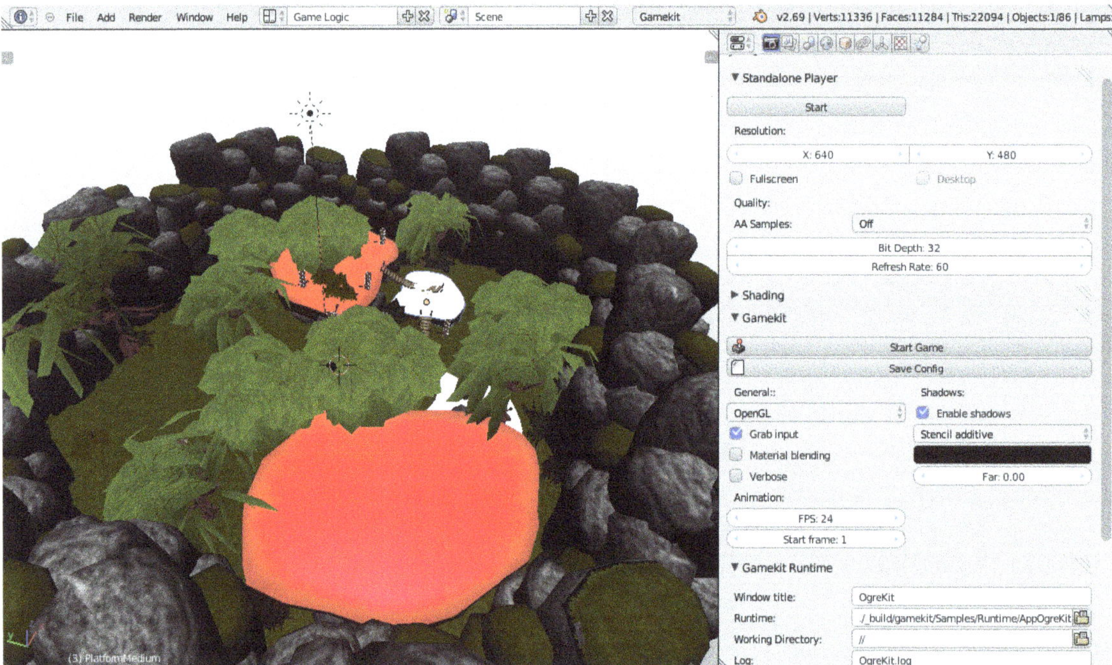

Illustration 4: «GameKit» under DirectX and OpenGL, fully integrated into Blender in the form of an Addon

Game Consoles (Wii, PS4, Xbox One):

There's nothing today to export for game consoles. You could be the person that will be undertaking the work. However, BGE allows for a rapid development of a prototype. All prototypes can be exported to others engines such as Unreal Engine or Unity.

STUFF YOU SHOULD KNOW BEFORE BEGINNING

Very quickly, you should be able to developing a 3D game by following recipes developed in this book.

A preliminary knowledge of Blender and the language Python would allow you however to appropriate more the conception of your game.

If you already know Blender and have knowledge in games development, you can go directly to recipes.

Otherwise, I deeply recommend you to consult the sheet at the end of the book which should allow you an accelerated upgrade.

According to your level and your method of learning, we advise you to do a training course or to complete your readings by others in the field of modeling with Blender.

IS IT POSSIBLE TO CREATE A 3D VIDEO GAME ALONE?

YES, you can! (it sounds strangely now). Some 3D games were developed by one or two people.

Go to www.deadcyborg.com. Visually, the product is very accomplished but it has a simple Gameplay. "Dead Cyborg" is an adventure game situated in a post-apocalyptic universe in which you explore the levels in subjective view and where you have to solve enigma to move forward.

The game was developed with Blender Game Engine and you can download it free of charge.

Illustration 5: Free game Dead Cyborg d'Endre Barath, a small donation would be welcome: www.deadcyborg.com

"Minecraft" was also introduced by a single person, Markus Persson, more known under the pseudonym of Notch by the community. Naturally, the product evolved a lot because Notch was equipped with a big team further to the success of the sales of its game in beta version.

It's a modulation of our previous answer: it's possible with **setting realistic goals**. No, you'll never be able to create a game such as "World of Warcraft" alone for example. It's more than a game, and it's a very huge virtual world with a lot of game assets.

Create a game needs important resources: a scenario, design art, modeling, animation, sounds, musics, voices, programming, etc.!

The more the world you wish to develop is vast, the more it's necessary for you to obtain some help.

Fortunately, there are numerous external resources (paying or not) which can be integrated into your game. There are numerous libraries of sounds, models 3D, textures.

It's also possible to return easily in touch with independents to realize such model or such art design (see **sheet #10**).

Games developed in this book remain accessible for only one person or a small team. It's a question of motivation, perseverance and competence. Also note that more and more games pass by crowd-funding allowing them to have consequent team.

Illustration 6: **Krum**, RPG made with BGE – Official Web Site: www.krum-game.com

In a cartoonish style, «**KRUM,** Edge Of Darkness» is a third person role playing game which uses BGE as game engine. All the assets were made with Blender. Its author, Orlin Doutskinov, has worked alone on this game during 5 years and try a crow-funding campaign at the end of 2014 on Indiegogo. It was a failure (funded at 6% of the 5000$ asked), but the author will continue. Be patient!

Is it possible to create a game alone **at any age**? The author of the game « **Z-Virus** », Fajrul Falakh, has an interesting hobby: video game creation. Indonesian, he was 15 when he created Z-Virus 2 and took 1 year to learn Blender.

A little more information about this game: http://bit.ly/1M4y0SO

From the first edition of this book, several teenagers studied it alone or with one of their parents, on video game projects. So there's no age to begin.

WHERE TO BEGIN?

Best is probably to begin by consulting some "making of" of games developed by independents. **«Post-mortem»** are also very rewarding: what has worked, what was badly thought from the beginning?

You'll find a mine of information at this address: http://tinyurl.com/6nnkxp3

It's also advised to practice sometimes the "modding":

Games like "Skyrim", "Starcraft" or "Unreal Tournament 3" propose a complete editor to create new cards and even new rules of set.

It's a very fast way of entering the universe of the game conception.

There are numerous games developed with BGE what you can download with sources. We advise you to begin there: study them, modify them.

You have a " game concept ", you need to begin by drafting a small document which details the main ideas: the gameplay, the environment, the main history, the game interface, the target, etc.

Others prefer the "storyboard" approach, by drafting a kind of small comic strip. From there you can develop your "Game Concept".

If you are alone and have time to mature your project according to the development, you can pass this chapter.

Otherwise, you have a «dead line», to define the time for the development of your game, you have to write a **«Game Design»** document. That resumes the elements of "Game Concept" by detailing at the most all the aspects. If your game has 10 levels, you have to describe them in detail, most possible here. All the characters, the monsters, the objects, the landscapes everything must be described in detail, with at least a sketch of every element or an approaching image taken on Web.

The scenario must be complete, the dialogues written, indications for the sound and bright atmospheres... It's a very big creative phase, for a "small game". But it's also probably the most interesting part where the main problem is not to find ideas, but not having too much ideas!

Then, it'll be necessary to go a little more into the technical aspects and to draft "technical design".

If you're using BGE, you'll have to describe all the game logic in the "logic bricks" of BGE, with a description of the necessary scripts (main algorithms).

We often use a python script when we don't find what we need in bricks, or sometimes for optimization.

The following stage consists in defining how long you'll need to put all this ready. You need to listing in a picture all the necessary tasks, by cutting them as much as possible to reach an elementary level («divide and conquer»). You can separate the technical aspects tasks from the graphic, music, tasks, etc.

You'll need to know the time required to animate such or such character.

It's important, because it's from there that you'll have to make an important decision: to reduce the volume of the project? To find a team? To find funds for the development? It's not very probable that you can finish a project which asks 2 years of development alone, without an external funding. Studios indies try most of the time to limit themselves to projects for 6 months to 2 years, with a reduced team from 3 to 10 people. And most of the time, the development sets twice more time than planned and thus costs, twice as expensively!

The purpose is not, here, to discourage you, but to say you that we can make very nice 3D games, without leaving in a Hollywood project.

In other words: it's better to have a nice little one wooden house that the western wall of a lame cathedral. It's wiser to succeed a version "alpha" and to intend afterward to develop a more ambitious project by basing itself on this version.

You are decided, you are motivated, it's time to do it. It's the least creative, but enriching phase however on other plans. And when the game begins to take life, a new motivation appears.

Don't especially hesitate to make test your game by friends, see by Internet users, or to publish videos of gameplay to get feedback. You'll find lit advices, feedback of players and there, with a little luck, of which to boost your ego.

You are the architect of a world which existed only in your imagination and which begins to take life right before your eyes.

It's the sharing of this reality with others whom give rise to the creation of a new universe in the even unsuspected and unlimited possibilities. Sometimes, a character seems to exceed his own algorithm which defines its intelligence. Are you certain that's not the case?

«Adopt, Adapt, Improve» recommends the motto!

FROM 3D TO GAMES

3D is a three-dimensional representation of a scene on a 2D surface (screen).

This should not be confused with stereoscopic display which is also supported by Blender.

In 3D, one point have 3 position components: X, Y and Z. On Blender, Z is height (Up).

Axis are visible by default at the bottom left of the «3D View» window. The units used are arbitrary: meter, centimeter, inch, light years, …).

Each face of a cube (3D object) consists of 4 points (a square, a 2D object). The coordinates of the points can be as follows: (-1,-1), (-1,1), (1,1) and (1,-1) in space 2D.

In 3D, there's a height in addition. Then, a cube is a set of 6 faces, each face has 4 points.

Faces are polygons, but in gaming, we often use faces made by 3 (triangles) or 4 points (Quads). **Edges** are lines joining a point to another from a same face.

Major **transformations** in 3D applying in a point, an edge, a face, an object are:
- **Grab**: it's movement in space. We move the item.
- **Rotate**: from a point called «rotation center», do a circular motion corresponding to an angle. Simplest rotates are axial rotates: Turn the figure (frontal view) by 180° in relation to the Z axis to see it by a back view.
- **Scale**: to change the size of the object, either proportionally or solely based on a reference axis. A scale along the X axis of a cube is scale its (scale or reduce) along the X axis. A scale along an edge distorts the object by reduction or scalement only on a face.

A 3D object is is made up of **mesh**, I.e. a combination of points, edges and faces.

To each face (or all at once), it's possible to assign a **material.** Material gives to the 3D object its color and sets the influence of light. To each material, it's possible to assign one or more **textures** (pictures plated on sides to make it seem that's more complex (example: texture «brick» on a plane make it feels a brick wall).

Two or more textures can be layered on an object to do specific effects (natural shadows or imperfections).

Lamps light up the scene, there are various kinds of lamps:
- «point» (example: a candle),
- «sun»,
- «Spot» (example: a flashlight),
- «Hemi» (ex: albedo returned by floor on an object – axial and directional light).,
- «Area» (ex: neon or any surface which emits light).

Cameras allow the configuration of shooting like in physic world. 3D Cameras have the same characteristics as real cameras. Cameras can be configured to track a character or to fly over a scenery along a defined track in three dimensions, etc. It's an important part of animation.

Animation: Succession of images (Frames). When there's more than 25 pictures per second (Frame per Second, FpS) it feels like a fluid movement, eye can't see more frames per second. There is, however, controversy over the issue (30 FPS vs 60 FPS in Games).

An animated character is a 3D object with:
- **deformation «shape keys»** (like cartoons): a walk can be divided into 10 pictures, each picture is a part of the moving. It's possible to set 2 key frames and Blender will create intermediates steps with **morphing** (interpolation).
- Or deformations with **armature** (skeletal bones)

Blender has a physic engine (Bullet) capable of creating animations with use of gravity, collisions and other physics objects parameters.

A character is made up of many animations. For example, one for walking, one for crouching, one for raising the arm, etc. An **action** like shooting can be done along with running: to mix the animation «to run» with the animation «to raise the arm».

To animate a character when one key is pressed, the «**keyboard logic**» must be programmed.

So we use:
- a «sensor» brick - type «Keyboard»
- an «actuator» brick - type «Motion»
- an «actuator» - type «Action» to select the associated animation
- a «controller» «And» brick to connect everything

It's not complicated. It's also possible too to make a python script. Put another way, why make life any harder on yourself than it already is?

All game logic can be done with theses bricks: collect an item, enemy following the hero, open a door, etc. And when there's no function, obviously, it's possible to use a script (example: to eave some bullets scars on a wall).

RULES TO MODELING FOR A GAME

1 – «Lowpoly» Models

A game requires realtime display, therefore there must be at least 25 frames per second (Fps).

To limit the number of faces, we talk about Lowpoly Modeling (LPM).

For information:
- A «DOOM 3» character is made of between 2000 and 6000 polygons. A «WoW» character, less than 2000 polygons, a building between 1000 and 5000 polygons.
- A «Metal Gear Solid 2» hero, is made of 4000 polygons.
- A «Half-Life 2» character: 7500 polygons, a monster 3000 polygons.
- A current graphics card support a scene between 500.000 and 1 Million polygons – «Clipping», «LoD» and «continuous loading» allow to support more larger scenes (**recipe III.17**)

To know the number of faces for an object, select the object, go to «Edit Mode» and see at top right of the screen: the field «Fa:x-y» indicates the number of faces for the object (y) and the number of faces selected (x). Be careful, Blender count the number of faces, composed of 3 or 4 vertex. A realtime motor engine only displays triangles, so to have significant statistic, you must multiply by 2 the number of faces given by Blender.

Avoid Subsurf, stay in Lowpoly.

2 – Pay attention to materials

Textures and bump-map effects allow meshes to seem more detailed. Details are important for the atmosphere in the game. For texturing, UV Mapping is used by BGE.

Textures used are in theses formats: TGA, PNG and DDS.

Sizes should be: 128x128, 256x256, 512x512, 1024x1024, etc... (power of 2)

For more complex materials, use **shaders GLSL**

3 – Use Baking at the most

When it's possible, use Lightmaps, Ambient Occlusion and anything baked (precalculated) to relieve the graphic card and the processor.

Most special effects (flow simulation, particles systems, radiosity...) achievable with Blender are unusable in realtimer.... directly!

4 – Animations

To run under BGE, animations are recorded as **Actions**. Constraints on frames (IK Solver, Copy Rotation, etc) are not being fully covered by BGE, but you can use them for actions creation.

TO INSTALL BGE

Download and install Blender on PC: www.blender.org/download/

Windows 32 or 64 ? See on C:/. If there's a folder «Program Files» AND a folder «Program Files (x86)», it's Windows 64 bits, else it's a 32 bits.

Linux: frequently, there's already Blender. See package manager/installer.

Mac: download the correspondent version (Power PC or Intel). Mount the drive, open it and copy the program in the folder «Applications».

Problem ?
Go to http://wiki.blender.org/, section «installation».

NEW FEATURES SHIPPED WITH 2.7X VERSIONS

The major new release of the **2.70 version**, is the **LOD** support (Level Of Detail) to allow scene optimization, especially to display large landscapes. We'll use it in different projects and you'll find a recipe especially for this release (**recipe VII.10**).

It's possible too to import the PSD files generated by Photoshop for textures for example.

A new navigation mode allows movements in the scene like for a FPS (First Personal Shooter).

The **2.71 version** introduces the notion of «**deactivation**» of logic bricks to make tests and debugging easier without having to delete the links.

The **animations** benefit of **multithreading**, so, performances on moderns processors are better. The option «**Cast Only material option**» allows to have objects invisible casting shadows (Useful to make a game like «Contrast»).

The action layers are now virtually unlimited (32K and next 64K).

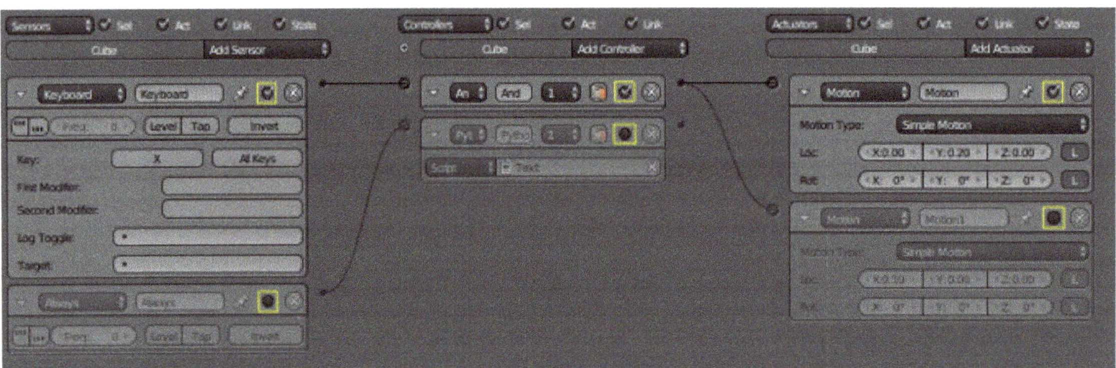

Illustration 7: Deactivating Logic Bricks

The **2.72 version** introduces a new **actuator «Mouse»** to do «MouseLook» effect. The sensor «Property» has new evaluation types and the actuator «Property» has changed. The actuator «Edit Object» (Track To) has a new menu to select the axis «Up/Track». The event «Mouse Over Any» of the sensor «Mouse» has new options (detection «Property/Material», «X-Ray»). And the API has changed to improve the debugging and the constraints management.

The **2.73 version** don't give improvements to Game Engine, but to the importation plugin for Collada files (3D format, standard XML), and to the motion tracking used in the recipe III.20.

The **2.74 version** allows to access to the first contact point of colliding from Python, and adds usability improvements. A new option "Lock Z Velocity" to avoid micro-jumping. The Python function makeScreenshot now supports writing the screenshot number to the created image's file name. The numbering replaces the last optional # in the provided filename (example: "//test-#" .blend).

The **2.75 version** adds a new hysteresis parameter for smoother transitions between LODs. Material and World mist attributes now support animation. Debug drawing of Sun Lamps shadow range. Improved collision masks and groups. Replication of rigid body joint constraints for group instances. Python API improvements with subclassing, new options and methods. Over 40 bug fixes.

The **2.76 version** allows to change camera Lens Shift during game. Python API improvements. Alpha Anti-Aliasing. Improved Game Publishing Add-on.

In the **2.77 version,** we'll find a new screenshot actuator (the python function still applies). The Max Jumps value (1 to 255) allows to set the maximum amount of jumps the character can make before it hits the ground.

For more information, check out regularly the development blog at this address: https://code.blender.org/

HOW TO READ THIS BOOK ?

Frequently, we use shortcuts for one action.

For example, to «add a cube», we use ⇧Shift+A → «Mesh» → «Cube». This replace: go to «3D View» window, click on «Add», select «Mesh» and click on «Cube».

⇧Shift+A = Press the ⇧Shift key and A key simultaneously.
«LMB» (Left Mouse Button): click with the left mouse button

(Right Mouse Button): click with the right mouse button.
When it's impossible (for example to parameter a material), we give the name of the window, the name of the tab, then the name of the panel, if there's zones in the tab, etc.

«Game Engine» is accessed by the «info» window with: «Blender Render», «**Blender Game**» and «Cycles Render». Select the second option (else for «baking»). If most functions are accessed in the same way under «Blender Render» and «Blender Game», some are accessed in only one mode.

Be careful to the **indentation of scripts in python** : 1 tabulation error can create a big difference !

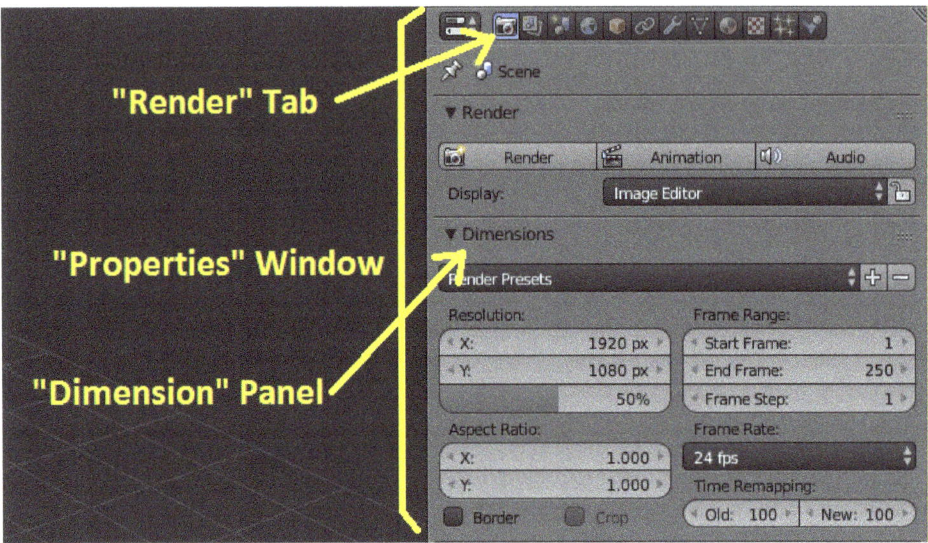

Illustration 8: Window, Tab et Panel

THE LAST WORD

Are you ready? You don't want to read 400 pages of theory on modeling, animations and programming... Good thing, this book was written for you.

I propose to get to the very heart of the matter. Your neurons will be severely tested, and if you are a beginner (creating game, 3D modeling, Blender, BGE), you'll often need to consult sheets at the end of this book.

Don't read the book like a novel, I can already tell you the end: you'll create your own game and share it with your amazed friends.

Let your imagination be your guide. If, there's a question, go to the sheets to find an answer.

You're now sick... with virus of 3D. You'll see all games with a new, more critical, eye: «How did they do that?», or «which A.I. script for this NPC (non player character)».

It's more fun to create a game than playing to the last blockbuster. You'll become the architect of a new World and you'll set the rules. These rules don't do everything: you'll be surprised to see unanticipated things !

In any case, I wish you an interesting reading! I hope that you'll enjoy reading this book as much as I enjoy writing it!

«Finally the purpose of a game is entertainment» (Monster)

II -   CREATE ANY TYPE OF GAME

Picture based from a scene made by **Dennis Haupt**:
http://www.blendswap.com/blends/view/67567

Armed with the recipes of the second part of this book, you can make any kind of game. However, especially if you're a beginner, It's better to study some matures projects. These projects will help you in your process of creating.

It's why we propose several **games projects:**

1. The First project is written to familiarize you with basic concepts in BGE, particularly programming with logic bricks. This is a little **labyrinth game.** If you tilt the plane, the ball rolls and the aim of the game is to roll it, to guide it through the labyrinth to the exit, whilst care it taken to avoid letting the ball falls into the holes.

2. The Second project is **a platform game** where the character, a squirrel, runs and jumps to collect some apricots, throws nuts on other critters and tackles the obstacles to the exit. Attention: it's a Flying Squirrel ! Here, we'll particularly see the set modeling and the various actions. To simplify the process of creating, we use some assets from «Yo Frankie» from Blender foundation.

3. The Third project is a **car race simulation** on Mars. We'll see how to create a broad landscape and an infernal racetrack, to set the car suspensions and to play until one or more players. This is an opportunity to learn python scripting.

4. The Fourth project serves to create an «unlimited» landscape generated from «3D tiles» with the advanced system Level of Detail (LoD) in the 2,70 version of Blender, for a **flight simulator**. You'll be able to make a space combat simulator with its physic and mutual interactions.

5. The Fifth project shows you how to build a **Minecraft clone**. The basis for Procedural generation and methods to dig or to add elements are given.

6. The Sixth project is a **First-Person Shooter (FPS)** in a FarCry atmosphere, on island with giant spiders. Armed with a rifle, the character must join a hut in the center of the island. He must survive. We'll learn how to model a land, add randomly objects to create realistic maps. This project allows you to learn how to model wildness scenes. It's easy: you don't have to animate the character !

7. The Seventh project is a **Third-Person Shooter (TPS)** like Tomb Raider. This project is based on camera movement, character animation and archery. We'll learn how to use a Motion Capture database to give to your character some complex movements and how to make movements sequences.

Other types of games are approached, like adventures games or Internet games like the Massively Multi-player Online (MMO).

After the first project, you can continue with the project you want. However, to see all aspects of game creation, you have to learn and test all the projects.

II.1.   PROJECT #1: INITIATION

Gameplay: one of the easiest games to learn, how to make a labyrinth: a ball, holes and an exit. The board must be titled, so the ball avoid holes and reach the exit.

Step 1: Main Elements modeling for the game

This step requires a basic knowledge of modeling (sheet #4 at the end of this book).

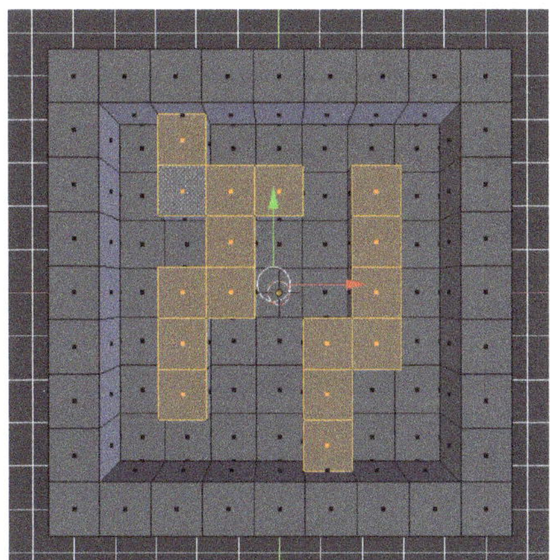
Illustration 9: Modeling the Labyrinth board

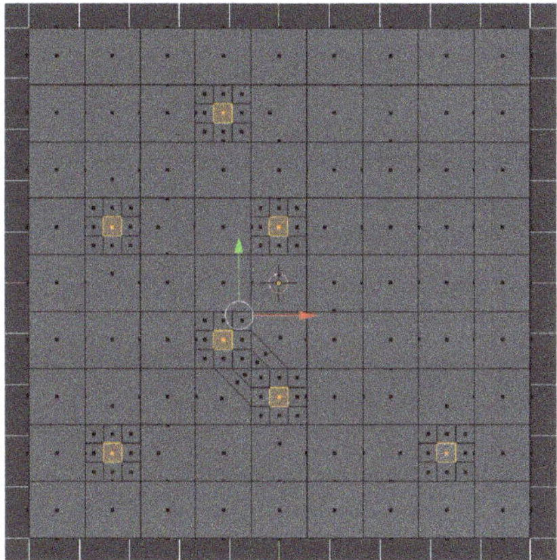
Illustration 10: Selection of boxes for being holes

1. Add a plane (Shift+A → «Mesh» → «Plane»). Name it «laby». Scale by 5 («S 5»). Go to «Edit Mode» (Tab) and Subdivide 8 times («W» → «Subdivide»)

2. Top View («7»). Select the boxes (in Face mode) cf. Illustration 9, extrude one unit by box («E 1»). Ditto for the edge of the board but with 2 units extrude («E 2»)

3. Select boxes with hole (Illustration 10) in face mode. Subdivide them 2 times. Select news boxes in the center and remove faces («x»)

4. Stay in «Edit Mode». «Properties» Window, «Material» Tab, add a new Material («+»). Name it «Standard». Choose a diffuse color «brown». Add a second Material. Name it «Arrival» and choose a «diffuse» color green. Select the big box at the bottom right, to the left of the hole, and only this one, then click on the «Assign» button of «Material» Tab to assign this color to this box. This Material is a test for detecting if ball is at the arrival.

5. Select the box at the top left «Space» → «Snap cursor to Selected». Go to «Object Mode» to add an object distinct of the first one.

6. Add a sphere (Shift+A → «Mesh» → «UVSphere»). Name it «Player». Resize x 0.15 («S 0.15»). Add a new Material with diffuse color blue. Move it from Z+0.5 («G Z 0.5») to raise the player.

7. In «info» window, make sure to be in «Game Engine» mode and in the «Physics» Tab of the «Properties» window, select «Type»: «Dynamic».

8. «Space» → «Snap cursor to center». Add a lamp (Shift+A → «Lamp») with «point» type. Move Z+5 («G Z 5»).

9. Test the level (P). If all is according to plan: the ball drop onto the plate.

Step 2: Gameplay Programming

This step requires a basic knowledge of programming with logic bricks (sheet #5 at the end of this book).

1. Select the board (object «laby»), then open «Logic Editor»
2. Add a sensor with type «Keyboard», name it «KeyUp» and select the key «↑».
3. Add an actuator with type «Motion», name it «LabyUP». «Rot» «X»: -1 . Connect the sensor and the actuator with an «AND» controller.
4. Repeat the operation for key «↓» («KeyDown», «Rot» «X»: 1), the key «←» («KeyLeft», «Rot» «Y»: -1) and the key «→» («KeyRight», «Rot» «Y»: 1) – you get the same configuration as Illustration 11.

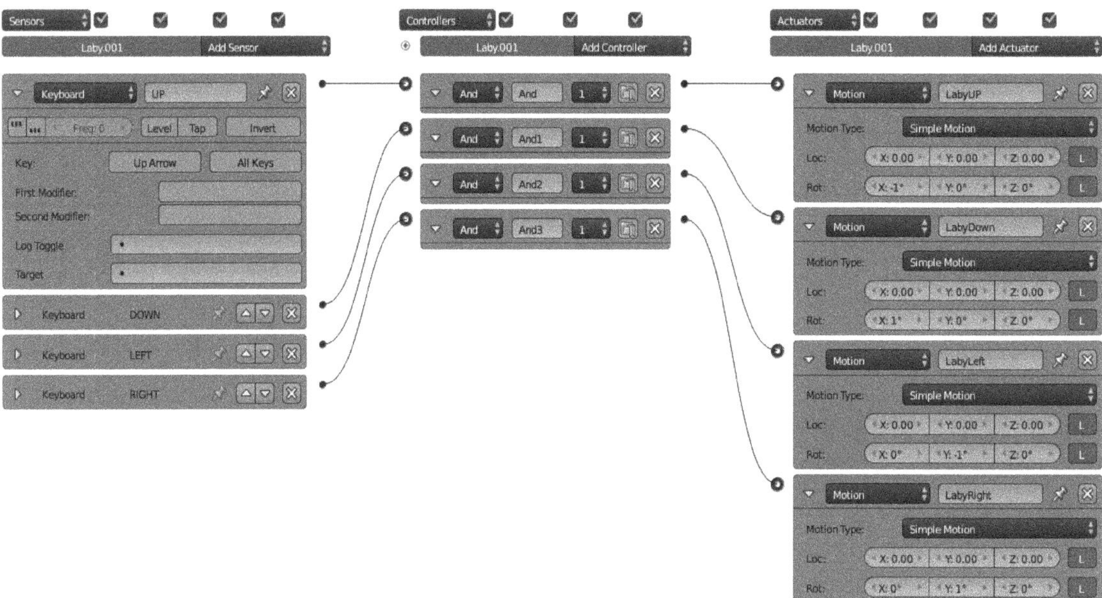

Illustration 11: «Logic Editor» view of Labyrinth gameplay (simple version)

5. Test the level (P). With the keys, we can move the board and the ball along the inclined plan of the board. We can move it to the green zone or feel it in a hole.

To prevent ground adhesion of the ball, and too much friction, go to the «Properties» window, «Physics» Tab, and set «Anisotropic friction» with X,Y and Z to 0.

Step 3: Game won?

Use a vertical ray («Ray» sensor) joined to the ball to detect the presence of a green object under the ball. The sensor must be joined to an «exit» box. This box was in the labyrinth but you must do modifications on it for the sensor functioning. The box must be separated from the labyrinth.

1. In «info» window, change the current scene name into «Game»
2. Add a new scene by copying only «settings» and name it «Win»
3. Add a camera and go to camera mode («0»). Add a text: «You Win !!!» at the center of the camera view (cf. recipe VI.7)
4. Go to scene «Game» and select the ball (object «Player»), then go to «Logic Editor»

5. Add a sensor «Ray» «Ray Type»: «Material» and select «Arrival» Material. «Axis»: «-Z axis» (direction: down). «Range»: 0.5.

6. Add an actuator with type «scene». Mode «add Overlay Scene» to display this message above the game scene. Select the «Win» scene.

7. Add a second actuator «scene». Mode: «suspend scene» to freeze the game. And Select the «Game» scene.

8. Link the sensor and these 2 actuators.

9. Test the level (P)

Step 4: Game over?

Alternative method to play with python. We use 2 variables: one to display the ball Z position and the other to detect when the ball is outside the board.

1. Open a script window and create a new text file :«verifyPos.py». Copy the script below.

2. «info» window, Menu «Game» → select «Show Debug Properties» to see all properties («i» selected in «Logic Editor») on the screen since execution.

3. Select the ball (object «Player»). Go to «Logic Editor»

4. Add a property «posz» with «Float» type, check «i» (information Debug).

5. Add another property «out» with «boolean» type, leave this checkbox unchecked (=false) and check «i» too.

6. Add a sensor «Always». Check «Activate True Level Triggering» and Freq: 50 (= verify every 50 frames).

7. Add a controller «Python» and Select the «verifyPos.py» script. Link the sensor and the controller

8. Test the level (P). The ball Z position can be seen on the screen. To verify if the game is lost, test the «out» variable.

9. Add a new «Lose» scene by copying it («full copy») from «Win». Modify the text with «You Lose !»

10. Select the ball (object «Player»). Go to «Logic Editor»

11. Add a sensor «Property». Check «Activate True Level Triggering» and Freq: 50. «Evaluation type»: «equal». «Property»: Select «out». Value «true».

12. Add an actuator «scene». Mode «add Overlay Scene». Select the «Lose» scene.

13. Link the sensor and the actuator. Link also the sensor with the actuator which suspends the scene.

14. Test the level (P)

Script python «verifyPos.py»:

```python
import bge
cont = bge.logic.getCurrentController()
own = cont.owner
pos = own.position

own['posz'] = pos[2] #z
if pos[2] < -20:
    own['out'] = True
```

We use a «own» variable which recovers the object on which the script is applied: here, the player (object «player»). «Pos» is a vector with the object position. Pos[0] → x, Pos[1] → y and Pos[2] → z.

The property «posz» value can be read and written through own['posz']. This lets you print the z position on screen. The condition «if z < -20» serves to establish that the ball is fallen (Let's modify this value according to the size of the board. Indeed, when we turn the board, the edge of the board could move too low). If the ball is fallen, set True in «out» game property to display the «You Lose!» message by the Logic Editor.

Step 5: restart the game

1. Go to «Lose» scene and start the «Logic Editor».
2. Add a sensor «Keyboard» and assign the «R» key («Restart»).
3. Add a first actuator with «scene» type, name it «restart1». Mode: «remove scene». Select the «Game» scene.
4. Add a second actuator with «scene» type, name it «restart2». Mode: «remove scene». Select the «Lose» scene.
5. Add a third actuator with «scene» type, name it «restart3». Mode: «set scene». Select the «Game» scene.
6. Link the sensor and the 3 actuators.
7. Test the level (P)

Attention, the «restart» sequencing order is significant.
Actuators can be moved, and then the sequencing order is modified. To do that: reduce them, and 2 new icons appear (Move Up and Move Down).

Step 6: Improve the game

Here is a non-exhaustive list of improvements for practicing:

- Add over the ball a transparent plane (with «collision bound» with «Box» type) to avoid the situation where the ball go above the walls.
- When no key pressed («Keyboard» sensor, «All keys», check «inv»), make the board returning in the horizontal position.
- Improve the board with a Heightmap (recipe III.1) to generate a land with other than just boxes. It's quite possible to modify the plan in «Sculpt Mode».
- Add different materials to change the way the ball moves (like on water) (recipe III.12).
- Add a «Skybox» with playroom atmosphere (recipe II.3)
- Add lights (recipe III.22) and apply an «Ambient Occlusion» and Lightmaps (recipes VII.1 and VII.2)
- Add some animated backgrounds elements or some elements which are animated when the ball is close to them (recipes V.6, V.7 and V.11)
- Randomly, add obstacles (recipes III.15) and make them disappear by hitting. Similarly, for collect lives or time bonuses
- Limit the time available to win each level, and manage the score (recipe V.8)
- Place teleporters (recipe V.6) to go to hidden levels and collect bonuses.
- Create platforms taller than screen and redirect the camera depending on the ball moves (recipe V.4)
- Add a character (recipe IV) who runs over the ball (without any physical interaction with the set). Make it fall when the ball is too fast, stop the game, make it climb above it and, then resume the game.
- Add sounds and musics (it's more fun)
- Create a menu: Play, Pause, Replay, Save, Charge, Scores (recipes VI.1 and VI.3)
- Create galleries with mirrors to lose the player (recipe VII.6)
- Add some radiosity for a «Tron» effect (recipe VII.8)
- Add fire effects (recipe VII.18), smoky effect (recipe VII.19) and explosions (recipe VII.17) with board vibrations for more immersion.
- Plenty of levels for more lifetime. We can imagine when the character fall into a hole, he returns to the precedent level. It's the Towering Inferno.

- Manage difficulty settings with time, the number of obstacles, the number of lives... and even gravity ! (for «veterans», play this game on Jupiter!)

With all these improvements, you won't have this «hello world» game, made to learn «BGE». You have a full game you can share or distributes for kids and olders.

Step 7:«Pacman» Transformation

History: «Pac-Man» («Puck Man») is a video-game created by **Tōru Iwatani for** Namco, published in Japan on 22 may 1980. «Pac-Mania» developed by Namco in 1987 is a «Pacman» 3D adaptation.

Gameplay: The hero must eat some white «pacgums» by avoiding randomly moving bad ghosts.
- If he eats a red «pacgum», he becomes a ghost eater and these run away from him.
- If he eats a yellow «pacgum», the ghosts become hunters.
- To go to the next level, Pac-Man must eat all the white «pacgums».

What are the **differences** with «Labyrinth» game?
- We don't move the board but the ball (recipe V.5)
- There's enemies (recipe V.13)

These differences are practically the only ones in game development.

Possible improvements:
- Almost all improvements from «Labyrinth» game can be used. The ball rolling can be used to add «flipper» effects (game «Sonic»).
- Use different views (FPS for «Doom» style, camera which follow for big game levels, or static view from the top)
- Add a multiplayer mode, in split-screen zoom mode (recipe V.16) or in a network version and Internet (recipe V.17)

Of course, «Pacman» could be revisited based on your imagination.

Step 8: «Marble Madness» Transformation

History: «Marble Madness» is a video game created by Atari Games, released in 1984 in an arcade version. The game was designed and programmed by **Mark Cerny** and **Bob Flanagan.** The game «**super monkey ball**» from **Amusement Vision** and published by **Sega** is a good 3D adaptation of the game.

Gameplay: To «Pacman», we add height and physic. It's a mix of the 2 precedents games. The player moves a ball over uneven ground with obstacles. The purpose of the game is to cross the finish line within the time limit.

You have everything you'll need to make this game.

Possible improvements:
- Use the mouse as a «trackball», the mouse influences the ball movements
- Change the observation angle with camera

II.2. PROJECT #2: PLATFORM GAMES

History:

The first platform game which has been reasonably successful was «**Donkey-kong**», published by Nintendo in 1981. Ill-treated by the carpenter, Donkey Kong, the gorilla escapes and kidnaps Jumpman's girlfriend, originally known as Lady. The player takes the role of Jumpman and must come to the rescue of his beloved climbing platforms; this is the first appearance of the theme of the damsel in distress in a video game, theme which becomes a recurring theme.

«**Super Mario Bros**», from the same publisher, was published in 1985. It's the first game from the *Super Mario* series. The player controls Mario and travels to various parts of Mushroom Kingdom to save princess Peach from Bowser, the Mario's enemy. It was the best-selling game of the years with more than 40 millions copies sold worldwide, until it's been beaten by *Wii Sports* in 2009.

«**Super Mario 64**» is the first game from the series in 3D realtime. It gives you complete freedom of movement, some big levels, but it's no longer a platform game. Mario can do 28 movements, more numerous and varied than in the previous episodes. He walks, runs, jumps, flies, swims, climbs or attacks.

In Blender community, **YO Frankie** has the same Gameplay (www.yofrankie.org). A fan has also produced a clone with Blender, it's **Super Blender Galaxy** ! (http://tinyurl.com/o4lnczm)

Our game model is «**Super Mario 3D Land**», published in 2011. This game is different from others in the series, having a combined elements from traditional Mario games with a side-scrolling presentation and moderns 3D games.

Gameplay:

A platform game usually presents a simple objective requiring moving along several levels, with traps and spanners. In typical 2D platform games, the avatar jumps from platform to other, from right to left, from bottom to top, or in all directions.

These games revised in 3D have the same Gameplay: combination of jumps to test the player.

«*Super Mario 3D Land*» *is a 3D Mario playing like a Mario 2D*» according to **Shigeru Miyamoto.** It combines elements from traditional games with a side-scrolling with elements from modern games (to control Mario in 3 dimensions and do various actions).

Step 1: Project implementation

In this project, we are focused on interactions between the player and his environment. For that purpose, we use an animated character: the «Yo Frankie» game main character, created by Blender Foundation to show BGE capacities.

1. Download the source code of the «Yo Frankie» game:

    http://www.yofrankie.org/yofrankie-11/. It's a Zip archive of 120Mo. The downloaded file has to be unpacked before installation in the directory of your choice.

2. Copy the files ./chars/frankie_actions.blend and ./chars/frankie.blend in the project directory. Rename «frankie.blend» in «project.blend». The game was developed in an older version of Blender, so it was not possible to efficiently use the Blender function «Append» to add the character to a project.

3. In the «info» window, remove the «HUD» scene and rename the «frank_logic» scene «main»

4. Retaining only the layer #2, remove the other layer objects (on each layer: «a», then «x» - eventually `Alt`+`H` to display hidden object). From layer #2, only remove the object «Throw_PlaceCarryFrank». At the end, only objects on Illustration 12 remained.

5. Select «RigFrankie», open the «Logic Editor», remove all the «game properties», all the sensors and controllers from each state logic layer. Only keeping the actuators with «Action» and «Sound» type (character animation), and a number of sounds.

6. Open the «Dopesheet» window in the «Action Editor» mode and for each action beginning with «LF Frankie», repeat the next step:

7. Click near the name on the icon look alike folder («Direct Linked Library Datablock») to make the action local (normally in the folder frankie_actions.blend)

8. Click on «F» to preserve it even although it's not necessary

9. Remove («unlink») all the project scripts one by one

10. Save the project and remove the «frankie_actions.blend» folder

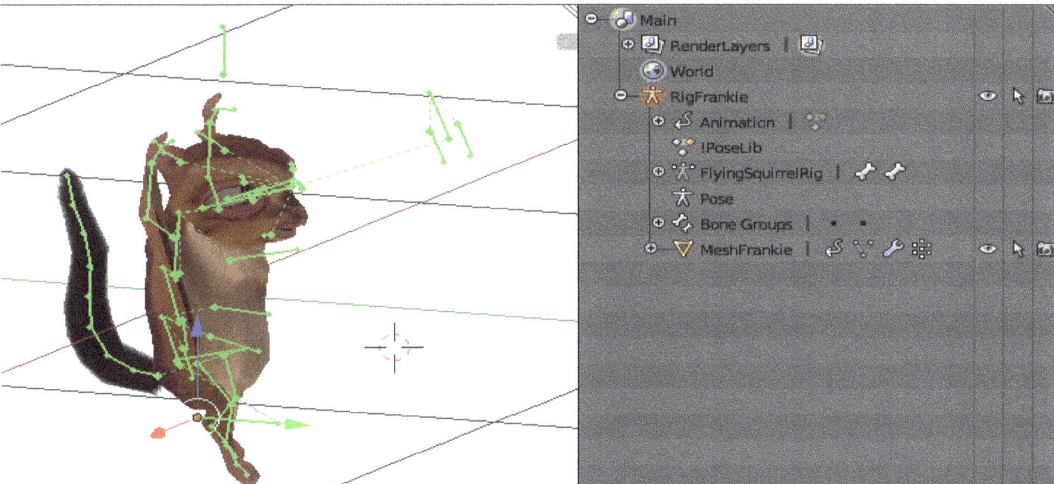

Illustration 12: Squirrel, the main character in the «Yo Frankie» game from Blender foundation

This results in an **animated character ready for use**. It's best to create its own character and to animate it according to games needs. However for this type of project, we prefer to focus on others aspects. The game project #7 is based on character animations.

Step 2: Modeling the scenery

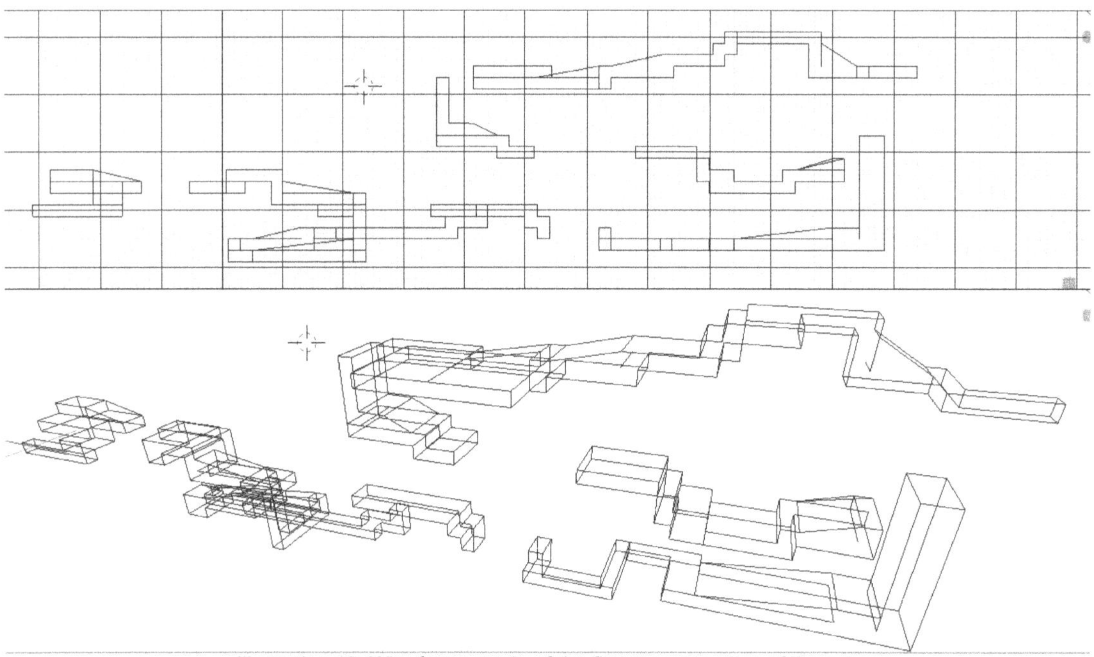

Illustration 13: Wire-frame mode of the first reconstruction of the set

Let's model a scenery with grass and soil to host our small rodent. The purpose is to realize a set with horizontal and vertical scrolling while fully exploiting depth.

1. Select the layer 1 and add a cube (⇧ Shift + A → «Mesh» → «Cube»). Rename it «Landscape». With this cube, we model all the scenery.
2. With a series of extrusions and deletions of faces, do a model like on Illustration 13.
3. «Properties» window, «Modifier» Tab→ «Add Modifier» → Select «Triangulate» and check «Beauty Subdivide».
4. «Add Modifier» → «Subdivision surface»: «View: 1» / «Render: 1». → result close to Illustration 14.
5. It's possible to keep the «modifiers» just like that, without applying permanently them. However, each time BGE is started, the «modifiers» are applied, using some time for computation. For this type of scenery, it's not too annoying, but if the set is more complicated, it can take a few minutes.
6. In «Edit Mode», do an UV unwrap («U»→ «Unwrap»). After each subsequent change of object geometry, redo this step.
7. «Properties» window, «Materials» Tab, add a new material («+»), name it «Ground». «Textures» Tab, add a new texture («+») with «Image or Movie» type and add a texture with «dirt-floor» type. «Mapping» Panel, Select «Coordinates»: «UV», «Map»: «Uvmap».
8. Do the same for a material with «grass» type, name it «Grass».
9. Then, in «Edit Mode», Select all the faces, Select the «Grass» Material and click on «Assign». All the scenery is made of grass. Select only faces that correspond to bottom of the surface of the set, Select the «Ground» material and click on «Assign».

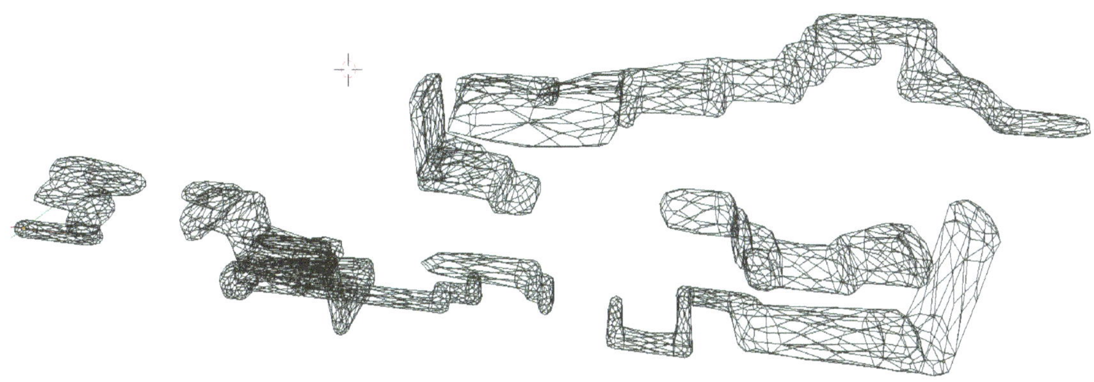

Illustration 14: The scenery after modifiers

We obtains a set like Illustration 15 used for the game and that we can populate by different objects more or less interactive.

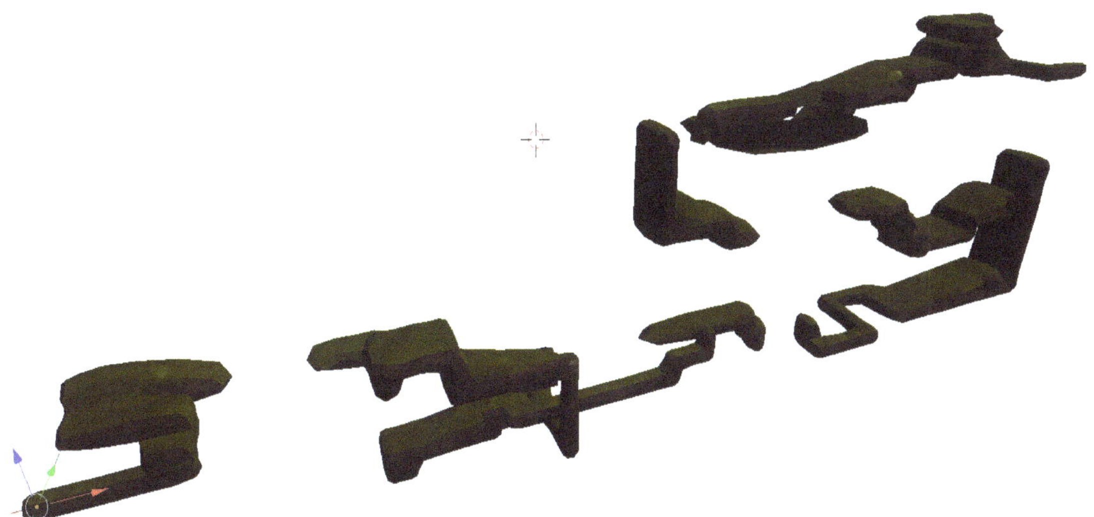

Illustration 15: Scenery with textures applied

Step 3: Adding objects to scenery

There are quite a few interesting objects in «Yo Frankie» game. You can find them in the project folder «./props». We invite you to discover:

- «newbridges.blend»: the whole objects forms a bridge between boards.
- «signpost.blend»: «signpost_medium» allows to leave messages for player when the character is right in front of you.
- «rocks.blend»: different models to decorate scenery.
- «Platforms.blend»: mobiles or fixed platforms as decor.
- «fences.blend»: fences prevent the player from falling, invisible fences to limit the character's movements.
- «Flowers.blend»: numerous flowers used with the automatic object generation script, like «plants.blend» (plants) and «mushrooms.blend» (mushrooms).

- «pickups.blend»: the object «apricot_001» (rename it «apricot») is used to collect score points, the object «item_acorn_001» (rename it «nut») is used to drop nuts on your enemies.
- «Trees.blend»: trunks or trees.

With that:

1. Select the most suitable objects for project and import them («info» window, «File» → «Append») in the layer #3. This layer is an object's storage.
2. For each object, remove all logic associated with the object in «Logic Editor», and all properties.
3. Add elements on scenery, except the flowers, plants and mushrooms.
4. Use the `recipe III.15` to put flowers, plants and mushrooms instances on scenery. This script gives an example of generation of these objects.

We obtain an exploitable scenery for the game (Illustration 16).

Illustration 16: Setting with several objects and plants

Script for generation of objects:

```
scatterObject("Scene", "Ground","mushroom_or_001", 50, "mushroom_or_001Scatter", True)
scatterObject("Scene", "Ground","mushroom_red_001", 50, "mushroom_red_001Scatter", True)
scatterObject("Scene", "Ground","grass_002_brown.001", 1000, "grass_002_brownScatter", True)
scatterObject("Scene", "Ground","flowers_s_colors_01",50, "FlowersScatter", True)
scatterObject("Scene", "Ground","flowers_s_colors_02",50, "FlowersScatter", True)
scatterObject("Scene", "Ground","flowers_s_colors_03", 50, "FlowersScatter", True)
scatterObject("Scene", "Ground","flowers_s_pink_01", 50, "FlowersScatter", True)
scatterObject("Scene", "Ground","flowers_s_red_01", 50, "FlowersScatter", True)
scatterObject("Scene", "Ground","flowers_s_white_01", 50, "FlowersScatter", True)
scatterObject("Scene", "Ground","flowers_s_purple_01", 50, "FlowersScatter", True)
scatterObject("Scene", "Ground","flowers_big_01", 30, "FlowersScatter", True)
scatterObject("Scene", "Ground","flowers_big_02", 30, "FlowersScatter", True)
```

Other simpler and more ornamental can be added: the Billboards (`recipe III.14`). The advantage is that a simple image is enough to result in smarter scenery. On the Internet, you can found numerous copyright-free versions of pictures to be used in the game (search with the word «sprite»).

It's also possible to set up a «Skydome» (`recipe III.3`). However, we limit the camera movement so that the bigger part of the sky dome is never displayed. For a best result, use different plans with different depths: one to display the sky and the earth and another to display trees and others closer objects, etc. It's an old technique used in video games: the differential scrolling that gives the impression of depth with number of superimposed planes.

Illustration 17: Final setting with sky and sea

Step 4: control of the character and the camera

Prepare the **physical mesh**:

1. Add a new cube (⬆ Shift + A → «Mesh» → «Cube», superimpose it to the character, so in «Edit Mode», resize it to surround the character as on the Illustration 18. Rename it «Player»

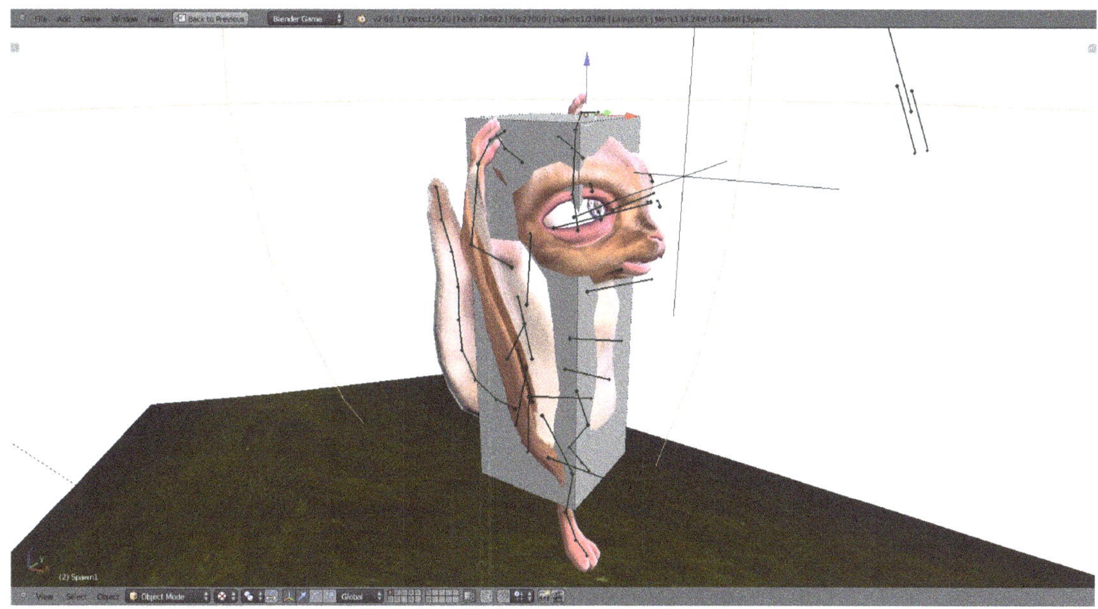

Illustration 18: Frankie and his collision box

2. Parent the object «RigFrankie» to the object «Player» by holding down the ⬆ Shift key and clicking on each object individually (character, then «Player»), and Ctrl + P → «Parent to Object»)

3. Select the «RigFrankie» object. In the «Properties» window, «Physics» Tab, «Physics Type»: Select «No Collision».

4. Select the «Player» object. «Properties» window, «Physics» Tab, «Physics Type»: Select «Dynamic». It's not yet possible to manage the friction on a physical object with «Character» type, so it's not possible to choose this type. The friction not allows the character to be led down a path. Check «Actor» to be detected by the «Radar» and «Near» sensors, and by the «invisible» sensor, since «Player» is only used by the physical mesh management. Check «Use Material Force Field» (see the Material configuration after). Check «Collision Bounds» too, select «Box» and set «margin» to 0.04.

5. «Materials» Tab, add a new Material («+»). «Physics» Tab, check «Physics» and «Friction»: 1.0 so that the character don't be led down a path (or as you wish!).

6. Add a **camera** following the character with the same orientation all the time, as in an arcade game:

    Select the «Player» object and position the cursor over the selected object (⇧ Shift + S → «Snap cursor to Selected»)

7. Add a camera (⇧ Shift + A → «camera»). Do an axis X rotation of 80° and the camera may be moved away from: y -10 and z + 2.

8. «Properties» windows, «Object» Tab, panel «Relations», «Parent»: Select «Player» and «Type of Parent Relation» (just below): «vertex». Don't parent the object so as not to suffer its orientation transformations. Like this, the camera follows the object, without changing its orientation.

Now, the character has collision with statical objectsthe sensor with when falling, but he's not able to **walk**. He has to learn:

9. Select the «Player» and «RigFrankie» objects and open the «Logic Editor».

10. To the «Player» object, add a «Keyboard» sensor, name it «KeyForward» (to move forward) and choose a key (example: «↑»).

11. Add a «Motion» actuator, «type»: «Simple Motion», «Loc» «Y»: 0.10 and check «L». Verify the Y axis corresponds to a vertical displacement in front of the character. If not, choose the good axis. «L» indicates a movement along the «local» axis and not along the «world» axis. Thus, even by changing the «Player» object orientation, the movement is always effected to the front. Link the sensor and the actuator with an «AND» controller.

12. To the «RigFrankie» object, select the «walk_forward» actuator. Set «Blending»: 4, «Priority»: 3, «Layer»: 1, «Layer Weight»: 0.5. If the actuator has not been unloaded, its characteristics are these: type: «Loop Stop», action: «Frankie_Walk», «start»: 1, «end»: 19, «continue» checked. Link the actuator with the precedent «AND» controller.

13. To the «Player» object, add a «Keyboard» sensor, name it «KeyRight» and choose a key to turn the character to the right (example: «→»).

14. Add a «Motion» actuator, «type»: «Simple Motion», «Rot» «Z»: -3,0 and check «L». The same remark as above applies. Link the sensor and the actuator with an «AND» controller.

15. To the «RigFrankie» object, Select the «turn_right» actuator. Set as follows «Blending»: 10, «Priority»: 3, «Layer»: 0, «Layer Weight»: 0.0. If the actuator has not been unloaded, its characteristics are these: type: «Loop Stop», action: «Frankie_Turn.R», «start»: 1, «end»: 13, «continue» checked. Link the actuator with the precedent «AND»controller.

16. Repeat the 3 last actions to turn left («KeyLeft», «Rot» «Z»: 3.0 and the «turn_left» actuator).

When the character is not in movement, it remains static. The character's animation when he does nothing is often named «**IDLE**». How to implement that:

17. To the «RigFrankie» object, add an «Always» sensor, name it «IDLE», check «Activate On True Level Triggering» and frequency: 10.

18. Select the «idle» actuator. Set as follows «Blending»: 5, «Priority»: 6, «Layer»: 0, «Layer Weight»: 0.0. The priority is less than the walk (6 is a lower priority than 3), the character quickly takes the attitude «IDLE» when he's not in movement. There's not condition to set. If the actuator has not been unloaded, its characteristics are these: type: «Loop Stop», action: «Frankie_idle1», «start»: 1, «end»: 269, «continue» check. Link the actuator with the precedent «AND» controller..

Our character can move but can't overcome barriers. He have to learn how to **jump:**

19. To the «Player» object, add a «Keyboard» sensor, name it «KeyJump» and choose a key to make the character jump (example: «Spacebar»).

20. Add a «Ray» sensor, name it «RayGround» and Select the axis «-Z axis» and «range»: 0.75. This sensor verifies if «Player» is still more or less in contact with the floor. By increasing «range», you can do higher jumps.

21. Link the 2 sensors with an «AND» controller.

22. Add a «Motion» actuator, «type»: «Simple Motion», «Force» «Z»: 50 and check «L». A 50 force is applied to «Player» which, by default weighs just 1 unit (1 kilogram for Bullet). If the mass is 10 units, the applied force must be 500. Link the actuator with the precedent controller.

Regarding the jump, it's possible to define a filter for the «RayGround» sensor to choose surfaces from which the character can't jump. Add a property to all object that might be a support.

The character has a particular **running** movement: it runs with legs (action «Frankie_Run»). Regularly, we can do that by adding a key (⬆ Shift) to run.

Because of the movement, we'll do that like this: running is possible only after walking:

23. Add to «Player» a «run» property with «integer» type, initialized to 0.

24. Add a «Property» sensor, name it «RunMode», check «Activate on True Level Triggering» and determine the frequency to 0, «Evaluation Type»: «Interval», Select the property «run», then choose a minimum of 10 and a maximum of 10000.

25. Add a «Property» actuator, name it «Run-», mode «Add», Select the «run» property and determine «value»: -10.

26. Link the sensor with the actuator. Automatically, the «run» value will decrease over time to reach 0.

27. Add a «Property» actuator, name it «Run+», «Add» mode, Select the «run» property and determine «value»: +11.

28. Link the actuator with the controller that's linked to «KeyForward». In this way, when the character moves, the rue value earns +1 (+11-10). Then all you have to do is to define a threshold above which the character runs.

29. Modify the controller that's linked to «KeyForward» into «Expression», name it «walk» and write «KeyForward AND (run<30)» into «value»

30. Add an «Expression» controller, name it «run», and write «KeyForward AND (run>=30)» into «value».

31. Add to «Player» a «Motion» actuator, «type»: «Simple Motion», «Loc» «Y»: 0.15 and select «L».

32. Regarding to «RigFrankie», modify the «run» actuator with «action» type. Set as follows «Blending»: 4, «Priority»: 4, «Layer»: 0, «Layer Weight»: 0.0. If the actuator has not been unloaded, its characteristics are these: type: «Loop Stop», action: «Frankie_Run», «start»: 1, «end»: 20, «continue» checked.

33. Link the 2 actuators with the «run» controller.

The character is a **Flying squirrel**, he has a particular fall, **he can fly on a few meters**:

34. Select the «Player» object and add a «Ray» sensor, name it «RayFall», «axis»: «-Z axis», «range»: 3.5. This sensor will detect a «fall» event.

35. Modify the «run» and «walk» controllers adding the «AND NOT RayFall» condition and Link them with the precedent sensor.

36. Add an «Expression» controller, name it «fly» and write «RayFall AND KeyForward». Link it with the «RayFall» and «KeyForward» sensors.

37. Add an «Expression» controller, name it «fall» and write «RayFall AND NOT KeyForward». Link it with the «RayFall» and «KeyForward» sensors.

38. Regarding to «RigFrankie», modify the «fall_down» actuator with «action» type. Set: «Blending»: 12, «Priority»: 1, «Layer»: 0, «Layer Weight»: 0.0. If the actuator has not been unloaded, its characteristics are these: type: «Loop Stop», action: «Frankie_Falling», «start»: 1, «end»: 12,

«continue» checked. Link the actuator with the «fall» controller.

39. Modify the «gliding» actuator with «action» type. Set: «Blending»: 15, «Priority»: 5, «Layer»: 0, «Layer Weight»: 0.0. If the actuator has not been unloaded, its characteristics are these: type: «Loop Stop», action: «Frankie_Glide», «start»: 1, «end»: 13, «continue» checked. Link the actuator with the «fly» controller.

Step 5: teleportation

We have already created actions to explore the environment. It's time to refine the movement and to work the settings. Before, we'll create a tool to make tests on the different parts of a level. After, we must deactivate this tool and use it in another way: **teleportation**. The character will be able to go from one point to the other with little stroke of key. This tool can be used for debugging or for restart a level at the next point in case of a fall.

1. Select «Player» and add a «spawn» «Integer» property, initialized to 0. This variable will contains the last teleportation point for the player.

2. Add an «Always» sensor, name it «RunOnce».

3. Add a «Keyboard» sensor, name it «Spawn+» and choose a key to select the next teleportation point (example «Numpad+»).

4. Add a «Keyboard» sensor, name it «Spawn-» and choose a key to select the preceding teleportation point (example «Numpad-»).

5. Add a «python» controller, select «module» and write «player.spawn». Link the controller with the 3 sensors.

6. Add a python script «player.py» and insert the following lines.

7. Go to «3D View» and add an Empty (`Shift`+`A` → «Empty» → «Sphere»), name it «Spawn0» and move it to the location of the first teleportation point, it's the character's location at the beginning of the level.

8. Repeat the operation as often as you want with «Spawn1», «Spawn2» … «SpawnX».

Script «player.py»:

```python
import bge

def spawn(cont):
    own = cont.owner
    scene = bge.logic.getCurrentScene()

    if cont.sensors["Spawn-"].positive and own["spawn"]>=1:
        own["spawn"] -= 1
    if cont.sensors["Spawn+"].positive:
        own["spawn"] += 1

    spawn = scene.objects["Spawn"+str(own["spawn"])]
    own.worldPosition = spawn.worldPosition
```

This simple script copy the location coordinates of the selected teleportation point on the object «Player».

Step 6: Examples of Interactions with the environment

What is the goal of the game? Go to the last platform to finish the level collecting a maximum of points. How collecting points? Picking up some «Apricots»!

1. Select the «Apricot» object and open the «Logic Editor»

2. Add an «Always» sensor, name it «Anim»

3. Add a «Motion» actuator, «type»: «Simple Motion», «Rot» «Z»: 2° and check «L».

4. Link the sensor with the actuator. It's a little animation which right the object herself.

5. Add a «Collision» sensor, and write the «Property»: «player».

6. Add a «Message» actuator, «To»: Select «Player», «subject»: «Apricot».

7. Add an «Edit Object» actuator: Select «End Object».

8. Link the 2 actuators and the precedent sensor with an «AND» controller. Then, when the character contacting the object, this object disappears and sends a message «apricot» to the Player object. Handle the message.

9. Select the object «Player» and add a property «score» with «Integer» type initialized to 0.

10. Add a «Message» sensor, name it «points+», subject «apricot».

11. Add a «Property» actuator, «mode»: «add», «Property»: Select «score» and write 10 into «Value».

12. Link the sensor with the actuator. When the character picks up an «apricot», it wins 10 points.

13. Copy (`Alt`+`D`) the object «Apricot» as often you want. The best is to move it in places at risk, or difficult to access (at the jump limit). The end of the level can be reached when the player has a minimal score for more difficulty.

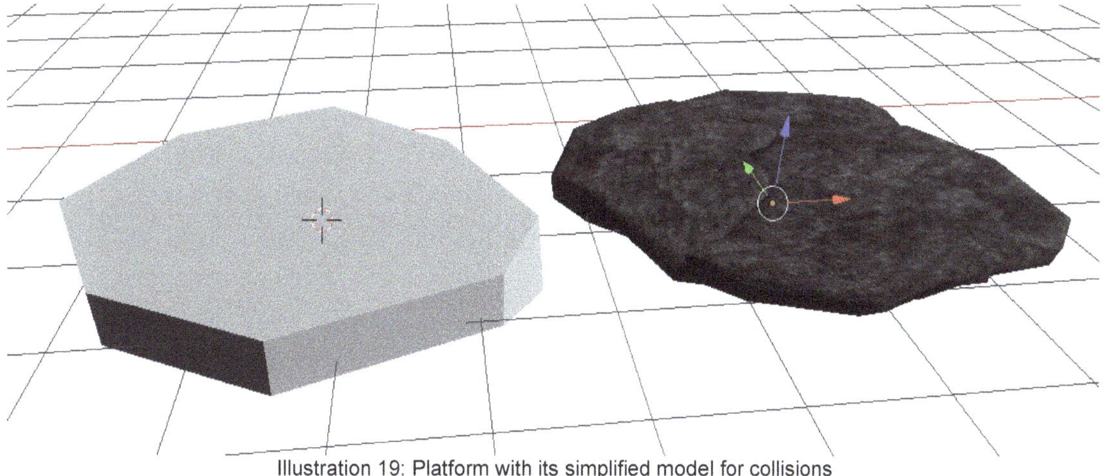

Illustration 19: Platform with its simplified model for collisions

A platform's game needs mobile platforms!

14. Use, for example, the «lava_platform.001» template. To illustrate the templates replacement by simplified models for physical object management, we use a simpler model than mobiles platforms: a cube with the platform size and another cube more complex as you can see at the Illustration 19

15. Set the simplified model «physics» type (at left) as «Dynamic» with a «collision bounds» with «Convex Hull» type, check «invisible» too. Set the other model «physics» type as «no collision». Parent the 2 models and move them at the same location (superposition).

16. To use the **recipe V.9** («navigation node system») to define a way for the platform's movement, parent the platform with an empty «LP1». Apply the recipe on this empty.

17. Define a way for the platform with 4 or 5 stages. For each stage, insert an empty (recipe). Each platform must have a name like «lava_platform-step.x», x is the stage number.

18. In the same way, it's possible to add some mobile objects, with some dangerous objects for the character, other objects that may be bonuses.

The problem we have with platforms is when the character jump on them. The character must run as fast as possible in order not to fall. We add a glue to it in order to **maintain it to the platform until the character jumps**:

19. Open «player.py» and add the script lines below.

20. Select the platform physical model and open the «Logic Editor».

21. Add a «platform» property with boolean type checked.

22. Select the «Player» object, add a «Ray» sensor, name it «RayStick», «property»: «platform», Select «-Z Axis» and «range»: 0.6

23. Add a «Python» controller, select «Module» and write «player.stickTo». Link the sensor with the controller.

24. Add an «Expression» controller and write «NOT RayStick».

25. Add a «Parent» actuator, «Scene»: select «Remove Parent» and link it with the precedent controller, and to the controller joined to the «KeyJump» sensor in order to remove the parent when the player is jumping.

The simplest method is to parent the character to the platform to ensure that it follows all the platform transformations. Our Character can move but can't jump (because it's a force which is applied). So, to jump, we remove the parental link. The character walks along the platform: when it falls, when it's pushed by an enemy or an obstacle, you must remove the parental link too. So, the «expression» controller «NOT RayStick» detects the platform under the character and breaks the link when the platform is not under the character.

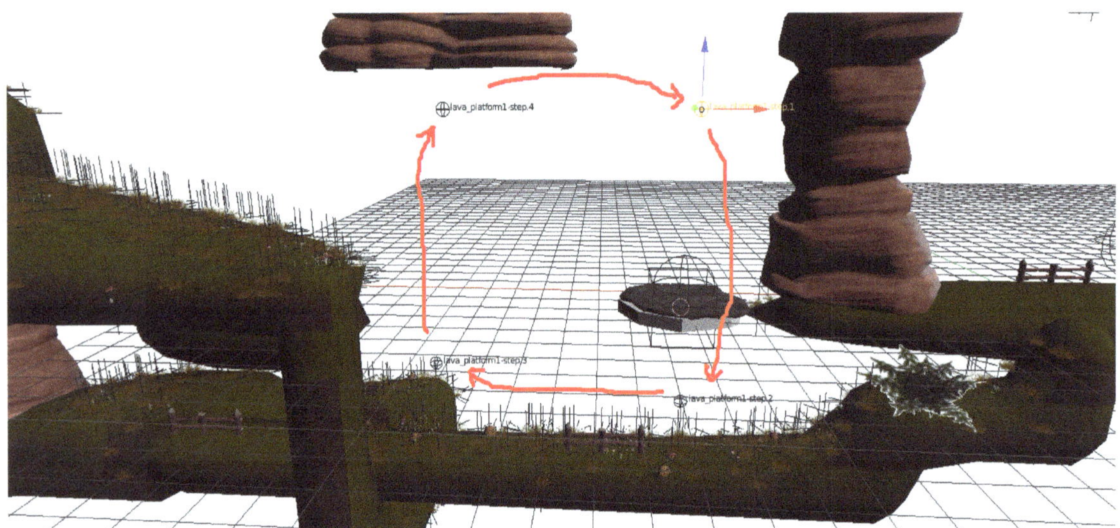

Illustration 20: Mobil platform using a pathfollow

Add to the script «player.py»:

```python
def stickTo(cont):
    ray = cont.sensors[0]
    own = cont.owner
    if ray.positive:
        own.setParent(ray.hitObject)
    else:
        own.setParent(None)
```

Step 7: Hazelnuts throw !

To increase interactions with the environment, we give the character the capacity of **throwing hazelnuts** (our poor squirrel prefers to throw his hazelnuts to eat them – he's be on a diet). He'll be able to trigger mechanisms by launching hazelnuts on cranks (**recipe V.7**) or on breakable objects (**recipe III.21**). Thereafter, the character'll be able to push dangerous animals off or knock out them.

1. In «3D View», add a new Empty, name it «FireStart» and move it in front of the character (illustration 17).

2. Select «Player» and open the «Logic Editor».

3. Add a «Keyboard» sensor and select a key for throwing a hazelnut (example: `Ctrl`).

4. Add the «throw» property with float type to the object «RigFrankie». This variable identifies the picture used for the hazelnut throw animation display, in order to generate hazelnut when the character has his arm straight.

5. Add an «AND» controller and link it with the precedent sensor. Link also this controller with the «Throw» actuator with «Action» type of «RigFrankie». If the actuator has not been unloaded, its characteristics are these: type: «Play», action: «Frankie_Throw1», «start»: 1, «end»: 36, «continue» deselected, «Blending»: 4, «Priority»: 2, «Layer»: 1, «Layer Weight»: 0.0. «Frame Property»: select «throw».

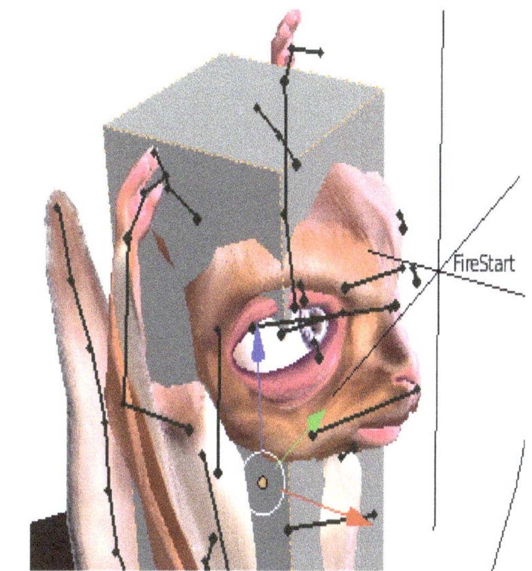

Illustration 21: Position of the Empty for hazelnuts throw

6. Add to the object «RigFrankie» a «Property» sensor, «Evaluation type»: select «Interval», select the «throw» property and write «Minimum»: 10 and «Maximum»: 25. That still leaves some leeway for the throw if the animation slows down.

7. Add a «Message» actuator, «To»: «FireStart», «Subject»: write «start». Link the actuator with the precedent sensor.

8. Select the object «FireStart» and add a «Message» sensor, check «Activate On True Level Triggering» and select a frequency at 15 (to limit the frequency of fire to 1, every 15 frames), «subject»: «start».

9. Add an «Edit Object» actuator, select the object «nut», «time»: 500, «Linear velocity» «X»: 10.0, «Z»: 5.0. Link the actuator with the precedent sensor.

10. Select the object «nut», go to the «Properties» window, «Physics» Tab and select «Type»: «Rigid Body».

To manage collision with various objects, you can add a «collision» sensor to «nut» and filter by properties. You can also increase the mass of the object to ensure that collision with other objects is more important (to repeal a creature for example)

Note: if the squirrel aims carefully, jumping and orienting the camera, he should touch the player behind the screen. Of course, there'll be no impact on the player! (I hope…).

Step 8: Ambient sound and effects

Step 8: Ambient sound and effects

You can use the available sounds with the original game. Here are a few suggestions:

- «frankie_dielava.wav»: for the fall (actuator: «sfx_fall»). To link with the «Fall» controller with «Expression» type.
- «item_pickup»: to collect bonuses like «Apricots» (actuator: «sfx_get». To link with the controller already linked with the actuator «pickup_anim».
- «sfx_jump.wav»: to jump (actuator: «Sfx_jump»). To link with the controller already linked with the actuator «jumping».
- «sfx_throw.wav»: to throw nuts (actuator: «Sfx_Throw»). To link with the controller already linked with the actuator sending the message «start» to «FireStart».
- «nutfall.wav»: To link with the «collision» sensor of the object «nut». When the nut crashes into an object, the sound is emitted.

The folder «/Audio» from the project «Yo Frankie» contains more than 70 sounds which can be reused for this game project.

To create a «nature» ambient sound :

1. Select the «camera» and open the «Logic Editor»
2. Add an «Always» sensor and an «And» controller then link the 2.
3. Add a «Sound» actuator, open the folder «msx_peachvalley.wav», «Play Mode»: «Loop End», «Volume»: 0.5
4. Add a «Sound» actuator, open the folder «amb_forest.wav», «Play Mode»: «Loop End», «Volume»: 0.7
5. Link the 2 actuators with the precedent controller. The music «peachvalley» and the ambient sounds type «forest» will be continuously played for the duration of the game.
6. Add a «Random» sensor, check «Activate On True Level Triggering», give a frequency of 500 (every 10 seconds, there's a draw with 50 % to be lucky enough to make the sound)
7. Add a «Sound» actuator, open the folder «amb_bird_1.wav», «Play Mode»: «Play Stop», «Volume»: 0.5, then link the precedent sensor with the actuator. A bird song will be played average 3 times per minute with a separation of 10 seconds.
8. Add a «Random» sensor, checked «Activate On True Level Triggering», give a frequency of 100 (there's a draw every 2 seconds with 50 % to be lucky enough to make the sound)
9. Add a «Sound» actuator, open the folder «amb_cricket_1.wav», «Play Mode»: «Play Stop», «Volume»: 0.5, then link the precedent sensor and the actuator. A locust sound will be played 15 times per minute with 2 seconds of interval.
10. Add a «Random» sensor, check «Activate On True Level Triggering», give a frequency of 250 (there's a draw every 5 seconds with 50 % to be lucky enough to make the sound)
11. Add a «Sound» actuator, open the folder «amb_frog_1.wav», «Play Mode»: «Play Stop», «Volume»: 0.5, then link it with the precedent sensor. A cry of a frog will be played 6 times per minute with 5 seconds of interval.

Then, using only little sounds and one music, it's possible to create a composition with numerous variations using random. It's also possible to use random with musics and modifying the intervals between sounds, etc.

Step 9: improvements

Here is a partial list of what you can add to this game to make it even more exciting:

- Some enemies **creatures**: use 2 recipes that we have seen before: the enemy walk, like for mobiles platforms using a «navigation node path» (**recipe V.9**), the detection of the character with a «radar» sensor or a «near» sensor (**recipe V.7**). The enemy can use too a «path finding» (**recipe V.14**) to charge at the character. See the game project #6 «FPS».
- The management of **life** (game project #6, step 8)
- The character drop detection (project #1) and a teleportation to the next point before the fall (modify the function spawn() of the script player.py)
- Take advantage of the physic engine: use objects collision (example: a big stone that we move with a stick to clear a path, or objects falling on others like dominoes).
- Some **traps** using proximity sensors (**recipe V.7**) like in the game «Rick Dangerous»
- **elevators** with forced-air heating (add a vertical force to the character) to allow the character to fly. Thanks to his flight capacity, the character can reach very distant bonuses plates forms.
- Give to the character the ability **to interact with objects** like barrels (**recipe V.14**) and throw them using the mouse, or using an approach with «elastic» type like in the game «Angry birds».
- Insert **teleporters** (**recipe V.6**) that carry the character in **hidden levels** with numerous bonuses. This bonuses can be hidden in breakable objects (**recipe III.21**) or behind doors needing keys.
- Add a **time limit** to finish the level with a time countdown for the last minute.
- **Play with lights**: create dark levels and give a torch to the character. Play with shadows and a scary music... but without doing a horror-survival game!
- Add some **flying creatures** (like bees) which follow the player and steal the bonuses within a defined radius of the site.
- Add **a 2 players mode** (**recipe V.16**) in which each character has a specific characteristic (one fly and the other jump to rattle the environment) and play in a cooperative mode like in the game «The Lost Vikings».
- Add some **explosives** (**recipe VII.17**) to reveal some parts of the environment and open passages like in «bomberman».

II.3.   PROJECT #3: RACE GAMES

The story:

The first game of this kind is «*Astro Race*» from Taito, came to market in 1973. It's a futurist race game, with 2 simultaneous players, the player controls a vessel seen in a top view, avoiding the asteroids on the way. In July 1974, «*Gran Trak 10*», created by Atari Inc., can be see like the first race car. The raceway is fully displayed to screen, in a top view, and the player must do a race against the clock to win a maximum of points. In 1988, «*Hard Drivin'*» from Atari Games is the first race game fully made with 3D graphics. The game that has inspired me was «***Stunt Car Racer***», made by **Geoff Crammond and published by** Micro-Prose in 1989 on most 8 and 16 bits computers of that time. The competition take place on tight and cluttered trails, rising to some dozen meters without any barrier. Raceways are made with important vertical drops, abysses, sharp turn, ramps, humpbacks and dynamic portions. It's a race against one concurrent, the player controls a hybrid vehicle between buggy and dragster with nitrogen pack.

Gameplay:

You drive your car. You can drive with direct view from cockpit or with view from outside the car. It's an infernal raceway and there are skilled adversary.

Technique:

BGE give us an object for vehicle simulation, it's KX_VehicleWrapper. We'll use this as an opportunity to improve scripting python and how to use the wrapper.

To begin, we need a car (name «car») and 4 tires (names «TireFD» front driver, «TireFP» front passenger, «TireRD» rear driver, «TireRP» rear passenger): Illustration 22.

Use Lowpoly models. To use a more complex model, use a substitution model, invisible, useful only for collisions. Parent to this last model the more complex model. The more complex model can't collide.

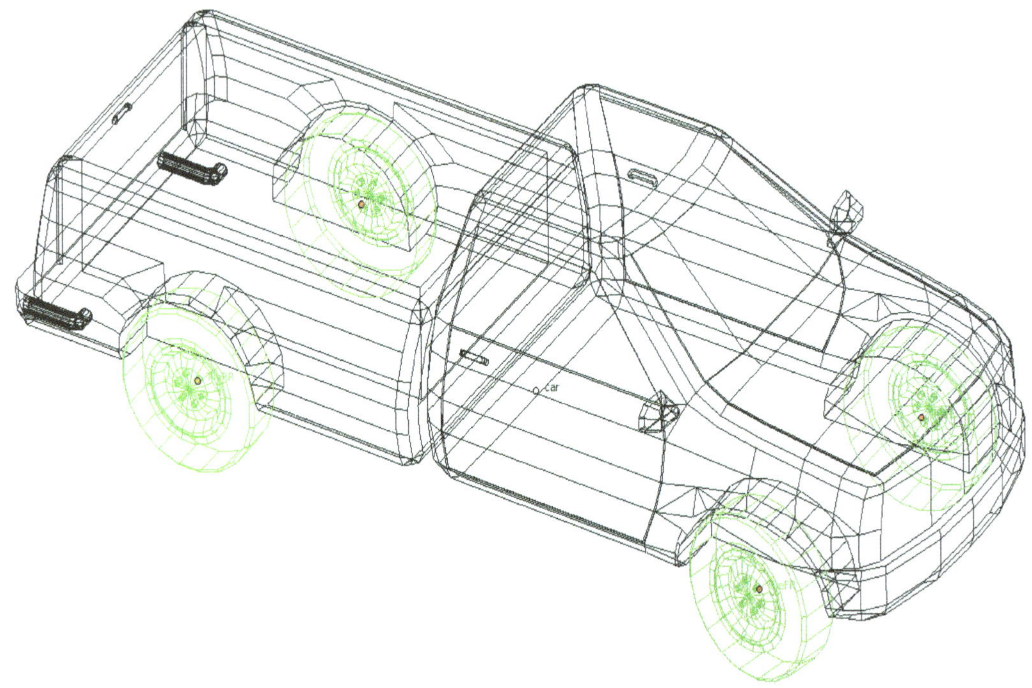

Illustration 22: Car and its 4 tires, free model downloaded from the internet

Step 1: Car preparation

1. Open a new folder «car.blend». All car configurations are here.

2. Place the «car» object in the Y axis direction. The Y axis corresponds to the car length, the X axis to its width and the Z axis to its height. Be careful, in what follows, everything is depending on the car's dimensions: values must be used according to these.

3. Place a plane under the «car» object to manage tests

4. Select the «car» object. «Properties» Window, «Physics» Tab, select «Type»: «Rigid Body» then check «actor» and set «Mass» to 250.

5. Check «Collision Bound» to activate collision detection and select Bounds: «convex hull» (box is too simple and can't do a good collision detection).

6. Select each tire and select «Physics type»:«no collision» in «Physics» Tab.

7. Create a new text document named «carsetup.py» and paste the following script.

8. Select the «car» object and open the «Logic Editor»

9. Add an «Always» sensor

10. Add a «python» controller and select the script «carsetup.py»

11. Link the sensor and the controller

12. Go to the «3D View» and make a test (P)

Now, results can be disappointing. You must configure the tires and other elements position. The car must be on its tires and when the car does a jump, she rebounds, showing its suspensions. The car is ready !

Script «carsetup.py» (source: www.tutorialsforblender3d.com – Licence CC3):

```python
import bge

def main():
        carObj = Car_Object()
        vehicleID = Car_Constraint(carObj)
        tireObj = Tire_Objects()
        tirePos = Tire_Positions()
        tireRadius = Tire_Radius()
        tireSuspension = Tire_Suspension()
        tireSuspensionAngle = Tire_SuspensionAngle()
        tireAxis = Tire_Axis()
        tireSteering = Tire_Steering()
        Add_Tires(vehicleID, tireObj, tirePos,
                tireSuspensionAngle, tireAxis, tireSuspension,tireRadius, tireSteering)

def Car_Object():
        # get current controller
        controller = bge.logic.getCurrentController()
        # get car the controller is attached to
        carObj = controller.owner
        return carObj

def Car_Constraint(carObj):
        car_PhysicsID = carObj.getPhysicsId()
        vehicle_Constraint =
                bge.constraints.createConstraint(car_PhysicsID,0, 11)
        constraint_ID = vehicle_Constraint.getConstraintId()
        vehicleID =
                bge.constraints.getVehicleConstraint(constraint_ID)
        carObj["vehicleID"] = vehicleID
        return vehicleID

def Tire_Objects():
        scene = bge.logic.getCurrentScene()
        objList = scene.objects
        tire_0 = objList["TireFD"]
        tire_1 = objList["TireFP"]
        tire_2 = objList["TireRD"]
        tire_3 = objList["TireRP"]
        return (tire_0, tire_1, tire_2, tire_3)
```

```python
def Tire_Positions():
        tire_0_Pos = [ -2.2,  4.2, -0.2]  # front driver
        tire_1_Pos = [  2.2,  4.2, -0.2]  # front passenger
        tire_2_Pos = [ -2.2, -3.6, -0.2]  # rear driver
        tire_3_Pos = [  2.2, -3.6, -0.2]  # rear passenger
        return (tire_0_Pos, tire_1_Pos, tire_2_Pos, tire_3_Pos)

def Tire_Radius():
        # tire radius
        tire_0_Radius = 0.90  # front driver
        tire_1_Radius = 0.90  # front passenger
        tire_2_Radius = 0.90  # rear driver
        tire_3_Radius = 0.90  # rear passenger
        return (tire_0_Radius, tire_1_Radius, tire_2_Radius, tire_3_Radius)

def Tire_Suspension():
        tire_0_suspensionHeight = 0.3  # front driver
        tire_1_suspensionHeight = 0.3  # front passenger
        tire_2_suspensionHeight = 0.3  # rear driver
        tire_3_suspensionHeight = 0.3  # rear passenger
        return (tire_0_suspensionHeight, tire_1_suspensionHeight,
                tire_2_suspensionHeight, tire_3_suspensionHeight)

def Tire_SuspensionAngle():
        tire_0_suspensionAngle = [ 0.0, 0.0, -1.0]
        tire_1_suspensionAngle = [ 0.0, 0.0, -1.0]
        tire_2_suspensionAngle = [ 0.0, 0.0, -1.0]
        tire_3_suspensionAngle = [ 0.0, 0.0, -1.0]
        return (tire_0_suspensionAngle, tire_1_suspensionAngle,
                    tire_2_suspensionAngle, tire_3_suspensionAngle)

def Tire_Axis():
        tire_0_Axis = [ -1.0, 0.0, 0.0]  # front driver
        tire_1_Axis = [ -1.0, 0.0, 0.0]  # front pass
        tire_2_Axis = [ -1.0, 0.0, 0.0]  # rear driver
        tire_3_Axis = [ -1.0, 0.0, 0.0]  # rear pass
        return (tire_0_Axis, tire_1_Axis, tire_2_Axis, tire_3_Axis)

def Tire_Steering():
        tire_0_Steering = True  # front driver
        tire_1_Steering = True  # front passenger
        tire_2_Steering = True  # rear driver
        tire_3_Steering = True  # rear passenger
        return (tire_0_Steering, tire_1_Steering, tire_2_Steering, tire_3_Steering)

def Add_Tires(vehicleID, tireObj, tirePos,
        tireSuspensionAngle, tireAxis, tireSuspension, tireRadius, tireSteering):

        for tire in range(0,4):
                obj = tireObj[tire]
                pos = tirePos[tire]
                suspensionAngle = tireSuspensionAngle[tire]
                axis = tireAxis[tire]
                suspension = tireSuspension[tire]
                radius = tireRadius[tire]
                steering = tireSteering[tire]
                # Add front driver tire
                vehicleID.addWheel( obj, pos, suspensionAngle,axis, suspension,  radius, steering)
main()
```

This script contains all you need to configure the car:

- **Tires position** and **distance** (en Blender Units) from each fire to the center of the car (function Tire_Positions). Adjust in accordance with the used model.
- Each **radius tire** (function Tire_radius). T calculate the radius, take the size y (or z) of the tire object and divide by 2 (here, the tire is 0.50x1.80x1.80 – the radius is 1.80/2 = 0.90).
- Add an «And» controller and link it to the «Always» sensor.

Step 2: Control of the car

- The **height** of **suspensions** (function Tire_Suspension)
- **The angle** of **suspensions** (function Tire_SuspensionAngle) and tires (function Tire_Angle) using a vector.
- If **tires** are **activated** for steering (function Tire Steering): rear-wheel drive, front-wheel-drive or 4x4 (4 tires).

Using a script allows you to easily change tires, to precisely manage the driving settings, etc. It's possible to use a number of car models with different settings.

1. Create a new text document named «Powertrain.py» and paste the following script.
2. Select the «car» object and go to the «Logic Editor»
3. Add a «State» actuator, «Set State» and select the state#2 (that we'll create)
4. Go to the state#2 (Select the state like for a layer selection). To reveal them, click on «+» near «car» under «Controller».
5. Add a «Keyboard» sensor, name: «Gas» and choose a key to to propel the vehicle («↑» for example). Do the same for «Reverse», «Brake», «EBrake» (emergency brake), «Right», «Left»
6. Add a «Python» controller and select the script «Powertrain.py»
7. Link all these sensors with the controller
8. Select the state# 1 as «starting state»: there are 2 lines for the state, the first line is for the running layer and the second line is to Select the starting layer, go to «3D View» and test (P)

Script «Powertrain.py» (source:www.tutorialsforblender3d.com – Licence CC3):

```python
import bge

def main():
        controller = bge.logic.getCurrentController()
        vehicleID = ConstraintID(controller)
        brakes = Brakes(vehicleID, controller)
        Power( vehicleID, controller, brakes)
        Steering(vehicleID, controller)

def ConstraintID(controller):
        car = controller.owner
        vehicleID = car["vehicleID"]
        return vehicleID

def Brakes(vehicleID, controller):
        brakeAmount = 40.0            # front and back brakes
        ebrakeAmount = 100.0          # back brakes only
        reverse = controller.sensors["Reverse"]
        brake = controller.sensors["Brake"]
        emergency = controller.sensors["EBrake"]

        if emergency.positive:
                front_Brake = 0.0
                back_Brake = ebrakeAmount
                brakes = True
        elif brake.positive and not reverse.positive:
                front_Brake = brakeAmount
                back_Brake = brakeAmount
                brakes = True
        else:
                front_Brake = 0.0
                back_Brake = 0.0
                brakes = False

        vehicleID.applyBraking( front_Brake, 0)
        vehicleID.applyBraking( front_Brake, 1)
        vehicleID.applyBraking( back_Brake, 2)
        vehicleID.applyBraking( back_Brake, 3)
        return brakes

def Power( vehicleID, controller, brakes):
        # set power amounts
```

```
        reversePower = 200.0
        gasPower = 800.0
        # get power sensors
        gas = controller.sensors["Gas"]
        reverse = controller.sensors["Reverse"]
        if brakes: # brakes
                power = 0.0
        elif reverse.positive: # reverse
                power = reversePower
        elif gas.positive: # gas pedal
                power = -gasPower
        Else: # no gas and no reverse
                power = 0.0
        # apply power
        vehicleID.applyEngineForce( power, 0)
        vehicleID.applyEngineForce( power, 1)
        vehicleID.applyEngineForce( power, 2)
        vehicleID.applyEngineForce( power, 3)

def Steering( vehicleID, controller):
        turn = 0.35
        steerLeft = controller.sensors["Left"]
        steerRight = controller.sensors["Right"]

        if steerLeft.positive:
                turn = turn
        elif steerRight.positive:
                turn = -turn
        else:
                turn = 0.0
        vehicleID.setSteeringValue(turn,0)
        vehicleID.setSteeringValue(turn,1)
main()
```

Step 3: Camera management

It's useful to change the point of view, from inside the car like a driver to an outside point of view, or to a rear view or to an upper view. To set up the 2 types of cameras (Illustration 23) go from one to the other:

1. Add a camera, name it «cameraFPS» and move it in place of the driver.

2. Select the «car» object, then the «cameraFPS» object, and parent them with `Ctrl`+`P` (Parent to). This camera follows the car.

3. Add a camera, name it «cameraTPS» and move it a few meters behind the car, the exact position is not important.

4. Open the «Logic Editor». Add an «Always» sensor, check «Activate on True Level Triggering», give a frequency of 10.

5. Add an «Edit Object» actuator, «Track To», select the «Car» object, set up «Time» to 10 and check «3D». Keep the default axes. The camera is turning towards the car.

6. Add a «Camera» actuator, «Camera Object»: select the «Car» object, «Height»:12.0, «Axis»: «+Y», «Min»: 5.0 , «Max»:30.0, «Damping»:0.03. From that point, the camera is «hampered» in car chase, that gives a good effect without programing.

7. Link actuators with the sensor.

8. Select the «car» object and go to the «Logic Editor». Go to state#2 (define the keys).

9. Add a «Keyboard» sensor and select a key corresponding to the «cameraFPS» view (ex: key «1»).

10. Add a «Scene» actuator, select the «Set Camera» mode and the «cameraFPS» camera. Link the sensor with the actuator

11. Repeat the same operation to select the «cameraTPS» view (key «2» for example)

12. Go to state#1, go to «3D View» and test (`P`)

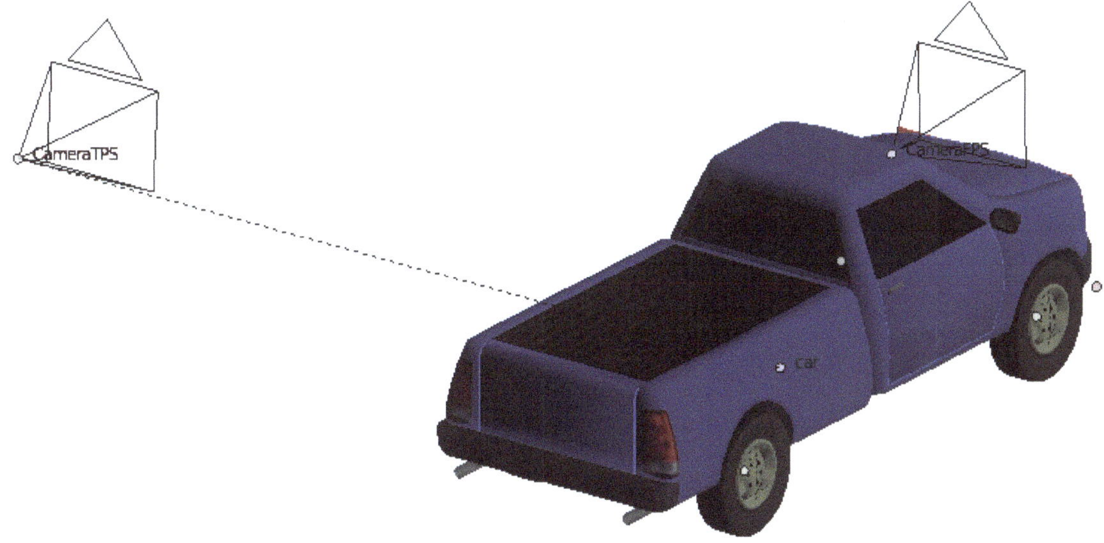

Illustration 23: 2 cameras positioned for 2 types of point of view

Possible improvements:

- Add a camera on the road to show the use of suspensions and to create interesting effects.
- Put all around the raceway some cameras and change of point of view when the sensor with «Near» type detect them. These cameras are in the «car» object «tracking» mode.

Step 4: Fine adjustment of suspensions

1. Create a new text document named «suspension.py» and paste the following script.
2. Select the «car» object and go to the «Logic Editor», go to state #3
3. Add an «Always» sensor
4. Add a «Python» controller and select the script «suspension.py»
5. Add an «and» controller
6. Add a «State» actuator, «Set state», and select the state #2 (to go back other driving control).
7. Link the sensor with the 2 controllers, then the «and» controller with the actuator
8. Go to state #1 and modify the actuator with go to state #3 and not in state# 2 (add a setup state)
9. Go to «3D View» and test (⌨)

Script «carsetup.py» (source: www.tutorialsforblender3d.com – Licence CC3):

```python
import bge

def main():
        controller = bge.logic.getCurrentController()
        vehicleID = ConstraintID(controller)
        Tire_Grip(vehicleID)
        Suspension_Compression(vehicleID)
        Suspension_Damping(vehicleID)
        Suspension_Stiffness(vehicleID)
        Roll_Influence(vehicleID)

def ConstraintID(controller):
```

```python
        carObj = controller.owner
        vehicleID = carObj["vehicleID"]
        return vehicleID

def Tire_Grip(vehicleID):
        grip_0 = 50.0    # front driver
        grip_1 = 50.0    # front passenger
        grip_2 = 50.0    # rear driver
        grip_3 = 50.0    # rear passenger
        vehicleID.setTyreFriction(grip_0, 0) # FD tire
        vehicleID.setTyreFriction(grip_1, 1) # FP tire
        vehicleID.setTyreFriction(grip_2, 2) # RD tire
        vehicleID.setTyreFriction(grip_3, 3) # RP tire

def Suspension_Compression(vehicleID):
        compression_0 = 2.0    # front driver
        compression_1 = 2.0    # front passenger
        compression_2 = 2.0    # rear driver
        compression_3 = 2.0    # rear passenger
        vehicleID.setSuspensionCompression(compression_0, 0)
        vehicleID.setSuspensionCompression(compression_1, 1)
        vehicleID.setSuspensionCompression(compression_2, 2)
        vehicleID.setSuspensionCompression(compression_3, 3)

def Suspension_Damping(vehicleID):
        damp_0 = 20.0    # front driver
        damp_1 = 20.0    # front passenger
        damp_2 = 20.0    # rear driver
        damp_3 = 20.0    # rear passenger
        vehicleID.setSuspensionDamping(damp_0, 0)
        vehicleID.setSuspensionDamping(damp_1, 1)
        vehicleID.setSuspensionDamping(damp_2, 2)
        vehicleID.setSuspensionDamping(damp_3, 3)

def Suspension_Stiffness(vehicleID):
        stiffness_0 = 12.5    # front driver
        stiffness_1 = 12.5    # front passenger
        stiffness_2 = 12.5    # rear driver
        stiffness_3 = 12.5    # rear passenger
        vehicleID.setSuspensionStiffness(stiffness_0, 0)
        vehicleID.setSuspensionStiffness(stiffness_1, 1)
        vehicleID.setSuspensionStiffness(stiffness_2, 2)
        vehicleID.setSuspensionStiffness(stiffness_3, 3)

def Roll_Influence(vehicleID):
        roll_0 = 0.15    # front driver's tire
        roll_1 = 0.15    # front passenger's tire
        roll_2 = 0.15    # rear driver's tire
        roll_3 = 0.15    # rear passenger's tire
        vehicleID.setRollInfluence( roll_0, 0)
        vehicleID.setRollInfluence( roll_1, 1)
        vehicleID.setRollInfluence( roll_2, 2)
        vehicleID.setRollInfluence( roll_3, 3)

main()
```

This script allows you to finely set BGE wrapper with values:
- The adherence of the tires on the ground (Tire_Grip). here: 50.0
- The compression of couple recoil spring of the suspension (Suspension_Compression). Here: 2.0
  The damping (Suspension_Damping). Here: 20.0
- The Suspensions Stiffness (Suspension_Stiffness). Here: 12.5. The lowest it's, the more you slide.
- The roll influence (Roll_Influence). Here: 0.15. The highest it's, the more the car turn over in a bend.

Step 5: An infernal Landscape

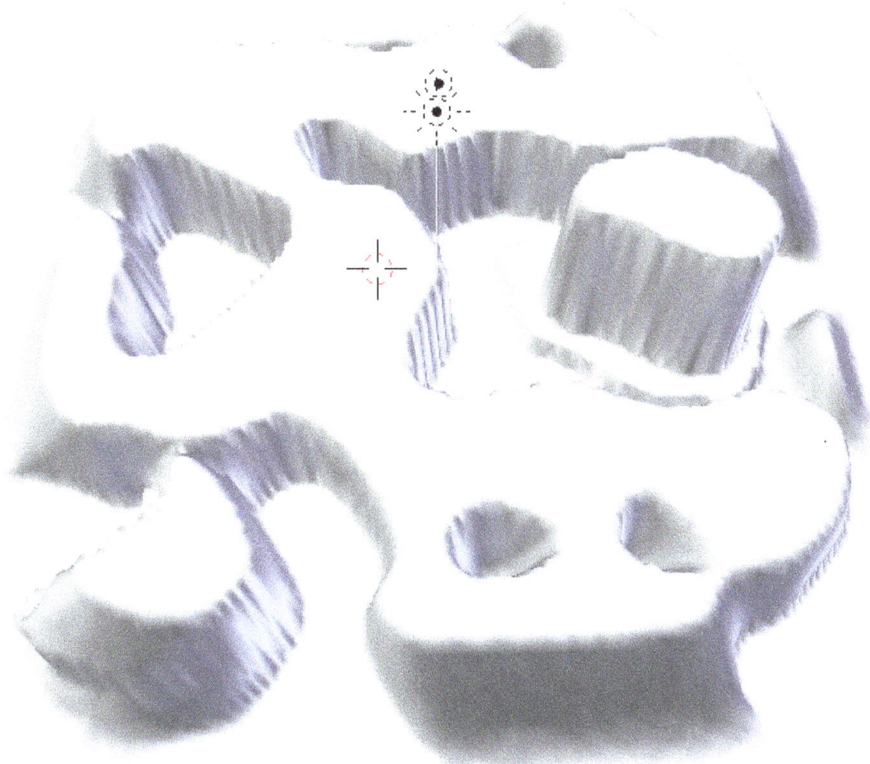

Illustration 24: Landscape generated by ANT, modified in «Sculpt mode» and in «Edit Mode» to increase some levels, and a displacement map slightly applied

We need a large landscape with wides and relatively flats parts.

1. Open a new file «Track01.blend»: a file per raceway.

2. Follow the **recipe III.1** («Ant Generator») to **model** the principal landscape. Type: «Multifractal», «subdivisions»:128, «mesh size»:6, «Depth:6», «lacunarity»: 1, check «Invert», «Height»:1.50, «Offset»:1.0, «Plateau»:0.75. Don't forget to do a «Flip Normals» in «Edit Mode», otherwise the landscape stay «black» in BGE (even if it's visible in 3D View GLSL).

3. You can add some details in «Sculpt Mode» like arch, gateway, etc: activate «Dynamic Topology» and use the «snake Hook» brush. Be careful: don't slow the game with an oversize landscape. Apply a «triangulate» modifier. Indeed, the physics engine can only process with triangular faces and the conversion will not necessarily be made by Blender: many errors can occurs by forgetting this step.

4. The landscape is automatically generated with flat places to allow the traffic. But for rodeoin', add a displacement map: in the «Properties» window, «Modifier» Tab, add a modifier with «Displace» type. Configure: «Midlevel» to 0.05, «Strength» to 30.0, «Direction»: Z, «Texture Coordinates»: Global. Add a new texture with «cloud» type, Basis: «Voronoi F1», «size»: 0.25, «Nabla»: 0.1 and «Depth»: 10.

5. Depending on the selected game machines, it's also possible to apply a «decimate» modifier to limit the number of faces (a decimate of 50% has no impact on visuals).

6. Do a scale (S) of 500 and apply (object → Apply → Scale). Go from viewport clippling (menu «Properties» of «3D View») to 10000 to see all the scenery in edition mode.

7. Do an UV Unwrap and add a material and 3 textures. As the landscape is very big, we you try to

see all the scenery, it seems « blurred», even in high resolution. Cheat by using 2 textures with repeating units (mapping size x300) with an inserted stencil (recipe III.2 – «**Texture Splatting**»). Choose 2 textures fairly closes representing a volcanic soil.

8. Prepare a lighting environment with the recipe III.4. Take a red color for the soil reflexion (RGB: 1.0, 0.05, 0.1 and intensity: 0.2) and **simulate the presence of flowing lava**, and a night blue color for the sky (RGB: 0.003, 0.003, 0.05 and intensity: 0.2). For the sun, choose 45° of inclination. Colors are marked on the car: its rocker Tab becomes brown.

9. Select the layer #2. Add a plane at a certain height to obtain a **surface with lava** and use the recipe III.12 to have an effect of water's surface. Modify the material: diffuse (1.0, 0.0, 0.0), «Shading Emit»: 2.0. Concerning the «watercolor» texture, «Diffuse»: «Intensity»: 25.0, «color»:1.0, check «RGB to Intensity» and choose an orange color (1.0, 0.35, 0.25). Check «Physics», «friction»: 0.0 and «Elasticity»: 1.0

10. Select the layer#3. Add a **skydome** by using the recipe III.3, choose a starry night, or a surrealist sky with night blue color.

11. Add a fog: recipe III.5. «Horizon Color»: RVB (0.0, 0.0, 0.01), «Horizon Color»: RVB (0.0, 0.0, 0.0), Quadratic – Start: 1m / Depth: 120m

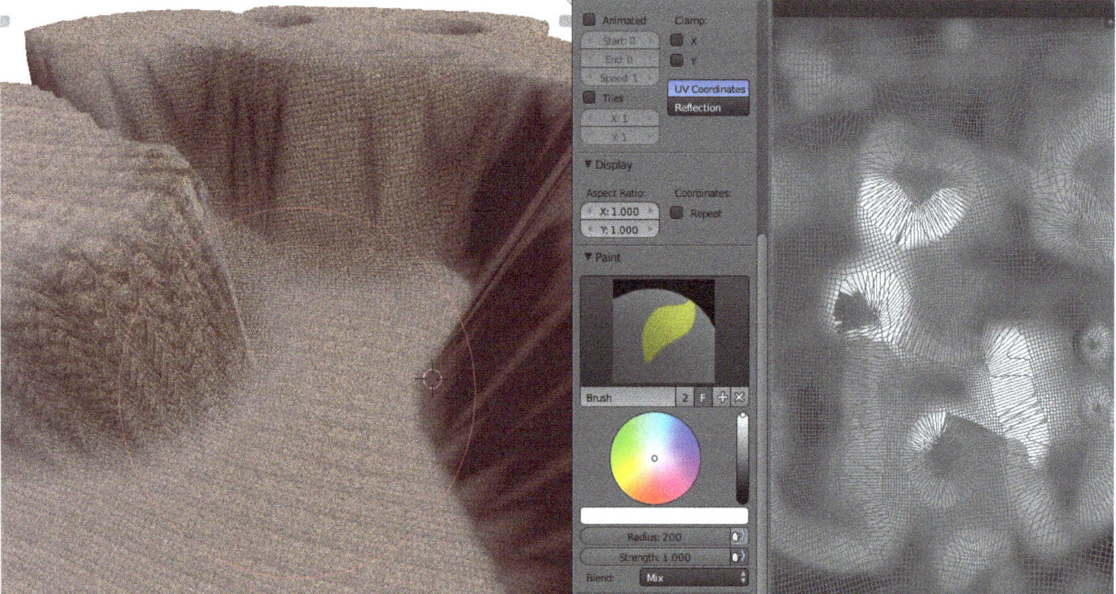

Illustration 25: «Texture Splatting» to break the "moire" effect due to a single texture repeated too much times on a big landscape

Step 6: Raceway design

1. Go to «3D View» and display only the landscape. In «Edit Mode», select a point from the landscape and position the cursor to this place («space» → «Snap cursor to selected»).

2. Add a Bezier curve (**Shift**+**A** → «Curve» → «Bezier»). Name it «RoadCurve». Resize it to be able to see it on the landscape (S x100).

3. Go to mode top view (7) to have a plane curve. The height is independently worked, otherwise the results will be will be unpredictable and be very hard to undo.

4. By successive extrusions, obtain a curve like on Illustration 26. In the beginning, only position the points, then, when the raceway is finished, click on each point and do a rotation to round the curve. If necessary, move on the axis X and Y the points to stick to the landscape. Don't hesitate to pass throw some elements of the scenery.

5. Work in free view and move the track points on the axis Z (G Z) to create relief on the raceway, like on Illustration 27.

Illustration 26: using a Bezier curse to model a road

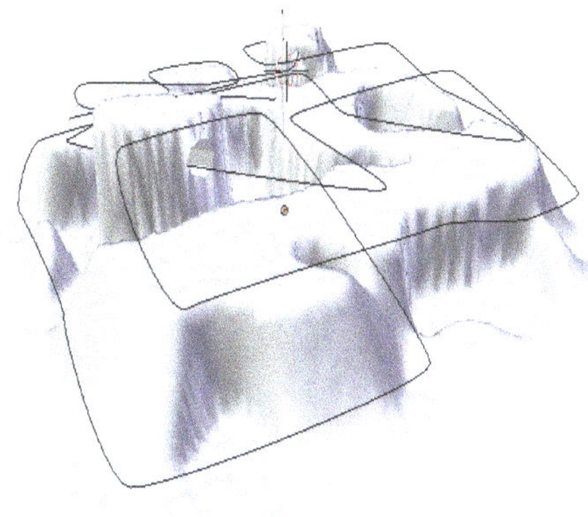

Illustration 27: Modify the height points to stick to the road

6. Take another layer. Draw a free form like on Illustration 28. This form will be the basis for the Bezier curse (bevel) to **draw the raceway**. Name it «RoadModel», then convert into curse (**Alt**+**C** → Curve from Mesh).

7. Come back to the principal layer and modify the curse settings «RoadCurve» in the «Properties» window, «Active Data» Tab, «Geometry» panel , «Bevel Object»: select «RoadModel». In the «Active Spline» Tab, we can modify the resolution to obtain a more detail geometry, be careful:!!! this action modify the number of vertex. A good compromise: 5. To have a flat track, in the panel «Shape», we can set «Twisting» to «Z-Up» and playing with the «smooth», we can modify the base of the way.

8. For **tunnels**, position the cursor near the entrance of the tunnel. Add a cube (name it «hole»), resize it and do a rotation to symbolize the tunnel. It's possible too to add a «modifier» with «Subsurf» type to have a rounder shape. The Illustration 29 give an example of this hole pattern. To apply it, select the landscape, then apply a «modifier» with «Boolean» type, «operation»: «difference» and select the «hole» object. We need only to hide the hole object.

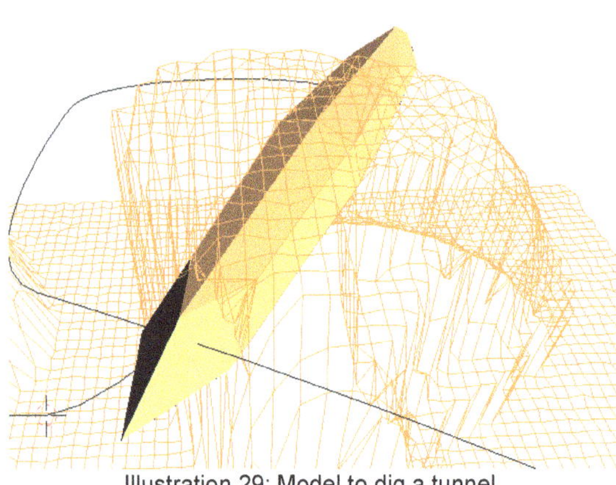

Illustration 29: Model to dig a tunnel

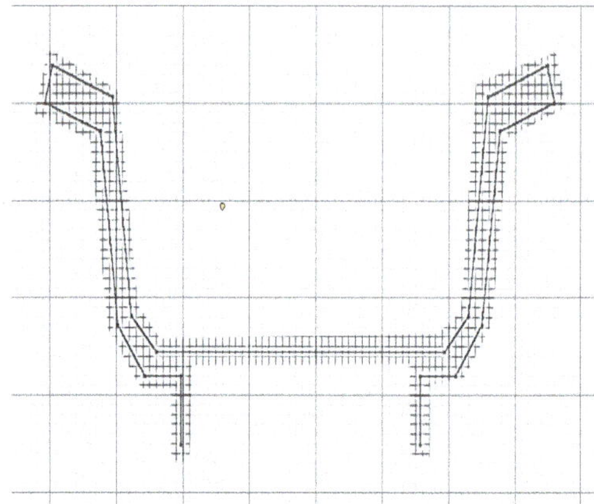

Illustration 28: Model to design the road

9. It's always possible to modify the curse for the moment. Please verify that all the track is practicable, but it's impossible to test in this way. Before, you need to transform it in a mesh. Select the «RoadCurve» object, duplicate it (**Shift**+**D**), rename it «RoadMesh» and convert into mesh **Alt**+**C** → «Convert Mesh from Curve». In the «Physics» panel, select the «Static» type. Move «RoadCurve» in the layer of «RoadModel». Apply to «RoadMesh» a modifier «triangulate».

10. Preserve the way in the form of «Curve» allows to do later modifications of the way. When it's in the form of «mesh», it's possible to modify the edges of the lower part of the way: we can add a support structure like on Illustration 30.

11. To distinguish the roadsides: create a new material «Track». Choose for example, a material with a texture which has an alpha canal of transparency, representing a grind (goods speed effects and allows to visualize the road). Go to «Edit Mode» and select all the faces corresponding to the part on which the vehicle can be driven. Assign the «Track» material to these faces. When the road is entirely done, apply a separation by material («space» → separate → By Material): we'll have 2 objects: «roadmesh.track» (the road) and «roadmesh.sides» (the sides). See Illustration 31.

12. Import the car by joining this folder to «car.blend». In the «info» window, «File» menu → Link. Place the car at the entrance of the road. Resize according to needs of use, but without forgotten ti apply the modification on the tires position and the tires radius.

13. Test (**P**)

Illustration 30: Add a support structure to the mesh

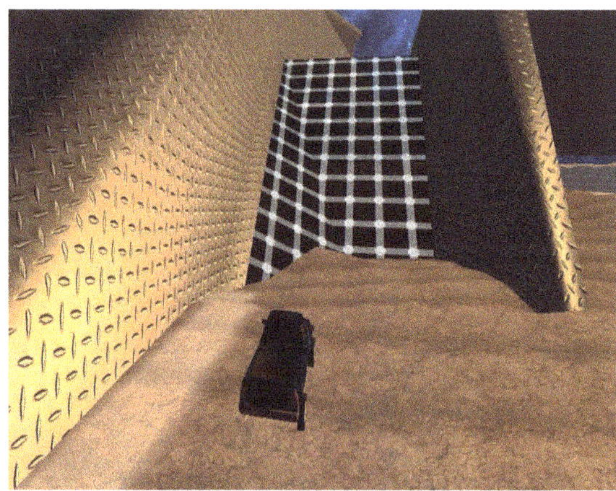

Illustration 31: Example of texture applied to the road

Illustration 32: Final result final: an infernal road !

improvements:

14. Create looping using the same method as for the road. Deactivate the curse «Twisting» and work with a side-view for the moment.

15. Create some semi-transparent tubes for more sensations: then, depending upon the speed of the vehicle, the tires «gripping» and the friction coefficient of the tube material, it's possible to drive upside down on all the tube faces.

16. An infernal circuit needs a final ramp ! Modeling it like on Illustration 33.

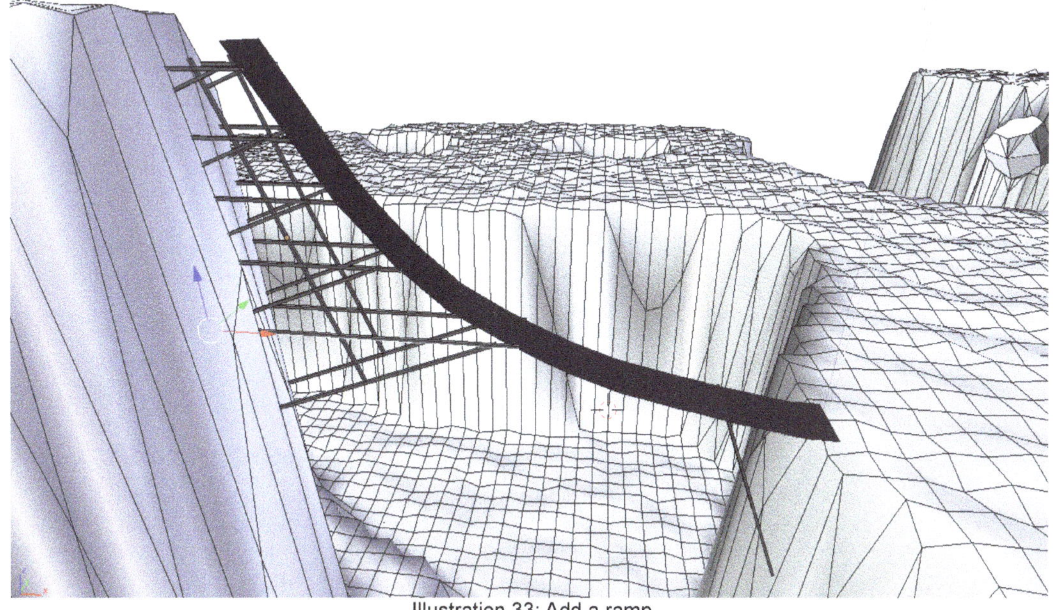

Illustration 33: Add a ramp

Step 7: Game-play Improvements

The vehicle is bouncing too high, easily flips, etc.

To obtain a car which lands on its tires:
1. Select the «car» object and go to the «Logic Editor». Go to the logic layer #3.
2. Add an «Always» sensor
3. Add an actuator with «Constraint» type, «constraint mode»: «Orientation Constraint», «Direction»: «Z Axis», «Damping»:50, «Reference Direction»: «Z»: 1.0
4. Link the sensor with the actuator

To avoid getting a fly:
1. Add an «And» controller and link the 2 sensors with the controller. The condition is: «the road is between 3 and 50 units».
2. Select the «roadmesh.track» object and go to the «Logic Editor». Add a «track» property with «boolean» type, checked.
3. Select the «car» object and go to the logic layer #3.
4. Add a «Ray» sensor, check «Invert», «Property»: «track», Select «-Z Axis», «range»: 3.0.
5. Add a «Ray» sensor, «Property»: «track», Select «-Z Axis», «range»: 50.0.
6. Add a «motion» actuator, «Motion type»: «simple motion», «Force» «Z»: -120000.0, check «L», «Damping Frames»:5.
7. Link the actuator with the controller. If the condition is respected: when the car flies, we apply a vertical force to create a fake gravity, as if the road has a force field.

To avoid car collisions on the circuit:
1. Select the «roadmesh.sides» object and go to the «Logic Editor». Add a «sides» «property» with «boolean», checked.
2. Select the «car» object and add a «Ray» sensor, «property»: «sides», «axis»: «+X Axis», «range»: 7.0 (to define according to the vehicular width)
3. Add a «motion» actuator, «Motion type»: «simple motion», «angular velocity» «Z»: 0.5, check «L», «damping frames»:20
4. Link the sensor with the actuator. The passenger side is «helped».
5. Add another «Ray» sensor, «property»: «sides», «axis»: «-X Axis», «range»: 7.0 (like precedent)
6. Add a «motion» actuator, «Motion type»: «simple motion», «angular velocity» «Z»: -0.5, check «L», «damping frames»:20
7. Link the sensor with the actuator. The passenger side is «helped».

Illustration 34: smoke from the exhaust pipe

Step 8: Sound effects

Download the following sounds or use some other sounds:

1. Engine start (A): sound proposed #2097
2. IDLE engine (B): sound proposed #2096
3. Skidding (C): sound proposed #809
4. Small impact (D): sound proposed #4910
5. Big impact (E): sound proposed #4909
6. Fire (F): sound proposed #7451
7. Boost (G): sound proposed #10195
8. Music (H): sound proposed #10371

To download sounds on FreeSfx (www.freesfx.co.uk): open an account (free) and replace the number in the following address: http://www.freesfx.co.uk/download/?type=mp3&id=2097.

Engine start and music:

1. Select the «car» object and open the «Logic Editor». Select the logic layer #1
2. Add an «Always» sensor
3. Add a «Sound» actuator, select the sound (H), «Play Mode»: «Loop End», «Volume»: 0.25 and «3D Sound» unchecked.
4. Add a «Sound» actuator, select the sound (A), «Play Mode»: «Play End», «Volume»: 0.50, check «3D Sound», «Reference Distance»: 10.0
5. Link the actuators with the sensor
6. Go to «3D View» and test (P)

Engine noise:

Use a simple function: engine noise and sound are depending of the vehicle speed.

1. Open the «Text» window and add a new python script «car.py». Paste the following script.
2. Select the «car» object and open the «Logic Editor». Select the logic layer #3.
3. Add a «Delay» sensor, «Delay»: 140 (to give time to the engine to start)
4. Add a «Python» controller, select «module» and write «car.sound».
5. Link the sensor with the controller
6. Add a «Sound» actuator. Name it «SoundIDLE». Select the sound (B), «Play Mode»: «Loop End», «Volume»: 0.50, check «3D Sound», «Reference Distance»: 10.0
7. Link the actuator with the precedent controller.
8. Go to «3D View» and test (P)

Script python «car.py»:

```python
def sound(cont):
    own = cont.owner

    # Control Speed Sound
    speed = own.getLinearVelocity(0).length
    cont.actuators["SoundIDLE"].pitch = speed / 150 + 1
    #cont.actuators["SoundIDLE"].volume = speed / 35

    cont.activate(cont.actuators["SoundIDLE"])
```

Use the function getLinearVelocity() to have a speed vector (convert in speed using length). Change the pitch to boost the sound reading when the speed increases.

Skidding:

See if there's skidding. Detect a rapid gear change. The rule used here is: «when the vehicle lost 15 % of speed between 2 function calls (change with tests)».

1. Open the«car.py» script and add the following lines between the speed control and the actuator activation.

2. Add a «speed» property to «car» with «Float» type, initialized to 0.0

3. Link the controller managing this script with the sensors «Gas», «Left», «Right», «Brake» and «eBrake».

4. Add a «Sound» actuator. Name it «SoundSkid». Select the sound (C), «Play Mode»: «Play End», «Volume»: 1.0, check «3D Sound», «Reference Distance»: 10.0

5. Link the actuator with the controller.

6. Go to «3D View» and test ([P])

Script python «car.py»:

```python
# Detect Skid
if (own["speed"] > (speed*1.15)) & (speed > 40.0):
    cont.activate(cont.actuators["SoundSkid"])
# update Speed
own["speed"] = speed
```

Little collisions:

When the car flies and heavily fall back, or when it touches a rock with its body, it's possible to use the «collision» sensor to launch a sound. And Manage the damages too.

1. Select the «Landscape» object, open the «Logic Editor» and add a property «choc» with boolean type, checked.

2. Idem with the «RoadMesh.sides» and «RoadMesh.track» objects. Give another property to have different sounds depending the object.

3. Select the «car» object and open the logic layer #3. Add a «damage» «Integer» property initialized to 0. Check «i» for the display at debug.

4. Add a «Collision» sensor, «property»: «choc»

5. Add a «Sound» actuator, select the sound (D), «Play Mode»: «Play Stop», «Volume»: 1.0, check «3D Sound», «Reference Distance»: 10.0

6. Add a «Property» actuator, «Mode»: «Add», «Property»: «damage», «Value»: 1

7. Link the sensor with the actuators.

8. Go to «3D View» and test ([P])

Big collision:

To detect when the car flip to play a special sound:

1. Select the «car» object, open the «Logic Editor» and select the logic layer #3

2. Add a «Ray» sensor, «property»: «choc», «Axis»: «+Z Axis», «Range»: 10

3. Add a «Sound» actuator, select the sound (E), «Play Mode»: «Play Stop», «Volume»: 1.0, check «3D Sound», «Reference Distance»: 10.0

4. Add a «Property» actuator, «Mode»: «Add», «Property»: «damage», «Value»: 10

5. Link the sensor with the actuators.

6. Go to «3D View» and test ([P])

Improvements: Substitute a damaged model according to the accident.

Fire sound:
2 circumstances: when the car takes fire (too much damages) and when the car is on lava.
1. Select the «Lava Surface» object and open the «Logic Editor». Add a «lava» property with boolean type, checked.
2. Select the «car» object, and go into the logic layer #3.
3. Add a «Ray» sensor, «property»: «lava», «Axis»: «-Z axis», «range»: 5
4. Add a «Sound» actuator, select the sound (F), «Play Mode»: «Play End», «Volume»: 1.0, check «3D Sound», «Reference Distance»: 10.0
5. Link the sensor with the actuator.
6. Go to «3D View» and test (P)

Improvements:
*   Use the **recipe VII.18** to create flames around or into the vehicle, as you want.
*   Use a «Property» sensor, «Evaluation type»: «Interval» and give an interval between 50 and 100 to the «damage» property for example. Then, the fire on the car only trigger between these 2 values.

Boost:
A «nitro» kit to gain speed ?
1. Select the «car» object and open the «Logic Editor». Select the logic layer #3
2. Add a «boost» «Integer» property initialized to 3 (3 available boosts since the game beginning)
3. Add a «Keyboard» sensor, and choose a key for the «Boost» (example: «B»)
4. Add a «Property» sensor, «Evaluation Type»: «Interval», «Property»: «boost», «Minimum»: 1, «Maximum»: 9999 (This should be enough!)
5. Add a «Motion» actuator, «Motion Type»: «Simple Motion», «Linear Velocity» «Y»: 120.0 and check «L» (to ensure that the force be applied in the vehicle Y axis)
6. Add a «Property» actuator, «Mode»: «Add», «Property»: «boost», «value»: -1. Name it «boost--», it'll be removed.
7. Add a «Sound» actuator, select the sound (G), «Play Mode»: «Play End», «Volume»: 1.0, check «3D Sound», «Reference Distance»: 10.0
8. Link the sensors with the actuators using an «And» controller

Add too a little filter to give a speed effect. With an ATI/AMD graphic card, the «Motion Blur» filter could not give good results. In that case, choose another filter like «Laplacian» to give a «surrealist» effect to the scenery.
9. Add an actuator «Filter 2D», «Type»: «Motion Blur» (speed effect).
10. Add an actuator «Property», «Mode»: «Assign», «Property»: «filterTime», «Value»: 5
11. Link the 2 actuators with the precedent controller.
12. Add a «property» «filterTime» with «Integer» type
13. Add an «Always» sensor, check «Activate On True Level Triggering» and give a frequency at 50
14. Add a «Property» actuator, «Mode»: «Add», «Property»: «filterTime», «Value»: -1
15. Link the sensor with the actuator
16. Add a «Property» sensor, «Evaluation Type»: «Equal», «Property»: «filterTime», «Value»: 0.
17. Add an actuator with «Filter 2D» type, «Type»: «Remove Filter»
18. Link the sensor with the actuator
19. Go to «3D View» and test (P)

Get the smoke out of the exhaust pipe:

1. Select an invisible layer (where there are «curves» for example) and add an «icosphere» (one subdivision is enough). Name it «Smoke». In «Edit Mode», do an UV mapping («U» → «Sphere Projection»). Add a semi-transparent material to it,representing smoke with recipes III.6 and VII.17.

2. Position the cursor in place of the exhaust pipe, slightly separating. Add an «Empty» with «Sphere» type. Name it «SmokeEmit.P» (passenger side).

3. Parent it to the vehicle (Select first the children (the empty), then the parent (the «car» object, and `Ctrl` + `P`)

4. If necessary, do the same on the other exhaust pipe («SmokeEmit.C» driver side).

5. Open the «Text Editor» and add the following script lines to the script car.py. Adapt according the number of empty (blocs: *if random()... cont.activate*)

6. Select the «empty» (ies), open the «Logic Editor» and add an «Always» sensor, check «Activate on True Level Triggering», tune «Freq» to 2.

7. Add a «Python» controller, select «Module», then write «car.emitSmoke». Link the controller with the precedent sensor.

8. Add to «SmokeEmit.P» an actuator «smoke.P» with «Edit Object» type, «Add Object», select «Smoke», «time»: 50, «Linear Velocity»: 0.0, -20.0, 2.0 and check «L».

9. Do the same with «SmokeEmit.C» and its actuator «smoke.C»

10. Link the 2 actuators with the precedent controller.

11. Go to «3D View» and test (`P`) – Illustration 34.

Script car.py (addition):

```python
from random import random

def emitSmoke(cont):
    own = cont.owner
    speed = own.getLinearVelocity(0).length
    if random() < (speed/50):
        cont.actuators["smoke.P"].linearVelocity = [10*random(),-10*random(),10*random()]
        cont.activate(cont.actuators["smoke.P"])
    if random() < (speed/50):
        cont.actuators["smoke.C"].linearVelocity = [-10*random(),-10*random(),10*random()]
        cont.activate(cont.actuators["smoke.C"])
```


Add a 3D compass:

1. Open the «Text Editor» window and add to the «car.py» script the following script lines.

2. Download a compass picture (ex: Google picture «compass filetype:png»). Make sure that the picture has an alpha transparency or delete the fund with a software like «The Gimp».

3. Add a new scene «GUI». This scene allows to display all the game information.

4. Add a camera at (0,0,50.0) pointing down (axis: -Z)

5. Go in camera view (0) and add a plane at the bottom right of the screen (Illustration 35), name it «Compass». Go to «Edit Mode», do an UV mapping (U → Unwrap) then come back to «Object Mode».

6. Ensure to be in «Blender Game» mode. Create a new Material. Check «Shadeless» to be independent from the light. Check «Transparency» (Z Transparency, Alpha: 0.0). «Game Settings» → «Alpha Blend: Alpha Blend»

7. Add the downloaded picture as a new texture, «Mapping Coordinates: UV», «Map: UVMap», «Projection: Cube». Check «Show Alpha» to verify the transparency. Check «Diffuse» → «Alpha»: 0.1.

8. Test (`P`): the compass must be transparent.

9. Come back to the principal scenery and select the «car» object, then go to «Logic Editor» mode.

Select the logic layer #1.

10. Add an «Always» sensor

11. Add a «Scene» actuator, «Mode: Add Overlay Scene» and select the «GUI» scene. Link the sensor with the actuator.

12. Select the logic layer #3. Add an «Always» sensor, check «Activate on True Level Triggering» and select 10 as frequency.

13. Add a «Python» controller, «Module» and enter «car.updateOverlay». Link the sensor with the actuator.

14. Come back in «3D View» and test (P).

Script car.py (addition):

```python
def overlayUpdate(cont):
    own = cont.owner
    scenes = bge.logic.getSceneList()
    screen = [scene for scene in scenes if scene.name=="Gui"][0]
    compass = screen.objects["Compass"]
    rotation = own.worldOrientation.to_euler()
    compass.worldOrientation = rotation
```

We simply apply to the compass the «car» object rotation matrix. So, we can see the change in direction, and the change in bases. To reorient the north, modify the precedent script to do a rotation on the Z axis.

Add a speedometer:

1. Open the «Text Editor» window and add to the «car.py» script the following script lines in the Over-layUpdate function, after the existing lines.

2. Download a speedometer picture (ex: Google picture «speedometer filetype:png»). Make sure that the picture has an alpha transparency or delete the fund with a software like «The Gimp». In every case, you must delete the needle.

3. Repeat the operations 5, 6 and 7 of the precedent recipe (compass). Place the speedometer at the bottom left of the screen in camera mode (Illustration 35).

4. Place the cursor at the center of the speedometer (needle axis of rotation), with a little Z gap of 0.1: to avoid the needle is on the speedometer plane.

5. Add a new plane, name it «Needle», go to «Edit Mode» and move the 4 points to obtain a needle that points to the speedometer 0. Select the future object center of rotation and Shift+S → «Cursor to selected». Go to «Object Mode» and «Object» → «Transform» → «Origin to 3D Cursor». Do a test rotation on the Z axis, the needle must follow the speedometer. Apply the rota-tion (Ctrl+A → Rotation). Repeat for the maximal speed, take note of the Smax and the angle Amax. Apply an angle of (Amax/Smax) in degrees for 1 speed unit. With Python, angles are in radians. 1° = (3.14159/180) radians. The coefficient to apply to the speed is: (Amax/Smax)*(3.14159/180). Adapt the script with this value.

6. Go to the principal scenery, go to «3D View» and test (P)

Script car.py (addition):

```python
    speed = own.getLinearVelocity(0).length
    needle = screen.objects["Needle"]
    rotation = needle.worldOrientation.to_euler()
    rotation.z = speed * (-271/140)*(3.14159/180) #(Amax/Smax)
    needle.worldOrientation = rotation
```

Add boosts display:

1. Download a boost picture (ex: Google picture «dynamite filetype:png»). Make sure that the picture has an alpha transparency or delete background with a software like «The Gimp».

2. Repeat the operations 5, 6 and 7 of the compass recipe. Place the boost at the right of the speedometer. Name it «boost.1»

3. Copy it 2 times (⇧ Shift + D) to have 3 boosts aligned (Illustration 35). Name them «boost.2» (at the center) and «boost.3» (at right).

4. Modify the «car.py» script and add the following function. The boost indicator is modified by this function. Delete the actuator that decrement the boosts.

5. Go to principal scene, select the «car» object, open the «Logic Editor» window and choose the logic layer 3.

6. Delete the «boost--» actuator

7. Add a «Python» controller, select «Module» and write «car.boostOverlay».

8. Link this controller with the «Keyboard» sensor launching the boost.

9. Go to «3D View» and test (P).

Illustration 35: Overlay of the speedometer, compass and boosts

Script car.py (addition):

```python
def boostOverlay(cont):
    if not cont.sensors["Boost"].positive:
        return

    own = cont.owner
    scenes = bge.logic.getSceneList()
    screen = [scene for scene in scenes if scene.name=="Screen"][0]

    boost1 = screen.objects["boost.1"]
    boost2 = screen.objects["boost.2"]
    boost3 = screen.objects["boost.3"]

    own["boost"] -= 1

    if own["boost"]<1:
        boost1.visible = False
    else:
        boost1.visible = True
```

```
if own["boost"]<2:
    boost2.visible = False
else:
    boost2.visible = True
if own["boost"]<3:
    boost3.visible = False
else:
    boost3.visible = True
```

Step 10: Interactivity

Like examples: add some meteors falling from time to time and which cause the ground to shake and can cause the vehicle to roll over frontwards.

According to the environment type, it's possible to pass an airplane, to run a mil, to move the trees leaves, etc.

It's time to add some interactive objects in the scenery to give more gaming fun.

BE CAREFUL: In the later stages, you need to use an object «X» made by any third parties, go on:
http://www.blendswap.com/blends/view/X
and replace X by the corresponding number

Example with a meteor shower:

1. Download a «rock» or «meteor» model. For example, use the object #71209 from OliverMH. Name it «Rock» and place it in an invisible layer.

2. Add to the «car.py» script the function which is in the following script lines.

3. Measure the maximum height of the skydome, note Zmax. Measure too the width and the height of the land: Xland and Yland.

4. Add an Empty at (0.0, 0.0, Zmax), name it «rockEmit».

Open the «Logic Editor» and add an «Always» sensor, check «Activate on True Level Triggering» and put the frequency to 3000 (1 minute – frequency of meteor generation).

5. Add a «Python» controller, select «Module» and write «car.rockRain».

6. Add an «Edit Object» actuator, «Add Object» and select the «Rock» object. «Time»:3000 (it disappears over after 1 minute – it's possible to give a more important value but the collision management take time to the processor, even if the object geometry is simple).

7. Link the sensor with the controller and the controller with the actuator

8. Select the «Rock» object and add a «Rock» property with Boolean type checked.

9. «Properties» window, «Physics» Tab, configure like for a «Rigid Body» with «Mass» 100.00. Activate «Collision Bounds» and select «Triangle Mesh». Make sure that the «skydome» is with «no collision».

10. Select the «Landscape» object and add a little animation with 10-15 frames in which the coordinates changes every 2 or 3 frames, coordinates (X,Y,Z) with a few units (-2 to +2). Effect o shaking. `recipe III.7`.

11. Add a sensor with «collision» type, check «activate on True Level Triggering» and select a frequency of 1500 (to not have shake at each collision when the object rolls).

12. Add an «Action» actuator, «Play», select «LandscapeAction», and setup the «start» and the «end».

13. Add a «Sound» actuator, choose an explosion or impact sound (#3632 of the precedent internet site). Don't activate «3D Sound».

14. Link the actuators with the sensor using an «And» controller.

15. Go to «3D View» and test ([P]) – Illustration 36.

Illustration 36: Meteors falling !

Script car.py (addition):

```python
def rockRain(cont):
    own = cont.owner
    own.position.x = (random() - 0.5) * 1000 # Xland / 3
    own.position.y = (random() - 0.5) * 1000 # Yland / 3
    act = cont.actuators["rockEmit"]
    act.linearVelocity = [(random()-0.5) * 500,
        (random()-0.5) * 500, -500] # Modify to accelerate Fall
    cont.activate(act)
```

Example of animation:

Take a futuristic plane (like the «Futuristic combat jet» from Dennish2010 on BlendSwap, #67546) and with the **recipe V.9.** Create a navigation curse like in the Illustration 37.

Teleporters addition:

When the player fall off the road, he can only come back on the road at the point of origin. To make it easier, install teleporters, elevators, bridges, airflow propulsion devices, etc.

Use the **recipe V.6** to adjust some teleporters (without changing of scenery) on the terrain, and «empties» on the road. Orient axes so that empty has +Y in the road direction if the vehicle use the Y to move.

Download the object # 70335 from gogo199432 as teleporter (apply the «modifiers» to avoid problems and merge to have only one object).

Other ideas:

- **Rocks** that falls near the car when the car moves alongside. Use a radar sensor radar with angle. Object #71506 from OliverMH or # 21177 from mtalhalodhi. Object #69268 from Signovinces (container). The player must speed up the car, slow or avoid the obstacle in another way !

- **Traps to cut the tires.** Setting of with a Ray +Z. Adding damages, or put the car on the top. Object # 66754 from Danimal. Or mines with explosion: object #67071 from pasilan. We can imagine dropping mines by a concurrent too.

- **Airflow propulsion devices** to throw the car in the air. Use a ray +Z for detection and a force +Z for propulsion. Object # 71189 from OliverMH. Or **mechanical lifting device**: object #67103 from pasilan.

- Blocking parts of the road by **force field**. When the car approach this part, apply a force -Y (locale) strong enough to repel the car. Object # 71185 from OliverMH.

- **Defense tower** shooting at anything near. Object # 67094 from pasilan.

- **Big bots to obstruct the road**. Object # 66930 from OliverMH (mechanical spider).

- **Large items** with «rigid bodies» type more or less heavy to slow-down or stop the vehicle. Object # 69774 from Flight King (case), #67492 from bapsite (wheel), barriers: Object #69225 from Signovinces

- **Cameras** following the vehicle and taking photos when accelerating. Object #71872 from dsdlm. A surveillance **drone** to film when viewed from above. Parent to the camera TPS. Object #66686 from Dulon.

- **Walls** made with cubes, the wall is broken when the car gets throw (rigid bodies with mass 1 with «Box» as«collision node»).

- **Fuel reserves**. Add a property «gas» and continue decline using the vehicle «speed» factor. For the collect, `recipe V.8`. Object #69219 from Signovinces or 67825 from Protomace.

- **Signalization,** to give the road, steps,... and the teleporters direction!

- Lumps of rock during high energy collisions from. Object #70244 de RookieProject

- **Buildings** and other parts of scenery. Object #67968 from Blender2012.

- **Lamps**, with different colors! To modify the game atmosphere according to the area. These lamps will be probably «baked» to down the real machine time.

- Bonus with «reparation» type to reduce the damages. It could be a garage, tools, etc. It's possible too to have a counter which reduce the damages when the time pass.

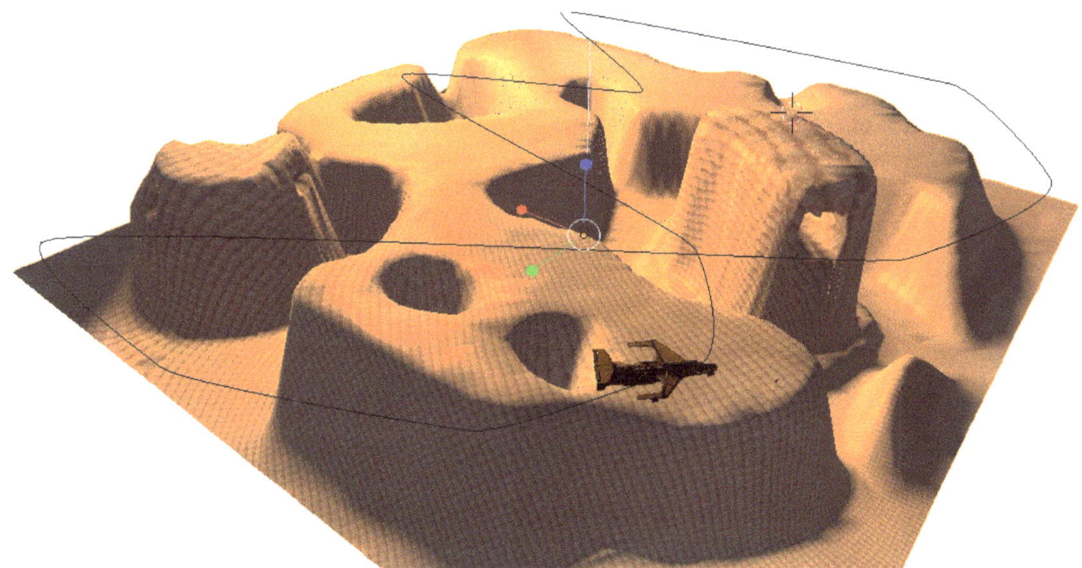

Illustration 37: Navigation Path created from a curse

Step 11: Cameras movements with points of view

The **recipe V.15** explains the creation of this type of camera. Replace «player» by «car» and place the cameras (configure the first camera, and then duplicate it ⏷Shift+D) in strategic locations on the raceway. Don't forget to configure the clipping.

Cameras move when the car arrives and return automatically on the active camera when the car passed. Store in the «cam» property the name of the active camera («cameraTPS» or «cameraFPS»). So, to allow the player to ask a camera change with the keyboard, you must add to each key a «Property» actuator. This actuator assigns to the camera «cam» the name of the new camera.

For the ramp example, you must modify the recipe: use an empty with a radius placed at the ramp entrance. Add, on this empty, the recipe logic, activate the good camera (modify the script).
Place a camera far away to have a best view.

Step 12: 2 player game

Duplicate the «car» object and choose other keys for the control of the vehicle, then, you can add another player.

The **recipe V.16** allow to divide in 2 the screen.
Apply a horizontal separation like in the principal recipe, using cameras «CameraFPS» and «CameraFPS2».

1. Select the «car» object and duplicate it (⏷Shift+D). Modify the basic color and name it «car2» (the Material is the same for the 2, then you have to create a new material: in «Edit Mode», select the Material, click on «select», create a new Material, then «assign»).

2. Duplicate «CameraFPS» and «CameraFPS2» too and parent to the «car2» object. Position as needed.

3. A «carsetup.py» script modification allows to manage several vehicles.

4. Add a «name» property with string type to each «car» object with «player1» for the first and «player2» for the second.

5. Add the «viewports.py» script of the **recipe V.16** and add an «Always» sensor to «Landscape», then a «python» controller, select the «viewports.py» script, link the sensor with the controller.

6. Modify the sensors «Keyboard» of the «car2» object. Then it's possible to play with 2 players, to block each other, to collide, to take or not the same way (Illustration 38). Go to «3D View» and test (P)

```
def Tire_Objects(name):
        frontDriver    = name+".TireFD"  # front driver
        frontPassenger = name+".TireFP"  # front passenger
        rearDriver     = name+".TireRD"  # rear driver
        rearPassenger  = name+".TireRP"  # rear passenger's
```

Going further, modify too the overlay to take into account the 2 vehicles, and duplicate too camera TPS.

Step 13: Some intelligent competitors

To create competitors (NPC) which stay on the road, there a 3 simple approaches:
- Record a «navigation mesh» created from the raceway and create an arrival point at the end of the road. The NPC will try to join this point. Use the **recipe V.13**
- Record checkpoints (**recipe V.9**) the NPC must follow these checkpoints.
- Execute several times the raceway and use a script to record every 50 frames for example, the «car» object position and rotation. Save these information in the form of a «navigation node system».

It's possible to modulate the NPC «intelligence» spacing checkpoints and playing with speed and acceleration.

Illustration 38: Mode 2 players in Multi-view

The NPC intelligence is limited to path seeking. Now you must program these rules in a script. These rules can be more or less followed.

Example of rules:
- With a «Ray axis +/- X», try to be at the raceway center
- With a «Ray axis +/- X», detect the concurrent and try to collide them
- With a «Ray axis -Z», if the vehicle is not on the road, use a «radar» to find the next teleporter
- With a «Ray axis +Y», detect if a concurrent is before and use a «boost» to pass him.
- If «ramp» near, accelerate to fly (Ray -Z)
- If concurrent just before(«Ray axis +Y») for more than 10 seconds, honk or/and push.

The rules must be written in a Python script with appropriate sensors, controllers and actuators. According to the NPC settings, the rules will be kept or not. A «boolean» properties list can be enough. The NPC intelligence can be increased with the time.

II.4. PROJECT #4: OTHER SIMULATORS

Ex #1: Flight simulator (and battle)

The story:

Before being a game, flight simulators are simulator for armies, for studying and conception of new flies, arms and for the training center for pilots.

Microsoft Flight Simulator is one of the most emblematic games: its development began in 1976 as a set of articles on 3D graphics by **Bruce Artwick.** When the editor said to him that the readers wanted to buy the software, Bruce Artwick founded a compagny named LOGIC Corporation in 1977 and sold flight simulators. In 1982, Microsoft purchased these licenses. Since, the product has come a long way: the last simulator versions, MS Flight Simulator 2004 and MS Flight Simulator X, are made to satisfy pilots or futures pilots, or people who dreams to be a pilot.

Emblematic flight simulators: **Falcon**, **Apache**, **Combat Flight Simulator** or **FlightGear**.

Gameplay:

The Gameplay is simple: to learn to take off, to land and eventually to battle against other planes. Controls are more or less simple and the player needs joysticks. Some games need a good deal of knowledge about aeronautic (MS Flight Simulator), others are arcade-style games. The game system looks like a camera with «freeview» type with the possibility of to push the throttle control and to manage the horizontal and vertical bases.

Step #1: Landscape implementation

A flight simulator is characterized by a vast landscape. The **recipe III.2** is used («optimize for big land-scape).

1. Use the **recipe III.2** to generate a landscape with a size of X,Y = 1000,1000, made with 130,000 faces. Add a water body too using the **recipe III.13**.

2. Apply an automatic LoD (version 2.70 of Blender) as seen in the **recipe III.17** to generate 2 new geometries: a first (MD) displayed with 750-1500 units, with a «modifier decimate» of «0.1» (13000 faces), a second (SD) displayed after 2000m, with a «modifier decimate» of «0.01» (1300 faces). Place the first geometry in the layer #2 and the second in the layer #3. On the layer #1 with the landscape in «high resolution».

3. Make a landscape with the **tiles approach** (**recipe III.16**). The map is made of several Tiles. The Illustration 39 gives a landscape example made by 16 units on a matrix 4×4. There's only one object duplicated 16 times, but it's possible to use a lot of different models. We can create land-scapes with big size, varied with a limited number of tiles.

4. Add a camera with «Freeview» type like on **recipe V.1**. In the «Properties» window, «Object Data» Tab, «Lens» panel, set «Focal Length» to «15» and «Clipping End»: «3000».

5. Place the camera at the center of the landscape. The Illustration 40 shows the display of this type of scenery using LoD.

This landscape should include 16 x 130,000 faces, that's to say more than 2 millions of faces. With this method, we average:
- 1 tile HD, ie 130,000 faces
- 3 tiles MD, ie 39,000 faces
- 12 tiles SD, ie 15,600 faces.

In total, there are 200,000 faces to display instead of 2 millions. Without calculate on the camera clipping ! We could too decrease the clipping, but, in that case, the view would be limited. The clipping, is the poor 's LoD ! A good combination of both is interesting.

A system Improvements can be done with continuous loading, like streaming, using the libload function of the recipe III.18. In this way, we can obtain an unlimited landscape.

Step #2: Adding a plane and advanced controls

1. Model a plane or download a model (like object #67546 on Blendswap).
2. Parent the plane with the camera. Now, move the camera to move the plane. In reality, we are interested by the camera to make hiding the plane possible if necessary.
3. Modify the «freeview.py» script to insert the following modification.
4. Select the camera and open the «Logic Editor»
5. Add an «Always» sensor, check «Activate on True Level Triggering» and choose a frequency of 0
6. Add a «Motion» actuator, «type»: «Simple Motion» and «Loc» «-Z»: -1.0, check «L».
7. Link the sensor with the actuator. This allows the traveling along the local axis -Z (frontward) of «cameraFreeview», simulating the engine thrust.

Modifications of freeview.py:

```
invert = -1 # Line 11
act_LeftRight.dRot = [ 0.0, 2*leftRight, leftRight] #line 34
```

The first line allows to inverse the movement according to the mouse movement. The second line allows to add a tilting movement to the right or to the left. Use a collision sensor to manage the possible engine crash.

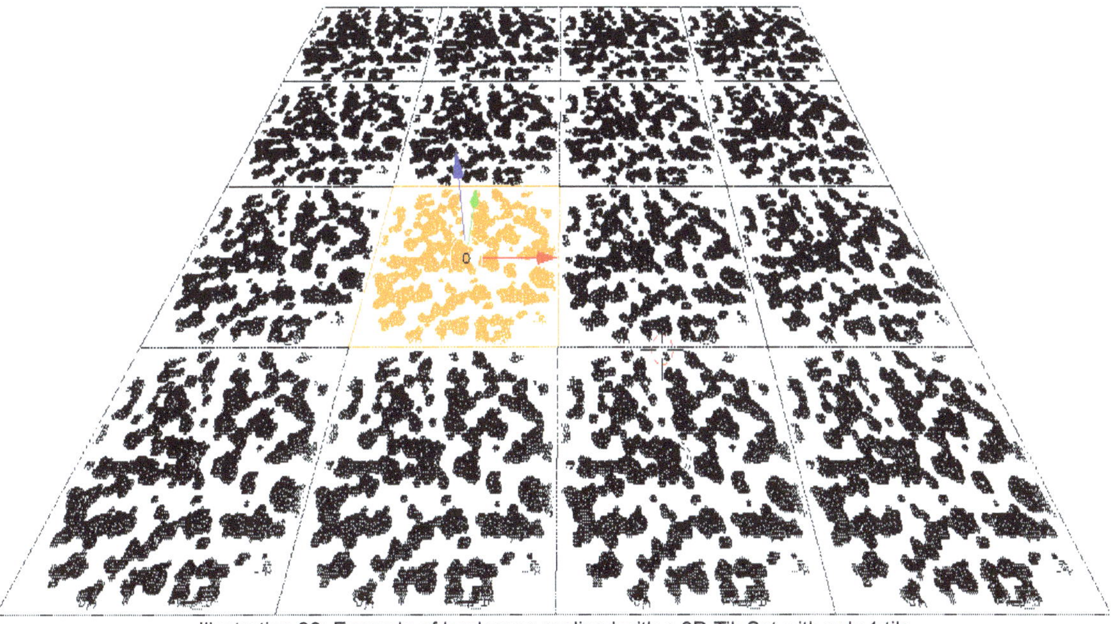
Illustration 39: Example of landscape realized with a 3D TileSet with only 1 tile

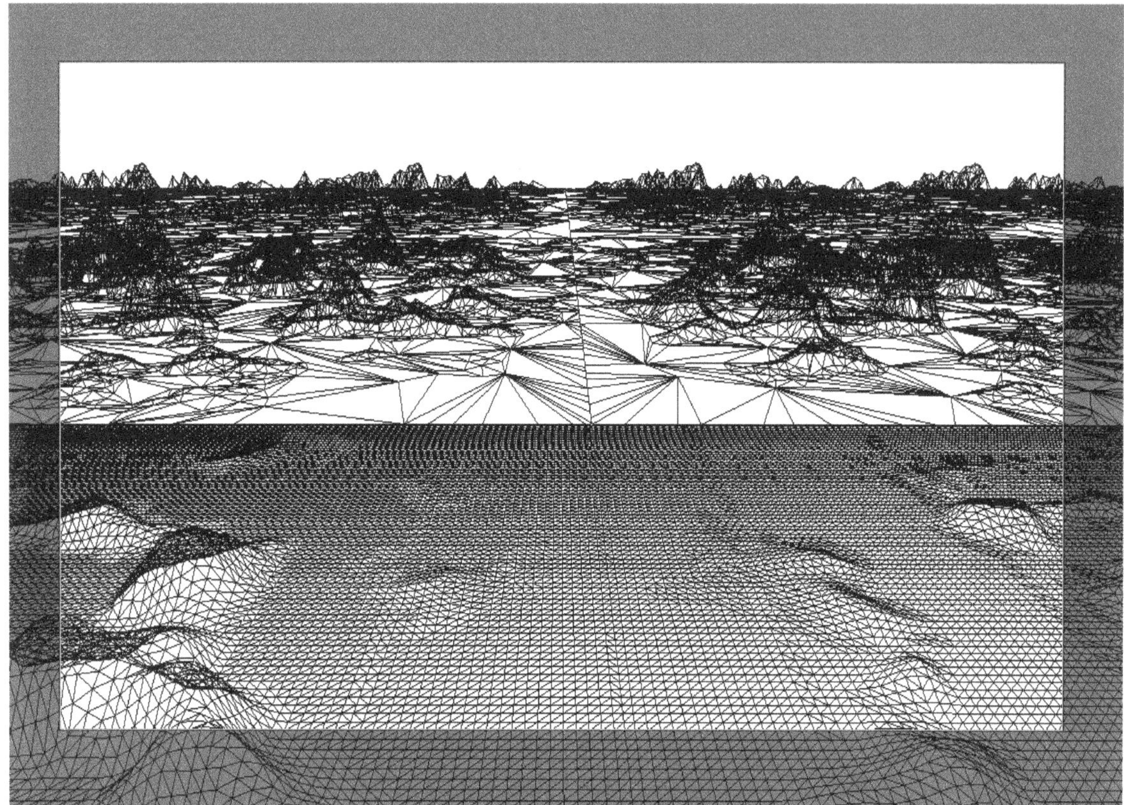

Illustration 40: Landscape tiles display using a LOD – mesh size in the nearest part of the camera is tight because the display takes the HD model.

Step #3: Addition of enemies

Use the script developed for the `recipe V.9` to create a covered way. Add a «radar» sensor or a «near» sensor to detect the presence of the player and add a «steering» actuator.

Add gun sites with ground-to-air missile and use a «radar» sensor to adjust the shooting. The `recipe V.7` shows this kind of sensor.

Shooting handle:

Add a missile launcher and use a collision sensor on the missiles. To do that, use the `recipe V.12` and the example of projectile fired studied in the game «Doom» type.

Regarding the enemies, we can copy the empty that started the missile launch and join it to the enemies. A projectile «Ray» sensor allows to know if the player's plane is in sights.

To create homing missile, add them a «Steering» actuator like in the `recipe V.13.`

Step #4: Improvements

1. Add a «Lens Flare» (very important for this game type) using the `recipe VII.21.`
2. Add a fog (`recipe V.3`) and a volumetric fog (`recipe V.4`) in certain areas, above water to hide some missile batteries.
3. Add a speed-up and a «motion blur» effect for a landscape more or less blurred depending on speed. Use the `recipe VII.9`
4. Add flames and smoke leaving the reactor with the `recipes VII.18` and `VII.19`
5. Add a «Bullet Time» effect when the missile collide an enemy (`recipe VII.22`) and an explosion (`recipe VII.17`).

6. Blow down some debris from shot down aircraft and if it falls on ground, use the **recipes VII.18** and **VII.19** to create a fire and some smoke during 2000 cycles.

7. Add some trees in the form of billboards (**recipe III.14**) and other objects that, seen from the sky, won't take too machine time and are realistic enough. Use the **recipe III.15** to dispose them automatically.

8. Add some buildings to destroy with missiles. The **recipe III.21** shows how to broke some objects, the **recipe VII.17** how to explode them (combine the two) and let it burn with the **recipes VII.18** and **VII.19**.

9. Add an objective mission control: escort a plane (use the **recipe V.9** to create a flight path), destroy building, kill them all !

10. The game «car simulation» developed in this book uses a compass. Add an altimeter too, and a radar to detect enemies close. A cockpit view allows to add a scene with «Overlay» type and all these elements.

11. The **recipe V.21** allows to add a 2 players mode: cooperative for some missions or «only one will survive».

12. The **recipe V.15** allows to add different points of view when the player is near some places. It's possible to highlight an enemies airbase or a particular object thanks to this type of view.

13. According to the number of enemies destroyed, the player can win bonuses in an inventory (**recipe VI.6**): missiles more powerful, lives, time for the mission... or an aircraft to help the player.

14. Add some weather effects with the **recipe VII.20** (rain, snow) and a night mode (a 2D filter with the **recipe VII.9** can be used, in cockpit view).

These are only simple ideas, the more important is to realize that each type of game has its specifications, but the recipes can be used for the most part of the games.

To inspire you, Martins Upitis has developed a flight simulator adding his landscape manager system (using a shader doing by himself). http://tinyurl.com/nl8467n

Another examples on Blender: http://devlog-martinsh.blogspot.fr/

Tutorial to create a helicopter game: http://tinyurl.com/obmo8q9: it's made with 3 documents and with videos unveiling a complete creation project.

Ex #2: Spatial Combat and Simulation

The story: Spatial combat games appeared quite early, before 3D can brings to this type of games a whole new dimension. In 1962, **Nolan Bushnell** discovered the spatial shooting game «**Space War**», made on a DEC PDP-1, by MIT students. Bushnell took the idea and created the first arcade terminal in mass production with a Space War clone, «**Computer Space**», in 1971. «**Deep Space**», developed and published by par Psygnosis, in 1986, is one of the firsts in this type. «**Frontier: Elite II**», in 1993, was the first 3D game, with plain surfaces and using Bezier curves. The «tour de force» of the engine was that it generated more than 10 millions of planets with 700 KB of memory ! More recently, games like «**Freespace**» (1998) and «**X³: Reunion**» offered an additional dimension, the «space opera»: a game with combat and economic simulation, and incredible graphics.

In another category, there are games like «**Microsoft Space Simulator**» (1994). Like the other flight space simulators, the player needs to know some celestial mechanics and astronomy concepts.

Gameplay:

The player is on board of a spaceship or at the head of some spaceships facing spatial enemy forces and avoiding asteroids.

Technique:

When there's only one spaceship, mechanisms are near to flight simulators, excepted for gravity (even if some games ignore this consideration). When there's a set of spaceship, use a big part of technics from strategic games like «Age of Empires», with «3D» combat tactics based on «Starfleet Academy» !

Moving and impact force

We can use a camera with TPS type (recipe V.4) with a view focused on the spaceship, or o view from the interior using a camera FPS (recipe V.2).

The ship must have a «rigid body» to apply forces for moving. Define an approach for the movement:

- **Realist:** apply 6 different forces (-X, +X, -Y, +Y, -Z, +Z). Normally, the player needs 2 joysticks to do that.

- **Arcade:** on key for acceleration or deceleration with a determinate axis, and the mouse to direct the other axes, like for the Freeview camera (recipe V.1).

Thanks to the game engine, it's possible to determinate the **impact force** at the time of a celestial body collision. Add the speed of the 2 objects in collision (with getLinearVelocity() before the choc), multiplied by their mass.

Another approach, simpler, is to let the game engine work and note the result after:

```
if collision.positive:
        linv_now = Vector(own.getLinearVelocity())
        applied_vec = linv_now - own["linv_before"]
        print ("For object:", own.name)
        print ("Impact magnitude:", applied_vec.magnitude)
        applied_vec.normalize()
        print ("Direction vector:", applied_vec)
else:
        own["linv_before"] = Vector(own.getLinearVelocity())
```

We get the new direction vector too. This script can be used for asteroids collision. Depending on the impact force (applied_vec.magnitude), it's possible to disintegrate the asteroid or to generate smaller asteroids instead.

Gravitation management:

The first thing to do is to disable the gravitation management with Bullet like in the following recipe.

The force of gravity of a body A on a body B is:

$$F_{\frac{A}{B}} = G \times \frac{m_a m_b}{d^2}$$

With M, the mass, d, the distance between A and B, and G, the universal constant of gravitation = $6{,}6742 \times 10^{-11}$ N·m^2·kg^{-2}

With these values, the game engine can't work. Use another scale.

The force applied is proportional **to the mass** and **inversely proportional to the square of the distance**. For a more basic management, use only the distance instead of the square of the distance.

The more heaviest the object is, the more this object attracts other objects. The more farest it is, the less this object can attract other objects.

This recipe can inspire you:

1. «Properties» window, «World» tab, «Physics» Panel and set «Gravity» to 0.

2. Add a new script «simul.py» and copy the folowing lines.

3. Add a sphere (⇧ Shift + A → «Mesh» → «UV Shpere»). «Properties» window, «Physics» panel, «Physics Type»: Select «Rigid Body» and make sure that the «Actor» is checked (the sensor

«Near» must work).

4.   Open the «Logic Editor» and add a «Near» sensor, set «Distance» to 1000 and «Reset Distance» to 0.

5.   Add a «Python» controller, select «Module» and write «simul.attraction». Link the sensor with the controller.

6.   Copy other sphere instances (`Shift`+`D`), varying the mass and test (`P`). The spheres will attract each other depending to their mass and their distances.

Script simul.py:

```python
def attraction(cont):
    own = cont.owner
    if cont.sensors["hit"].positive:
        for object in cont.sensors["hit"].hitObjectList:
            dist = own.getDistanceTo(object)
            force = (own.mass * object.mass)/dist
            vect = object.getVectTo(own)[1] # unit vector / angle
            object.applyForce(vect * force)
```

For the shooting management:

Use the **recipe V.12** to launch projectiles or for a laser (immediate impact), use a «ray» sensor.

A.I. Script for enemies starships or for the movement of troops:

The **recipe V.9** can be used for the movement of troops in space, with a path follow. We can use «near» or «radar» sensors to detect player.

Illustration 41: View with fog effects

II.5.   PROJECT #5: «MINECRAFT-LIKE»

The story:

«Minecraft» is an independent video game «sandbox» type (construction completely free) developed in 2009 by **Markus Persson**, alias **«Notch»**. The game is based on older games like «Infiniminer», «**Dwarf Fortress»**, or «Dungeon Keeper» (an underground world that the player must excavate to create its own dungeon). Note that the first game version was developed by 1 person and that it was sold to **10 millions of people**. There are numerous clones, one of these is **Terasology** which is Open Source.

Gameplay:

The game immerses the player in a world created dynamically, made with blocks («8 bits» style), by different materials representing soil, sand, stone, water, trees, animals, etc. The concept is the player can modify this world as he wants, adding or deleting cubes to survive as long as possible. The player can freely create buildings, it's like «Legos».

Step 1: Generate blocks for game

We can model a cube, apply a texture and use it directly in step 2. But it would be necessary to create as many cubes as block types needed in this game. So, we create the cube directly with Python using the **recipe VII-16**.

Illustration 42: set of blocs with 'Minecraft' type and only1 texture

The texture used is composed of a set of blocks like on Illustration 42. On Google, search the pictures with the following word «texture Minecraft».

1. Download a block picture, save it in the same folder than the blend file, name it «texturepack.png»
2. In the «Text Editor» window, create a new text file, name it «generateWorld.py» and paste the script of the **recipe VII.16.** Add the following script lines at the end.
3. Test running the script directly (click on «Run Script»)

script python additional lines:

```
createCube('ground',' texturepack.png',2*(1/16),15*(1/16), (1/16),(1/16))
createCube('water',' texturepack.png',15*(1/16),2*(1/16), (1/16),(1/16))
createCube('grass',' texturepack.png',1*(1/16),6*(1/16), (1/16),(1/16))
```

Step 2: Generate a world with a Heightmap

In «Minecraft», the world is procedurally generated: we use a function to generate some noise to create a kind of Heightmap, then we define biotopes (desert, forest, etc.) according to criteria like altitude and distance from the water. According to the biotope, we include plants, animals, etc. That won't be addressed here, bust the post-generation management is almost identical.

Illustration 43: Generation of a world in 32x32x8 blocks max

We generate a world duplicating some blocks, and we position these blocks according to a Heightmap.

To understand, you need to know the **recipe III.1**, even if we don't use it directly.

1. Download a picture with «heightmap» type and name it «heightmap.png», save it in the current folder of blend.
2. Add to the script «GenerateWorld.py» the following script lines, and the function duplicateInstance() of the **recipe III.15**

3. In the CreateCube function, add thes lines:

```python
ob.hide = True
ob.select=True
bpy.ops.group.create(name=name)
bpy.ops.object.group_link(group=name)
```

«ob.hide = True» just after «ob.location» to use the blocs only as models, they are not displayed in the scene

The function duplicateInstance() use a group like support, so it's necessary to create before this group and to add the model to copy in this last.

4. Add a «Point» lamp with type location = (0.0,0.0,25.0) and Energy = 10.0

5. Test running the script directly (click on «Run Script»). We obtain a scenery like in the Illustration 43

Script Python:

```python
import bpy,os
from math import *

def createWorld (xblocs,yblocs,zblocs):
    print ("Pass 0: Cubes Generation")
    createCube('ground','terrain.png',2*(1/16),15*(1/16),(1/16),(1/16))
    createCube('water','terrain.png',15*(1/16),2*(1/16),(1/16),(1/16))
    createCube('grass','terrain.png',1*(1/16),6*(1/16),(1/16),(1/16))
    createCube('rock','terrain.png',0*(1/16),14*(1/16),(1/16),(1/16))
    createCube('lava','terrain.png',14*(1/16),0*(1/16),(1/16),(1/16))

    maptext = bpy.data.textures.new('map',type='IMAGE')
    realpath = os.path.expanduser('heightmap.png')
    map = maptext.image = bpy.data.images.load(realpath)
    blocradius = 2
    texcolor = 4 # R,G,B,I
    xtex = map.size[0]
    ytex = map.size[1]
    x_dt = round(xtex / xblocs)
    y_dt = round(ytex/ yblocs)

    #First pass: find height max
    print ("Pass 1: Calculate HeightMax")
    heightmax = 0
    for x in range (0,xtex, x_dt):
      for y in range (0,ytex,y_dt):
        idpix = ((x + y*xtex) * texcolor)
        height = sqrt(map.pixels[idpix]*map.pixels[idpix] + map.pixels[idpix+1]*map.pixels[idpix+1] +
                    map.pixels[idpix+2]*map.pixels[idpix+2] )
      heightmax = max (height, heightmax)
    z_dt = heightmax / zblocs

    #Second pass: Generate World !
    print ("Pass 2: World Generation")
    for x in range (0,xtex, x_dt):
      for y in range (0,ytex,y_dt):
        idpix = ((x + y*xtex) * texcolor)

        #lava
        for z in range (0,blocradius,blocradius): # 1 bloc
          myobj = duplicateInstance(bpy.data.scenes["Scene"],"LavaBloc","lava",
                        x / (x_dt/blocradius) - xtex / x_dt + 1,      y / (y_dt/blocradius) - xtex / y_dt + 1,z)

        #rock
        for z in range (2,blocradius+1,blocradius):
          myobj = duplicateInstance(bpy.data.scenes["Scene"],"RockBloc","rock",
                        x / (x_dt/blocradius) - xtex / x_dt + 1,      y / (y_dt/blocradius) - xtex / y_dt + 1,z)

        #water
        for z in range (4,blocradius *2+2,blocradius):
          myobj = duplicateInstance(bpy.data.scenes["Scene"],"WaterBloc","water",
                        x / (x_dt/blocradius) - xtex / x_dt + 1,      y / (y_dt/blocradius) - xtex / y_dt + 1,z)

        #ground
        lastz = 4
        height = round( sqrt( map.pixels[idpix] * map.pixels[idpix] +
                    map.pixels[idpix+1] * map.pixels[idpix+1] +
                    map.pixels[idpix+2] * map.pixels[idpix+2] ) / (z_dt/2))
        for z in range (6,height,blocradius):
          myobj = duplicateInstance(bpy.data.scenes["Scene","GroundBloc","ground",
             x / (x_dt/blocradius) - xtex / x_dt + 1, y / (y_dt/blocradius) - xtex / y_dt + 1, z)
        lastz = z
```

```
    #grass
    if (lastz > 4):
        myobj = duplicateInstance(bpy.data.scenes["Scene"], "GrassBloc","grass",
                        x / (x_dt/blocradius) - xtex / x_dt + 1,
                        y / (y_dt/blocradius) - xtex / y_dt + 1, lastz + 1 + 0.25)
        myobj.scale.z = 0.25;

    print ("Progress: %.2f" % ((x*100)/(xtex-x_dt))," %")

createWorld(32,32,8)
```

Explications:
- The function before generates a scenery with 32 blocks in length (X), on 32 in width (Y), and at most 8 blocks in height
- Create a first layer of lava flows (Z=0). Then a second layer of rock (Z=2). At least 2 layers of water (Z=4). According to the Heightmap, we generate some soil. Then we add a layer of vegetation. We keep only 25% of the block height for aesthetic reasons.
- The step «Heightmax calculation» allows to know the maximal value for the Heightmap height. We can determinate the gradient to use to obtain a maximum of zblocs
- The height is determined according to the norm of the vector made by the components (Red,green,Blue,Intensity) of the picture pixel.
- x_dt and y_dt are used to match the picture size and the number of blocks wanted (xblocs,yblocs)

Step 3: Explore the landscape

1. In «Text Editor», add to the script «MouseLook.py» a Player with the **recipe V.2**, add the camera and the logic movement. The size blocks is 2x2x2, it's possible to double the player's proportions to give the impression that 1 block → 1 m. Adjust the focal length of the camera: 12.0 give a good view of the scenery.
2. Select «Player» and go to «Logic Editor»
3. Add a «Ray» sensor, «Axis: -Z axis» and «Range: 2.2». This condition detects whether something is under the object and is a condition for the jump.
4. Add a «Mouse» sensor, «Mouse Event»: «Middle Button»
5. Add a «Motion» actuator, «Motion Type: Simple Motion», «Force» «Z: 100.00». Apply a force upward
6. Link the 2 sensors with the actuator using an «AND» controller
7. Go to «3D View» and test (P)

Step 4: adding a crosshair

Graphically set the crosshair position:
1. Download a little picture to be the crosshair (ex: Google picture «target filetype:png»). Make sure there's an alpha transparency layer.
1. Add a new scene «GUI». This scene allows to display all the game information: life, blocks choice, crosshair.
2. In a position of top view (7) add a plan in the center of the screen. In «Edit Mode» do a mapping UV (U → Cube Projection) and return to «Object Mode».
3. Create a new Material. Check «Shadeless» to be independent of the light, check «Transparency» (Z Transparency, Alpha: 0.0). «Game Settings» → «Alpha Blend: Alpha Blend»
4. Add the downloaded picture as a new texture, «Mapping Coordinates:UV», «Map:UVMap», «Projection: Cube». Check «Show Alpha» to verify the picture transparency, if it's not possible, download another picture or delete the background with a software like Gimp. Check «Diffuse» → «Alpha» and test with 0.7 as value (it's the transparency index, let it at1,0).
5. Add a camera in (0,0,50.0) pointing down (axis: -Z)

6. Go to camera view (0) and test (P): the target must be transparent and at the center of the screen.

7. Go to the principal scene and select the camera, go in «Logic Editor» mode

8. Add an «Always» sensor

9. Add a «Scene» actuator, «Mode: Add Overlay Scene» and select the «GUI» scene. Link the sensor with the actuator.

10. In «3D View», test (P). The target is still at the center of the view.

Determine the block pointed:

1. In «Text Editor», add to the script «Action.py» and copy the following script

2. Add a cube of the same size that the blocks and name them «outline»

3. Add it a material with «Wire» type (and not Surface which is by default). Choose for example a diffuse color flashy like red, then check «Shadeless».

4. Select the camera and the «Player» object, go in «Logic Editor».

5. Add to the camera a new sensor with «Ray» type, name it «blockray», check «Activate True Level Triggering», choose the axis «-Z axis» to point in front of the camera (to verify axis, to display them), limit the radius to 6 (the greater the value is, the more the player will be able to use a block at distance).

6. Add a «Python» controller and select «Module» write «action.rayaction»

7. Link the sensor with the controller

8. Go in «3D View» mode, select the camera view (0) and test (P)

Script python:

```python
import bge
def rayaction(cont):
        own = cont.owner
        scene = bge.logic.getCurrentScene()
        outline = scene.objects['outline']
        blockray = cont.sensors['blockray']
        if blockray.positive:
            outline.visible = 1
            outline.position = blockray.hitObject.position
        else:
            outline.visible = 0
```

Step 5: to dig tunnels

Add a «property» to all the blocks to define if they are destroyable or not. Use the left mouse button to destroy a block. Manage the hold-click, according to this hold-click, advance the destruction of the block.

Generate 10 new blocks (destroy 1 to 10) containing some fractures to imitate the stone fracture or other type. Move these blocks in the layer 2. These blocks will be used to be superimpose to the existing blocks to give the impression of fractures.

Verify the type of block to destroy and according to this type, it'll be destroyed more or less rapidly.

Generate a «destroyX» object from the destruction. When the block is destroyed, delete «destroyX».

Recipe:

1. Add to «Player» an «Integer» property, named «destroy». This property will allow to know how much time the block was hit to know when destroy it.

2. Add the following lines to the script «GenerateWorld.py»

3. Modify the sensor «blockray» and select «Property: destroyable». The radius will pass through

other the block «outline» thanks to X-Ray and will touch the blocks with «destroyable» type.

4. Add to «Player» a «Mouse» sensor named «LMB», «Mouse Event: Left Button», and check «Activate True Level Triggering», check «Tap» and set freq to «10.0».

5. Add to «Player» a «Mouse» sensor named «holdclick», «Mouse Event: Left Button», check «Activate True Level Triggering»

6. Link the 2 sensors with the controller python launching the «Action.rayaction» module

7. Modify the script «Action.py» by replacing them with the following lines.

8. Delete all the landscape by keeping only the «Players», «Camera», «outline» objects and the objects with lamps type. Execute the script «GenerateWorld.py» manually

9. Test (P)

Additional lines to insert at the end of «GenerateWorld.py»

```python
#Add Game Properties to Objects
for obj in bpy.data.objects:
    if 'ground' in obj.name or 'grass' in obj.name or
            'water' in obj.name or 'rock' in obj.name:
        bpy.context.scene.objects.active = obj
        bpy.ops.object.game_property_new(type='BOOL', name="destroyable")
        obj.game.properties['destroyable'].value = True

#Add Destroy Blocs
layers = 20*[False]
layers[2] = True
for i in range (10):
    ob = createCube('destroy%d'%(i+1),'terrain.png', i*(1/16),0,(1/16),(1/16),True)
    ob.layers = layers
```

Script «action.py» modified:

```python
import bge

def rayAction(cont):
        own = cont.owner
        scene = bge.logic.getCurrentScene()
        outline = scene.objects['outline']
        blockray = cont.sensors['blockray']
        lmb = cont.sensors['lmb']
        holdclick = cont.sensors['holdclick']

        if blockray.positive:
          outline.visible = 1
          outline.position = blockray.hitObject.position
        else:
          outline.visible = 0

        if lmb.positive and blockray.positive:
    block = blockray.hitObject
    if 'ground' in block.name:
      own['destroy'] += 2
    elif 'water' in block.name:
      own['destroy'] += 5
    elif 'grass' in block.name:
      own['destroy'] += 3
    elif 'rock' in block.name:
      own['destroy'] += 1
    else:
      return

        def clearChildren(block):
    if len(block.children) > 0:
      for x in block.children:
        x.endObject()

    if block != bge.logic.lastblock and bge.logic.lastblock != "":
      clearChildren(bge.logic.lastblock)
      own['destroy'] = 0
    if own['destroy'] <= 10:
      if len(block.children) > 0:
        block.children[0].endObject()
        bge.logic.lastblock = block
        destroy = scene.addObject("destroy" + str(own['destroy']), block)
        destroy.setParent(block)
    else:
```

```
        bge.logic.lastblock = block
        if own['destroy'] > 0:
            destroy = scene.addObject("destroy" + str(own['destroy']), block)
            destroy.setParent(block)
    else:
        block.endObject()
        bge.logic.lastblock = ""
        own['destroy'] = 0
            elif not holdclick.positive:
    if bge.logic.lastblock != "":
        clearChildren(bge.logic.lastblock)
    own['destroy'] = 0
```

Step 6: To build and to craft

We are at the end of the lesson, we know how to pseudo-randomly generate a landscape and how to dynamically modify it during the game. To go further to create a «Minecraft-Like», you need to build and to craft.

To build, we need building blocks. In the game «Minecraft», we can cut a tree, create boards from the sliced elements, and build a piece of furniture.

When we break some elements of landscape, like stone, we can generate an object with «building stone» style. The player can pick up this object that will go in the inventory. To create an inventory, follow the **recipe VI.6**.

When the object is in the inventory, select it («⊞» for example), with another mouse click («Right Button» for example), add the block just above that selected by the mouse. It's a slightly modification of the step 5.

To craft, you need to combine objects. In the game «Minecraft», there are particular objects for that: the oven is an example. Create an object with «oven» type and add to it wood, flames, coal to create new materials.

Step 7: Improvements

In the game «Minecraft», everything or almost everything is made with blocks. The BGE is not an optimized engine such as the Minecraft's for the blocks display, some handicaps can become advantages: we can add any kinds of objects. To make grass, use the billboards technique in the **recipe III.14**.

Some suggestions:

- Thanks to the **recipes III.17** and **III.18**, it's possible to generate an **almost unlimited field** that can continue change. The **recipe VI.3** allows to add a copy of the modified elements from landscape «chunks». Add a fog effect for the distant elements with the **recipe III.5**, we obtain a good illusion of an unlimited landscape.
- The **skydome** in the **recipe III.3** allows to obtain a more realistic environment. «Minecraft» use blocks for clouds, it allows complex atmospheric animations.
- Create some **objects generators** for trees or another objects to use in the game (houses, castles, bridges). Write python procedures like the **recipe VII.16** considering the size, the type of blocks to use, etc. It's possible, in this way, to generate more elements by a pseudo-random process, under different conditions determined by biome classes.
- Add some **animals** to eat, and to brighten the landscape. Adapt the animals' artificial intelligence with a script (**recipe IV.11**).
- Add some **enemies creatures**, using the **recipe IV.11**.
- Allow to the player to manipulate objects directly on screen with the **recipe V.14**.
- Add a night mode, and a torchlight to the character, the character can put these torches in different parts of the scene. Use BGE, but if there are too much «lights», the rendering engine can be saturated. Optimization: use different blocks for each intensity of light (irradiance) (5 levels for example) and modify the Material («Shading» panel, value of «Emit»). Then, with a torch, we modify the

blocks around to increase the intensity. But we can't do shades...

- Add seasons (4 types of blocs). Use the declination according to the height (snow above a certain altitude for example).
- Add a snow mode and a rain mode with the **recipe VII.20**
- Add an explosive system to dig faster with the **recipes VII.17** and **VII.19**.

Another important Improvements could be done using only one cube subdivided into a number of vertex, then increasing the vertex meshing according to the soil height. Use the functions getVertex() and setXYZ() on BGE. The UV mapping can be adapted via python. To dig, we reduce the height of the 4 vertex closest to the point. In this way, we use only one object for the soil.

However, this greatly complicates the game logic. At that level, Select a block with «Fire» or «Oven» type to add to it any interaction.

It's possible to join the blocks, do a «remove doubles», apply a «modifier subsurf», but the notion of cube disappears.

Illustration 44: Minecraft Map directly imported with the tool MneBlend: https://sites.google.com/site/mineblend/

II.6. PROJECT #6: FIRST-PERSON SHOOTER

Or **Doom-Like**, it's a shooting game based on combats in thrilling first-person view. The player sees what the character sees. Opposite to shooting game in third-person action game control that saw the back character (TPS: Third-Person Shooter).

The story:

The 2 first-person shooters are **Maze War** and **Spasim** developed in 1974. But these games are not in 3D «realtime». It 's only a «wire frame» representing a section of a labyrinth.
Doom is a FPS developed and edited by id Software, in 1993. It's a **Wolfenstein 3D** evolution released 1.5 year before, and made by the same developers. Doom was one of the most popular games on PC like Tetris, with more than 30 millions of players in 3 years. Thereafter, doom-like or FPS peak at the top sales with **Duke Nukem**, the **Quake series** and **Half-Life**.
In 2001, on Xbox, «**Halo**: Combat Evolved» impresses the followers of this type of game. The game is known to draw the FPS into a new dimension, and to democratize it on consoles. The graphic rendering Improvements was progressive, using environments and textures increasingly more detailed, and using the physics (Half Life 2). There was more than 70 FPS developed during the year 2005. 2014 is the year of **Doom 4**, **HomeFront 2** and **Thief 4**. And now, **Takedown**, the multiplayer tactical FPS financed on Kickstarter.

Gameplay:

The player sees by the eyes of his character, the barrel of his weapon in incrustation in the foreground, if he has a gun in his hand of course! The goal is to shoot everything that moves and to find the exit or the next level.

Illustration 45: Land preparation for the FPS

Step 1: Create an environment for the game

For a «Doom's Like», use an opened environment with nature type.

1. Follow the **recipe III.1** («Sculpt Mode») creating a XY plane with size 100,100. Choose 1 m = 1 Blender unit. The land measures 2.4 acres. Subdivide this land into 64x64 cases. Each case represent approximately 21,52 sqft. Use a picture of texture of 4096x4096. Keep a flat zone (floor plan) for the houses. Try to obtain something like the Illustration 45.

2. Prepare a realistic environment with the **recipe III.4.** Don't take brown for the soil but a color green-grey for the effects. For the spot, everything is depending on its position. For example, move it in (-45,-80,40) with a rotation in (15,-50,50). Energy: 15 / Distance: 1000. Shadow size: 2048.

3. Select the layer #2. Add a plane at a certain height to obtain a water surface and use a **recipe III.12** to have an effect «body of water»→ land more realist (Illustration 46). Use the Improvements which enables to manage the height to make an effect «backwash».

4. Select the layer 3. Add a skydome using the **recipe III.3** (do a rotation of the l'UVMap so as to match the picture of the sun of the skydome with the position of the spot). Activate or not the clouds scrolling.

5. Like on the Earth, the distant objects seems to be blue because of the atmosphere. Add a fog like on **recipe III.5**. Parameters: RVB (0.20, 0.25, 0.40) – Quadratic – Start: 60m / Depth: 35m

6. Go to «3D View» and test (⌨P)

Set the vegetation position too and the different objects but more later. We work now on the game logic.

Illustration 46: Land with a lighting environment and animated body of water

Step 2: Insert the player

Use the **recipe «Camera FPS»** with modifications.

1. Select the layer #4. Follow the `recipe V.2` applying the following modifications.
2. Select the camera and adjust the focal: 12.0 gives a good view of the landscape.
3. Select «Player» and go to «Logic Editor»
4. Add a «Ray» sensor, «Axis: -Z axis» and «Range: 2.2». This condition detects whether something is under the object, condition for a jump.
5. Add a «Mouse» sensor, «Mouse Event: Middle Button»
6. Add a «Motion» actuator, «Motion Type: Simple Motion», «Force» «Z: 50». Apply an upward force
7. Link the 2 sensors with the actuator using the controller «And»
8. Go in «3D View», Select the camera view (0) and test (P)

Step 3: Arm the player

We need 2 arms and 1 weapon, correctly «rigged». We could model them, but on Blendswap, we found «FPS Assault Rifle» given by «turnpike101».

Use this model for this game, rendering thanks to him.

1. On   http://www.blendswap.com/blends/view/47984,   download   «FPS Assault Rifle». Unpack the archive.
2. Go on the layer#4 and in the «info» window, «File» → «Append», select the folder Blend downloaded (G36C.blend). The Blend folder is opened and it's possible to go in its directory «Object». Select the following objects: Arm_Hand_Mesh.000, Arm_Hand_Mesh.001, G36C Assault Riffle, Gun Armature, Left_Armature.001 and Left_Armature by clicking

    on each one while pressing the «⇧ Shift» key. When done, click on «Link/Append from Library». The import done, we have 2 arms, 1 weapon, correctly rigged. Rename all the objects and armatures «Left_XXX.001» in «Right_XXX» for a better management in the «Outliner» window. It's possible to do the same for the bones with the extension «.L» to rename in «.R» when the bones take parts of the right arm armature. Good names makes the animations easier (windows «Dope Sheet» and «NLA Editor»).
3. Resize everything (Scale: 0.2). Move the elements like on Illustration 47. Make sure, in camera-view (0), that arms and weapon are visible
4. Select the right arm armature, then the «Camera» object and parent them (Ctrl+P → «Parent to Object»). Repeat the operation for the left arm armature. The arms follow the body («player»), and the camera for the verticals movements too.
5. Select the weapon armature (Gun Armature), click on the left arm bone «hand.L» and parent them

    (Ctrl+P → Parent to Bone): the weapon follow the left arm.
6. Remove the material shadow management (uncheck «cast buffer shadows» in the «shadows» panel, in «Materials» Tab) for all the elements (arm, weapon).
7. Test (P) – If the armature seems to «explode» at the launching of BGE, it's probably a problem of

    parent object transformations. To avoid that: Select the «player» in «Object Mode», Ctrl+A → «Apply Rotation & Scale». Test too with Location. Repeat on the camera.

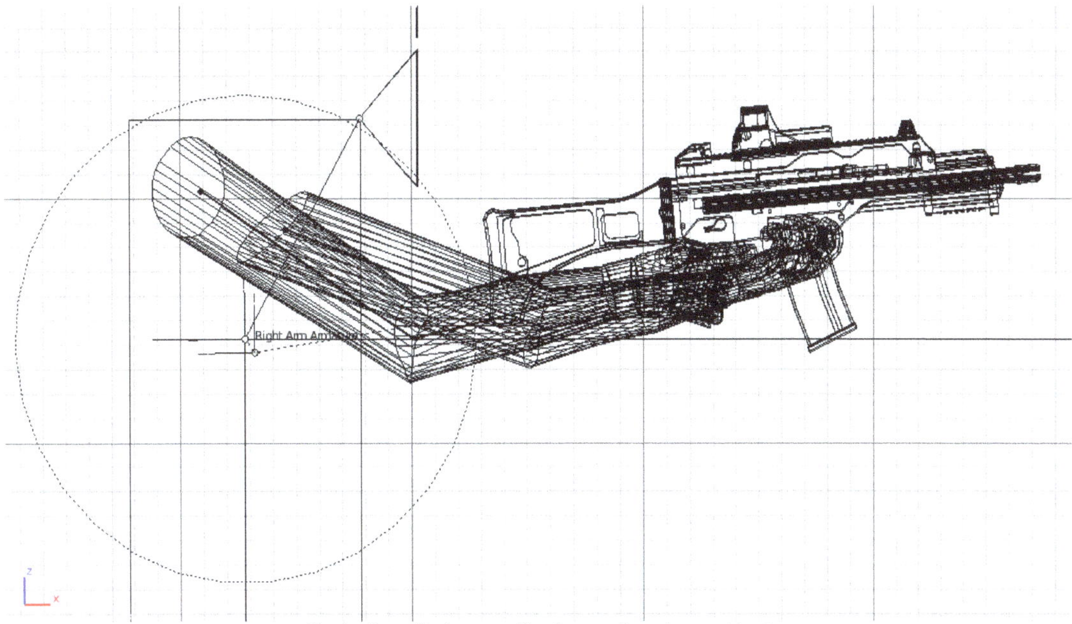

Illustration 47: Arm positioning on the player object

Step 4: Character animation

The FPS player animate only the arms and eventually the legs of the character. Here, we'll animate its arms.

There are 2 armatures to animate, so, each time, we realize 2 actions. 1 action applied on the 2 armatures will be worse off than 2 actions. To each action, we have the «.R» (right arm) and «.L» -(left arm).

Note that the objects are already «rigged», so we can use directly the step 14 of the **recipe IV.3.**

1. Use the **recipe IV.3** to create 2 actions «Fire.L» and «Fire.R» corresponding to motion of to point the weapon at in front of the character, to shoot and have the recoil effect. Use the interval of frame between 1 and 20 to do that, 10 frames are enough for this motion.

2. Idem for the actions «Walk.L» and «Walk.R» corresponding to the motion of balance when the character walks. If you don't want to see the arms and the weapon, don't make these actions. Use the interval of frame between 1 and 50 to do that.

3. Select the 2 arms armatures and go in the «Logic Editor»

4. Add to the left arm armature an «Action» actuator, «FireLeft» name, «Action Playback type»: «Flipper», «Start»: 1, «End»:20, select «Fire.L».

5. Link the actuator with the controller already linked with the shot («Fire»)

6. Add to the right arm armature an actuator with «Action», name: «WalkLeft», «Action Playback type»: «Loop Stop», «Start»: 1, «End»:50, select «Walk.L»

7. Link the actuator with the controller already linked with the walk («Forward»)

8. Start again from step 4, but using the right arm (replace .L by .R).

9. Go to 3D View, camera view (0) and test (P). If you don't see the arms during the walk, maybe you must scale the viewing angle of the camera (Focal Length, the lower the value is, the more important the angle is).

Step 5: let there be set !

Go on BlendSwap and look for models «Lowpoly» (in «low resolution») or for the game («realtime»). Choose the more appropriated models for the game, we propose the following elements (Append, menu of the «info» window):

- A chest: #47993, made by SebastL
- Mushrooms: #62557, made by DennisH
- A shed, #71027, made by OliverMH
- Grass, #71002, made by OliverMH
- A pontoon, #71243, made by Bishop
- A box, #69774, made by Flight King

1. Select the layer #5
2. Place the shed on the ground, in an accessible zone
3. Place the pontoon right by the sea
4. Place the box in a place where the player could test the weapon
5. Create the actions «Open» and «Close» for the chest. Place it in the shed.
6. Use the **recipes III.7** and **III.8** to import some animated trees, moving like the wind. Place a copy in the layer#6 and use the **recipe III.15** to generate 30 units on the map.
7. The imported grass use the **recipe III.14**, it's possible to add other billboards like flowers, like some plants for high realism. Animate the grass is easy using the **recipe III.7**. Populate with 3000 units like before.
8. Place manually some mushrooms in strategic positions.
9. To download these models, replace the number in the address given as example: http://www.blendswap.com/blends/view/47993 (for the chest).

Example for the automatic generation:

```
scatterObject("Scene","Ground","Foliage_Trees_01", True, 30, "Trees_01Scatter", True, -10.0, 30.0)
scatterObject("Scene","Ground","Grass", True, 3000, "GrassScatter",True, -10.0, 10.0)
```

A positioning example for the objects is given on the Illustration 48 and a game on the Illustration 49. A general map after grass and trees random generating is visible on the Illustration 50.

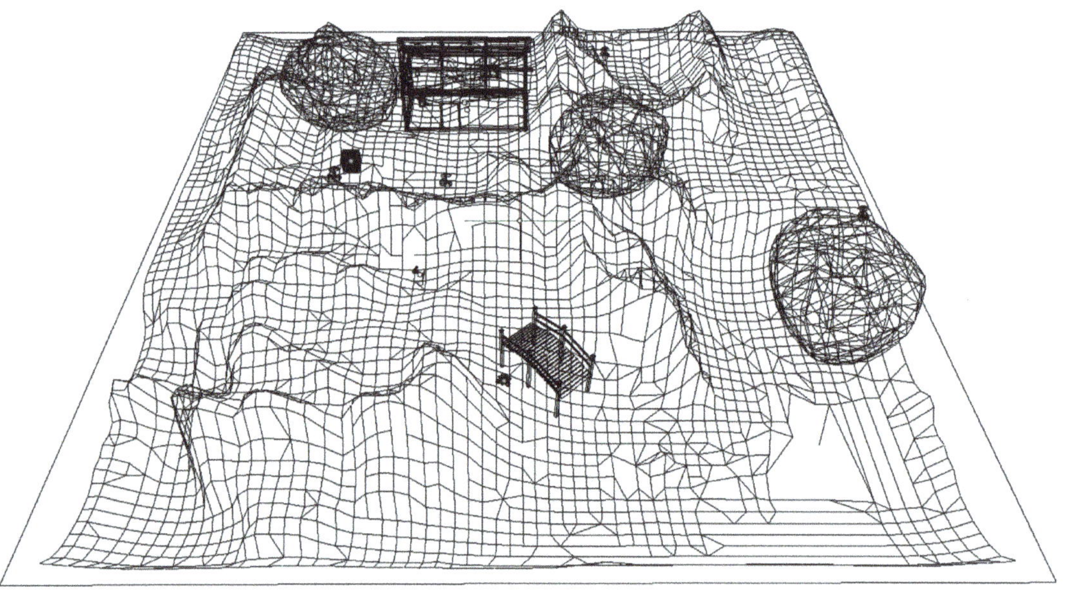

Illustration 48: Example of land in wireframe

Illustration 49: View on the pontoon in FPS view

Illustration 50: Game map after randomize generation of trees and grass

Step 6: Shoot and touch some objects

Define a property allowing some objects to receive impacts. The object must be «breakable». Move other objects according to the shoot.

1. Use the **recipe V.13** to shoot and to generate impacts on all the objects with the Boolean property «Impacts». Use, for the moment, the «space» key to shoot. For not modeling a bullet, use the BlendSwap #69108 of bheema.

2. At the precise time of the shoot, detect exactly the action fire picture when the bullet exit. Here, it's the picture #11, just before the barrel moves with the recoil effect. Create a new script script «Fire.py» and post the following script.

3. Select the empty and go to «Logic Editor»

4. Add a «Mouse» sensor / «Mouse Event»: «Left Button», check «Activate True Level Triggering».

5. Add a «Python» controller, select «Module» and write «Fire.fire».

6. Link the sensor with the controller.

7. Go to «3D View» and to (P): make sure that it's possible to shoot many times and the direction is good. Otherwise, modify the empty orientation.

8. Select the «box» object, go to the «Physics» Tab in the «Properties» window and modify the type into «Rigid Body».
   - Mass: 1 U → when you hit the box, it's flying away (arcade mode)
   - Or 10 U to have something realistic.

9. Select the «shed» object and give it a Property «Solide», with the **recipe V.12** to leave some impacts on the object.

10. Select the «Bullet» object and go to «Logic Editor».

11. Add a «Sound» actuator and add a sound with gunshot type / «Play Mode»: «Play End», check the «3D Sound» option (to listen the bullet straying from) and set «Maximum Distance» to 50.

12. Link the actuator with the existent controller. The sound is generated at the instance «Bullet» creation and the sound follows the bullet.

13. Add a recoil effect: Remove the corresponding lines of comments in the script «Fire.py»

14. Select the «Raycast» object and go to «Logic Editor»

15. Add a «Message» actuator, name it «MessagePlayer» / «To»: Select «Player» / «Subject»: «Fire» / «Body»: «Text» and left empty

16. Link the actuator with the controller managing the script «Fire.fire»

17. Select the «Player» object. Add a «Message» sensor, name it «MessageRaycast», «subject»: «Fire»

18. Add a «Motion» actuator / «Motion Type»: «Simple Motion» / «Loc» «X»: -0.20 and «Z»: 0.1. Link the sensor with the actuator

19. Test (P): with every shot, when the bullet goes out of the weapon, a message is sent to «Player» to push back the character.

This script is only an example. In the game project #2, we'll use a sensor with «property» type and an evaluation with «interval» type to run the actuator. This second approach is quicker at he execution but allows fewer opportunities. Using bullets with dynamical bodies like we have done, we can touch enemies by rebound.

Script «Fire.py»

```python
import bge
c = bge.logic.getCurrentController()
scene = bge.logic.getCurrentScene()
own = c.owner
armatureObject = scene.objects['Right Arm Armature']
fireright = armatureObject.actuators['FireRight']

def fire():
```

```python
frame = fireright.owner["frame"]
if (frame == 11): #Replace by Your Frame Number
    own["delayFire"] += 1
    if own["delayFire"] == 1:
        act = c.actuators["ActionFire"]
        c.activate(act)
                        #recoil effect
                        #act = c.actuators["MessagePlayer"]
            #c.activate(act)
else:
  if (own["delayFire"] >= 2):
    own["delayFire"] = 0
```

This method is far from accurate because some bullets have not enough speed. The collisions system is not optimized to manage the high speed objects. To increase the chances of hit, increase the value of «Physics Substeps» in the «World» Tab of the «Properties» window.

Possible Improvements:

- Add some bullets impacts («decals») according to the materials (a black trace on stone, a hole in wood, etc.)
- Add an animation with little blocks that explode to simulate the effect of fragments falling during the impact. Modify the impact script and add this animation, the physic engine let the fragments fall. Limit the object time life to 2 or 3 seconds.
- With the same technique, simulate a knife throwing. Throw like for the bullet, but at the time of the collision, test the object property to know if it's stuck. In this case, transform the knife into «static», then it stops moving.
- Impacts can be used only on statics objects. When the player shoot on the box, the impacts remain in place, even if the box moves. To avoid that, when the impact is created, determine the impact object and parent the impact object to the object (in python, objImpact.parent = objShooted).
- Add a «sniper» mode: change the camera adding a telescopic sight to the gun with a rather high «Focal Length» (mode zoom). Add a 2D filter with «Night Vision» type or just a color with a target in mode «overlay» scene.
- Add a camera on the bullet and slow down time with the `recipe VII.22`, just before hitting an object.

Step 7: Monsters in excursion

Shooting on boxes and leaving marks on the stones, it's just a training!

In a first time, we needs an enemy creature. Use the `recipes IV.3` to `IV.5` to model an enemy type (object «Spider» in the recipe), and provide the following actions: Walk, Attack, Die. It's possible to download the object # 26798 too, a rigged spider made by «DennisH2010» which have the goods actions.

With the model 26798, **do the followings modifications**:

1. At the time of import, we needs objects: 02_Spinnen_armature (rename it «spider»), Cube (rename it «spider.leg») and Cube.002 (rename it «spider.body»).
2. Actions are already set in «Logic Editor». Add one to reveal the others. Remove the useless actuators and spot the actions of the remaining actuators. Rename them to have the actuators «walk», «run» and «die».
3. Go to «Dope Sheet» window, menu «Action Editor» and to each action, click on «F» to save the datablock, even if the action is not employed. If it's not done, the actions will disappear at the next starting.

Configure the creature to charge player:

1. Place the enemy creature in the layer #10.
2. Select the «spider» object, «Physics» Tab / «Type»: «Rigid Body» and check Lock Rotation «Y» and Lock Translation «X». Doing that avoids the spider glides. Set the «radius» at 3.0 and «collision bound» with «Sphere» type

3. Go to «Logic Editor», add an «Always» sensor and select «Activate True Level Triggering» - choose a frequency: 25

4. Add an «And» controller and link the sensor with the controller, link the controller with the actuator action «Walk».

5. Add a «Steering» actuator / «Behaviour»: «path follow» / «Target Object»: «Player» / «Velocity»: 2 / The axis is in the same direction as the model: «-Y» for the «spider» model.

6. Link the actuator with the precedent controller «And», go to «3D View» and test (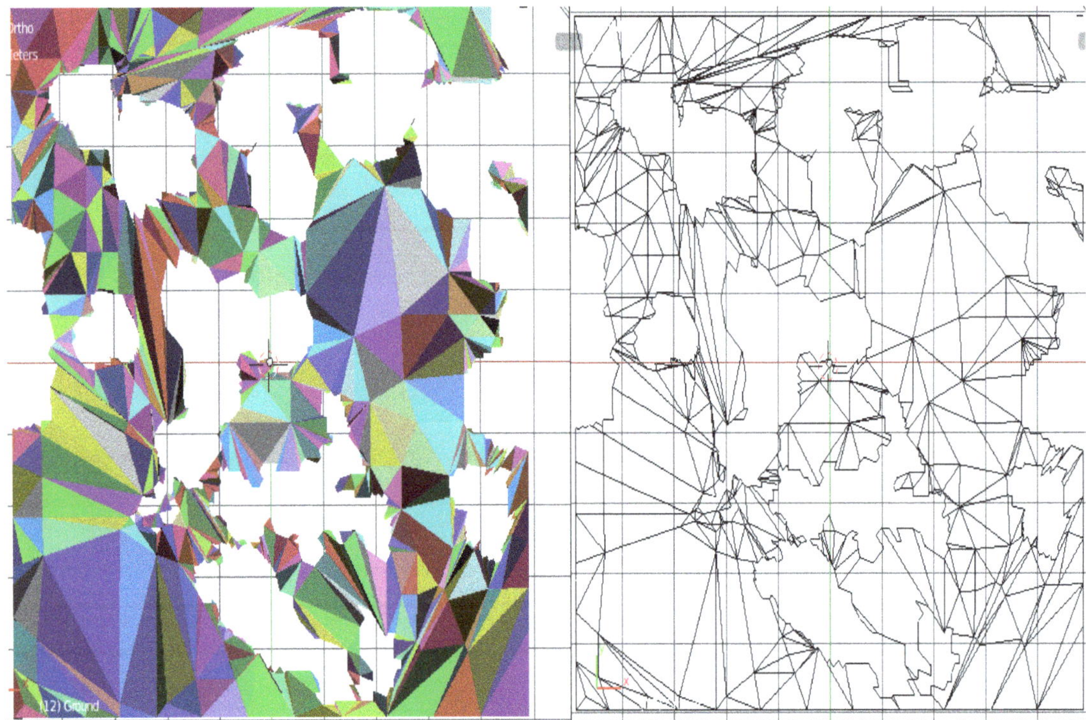)

The enemy runs on the player. When the player changes direction, the enemy needs 25 frames before turning forwards the player. If there's an obstacle, the enemy is blocked.

Illustration 51: «Navigation Mesh» for the playground. Creatures can swim on the water body and bump into an obstacle (stones, shed), but know how to avoid the trees.

Add a «**Path Finding**» to avoid enemies blocking by trees:

1. Use the **recipe V.13** to add a «navigation mesh» to the set. The navigation mesh can be used by all enemies with the same size or with a smaller size. Remove the zone corresponding to the trees, keep the grass. It's possible to keep the water body to allow to the spider to have a bath and to drown oneself when it follow the player. The navigation mesh allows to spiders to find a way around the obstacle course to reach a point. Leave other obstacles that the enemies can't avoid allow the player to have time to draw breath. Test, if the spiders are blocked too often at any place, modify this place and recalculate («physics» panel) the navigation mesh.

2. Modify the «Steering» actuator of the «Spider» object by selecting «Navigation Mesh»: «Navmesh» and «behavior»: «Path following»

Configuration used for the navigation mesh:

- Cell size: 0.50
- Cell Height: 2.00
- Height: 0.50
- Max Slope: 75°
- Radius: 0.50
- Max Climb: 100
- Min Region Size: 3.00

- Merge Region Size: 20.00
- Max Edge Length: 12.00
- Verts Per Poly: 6.00
- Max Edge Error: 1.30
- Sample Distance: 6.00
- Max Sample Error: 1.00

The spiders are now skillful to charge the player !

Illustration 52: Scene with giant spider in attack

Step 8: Kill monsters

Personally, I would not recommend to shoot giant spiders in daily life, but in this kind of game... It's not very dangerous.

1. Select «Spider» object and open the «Logic Editor»
2. Add a «Game Property» «Life» with «Integer» type with a default value of 3. Add a game property, «monster» with «boolean» type checked.
3. Click on «+» near Spider in the «controller» zone to display the different state layers. Select the second layer to define the sate «dead».
4. Add an «Always» sensor, name it «InitDie». Link it with the actuator «action» which defines the animation «die». When the spider «Spider» is in state 2, the death animation is played.
5. Add a «Delay» sensor, «delay»: 1000.
6. Add an «Edit Object» actuator and select «End Object».
7. Link the sensor and the actuator. When the spider is in state 2, after 1000 frames, the spider disappears.

8.   Add a python script «spider.py» and paste the following script.

9.   Select the «Bullet» object

10. Add a «Collision» sensor, «property»: «monster»

11. Add a «Python» controller, select «module» and write «spider.hit»

12. Link the sensor with the controller

13. Go to «3D View», test (P)

Script «spider.py»:

```python
import bge

def hit(cont): #fix mobious, thanks to him
    hit = cont.sensors["collisionMonster"]
    obj = hit.hitObject
    if hit.positive and "monster" in obj:
        obj["life"] -= 1
        if obj["life"]==0: #creature dead
            obj.state = 2
```

The hit function takes in parameters the logic controller (cont). Recover the object knocked by the projectile.

Decrease its life. When the life reaches 0, the object goes to state 2 (death).

Step 9: Monsters attack !

You can't hope to be able to shoot at these little and inoffensive beasts and not be attacked in return!

1.   Select the «Player» object and open the «Logic Editor».

2.   Add a «Game Property» «Life» with «Integer» type and a default value of 10. Add another game property, «player» with «boolean» type checked.

3.   Add a «Message» sensor, «Subject»: «attack»

4.   Add a «Property» actuator, «Mode»: «Add», «Property»: «life», «value»: -1

5.   Link the sensor with the actuator. When the message «attack» is received by the player, the player loose 1point of life.

6.   Select the «Spider» object, in the first state layer, add a «Near» sensor, check «Activate True Level Triggering», «Freq: 200» (for an attack every 200 frames), «property»: «player», «Distance»:2.0, «Reset Distance»:3.0.

7.   Add a «Message» actuator, «To»: «Player», «Subject»: «attack»

8.   Link the sensor with the precedent actuator, link also with the actuator using «action» type Attack (animation attack). When the monster is 2 meters away from the player, it attacks and send a message to the player with «attack» type

9.   To test, copy (Shift+D) several «Spider» and put them on the map, test (P)

Step 10: the sound

To download a sound on FreeSfx (www.freesfx.co.uk), open an account (free). Replace the number 9786 in the following address: http://www.freesfx.co.uk/download/?type=mp3&id=9786

Download the following sounds or use another sounds:

- Player walking (A): #5478
- Player shooting(B): #5905
- Monster grunt(C): #6304
- Monster attack (D): #5178
- Monster death (E): #9786
- Surrounding sounds with nature type (F): #6332
- Box collision (G): #9152
- Ricochet (H): #947

1. Select «Player» and go in «Logic Editor». Add a «Sound» actuator, open the sound (A) and select «Play Mode»: «Loop End» (the sound is played during the moving). Change the Pitch (3 for walking, 10 for running) to adapt to the speed.

2. Link the actuator with the controllers for moving (walking)

3. Select the «Bullet» object and add a «Sound» actuator, open the sound (B) and select «Play Mode»: «Play End» (play only on time). Check «3D Sound». Link it with the «bullet» object to ensure that the sound follows the bullet.

4. Link the actuator with the controller bounded to the sensor «Always».

5. Select the «Spider» object and add a «Random» sensor, check «Activate on True Level Triggering», «Freq»: 200.

6. Add a «Sound» actuator, open the sound (C) and select «Play Mode»: «Play End». Check «3D Sound».

7. Link the sensor and the actuator. From time to time, but with spaces of 200 frames minimum, the monster grunts.

8. Add a «Sound» actuator, open the sound (D) and select «Play Mode»: «Play End». Check «3D Sound». Link the actuator with the controller bounded with the actuator «action» managing the attack animation. Select the state layer#2. And add a «Sound» actuator, open the sound (E) and select «Play Mode»: «Play End». Check «3D Sound». Link the actuator with the controller already linked with the sensor «Always».

9. Select the «CameraPlayer» object and add a «Sound» actuator, open the sound (F) and select «Play Mode»: «Loop End». Add an «And» controller and link it to the actuator. Link the controller with the sensor «Always»

10. Select the «Box» object and add a «Collision» sensor. Check «Activate on True Level Triggering», «Freq»: 200, «Property»: «player»

11. Add a «Sound» actuator, open the sound (G) and select «Play Mode»: «Play Stop». Link the sensor with the actuator. When the player hits the box, a sound is played, it's played differently if the player continues hitting the box (play «stop»).

12. Select the «Raycast» object and add a «Sound» actuator, open the sound (G) and select «Play Mode»: «Play End». «Volume»: 0.50. Link the actuator with the controller launching the script «BulletHole»

13. Edit the script «Bullet Hole» and add the following lines:

```
if mouseclick.positive and ray.positive:
    ...
    #Sound
    c.activate(c.actuators["ricochet"])
```

A bounce noise is played when the surface (with a property «impact») is hit.

Improvements:
- When the player approach the 'ocean (sensor «Near» on an «empty» in the middle of the water body), the rumble of the waves
- A sound of reloading shotgun
- A sound of footsteps according to the soil: grass, stone, water...
- Aleatory noises of animals, wind, etc.

The more the surroundings sounds are worked, the more the player is immersed in action.

II.7. PROJECT #7:THIRD-PERSON SHOOTER

The story:

In 1996, **Tomb Raider** enjoyed a worldwide success making the heroine Lara Croft, created by **Toby Gard,** one of the best numeric values...sexier than Mario (it depends of your tastes).
The character was played by Angelina Jolie who has already a charmed geek public since «Hackers» in 1996. It's one of the firsts games in 3D with texture mapping. There are 12 episodes in this franchise, the twelfth at the end of 2015: « Rise of the Tomb Raider».

Gameplay:

Tomb Raider combines action scenes to adventure and enigmas. The heroine evolves in 3D landscape, with a background music to immerse the player in the landscapes or to highlight events (collapse, dangers, enemies coming…). The addition of vehicles in the second opus (snow-bike and motorboat) allows to cover quickly distances. In the fourth opus, a new movement is added: to hang on with rope.

Technique:

By contrast with a «Doom's Like», where the game is based on action, a game like «Tomb Raider» focuses on the landscape and the interactions with it. Otherwise, a big part of the elements made for this kind of game can be taken back here.

Step 1: Preparation

We use the model **Sintel** of the **Blender Foundation**, made by **Angela Guenette**. To use your own model, go at the step 2.

1. Download the model Sintel on Blendswap: http://www.blendswap.com/blends/view/54246.
   The model is complex, remove the existing armature, apply the modifications («Location», «Rotation» and «Scale») on all the objects, combine the objects, apply the texture with «normal map» type, remove the option «transparency» from the material, and for the hair, unselect «backface culling».
2. For a play ground, download from http://www.blendswap.com/blends/view/70593 the model Castle of **brothermechanic**. Keep only the layer with the cathedral and eventually lamps. Remove all the «dupli groups» selecting everything and «`⇧ Shift`+`Ctrl`+`A`» («Make Duplicates Real»).
3. Add to the character a camera type TPS (**recipe V.4**) integrating the obstacles management between the camera and the character. For specific footage, use the **recipe V.15**. According to the scene, the enigma or the action to realize, it can be interesting to use a slave camera.

Step 2: Animations

It's the heart of the system: the character must have numerous animations to be capable of interacting with the landscape: to jump, to roll, to pick up,...
It's possible to use the **recipe IV.5** to animate the character, but, here, we'll use the **recipe IV.6** to use a Mocap bank.
The Mocap bank proposed is the one of **Carnegie Melon University** (CMU).

For the animation folders importation (BVH), use the **recipe IV.4** to obtain a rigged model with the good armature. The best is to import a first animation of the CMU to use the armature. The bone names are the same in all folders. So it's not necessary to make a «retargeting».

Animations used:
- Walk (25 Frames),
- Run (20 Frames),
- Idle (don'thing: 200 frames),
- Jump (50 frames),
- Push (100 frames),
- Tract (100 frames),
- Climb (100 frames),
- Crouch (100),
- Salto (70 Frames),
- FootKick (50 Frames),
- SwordFight (450 movements),
- BowFire (150 frames),
- Die1 and Die2 (100 andt 50 frames).

Transform them in actions in the «Dopesheet Editor», removing bone locations «Hip» (not for the IDLE which allows to put the character back on their feet).

Each animation must be cleaned keeping only the most interesting part, by reducing the number of frames (table) thanks to a scale, by reducing the animation («Sample to Bezier» and/or «Simplify F-Curves»). It's possible to revert on any action at any time. The goal is to prepare the actions to be the nearest that we want.

Step 3: Give life to the character

1. Use the recipe IV.10 to configure the basics movements of the character: walk, run, jump and Idle, using the prepared actions (last step). It's a big job !

Use the walls as a support to jump further and/or higher:

Modify the jump to allow the character pour lean on the walls.

2. Select «Player» (the physical object with the joined armature) go to «Logic Editor»
3. Add a «Ray» sensor, name it «RayForward», «Axis»: «+X Axis» (in front of the character) and «range»: 2.2 (modify according to the distance between the character's origin and the wall).
4. Add an «Expression» controller, «value»: «Jump AND NOT RayGround AND RayForward».
5. Link the controller with the corresponding sensors: «RayForward», RayGround» and «Jump»
6. Add a «Message» actuator, name it «ActionSalto», «To»: select the armature, «subject»: write «salto».
7. Link the controller with the actuators «ActionSalto» and «Jump». If the character jumps and reaches a wall, the player can do a new jump and the character will do a flip before to fall back.

To push an object:

To prevent the character's body passes thought the objects pushing them, modify the Physics properties («radius» and «form factor»).

Another solution is to move the animation relative to the physical object «Player». Go at the beginning of the animation, in «Pose Mode», select the principal bone «hip» father of all the others, and move it rearward, then create (or modify) an animation key with «location» type. The character goes out of the bounding box and hangs back. To get the character returns at its first place, in the middle of the bounding box, it's necessary that the «IDLE» action has too a key with «location» type in «hip».

(This solution can't be used to squat because the character squats to be able to going where he can't when he stands up)

When the action is configured:

8. Select the armature and add a «Ray» sensor, name it «RayPushing», «property»: «pushing», axis: «+X Axis», «range»: 2.50
9. Add an «Expression» controller, «value»: «RayPushing AND (MoveForward OR Run)». Link it with the precedent sensor and with the sensors «MoveForward» and «Run»
10. Add an «Action» actuator, name it «actionPush», select the corresponding action, write

«start frame» and «end frame», «priority»: 1, «Layer»:1, «Layer Weight»: 0.1 (to keep walking movement).

11. Link the actuator with the precedent controller. When the character strikes an object with a «pushing» property, the character seems to push it, the physics pushes the object. According to the object mass, the character can more or less push it.

To pull an object:

It's more difficult because you need to create a traction force (to push use directly the collision system):

12. Add the following script lines to «character.py»

13. Select the armature and add a «Ray» sensor, name it «RayTracting», «property»: «tracting», axis: «+X Axis», «range»: 3.0 (shortly before the collision pushing the object).

14. Add a «Keyboard» sensor, name it «MoveBackward», choose a key to pull an object (ex: «⇧ Shift +↓»)

15. Add a «Python» controller, select «Module» and write «character.tractObj». Link the 2 sensors with the controller.

16. Add an «Action» actuator, name it «actionTracting», select the corresponding action, set «start frame» and «end frame», «priority»: 1, «Layer»: 1, «Layer Weight»: 0.1. Link the actuator with the precedent controller.

17. Select «Player» and add the sensor «MoveBackward».

18. Add a «Motion» actuator, name it «MoveBackward», «Motion Type»: «Simple Motion», «Loc», «X»: -0.02 and check «L».

19. Link the sensor with the actuator. The character can now pull all the objects with the «tracting» property. However, a force of 250 is applied, so everything is depending of the object mass.

This script recovers the object pulled then it applies a force with a direction corresponding to the couple of character and object, and directed to the character. This vector helps to apply a force to the object to push it «in the other direction» !

Script character.py:

```python
def tractObj(cont):
    for sensor in cont.sensors:
        if not sensor.positive:
            for act in cont.actuators:
                cont.deactivate(act)
            return
    ray = cont.sensors["RayTracting"]
    own = cont.owner
    obj = ray.hitObject

    vec = (own.worldPosition - obj.worldPosition).normalized()
    obj.applyForce(vec * 250.0, 0)

    for act in cont.actuators:
        cont.activate(act)
```

Step 4: Combat

Add 3 combat modes to the character: unarmed combat, sword fight and archery. The game project #6 integrate the firearms management.

Adding a monster:

1. Steps 6 to 8 of a «Doom» type conception or import a NPC with «Spider» type from this game (File → Append).

Sword fight:

2. Add to the script «character.py» the following script lines.
3. Download the model «Burster Sword» from Blendswap: http://www.blendswap.com/blends/view/68993. Parent the sword to the «lHand» left hand of the armature. Adapt the rotation and the size of the sword to make the animation «SwordFight» realist. Hide the sword (H).

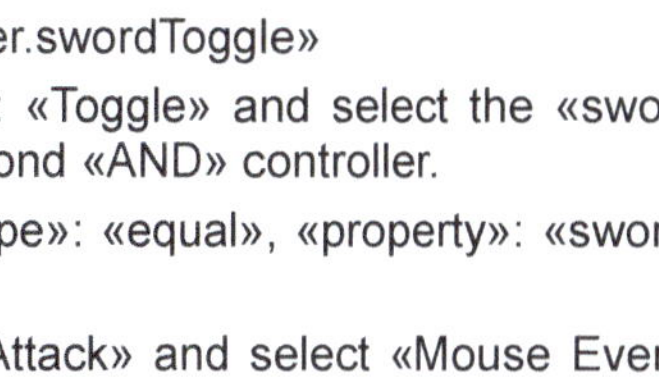

4. Select the armature and open the «Logic Editor».
5. Add a «sword» property with «boolean» type unchecked. This value allows to know if the sword is hidden or not.
6. Add a «Keyboard» sensor, name it «ToggleSword» and select a key offering the choice of selecting the sword fight mode.
7. Add a «Python» controller, select «Module» and write «character.swordToggle»
8. Add a «Property» actuator, name it «ToggleSword», «mode»: «Toggle» and select the «sword» property. Link the precedent sensor and the actuator with a second «AND» controller.
9. Add a «Property» sensor, name it «SwordON», «Evaluation type»: «equal», «property»: «sword», «value»: «True».
10. Add a «Mouse» sensor (or keyboard if you want), name it «Attack» and select «Mouse Event»: «Left Button».
11. Link the 2 sensors with a controller with «AND» type
12. Add an «Action» actuator, name it «ActionSword», «mode»: «loop stop», check «Continue», set «Start» and «End», «Blending»: 5 and «Priority»: 1. Link the controller with the actuator.

Addition to the script character.py:

```python
def swordToggle(cont):
    own = cont.owner
    scene = bge.logic.getCurrentScene()

    if own["sword"]:
        scene.objects["Sword"].visible = True
    else:
        scene.objects["Sword"].visible = False
```

«ActionSword» is a combination of several movements. Some of them allow to hit the high part of the body, another the low parts, …some shots are specifics and could be use with an intelligent way. Our character use continuously these movements in a cycle in all the attacks.

The other solution is to use only certain parts of the action and to determine some rules to condition the movement. We can, for example, take 3 empties parented to the armature or to player, one between the feet, one at waist, and the last above the head. Sensors with «ray» type can inform on the enemy position as: «don't strike the soil if the creature is jumping». We can use too different properties for each type of creature. For a more realistic fight, there are numerous conditions to determine.

A last solution is to let the player choose the kind of action, use only that solution in fighting game like «Street Fighter».

Using bow and arrows:

Unlike the precedent project where bullets and the physic engine are used, we exploit another mode: radius and impact point. The arrow is not materialized before the impact point is reached.

13. Download the «Gardian Bow» http://www.blendswap.com/blends/view/1500 of JG on blendswap: Import into the project (File → Append) the objects: «GOE-bow.JG» (rename it «bow») and «GEO-Arrow.JG» (rename it «arrow»). Parent «bow» to the bone «IHand» of the left hand of the armature. Adapt the rotation and the size of the bow for a realistic «DrawBow» animation. Hide the bow (H). In the «Physics» Tab, select «No Collision». Study the shapekey realized (you'll must do it again), then remove it. Apply the «mirror» modifier and apply a modifier with «decimate» type and with a value of 0.01. Put back in place the bow deformation shapekey during the shot. If it's not done, an action on which a modifier is executed for each picture, slowing down the animation !

14. Use the recipe IV.2 to make the bow animation. Go to frame 1, and configure the value of the shake key «Drawn» to 0, insert a key, do the same in frame 49 with a value of 0.4 (bent bow). In frame 50, value of 0. Rename the action «Keyaction» obtained in «DrawBow».

15. To display the bow, use the same approach as for the sword using a property «bow»: modify the script «character.py» to take account of the exclusive nature of the carrying of weapons like after.

16. Select the armature and go to «Logic Editor». Add an «Always» sensor, rename it «RunOnce» (launched only once at the beginning of the scene).

17. Add a «python» controller, select «Module» and enter «character.init». Link the sensor with the controller.

18. Select the «Bow» object. Add the same sensor «Attack» as for the armature.

19. Add an «Action» actuator, name it «ActionBow», «mode»: «Loop End», select «DrawBow», «Start»: 1, «End»: 50.

20. Add a «Message» actuator, «To»: «Bow», «Subject»: «fire». This actuator is used to launch the arrow later.

21. Link the sensor and the 2 actuators with an «AND» controller.

Addition to the script character.py:

```python
def init(cont):
    own = cont.owner
    scene = bge.logic.getCurrentScene()
    if not own["sword"]:
        scene.objects["Sword"].visible = False
    if not own["bow"]:
        scene.objects["Bow"].visible = False

def swordToggle(cont):
    own = cont.owner
    scene = bge.logic.getCurrentScene()

    if own["sword"]:
        scene.objects["Sword"].visible = True
        if own["bow"]:
            own["bow"] = False
            scene.objects["Bow"].visible = False
    else:
        scene.objects["Sword"].visible = False

def bowToggle(cont):
    own = cont.owner
    scene = bge.logic.getCurrentScene()

    if own["bow"]:
        scene.objects["Bow"].visible = True
        if own["sword"]:
            own["sword"] = False
            scene.objects["Sword"].visible = False
    else:
        scene.objects["Bow"].visible = False
```

Now, the character can do the gesture of taking an arrow and bending his bow. It's time to give it some arrows:

22. Add to the script «character.py» the following lines of script.

23. Add an «Empty», name it «RightHand» and parent it to the bone «rHand» of the armature.

24. Select «RightHand» and open the «Logic Editor». Add a «Message» sensor, name it «GenerateArrow», «subject»: arrow

25. Add a «Python» controller, select «Module» and enter «character.handArrow».

26. Add an «Edit Object» actuator, name it «SpawnArrow», «mode»: «Add Object», select the object «Arrow» and «time»: 35. While the character takes his arrow, the arrow is linked to the character's right hand.

27. Select the object «Bow», and a «Message» actuator, name it «GenerateArrow», «subject»: arrow. This actuator allows the arrow generation in the hand.

28. Add a «Message» actuator, name it «ArrowFire», «To»: «Player», «subject»: «arrow». This actuator allows the arrow generation in the target.

29. Link the 2 actuators to the controller linked to the actuator «ActionDraw».

30. Select the object «Player» and add a «Message» sensor, «Subject»: «arrow».

31. Add a «Ray» sensor, name it «RayBow», «axis»: «+x Axis», «range»: 500.

32. Add a «python» controller, select «module» and enter «character.cibleArrow». Link the 2 sensors with the controller.

33. Add an «Edit Object» actuator, «mode»:«Add Object», select the object «Arrow», «time»: 2000.

Addition to the python script «character.py»:

```python
def handArrow(cont):
    for sensor in cont.sensors:
        if not sensor.positive:
            return

    scene = bge.logic.getCurrentScene()
    spawn = cont.actuators["SpawnArrow"]
    spawn.instantAddObject()
    handArrow = spawn.objectLastCreated
    handArrow.setParent(scene.objects["RightHand"])

def cibleArrow(cont):
    for sensor in cont.sensors:
        if not sensor.positive:
            return
    ray = cont.sensors["RayBow"]

    arrowOnCible = cont.actuators["ArrowOnCible"]
    arrowOnCible.instantAddObject()
    arrow = arrowOnCible.objectLastCreated

    pos_vec = Vector(ray.hitPosition)
    normal_vec = Vector(ray.hitNormal)

    arrow.worldPosition = (pos_vec + normal_vec).xyz
    arrow.worldPosition.z += 1.5 #higher than origin
```

Unarmed combat:

When the character has nothing, we can assign another action like «FootKick» to the attack:

34. Add a property «monster» with «boolean» type to all the creatures to fight

35. Select the armature and add a «Ray» sensor, name it «RayMonster», «Axis»: «+X Axis», «Range»: 5

36. Add an «Expression» controller, enter «Attack AND RayMonster AND NOT sword AND NOT bow»

37. Add an «Action» actuator, name it «ActionFootKick», «mode»: «Loop End», complete «Start» and «End», «Layer»: 3 (to avoid conflicts with other animations).

38. Link the sensor with the controller, and the controller with the actuator.

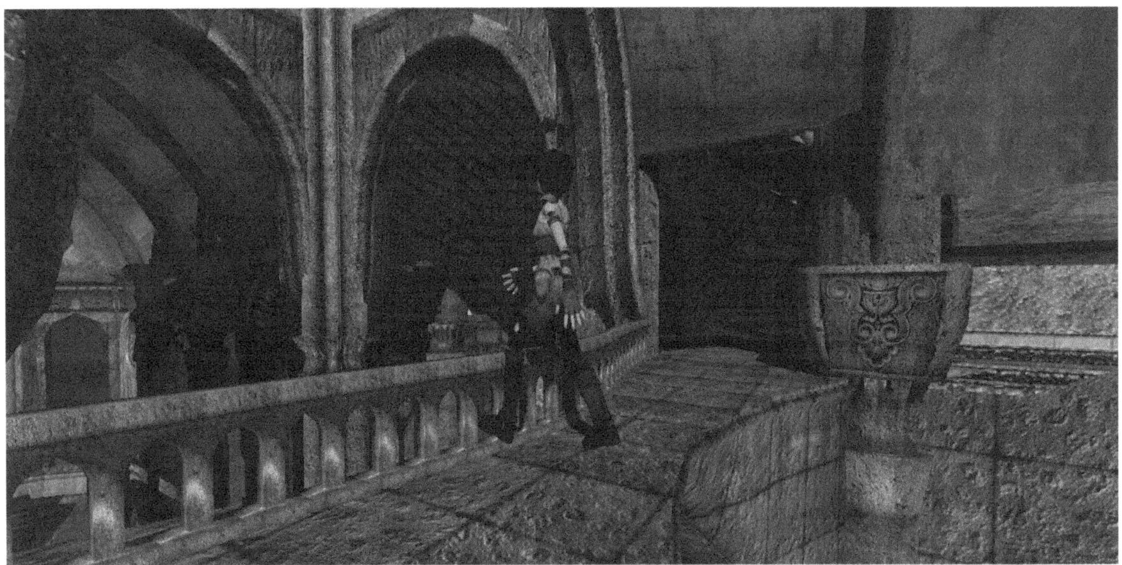

Illustration 53: Several scenes from the game

Life and death for the character and the creatures:

39. Add a «life» property to the «Player» object, with «Integer» type and enter the value of 100
40. Add a «life» property to the «Spider» object, with «Integer» type and enter a value of 10 (the character will win! According to the number of spiders....)

When a «spider» attacks the character, it sends to it an «attack» message (if the object was imported via «append», don't forget to modify the actuator «Steering» to indicate the «Player» and the corresponding «Navmesh»):

41. Select «Spider» and modify the actuator «AttackPlayer». Replace «attack» into «SpiderAttack» to identify the strokes origin.
42. Add an identical actuator but with «To»: armature to play an action corresponding to the be kicked. Link it with the same controller as «AttackPlayer»
43. Create an action «Hurt» on the armature, with a dozen images with a thrown backwards for the kick reception.
44. Select «Player», add a «Message» sensor, name it «SpiderAttack» and specify as subject: «attack».
45. Add a «Property» actuator, «mode»: «add», select the property «life» and enter as value: -1 (the damage of the spiders are light, we could use a random property too).
46. Link the sensor with the actuator.
47. Select the armature, add a «Message» sensor, name it «SpiderAttack» and specify as subject: «attack».
48. Add an «Action» actuator, «mode»: «Loop End», select the action «Hurt», specify «Start» and «End», «Layer»: 3

Link the sensor with the actuator.

Spider can damage the character, but the character can too:

49. Set «RayMonster» sensor to «radar», name it «RadarMonster», check «Activate On True Level Triggering», «freq»: 20, «Property»: «monster», «Axis»: «+X Axis», «Angle»: 30, Distance: 7 (modify according to the creature size).So, it's easier to hit than with a simple Ray (you need to aim straight ahead).
50. Select the armature and add a controller with «expression» type, «value»: «RadarMonster AND Attack AND sword».
51. Link the controller with the sensors «RadarMonster» and «Attack»
52. Add a «Message» actuator, «To»: «spider», «subject»: «SwordAttack». Link the actuator with the precedent controller.
53. Select the «spider» object. Add a «Message» sensor, «subject»: «SwordAttack»
54. Add a «Property» actuator, «Mode»: «Add», select the property «life» and «value»: -1
55. Link the sensor with the actuator.
56. Do the same things for the unarmed combat. The controller with «expression» type: «RayMonster AND Attack AND NOT sword AND NOT bow».

To kill a spider (state 2), you need to:

57. Select the «Spider» object, add a «Property» sensor, name it «IsDead», «Evaluation Type»: «Equal», «Property»: «Life», «Value»: 0. This sensor test the points of life.
58. Add an actuator «State», name it «DeadState» and select the second layer of state (state #2). Link the sensor and the actuator.

Now, to kill the character:

59. Select «Player» and go to layer #2. It'll be the layer for the state «Dead».

60. Add an «Always» sensor, name it «InitDie».

61. Add a «Message» actuator, name it «PlayerDie», «subject»: «die». Link the sensor with the actuator.

62. Add a «Delay» sensor, «delay»: 500

63. Add an «Edit Object» actuator, name it «Disappear», select «End Object». Link the sensor with the actuator. After 10 seconds, the character disappears.

64. Select the armature and add a «Message» sensor, name it «PlayerDie», «subject»: «die»

65. Add an «Action» actuator, name it «ActionDie», «mode»: «play», inform «start» and «end».

66. Add a «State» actuator, name it «DeadState» and select the layer 2. So, the character can no longer be controlled between the time of his death and the time of his disappearing.

67. Link the sensor with the 2 actuators using an «AND» controller.

To kill with the bow:

With the bow, you have just to add a message «ArrowAttack» to «Spider». It runs like «SwordAttack». For the message sender, modify the script «cibleArrow» and recover the object touched by «hitObject» and modify «Life».

Example:

```
cible = ray.hitObject
if "life" in cible:
    cible["life"] -= 5
```


Improvements:

- The spider can receive the message «PlayerDie» and position a property «PlayerDead». So, condition the «steering» to: «player is not dead» («Not PlayerDead»).

- Add some splattering of blood on screen (in overlay) when the character is hit

- Add some spattering of mucus when the spider is touched using the technique of billboards (recipe III.14) and generating them like particles with the actuator «Edit Object» in mode «Add Object».

II.8. PROJECT #8: ADVENTURE GAME

The story:

An adventure game is a video game in which the player assumes the role of protagonist in an interactive story driven by exploration and puzzle-solving. The first adventure game is «**Colossal Cave Adventure**», developed in 1975 by William Crowther on a PDP-10.

Very quickly, textual games become graphics games. It's time for games of «Sierra online» like the saga of King Quest, Space Quest and Leisure Suit Harry, game of «LucasArts» like Maniac Mansion, Zak McKracken (yes!), Monkey Island, Sam and Max, and Indiana Jones. Also known as «point & click» games, where the player needs to explore, associated objects to actions, combine objects and talk to other characters to evolve in the game. But these games were in 2D.

«**Myst**» is an adventure game made by the **Miller brothers**, developed at studio Cyan Inc and sold by Brøderbund in 1993. «Myst» had a big success, because of its immersive fiction universe. It generated «Myst-like», a sub-genus of adventure game. The games in this category have the same gameplay than «Myst» (subjective vision) as well as the same dreamlike ambiance where there's little dialogue.

Myst is one of the first game of this kind with a 3D universe. Levels are made up of several places more or less connected. Each place is shown as an image in 360°. So, the player can look in all the directions and numerous animations are proposed.

«**Little Big Adventure**» (LBA) is a action-adventure video game made by Adeline Software International in 1994. LBA is an OVNI made by **Frédéric Raynal**. He'll create too «Horror-Survival» in 3D, «**Alone In the Dark**» (1992). These games have a Gameplay based on the narration and the exploration, and not on killing monsters. Alone in the Dark is one of the first games which represents characters in polygons in a pre-rendered environment. It's the first game to use interpolated animated sequences to reduce the memory size of the game, and to propose a 3D animation adapted to the machine performance.

Games like «**Ankh**» (illustration 54), made by Deck 13 Interactive and published by Micro Application in 2006 use 3D to present an adventure in «point and click». The approach is closed to «Alone in The Dark» but the camera follows the character's movement, it's an immersion like cinematic. The studio **Telltale Games,** created by ex employes of LucasArts, produce this kind of game introducing the episode concept, it was a success for the adaptation of «**The Walking Dead**».

The principals characteristics of adventure game are: a scenario, exploration and a few action and dialogues. In 2015, **Dont Nod** encounter a great success with «**Life is Strange**» that cross genres.

Gameplay:

Example: a «point and click» game at the first person, the player can see the same view than the character. The player use the mouse to move, clicking on the place where he wants to go. The player can interact with some objects, clicking on these objects. There's no enemy, no time limit, no game over. There are numerous enigma more or less complexes. The player must read texts from books, press or signs.

Technique:

This kind of game is the simplest to realize on a technical level and one of the most difficult on graphical and narrative terms.

This kind of game use the following elements:
- A camera «Freeview» (**Recipe V.1**): we don't see the character, it provides substantial time savings for animation and rigging.
- Or a few fixed cameras (**recipe V.15**) according to the character position like in «Alone In The Dark».
- Interaction with objects with the mouse (**recipe V.14**), via proximity sensors (**recipe V.7**)
- Using point and click (**recipe IV.10**), with doors and teleporters (**recipe V.6**)
- Cinematics («cut scenes»)
- An inventory for objects (**recipe VI.6**)
- Text display (**recipe VI.7**)

The recipes of this book include all bases to do this kind of game.

It's one of the most attractive game for a beginner, it allows to tell a story, to learn something without the difficulty of animations. The other projects include all the notions needed to do this kind of game, so we don't present a complete project.

Illustration 54: Anhk, a point-and-click 3D adventure game by Deck13 Interactive

II.9.   IS IT POSSIBLE TO CREATE ANY GAME?

MMO ?

Massively multiplayer online Game engage **numerous** and **simultaneous** players via Internet. There are sub-genus like:

* MMOFPS (Massively Multiplayer Online First Person Shooter),
* MMORTS (Massively Multiplayer Online realtime Strategy),
* MMORPG (Massively Multiplayer Online Role Playing Game), the most popular today.

One of the principal characteristics of MMO is the persistent universe. The game is played at every time, player online or not.

Today, the MMO are focused on MMORPG with fantasy theme (medieval fantastic fictive universe): Lineage 2, EverQuest, or World of Warcraft.

Is it technically possible with BGE?

Creating a game that can be played in multiplayer on network is possible. The **recipe V.17** gives some perspectives...However, the volume of data to exchange must stay low, so the numbers of players should be small too. To do a chat, the volume of data is not important and it's possible to synchronize several hundred users. The realtime aspect is not important. For a 3D world with numerous objects and complexes physical rules, there's an explosion of the volume of data!

Games like «World of Warcraft» need servers to connect thousands of people. I think it's not possible to do a MMORPG like «Warcraft» with Blender.

And network games ?

To play on network, you must create a «universe» in which actions from each others are considered. The  simplest is «Master» (server) to manage all the world physics, the game logic and dispatch information to the different «Slaves» (clients). A game with 2 players can be done with a master and a server.

Blender Game Engine was not developed to do «multiplayer» game via network. There are some attempt more or less accomplished to synchronize objects via network. The most advanced is the one of Angus Hollands (Agoose77 on Blender-Artists). A discussion thread: http://tinyurl.com/pwtcwqx. It's an addon and a minimalist library, to create some simple games. Another discussion thread: http://tinyurl.com/pe9v9qa. This work is relatively advanced and based on the architecture of the «Unreal engine».

Bzoo is a 3D persistent virtual word created with BGE. A french adventure started in august 2006, but stopped. A development framework was made to allow to add network functions to a 3D universe, with the possibility to create a server, to connect clients, to add an avatar, to explore the world and to talk with other avatars using a chat. Official site: http://www.bzooworld.org/

The **«source engine»** developed by Valve (Counterstrike, Team Fortress, Left 4 dead 2 or Portal 2) use an optimized system for the network layer:

* State interpolation system (movement, animation, etc) between 2 states images, named «Entity interpolation»
* Users entries predictive system (key, click) on client: it generates movement, verifies the collisions etc ....
* Correction by the server if the prediction is not exact: a system of «lag compensation» recalculates the positions for each object when keys are pressed. The server reconstructs the general image of the state of the game at a given time «t» – the game engine «goes back in time» and has several images of the world in memory.

«Source Engine» has numerous others optimizations, but it can't allow MMORPG. The number of players max is 256 (theoretical limit), but it's optimized for 32 or less players.

Vindictus is a MMORPG using the «Source Engine», but the engine was optimized in the network layer. Vindictus is a dungeon's game.

II.10. CONCLUSION

The Blender Game Engine is not a ready-made toolkit to create video-game like Unreal Engine or Unity. The recipes developed in this book allow to respond to a lack of tools, and quickly make video games.

BGE has not a network layer to create MMO online.

Projects and recipes presented in this book **allow you to understand the difficulties** of developing 3D videogames. Difficulties are hidden by kits generally! indeed, BGE is one of the best tools to learn how to create a 3D video game.

Now, time has come for you to create a video game. Best is to start with an Improvements of a game presented in this book.

Illustration 55: BlenderArtists, Game Engine forums

In any case, visit and take part in the forum Game / WIP (Work In Progress) of blenderartists.org

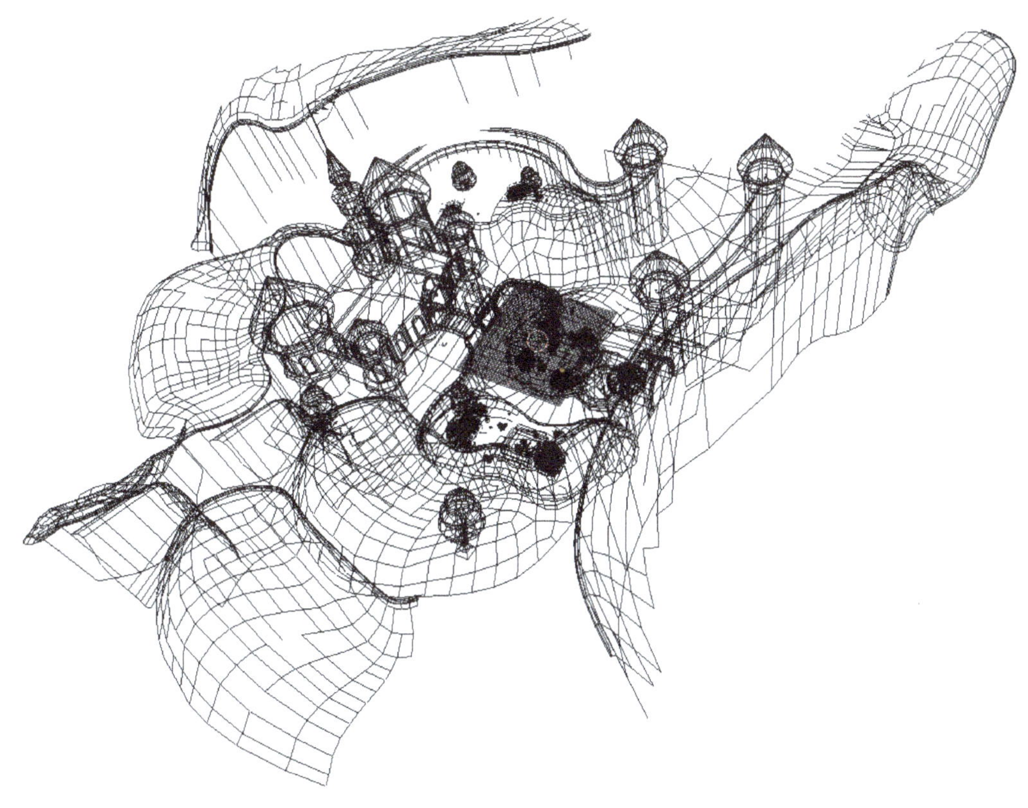

III - LANDSCAPE & DECORS RECIPES

Landscape model from **Super Blender Galaxy**: http://tinyurl.com/o4lnczm

III.1. LANDSCAPE MODELING

With a Heightmap

Purpose:

Obtain a game landscape using a picture with «Heightmap» as support. The advantage is **to be able to model quickly several decors and to modify the landscape by modifying the Heightmap** before with a drafting software like «The Gimp». The landscape will be textured (cf following recipe) to be directly exploited in the game.

Recipe:

1. Add a plane (`↑ Shift`+`A` → «Mesh» → «Plane»), then go to «Edit Mode»
2. Subdivide the plane 6 times («W» → «Subdivide») then go to «Object Mode»
3. In the «Properties» window, «Materials» Tab, add a Material («+»)
4. In the «Textures» Panel, add a texture («+») with «Image or Movie» type, select a file Heightmap like on illustration 49 (Google pictures «Heightmap» - avoid Jpeg compression which can produce bad results - size min 512x512)
5. «Modifier» Panel, add a «modifier» with «Displace» type
6. Configure height, etc. then apply

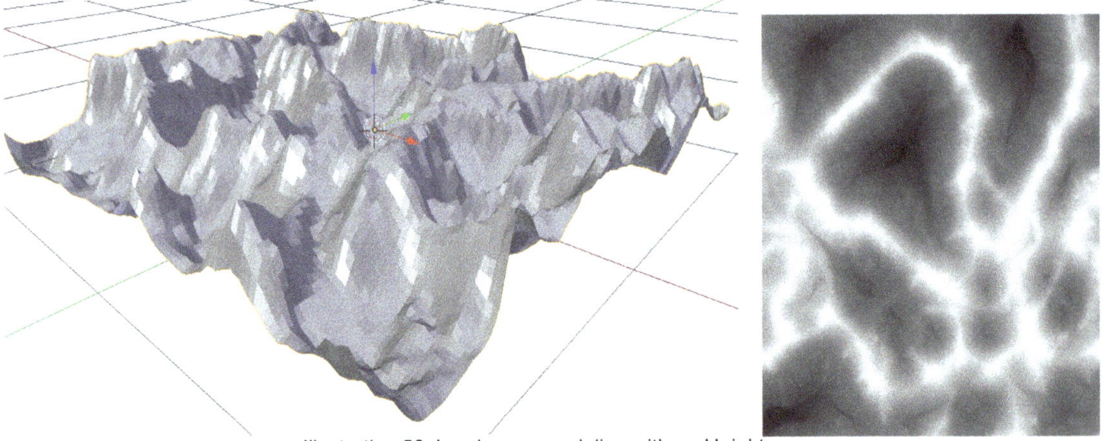

Illustration 56: Landscape modeling with an Heightmap

In «Sculpt» Mode

Purpose:

The landscape is modeled in the «3D View» window. In this way, you have **more realistic landscapes with tunnels** for example. However, each map must be completely reworked.

Recipe:

1. Create a plane and go to «**Sculpt Mode**»

2. Activate the «**Dynamic Topology**» (Ctrl+D): this mode avoid to subdivide the plane before. The mode add some details during the sculpt. Of course, don't work with a mapping UV done before. We can modify the size of the details in the menu «Tools», «Topology» panel, «Detail size».

3. Sculpt the landscape to give it specific forms (Illustration 63)

Advice:

Modify the brush radius as you need (key «F»). The radius works according to the zoom level on the landscape. Sometime, it's better to be near, rather than modify the radius.

To preserve the modifications zone: «Shift+Ctrl+LMB» and while keeping key pressed (mode lasso), draw the zone (Ctrl+I to inverse, and «Alt+M» to remove the lasso). You can use the brush «Mask» too.

Modify the brush shape by pressing the keys Ctrl+F

The key Ctrl **inverses the brush functioning**. Example: to deflate instead of to inflate.

For brushes, use:

- Standard «**Brush**» (key «D») to raise surfaces. The «**Blob**» brush does more or less the same things, but with a rounder shape (perfect for dunes).

- The «**Nudge**» brush to push surfaces such as play dough. «**Grab**» (key «G») is worse ! Use Grab to roughly model or to dig tunnels.

- The «**Fill/Deepen**» brush to raise the cavities. It erases imperfections of landscape. It's the lifting brush of the sculpt mode. Approaching of bump, this brush don't touch these and only raise the level of the holes. In «deepen» mode (Ctrl), the brush accentuates the holes.

- The «**Clay**» brush (key «C») to model as play dough.

- The «**Strips**» brush to leave truck tire or caterpillar marks, or to add this type of motif.

- The «**Crease**» brush (keys «Shift+C») to dig cracks in the ground, like to draw a canal.

- The «**Flatten**» brush (keys «Shift+T») to create flat landscape (for buildings, etc.). It's possible to activate or deactivate the dynamic topology.
    - activated, «Flatten» is like a «decimate» → remove the details.
    - deactivate, the brush levels the playing field.

- The «**Inflate**» brush (key «I») to inflate a zone, like air in a balloon.

- The «**Layer**» brush (key «L») to raise the surface, creating plates forms at one time (parameter Height)

- The «**Pinch/Magnify**» brush (key «P») to converge in the center of the brush everything below. If the cracks are to large, this brush can refine them.

- The «**Smooth**» brush (key «S») to erase imperfections, to simplify the zone, etc. However, the «**Polish**» brush is basically the same with a flatten more. Very handy for difficult topologies and with big levels of strength, the brush allows to create large and planes surfaces with sharp edges. For example, «Polish» is better to cut a stone than to cut a dune.

- The «**Scrap/Peak**» brush to smooth leaving an effect «play dough» like «**Clay**». In «Peak» mode (with Ctrl), to make sharp edges. In addition to «Crease», we can design a pretty valley.

- The «**Thumb**» brush to pull back while pushing. It's like press on play dough pushing laterally: the surface is extended in one direction. It allows to make rounded contours.

- The «**Twist**» brush to rotate the exterior around the center that's unchanged. Turning the mouse creates a whirlpool = Effect «cyclone».

- The «Snake/Hook» brush (key «K») to create «arches» and another specifics reliefs. This brush severely distorts so we can pull some landscape filaments. In «dynamic topology» mode, the brush will add mesh (unlike «Grab»)!

- The «Mask» brush (key «M») to preserve a modification zone from the other brushes. It's a very useful tool to create some crevices. We can use «⇧ Shift+Ctrl+LMB» and keeping them pressed (lasso mode), we draw the zone. In any case: «Ctrl+I» to inverse, and «Alt+M» to release the mask.

Each brush has its own configuration. It allows to have some tools highly functional.

Improvements

Work the model in a superior definition to add numerous details and imperfections. Bake the normals like in the **recipe IV.12** to obtain a High Definition map of these imperfections. Apply a «modifier decimate» like in this recipe (and/or use the LoD like in the **recipe III.17**).

With the Addon ANT Landscape

Purpose:

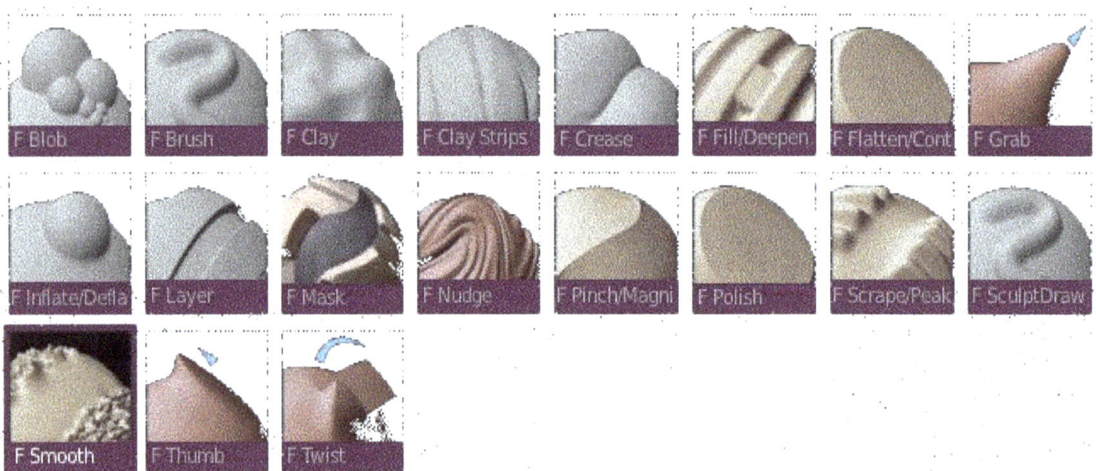

Illustration 57: Brushes on Blender

«Ant Landscape» is an addon written by Jimmy Hazevoet to easily generate some landscapes (Illustration 62 - tutorial: http://tinyurl.com/l2rcbgf). Thereafter, these landscapes can be modified in Sculpt mode. The tool is interesting to obtain some plates forms and to adjust the sea level.

Recipe:

1. Activate the module in the addons: go to «user preferences»

(Ctrl + Alt + U) «Addons» panel, search the module «add Mesh: ANT Landscape». Activate it and save the preferences, then exit from this menu.

2. Add a landscape: «Shift + A» → «Mesh» → «Ant Landscape».

3. In the «3D View», open the menu «Tools» (T), «Landscape» panel.

4. Position «Subdivisions»: 200, «Mesh size»: 6, «Heigth» at 2.0, «plateau» at 1.0

5. Test with «Lacunarity» at 1.0 (landscapes with «Far-west» type), see the result and reset at 2 (Illustration 58)

6. There are numerous generation functions, execute tests «Type» (Illustration 59,60 and 61)

7. At once, the model is finished, save the configuration clicking next to «Operator Presets», button «+»

8. Verify the normals which are sometimes reversed. To do that, in «3D View», go to «Edit Mode», menu «Properties» (N), «Mesh Display» panel check «display mesh normals as line» and increase the size to 1.0. If the normals point down, menu «Tools» → «Normals» → «Flip Direction».

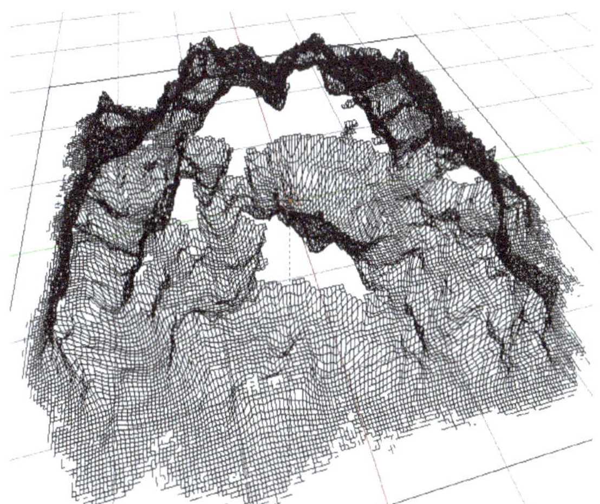

Illustration 58: Example in wireframe (Z) mode

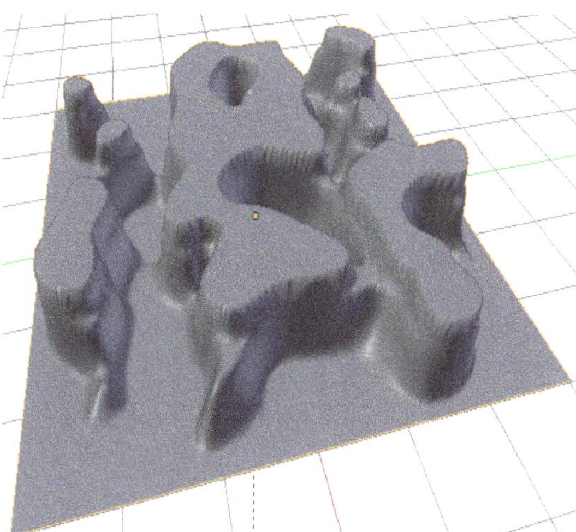

Illustration 59: Type «Multifractal», lacunarity: 1

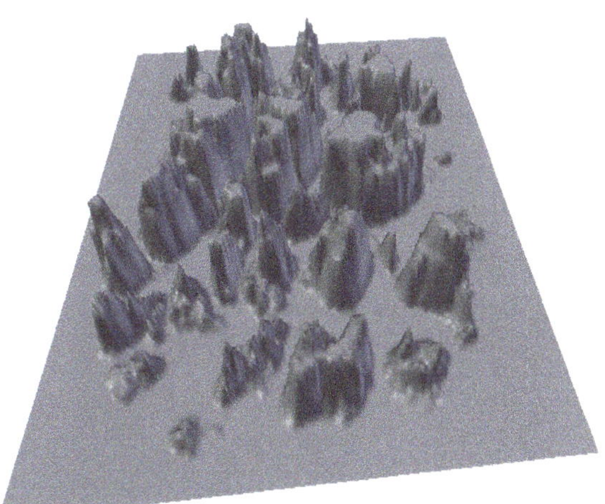

Illustration 60: Type «Shattered_hTerrain»

Illustration 61: Mode «Sphere»

III.2. BIG LANDSCAPES

In «Texture Painting» mode

Purpose:

When the model of landscape is created, you have to **color** it. We can do an UV mapping and then use another software to do the operation, but it'll be more complex to do, and it would be rather less funny. Fortunately, Blender has a fantastic tool: the Texture Painting. It allows to use some textures we can spray directly on the mesh.

Recipe:

1. Select the landscape, go to «Edit Mode», «U»→ «Smart UV Project»
2. Come back in «Object Mode», «Properties» window, «Material» panel, add a Material
3. «Textures» Panel, add a texture with «Image or Movie» type, create a new picture named «TextureMap» (choose a high definition like 2048x2048)
4. «Mapping» Panel, «Coordinates»: Select «UV» and the name of the generated UV (by default, «UVMap»).
5. Add some textures to be used as basic textures for the colorization of the landscape. Example: soil, sand, stone and grass. Load them without adding them to «Material». We can do an Append in a library of textures for example.
6. For a better view, cut the «3D View» in vertical direction to display the «UV/Image Editor» window. Select the picture «TextureMap» and the good UV. To do that, the landscape must be selected in «Edit Mode».
7. Go to «Texture Paint» mode in «3D View». Display the «Tools» menu (T) if it's not.
8. In Texture, select a picture, the stone for example.
9. Start to colorize the landscape with this last texture.
10. Idem with the other textures until we obtain something similar at the Illustration 62

Note: Several shortcut keys in «sculpt» mode may be used in «Texture Paint» mode, in particular to use layers.

Illustration 62: Example of landscape made with ANT Landscape by David Ward

<u>**Advices:**</u>

- **«radius»** to modify the brush size to paint more or less quickly ⬚F
- **«Strength»** to paint over another texture, leaving transparency. The closer to 1.0 the value is, the more the brush will be important.
- **«Brush Mapping»**
    - in «3D» for a quick first pass scanning the zone.
    - In «view plane» to have several texture resolutions (example: big and little stones from the same texture according to the zoom - varies with the mouse wheel, and with the angle).
    - In «random» for finish.
- **«Angle»** (available in brushing mapping: «view plane»): Change the orientation of the texture (⬚Ctrl+⬚F).
    - «random» to have a random effect when the landscape is overflew.
- «Rake» to follow the path of the brush and turn the texture. Useful for textures with «truck tire marks» or «caterpillar marks» type with a given direction.
- **«Paint stroke»**:
    - «Airbrush» to apply the effect when we click,
    - «space» distance interval.
    - «jitter» allows to overflow the brush when jitter is over 0.3.
- **«Blend»**:
    - «Mix»: standard mode, the texture is mixed with the existing textures, with color texture respect.
    - «Add» add to the existing color (ex: snow). «Substract» does the opposite.
    - «Darken» turns darker everything (ex: to highlight the relief) / «Soften» does the opposite.
    - «Erase Alpha»: make transparent / «Add alpha» does the opposite.

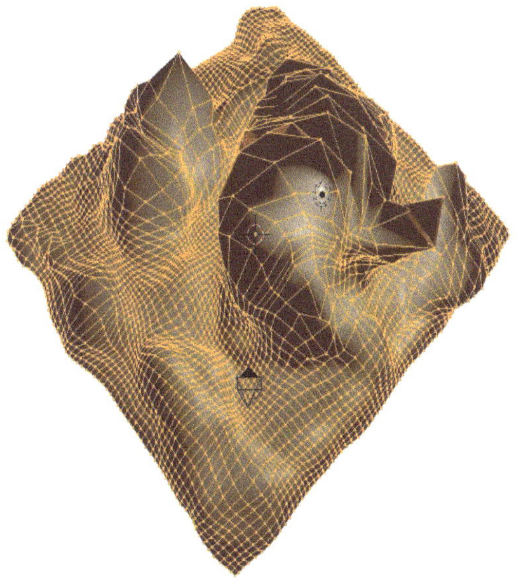

Illustration 63: Map after sculpt brush

Illustration 64: Texture after UV mapping

The «TextureMap» texture will be automatically painted like on Illustration 64. In the «UV/image Editor» window, we see in realtime the changes.

The «View» mode is selected by default, but it's possible to select the «Paint» mode to color directly the texture. This is a useful feature for doing some adjustments in inaccessible points en 3D. A general scanning is quicker too.

Illustration 65: Brush painting on the sculpted object

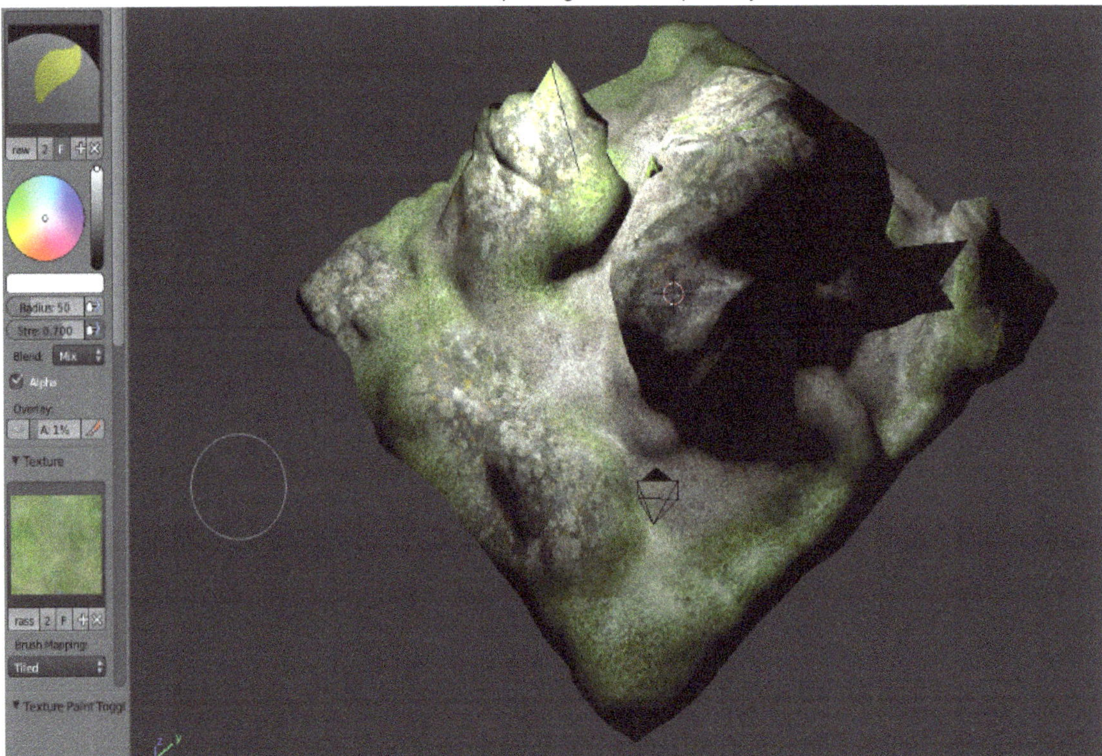

Optimize for vast landscapes in texture splatting mode

It's difficult to use bigger textures than 4096x4096 because it takes a lot of graphics memory. For vast landscapes, these textures seem to be blurred from up close.

Texture Splatting: this method allows a texturing with high resolution. You use a stencil like a layer between 2 textures (illustration 66).

Recipe:

1. Add a plane (`Shift`+`A` → Mesh → Plane). In «Edit Mode», do an «Unwrap».
2. «Properties» window, «Material» panel, add a Material (check «shadeless» for convenience, but remove it later when you'll add the lamps).
3. «Textures» Panel, add 3 textures with «Images or Movie» type: 1 of stone, 1 of sand and 1 of soil. Apply the Mapping with «UV» type.
4. Add a new texture «stencil1» and «stencil2» and create some new pictures. In the «Influence» panel check «RGB Intensity» and select a white (R:1.0,G:1.0,B:1.0). Check too «stencil».
5. In the display order of textures: Insert the first stencil between stone and sand, the second stencil between sand and soil.
6. Go to «Texture Painting» mode. Divide the screen in 2, in the vertical direction. On the right, choose the «UV/Image Editor» window and choose the texture «stencil 1». Divide this window in 2, choose the texture «stencil 2». For the 2, leave «View» mode to go to «Paint» mode. The screen is like on illustration 66
7. Select a white brush and draw in the «UV/Image Editor» window of the first stencil.
8. Do the same thing in the second. Test with a different color intensity (from black to white). The impact of a texture on another is managed in this way.
9. Another solution is: use the Material «nodes» and each texture needs a Material. This solution allows to obtain different bumps and specular effects and other modifications, for each texture.

Optimizations:

It's possible to mix 4 stencils in 1 picture by diverting the using of the channels. Le canal R(red) would be the first stencil, the G(green) the second and the B(blue) the third stencil and the canal A(Alpha) the fourth. With that, we have 5 different textures. We can do the same thing with a compilation of 3 into 1 picture for the Lightmap, the Specular Map and the Gradient Map (add noise to imitate imperfections). So, we limit the number of textures in memory to increase performances.

Another solution is to use the **«vertex colors»** instead of the stencils.

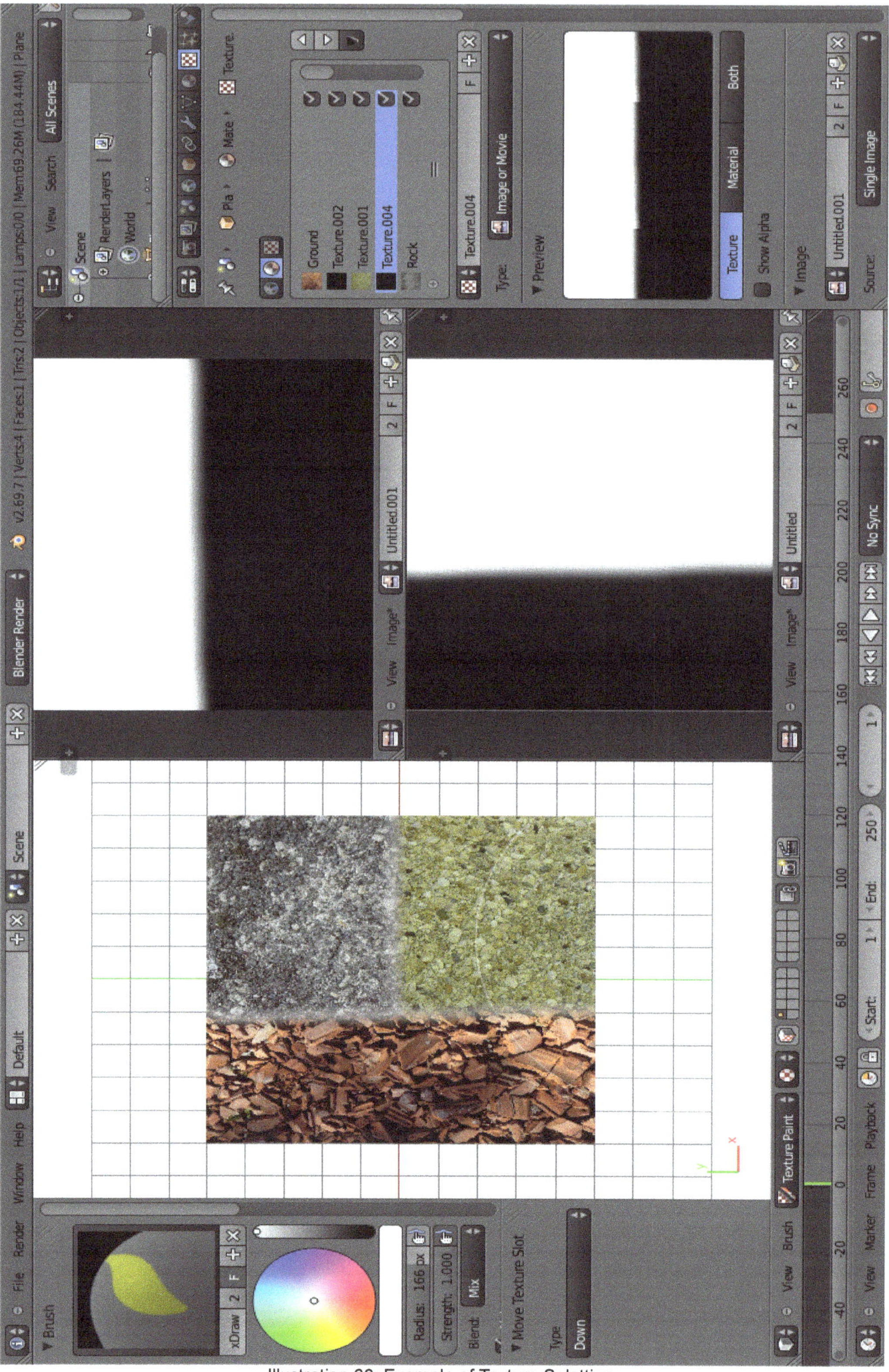

Illustration 66: Example of Texture Splatting

III.3. SKYDOME & SKYBOX

Purpose:

Create a decor placed around the playing field to make the scene appears more complex. This decor simulates a 3D landscape based on a 2D photography: a sky, some buildings and mountains.

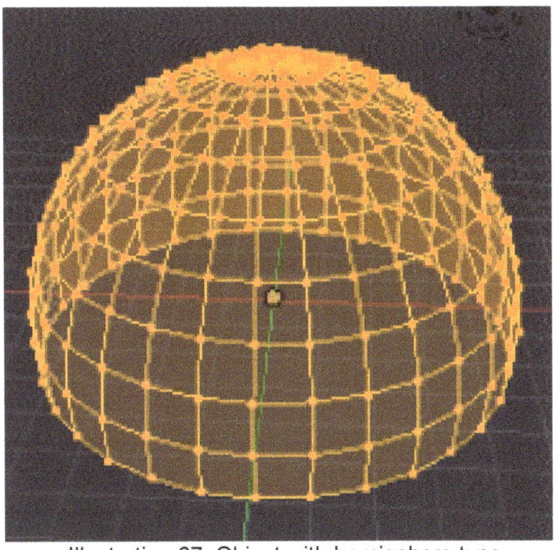

Illustration 67: Object with hemisphere type

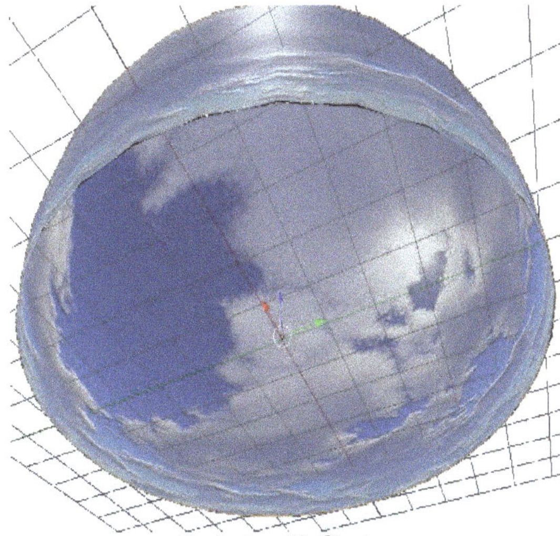

Illustration 68: Skydome

Recipe:

1. Model a hemisphere (half of this sphere is removed) Illustration 67
2. Go to Edit mode, UV mapping («U»→ «Unwrap»)
3. Go to Google/Images and look for a skydome picture (hemisphere)
4. Open the «UV/Image Editor» to open the picture and resize it («S») to correspond to the UV mapping
5. Add a «Material» to the hemisphere
6. Add a texture, load the downloaded picture, «Mapping Coordinates»: type «UV» with the good coordinates «Uvmap». Eventually, add to the texture a normal: 0.2 to give some relief to the clouds
7. In «Edit Mode», «Mesh» panel → «Normals»→ «Flip Normals» (normals face the hemisphere outward by default)
8. Add a lamp with Hemi type pointing upwards. We obtain a skydome like on Illustration 68.

For a skybox, do the same things with a cube and a picture like on Illustration 70.

Improvements:

It's possible to work with an integral sphere and a texture like on Illustration 71.
For high realism, add a **second sphere and using transparency move the clouds** → low impact on resources.

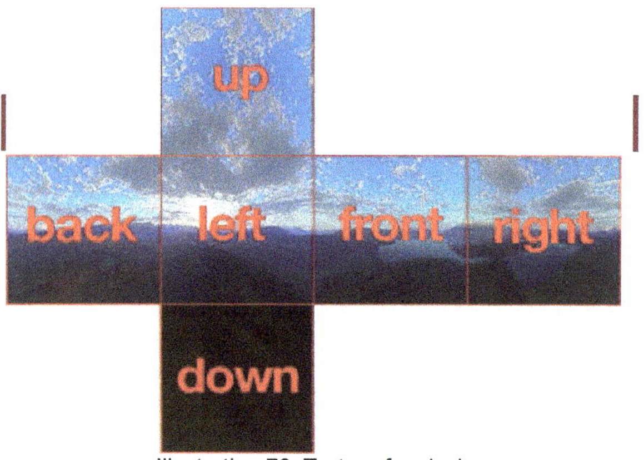

Illustration 70: Texture for sky box

Illustration 69: Texture for hemisphere

Illustration 71: Texture for skydome with sphere type

III.4. REALISTIC DAYLIGHT

Purpose:

Create a **light environment like on Earth** for the exterior scenes. Use 3 lights: 1 spot for the sun, and 2 hemi (1 for the sky reflexion and one for the floor reflexion).

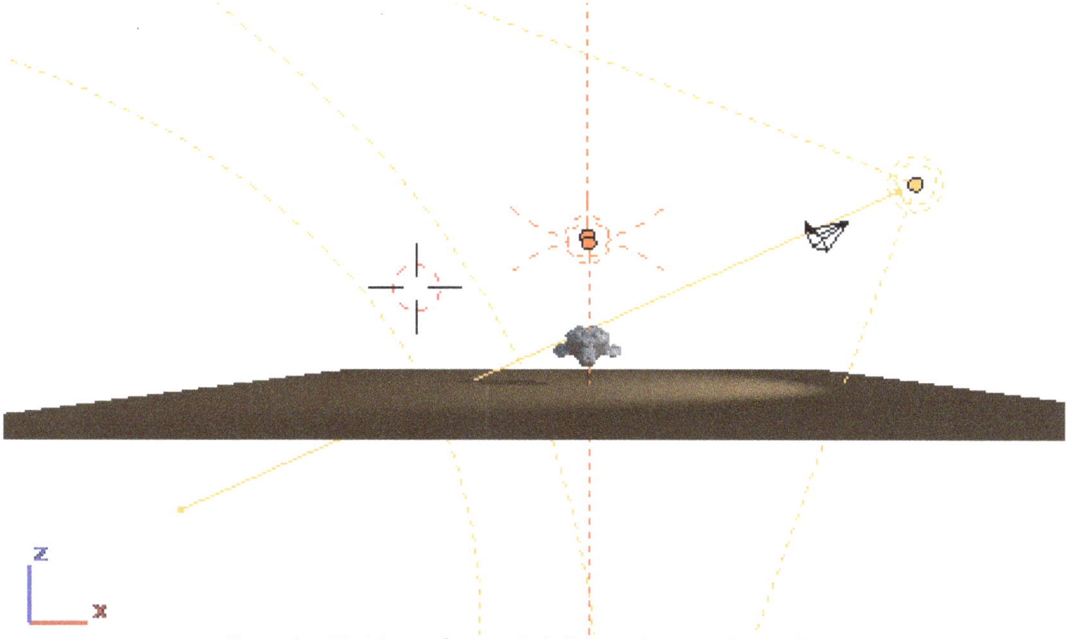

Illustration 72: 3 lamps for a realistic light environment like on Earth

Recipe:

1. Add a lamp (⇧ Shift + A → «Lamp» → «Hemi»). «Properties» Window → «Data Object» Panel → Lamp, modify the color into RGB (0.50,0.80,1) for a blue sky, «Energy»: 0.2
2. Orientate the hemi downward (Illustration 72)
3. Add a lamp (⇧ Shift + A → «Lamp» → «Hemi»). «Properties» Window → «Data Object» Panel → Lamp, modify the color into RGB (1,0.5,0.18) for a ground with soil (green for grass, etc.), Energy: 0.15
4. Orientate the Hemi upward (Illustration 72)
5. Add a lamp (⇧ Shift + A → «Lamp» → «Spot»). «Properties» Window → «Data Object» Panel → Lamp, keep the default color (or a sunset yellow for the evening hues), Distance of 80, Bias at 0.09 (shadows), Spot Shape size at 100° and Blend at 0.6.
6. Orientate the spot according to the time of the day.

The illustrations 73 to 76 show the different results based on these lamps. If you add a fog effect, don't forget to uncheck the option «use mist» in the materials. On Earth, distant objects seem to be blues thanks to the atmosphere which diffuse the blue preferentially. So, mountains at different distances have not the same blue color.

<u>Improvements</u>:

To rotate the sky continuously:

1. Select the skydome and go to the «Logic Editor».
2. Add an «Always» sensor, check «Activate True Level Triggering», configure «freq» at 30,0
3. Add an actuator with motion type and specify Rot: Z: 0.01 and link the sensor with the actuator

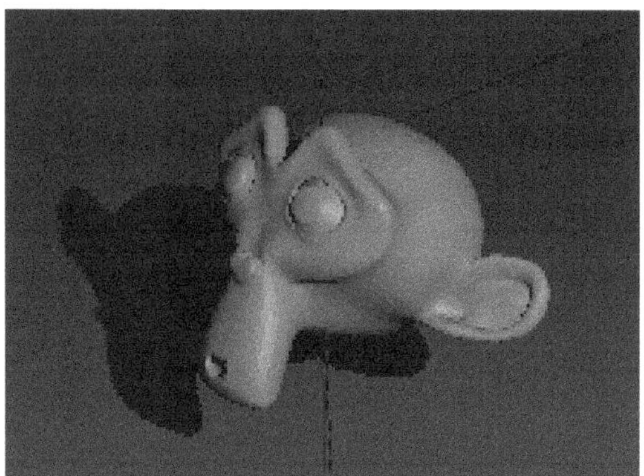

Illustration 73: Spot, without the Hemi

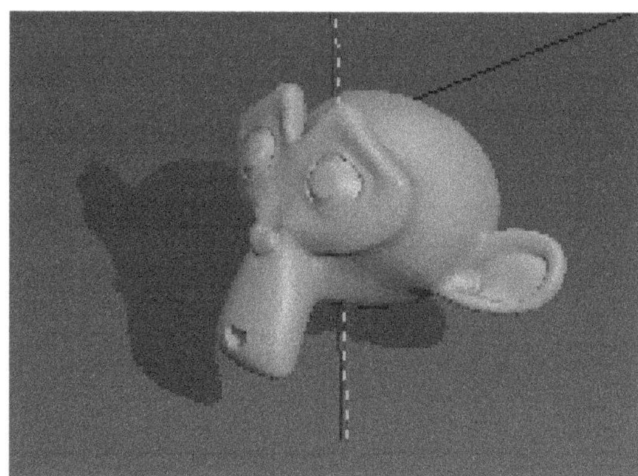

Illustration 74: Spot with the sky Hemi

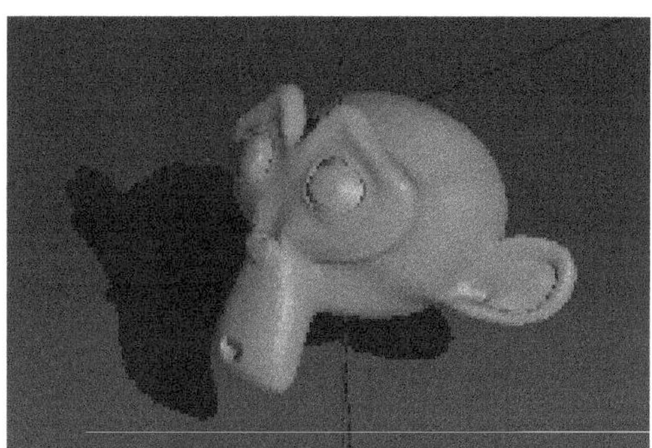

Illustration 75: Spot with soil hemi

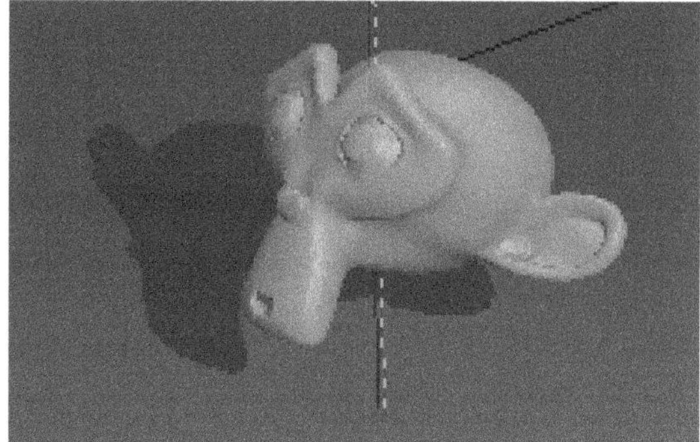

Illustration 76: Final result

III.5. SIMPLE FOG

Purpose:

When a fog effect is applied («Mist»), the **most distant objects become invisible (taking the fog color), adding to the illusion of depth to the picture.**
The fog allows to create a specific, enigmatic or «Horror-Survival» type atmosphere.

Recipe:

1. In the «Properties» window, «World» panel, check «**Mist**».
2. Configure: «**Falloff**»: allows to fix the mist proportion applied when the objects stray from the camera:
   - «**linear**», the simplest: the further we are, the more the fog is present.
   - «**Quadratic**» use a function in (1/x2)
   - «**inverse quadratic**» use a function in (1/ square root(x)). This last parameter gives an impression of volume, according to the distance.
3. Configure the distance parameters: the fog appears as from a distance of the camera with these parameters:
   - «**Start**»;
   - «**Depth**» distance from start over which the increase in density until everything is hidden. Any object further away from the camera than «*Start+Depth*» is no more visible.
4. The parameter «Minimum Intensity» sets the basic density for the fog.

Notes:

- To prevent an object's modifying by fog, uncheck the option «Use Mist» in the «options» panel of the Material.
- To see the depth of the fog in the editor, select the camera, go to the panel «Camera» of the «Properties» window, «Display» Panel and check the option «Mist».

Illustration 77: Application of simple fog: the most distant things are blurred

III.6. VOLUMETRIC FOG OR SMOG

Purpose:

The volumetric fog creates a fog effect in which the fog density is not constant (Illustration 78). To do that, use some pictures to disperse on the scene to create a volume effect. The recipe is the same for the smog.

Illustration 78: Example of volumetric fog

For this recipe, we need GIMP to create the fog image. It's possible to pass over this step, downloading a picture on Google Image with these parameters: «texture mist». Make sure that the alpha canal exists for transparency.

Recipe image:

1. Open «The Gimp» and create a new picture (1024x1024) – adapt the size as needed.
2. Menu «Colors» → Color to Alpha, then «Ok» to create our transparent background.
3. Select the tool «Paintbrush Tool», «Opacity»: 25, «Brush»: «smoke», «size»: 150 and step by step (little clicks without sweep), obtain something near the Illustration 80 (on transparency background, not black on the illustration).
4. Export to format .PNG and name the picture «fog.png»

Illustration 79: Example of volumetric fog with a light effect

Illustration 80: Texture type «Fog/Mist/Smoke»

<u>Recipe application</u>:

1. Load a scene which contains a space to use a volumetric fog (ex: along the strip roads).

2. Create a plane, do a rotation of 90° on the axis (R X 90) to set it in a vertical position. Go to «Edit Mode» and «U» → «Unwrap».

3. In the «Properties» window, «Material» panel, add a new «Material». Check the option «Shadeless» from the «Shading» panel to not be influenced by the lamps. In the «Game Settings» panel, uncheck the option «Backface culling» so that the plane is visible on both sides. «Alpha Blend»: Select «Alpha Blend».

4. «Transparency» Panel: check «Transparency», Select «Z Transparency» and «Alpha»: 0.0

5. «Texture» Panel, add a new texture with «Image or Movie» type. Select the picture created before (or downloaded).

6. Check «Show alpha» to verify the transparency of the background.

7. «Mapping» Panel, «Coordinates»: Select «UV», then select the good UV in «map».

8. «Influence» Panel, check «Diffuse: Alpha» and set the alpha at 0.2

9. The Illustration 81 gives us a glimpse into the disposition of the planes to create the needed effect along the lane. Copy the plane (⬆ Shift + D), resize it («S») and reorient it («R»).

10. To test: insert a camera with «FPS» type (recipe V.2) and walk along the path..

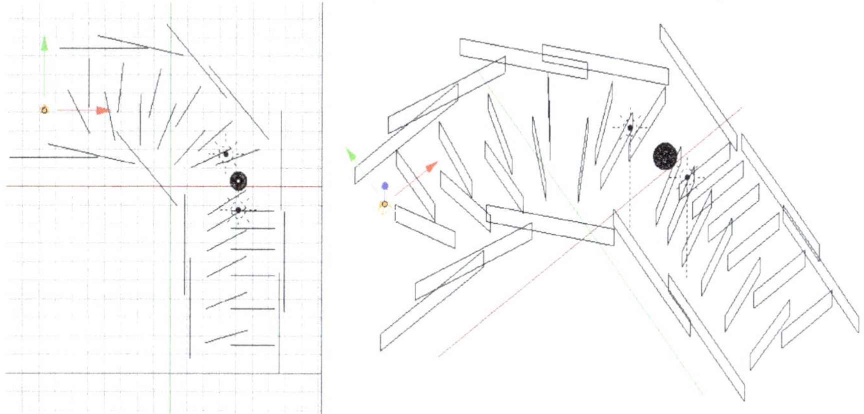

Illustration 81: Positioning of the different planes to create a fog

III.7. ANIMATE ELEMENTS OF DECOR

Purpose:

To add realism, we'll add some **animated elements like trees which move** like the wind. This recipe can be used for any decor animation.

Recipe:

1. Import an object «tree»

2. Separate the trunk («Edit Mode», «Border Selection», «P» → «Separate by selection») like on Illustration 82, put it in the layer 4

3. Select the rest of the tree (branches), go to «Edit Mode», unselect everything, faces mode, and select random

4. «P» → «Separate by selection», put it in the layer 2. So, the tree is cut into 3 layers.

5. Take the first part of the branches and an armature like the one on the Illustration 83

6. Select the tree, then the armature and parent them (Ctrl+P → «Armature Deform»)

7. «Weight Paint» mode, paint the elements ensuring the more distant leaves are painted too.

8. Repeat the operation for the other branches (with a second *armature*)

9. Take the first bone. Go to image 1, Insert Key frame («I» → «rotation»)

10. Go to image 50, rotation of bone on X of 2°, then Insert Key frame

11. Repeat the operation at image 100 (2°), then on image 150 (-2°) and on 200 (-2°).

12. Repeat the operation with the bone #2, on the axis Y

13. Limit the animation at 199. «Alt+A» to test. Change a few parameters to adapt the animation.

14. Select the first armature, go to «Logic Editor»

15. Add an «Always» sensor

16. Add an «Action» actuator / «Loop Stop» / Select «ArmatureAction» corresponding to the animation realized / «Start»: 1 / «End»: 199. Link the sensor with the actuator.

17. Repeat the operation for the second armature

18. Test the animation on the Game Engine.

Illustration 82: Trunk separation

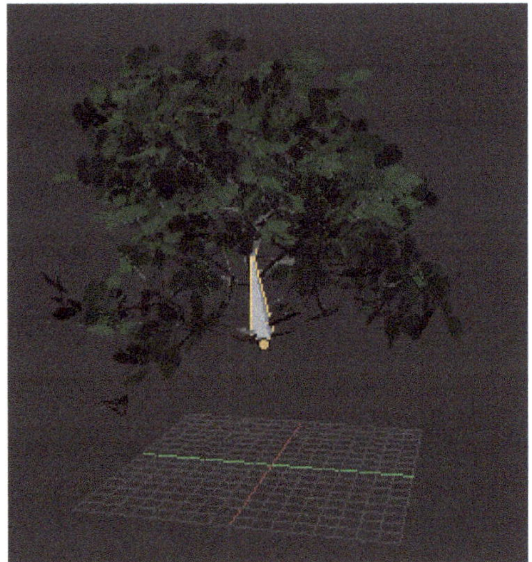

Illustration 83: Addition of an armature

Improvements:

For the shadows projection, use a floor which can receive shadows with transparency. For that purpose, select the «floor» object, then «Properties» window, «Materials» Tab, «Shadow» panel: check «receive» and «receive transparent».

The leaves material must be correctly configured, with «Influence Alpha» checked. → «Properties» Window → «Materials» Tab, «Game Settings» panel: «Alpha Blend»: Select «Alpha Clip».

III.8. REALISTIC TREES

<u>Purpose</u>:

When creating a scenery like an outdoor scene, we can insert numerous modelized objects or imported (internet). Blender has the Addon «Add curve: Sapling». This Addon allows to make some realistic trees with a large parameters choice. Thanks to Jason Weber and Joseph Penn for this contribution.

<u>Recipe</u>:

1. «info» window → «File» → «User Preferences» (or «`Ctrl`+`Alt`+`U`»): into «Addons» looking for «Sapling», check to make it usable, then save

2. «`Shift`+`A`» → «Add curve» → «Add Tree»

3. «3D View» window, display the menu «Object Tools» («T»), a new panel is available: «Sapling: Add Tree»

4. In «Setting» → «Geometry»:

   - «Bevel»: thicken the curse to draw a trunk.
   - «Ratio» to modify the trunk size.
   - Improve the resolution increasing «Be» and «Cu».

Illustration 84: Tree made with Arbaro

   - «Shape» offers some models for branches deployment and allows to modify the general form of the tree.
   - «Random Seed»: modify the pseudo-random generator and make some different trees with introduced parameters.
   - 4 «Scale» options, «Scale V» and 2 «radius» can be modified to change tree size.
   - Save the tree general configuration with the button «export preset», stating the name in the text field «preset».
   - The selection box «load preset» allows to load it. By default, the addon is given with some models to test.

5. «Setting» → «Branch Splitting»: this menu allows to modify the tree ramification.

   - Increase +1 «level» to see an additional ramification.
   - «Base Split» allows to split the principal trunk to create one or more additional ramification(s).
   - «Base size» allows to increase or decrease the trunk size which is located bellow the branches. Numerous parameters allow to personalize the way the branches separate and extend
   - «Branch Radius Ratio» allows to modify the branches size ratio (the bigger it's, the finer the branches are)

- «Setting» → «Branch Growth»:

   - «vertical attraction» to define the way of the branches grow. For a weeping willow, we'll use a negative value to a growth downward.
   - Numerous parameters allow to improve the modeling.

- «Setting» → «Pruning»: allow to generate the pruning of the trees with a visual tool and a set of parameters.

6. «Setting» → «Leaves»:

   - «show leaves» to display the leaves.
   - «Leaves» is the number of leaves by branch (25 by default). You can decrease this number to 10 to help the grapic card in the GLSL display.
   - «Leave Shape»: «rectangular» decrease the number of vertex.
   - The selection box «Leaf distribution» allows to choose different types of leaves distribution along the branches
   - «Leaf Scale» allows to scale the leaves size. We prefer scale the leaves and reduce the number of leaves to have a simpler object to display (type Lowpoly).

7. «Setting» → «Armature»: allows to animate the tree and to simulate the wind (**recipe III-7**), automatically.

- Check «Armature» and «Armature Animation», then launch the animation (`Alt`+`A`) to test.
   - «Frame rate» allows to change the animation speed. We can wish the tree moves only every 5 frames.

8. The object produced is made by one object «tree» corresponding to the trunk and the branches, and one object «leaves» corresponding to the leaves. Then, it's possible to apply materials and textures needed. To modify it when it's generated, transform it into mesh with `Alt`+`C` → «Mesh from Curve».

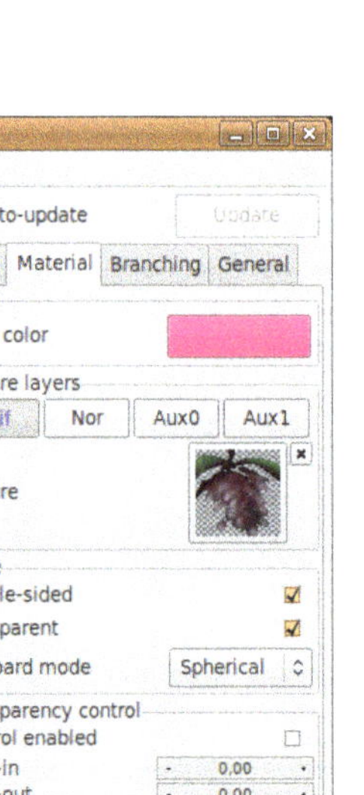

Alternative:
«**Arbaro**» (http://arbaro.sourceforge.net/ - Windows, Linux and Mac OS X) and«**ngplant**» (http://ngplant.sourceforge.net/ - Windows and Mac OS X) are 2 interesting projects to model trees and plants. With Windows: **tree[d]** (www.frecle.net/) in the projects section. Thank to this tool, it's possible to make some realistic trees that we can export to the Wavefront OBJ format.

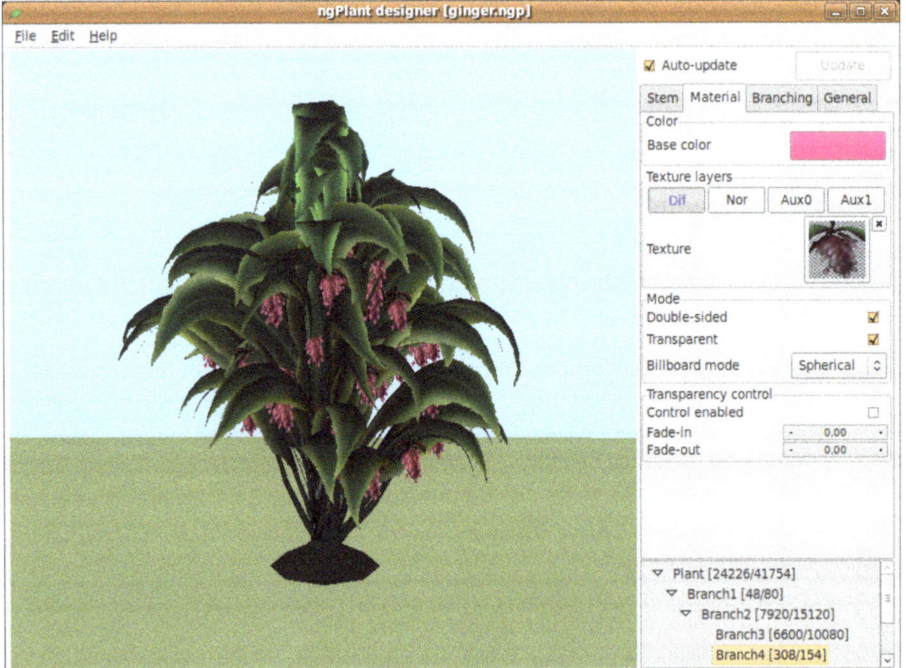

Illustration 85: ngPlant Designer

III.9. FLEXIBLE OBJECTS AND THE PHYSICAL ENGINE

Purpose:

The physical engine «Bullet» from BGE allows to use soft bodies by opposition to rigid bodies that we can't deform. To animate a soft body, **the object must have a sufficient mesh, if it's necessary, subdivide it to improve the physical simulation.**

In this recipe, we'll **animate directly an object with BGE**: curtains that waft, but without using the wind, not available on BGE! This recipe allows too to animate a rope, hair, clothes, etc.

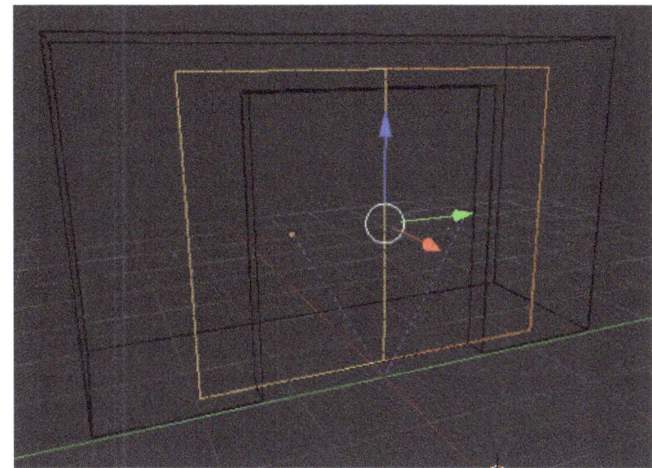

Illustration 86: Modeling of 2 curtains and 1 support

Recipe:

1. Model the scene: curtains (2 plans) and a background. Careful to realize some «double side» planes. Illustration 86

2. Subdivide to have at least 25 faces on one curtain line (in «Edit Mode», «W» → «Subdivide»)

3. «Properties» Window → «Physic» panel (Game Engine) → «Physics Type»: «Soft Body» / «Mass»: 0.1 / «Position iterations»: 6 / «Linear Stiffness»: 0.150 / «Friction»: 0.200 / «Margin»: 0.01 and uncheck «shape match»

4. For the first curtain, define the following constraints: we need 5 constraints because we have 5 support points. Go to the «Properties» window, «Object Constraints» panel → «Add object constraint» with «Rigid Body Joint» type. Check «Display pivot» and Pivot (X:.,0; Y:-1.0; Z:1.5) for the first, vary Y for the next constraints with the following values: -1,-0.5,0,0.5,1

5. Do the same with the second curtain

6. For the first curtain, go to the «Logic Editor»

7. Add a «Random» sensor / Check «Activate On True Level Triggering» / «Seed»: 28 (random number for the generator)

8. Add a «Motion» actuator, «Motion Type»: «Simple motion», «Force» «X»: 0.50 / «Torque» «Z»: 8.0

9. Link the sensor with the actuator

10. Repeat these operations with the second curtain

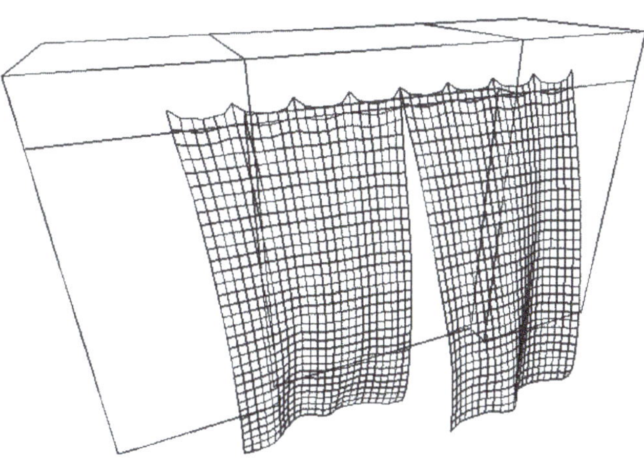

Illustration 87: Curtains moving in BGE (wind effect)

III.10. USE BLENDER PHYSICAL SIMULATIONS WITH BGE

Blender (not the Game Engine) has numerous interesting functions for physical simulation: simulation for fluid dynamics, particles system (for hair, snow, grass, explosion, fire), forces like the wind, etc.

In the preceding recipe, we saw how to reproduce the wind effect on the curtains in BGE. In another recipes, we'll see how to make an explosion, a fire or some smog.

Why don't use the Blender functions in the Game Engine? **It's not yet possible!** In the futures versions there will be more and more simulations, until BGE will be the realtime engine for Blender.

Example of a fluid flow: Blender allows to bake the animation, in other words, to precalculate the object «fluid» deformation at each frame. It's not possible to play the animation with series of interpolations. Today, the animation system needs that each frame has the same number of points, that's not the case in a fluid flow via Blender.

Illustration 88: Blender Fluid Simulation (cycles)

In **conclusion**, numerous recipes in this book allow to ignore BGE limitations in terms of physical simulation. The **recipe VII.17** explain how to transform a simulation in animation with «Billboard» type with the example of an explosion. For the rest, you need to be patient.

III.11. BAKE A SIMULATION OR AN ACTION

Purpose:

The physic engine from the Game Engine allows to make some interesting effects, but it needs a lot of resources. However, we can easily transform a simulation into an animation said «Keyframed». Even the player movements can be recorded. **Each position, rotation, scale is transformed into a key picture.**

We don't use the physical simulation of Blender. We saw in the precedent recipe that it's not possible presently. We use the physical engine of BGE to make a simulation and transform this simulation into an animation to reduce the machine-time costs. It's **important to understand the difference.**

Recipe:

1. Add a plane (**⬆ Shift**+**A** → «Mesh» → «Plane») in (0,0,0), resize (S) x10, and add 2 Suzanne («monkey»): the first in (0,0,3.5) and the second in (0,0,6.0)

2. In the «Properties» window, «Physics» panel, select «Rigid Body» for the 2 Suzanne. Check too «Collision Bounds» and select «Bounds»: «Convex Hull» (ask more calculation than a simple «box»)

3. Test (**P**) – the 2 Suzanne must fall and the second roll over the first.

4. In the «info» window, menu «Game», check «record animation» and «autostart»

5. Test again (**P**) and let the animation play until the Suzanne come to a standstill, then stop (**Esc**)

6. Rift horizontally the «3D View» and display the «Graph Editor» window. Each Suzanne has a complex animation curse based on numerous keys pictures.

7. Display the user preferences («**Ctrl**+**Alt**+**U**») and look for the addon «Add Curve: Simplify curves». Check it if it's not and save.

8. Select the first Suzanne. «Space» → «Simplify F-Curves». In «3D View», display the menu «Tools» («T»), «Simplify F-Curves» panel, change «error» into 0.9 (we admit a high error ratio in the animation, for a best result, we can reduce it, but now it's sufficient). The animation curse of the first Suzanne become simpler, with less than 5 key pictures!

9. Do the same for the second Suzanne without forgot to put the error at 0.9 and to valid it.

10. Limit the animation at 250 and verify the result with **Alt**+**A**.

11. For the first Suzanne, go to the «physics» panel and select «physic type»: «no collision». There will be no more heavy physical calculations.

12. «Logic Editor» window, add a «Keyboard» sensor and choose a key to launch the action («All keys» for example)

13. Add an «Action» actuator, «Action type»: «Play», «Start»: 1 / «End»: 250. Select the action «SuzanneAction». Link the sensor and the actuator.

14. Select the second Suzanne and do the same operations with the action «Suzanne.001Action»

15. In the «info» window, menu «Game», uncheck «record animation» and «autostart»

16. **Go to «3D View», remove and test(P)**

Note: by default, only the movements of the dynamics objects are recorded. To save the statics objects movements: for each object, go to «Properties» window, «Physics» panel, and check «Record Animation»

III.12.　　LAKE & ANIMATED NORMAL MAP

Purpose:

There are several ways **to obtain an ocean effect**. One of the simplest is to use a «normal map» and to animate it playing with the object geometry. This recipe can be applied when we need an animated «Material» to create some effects.

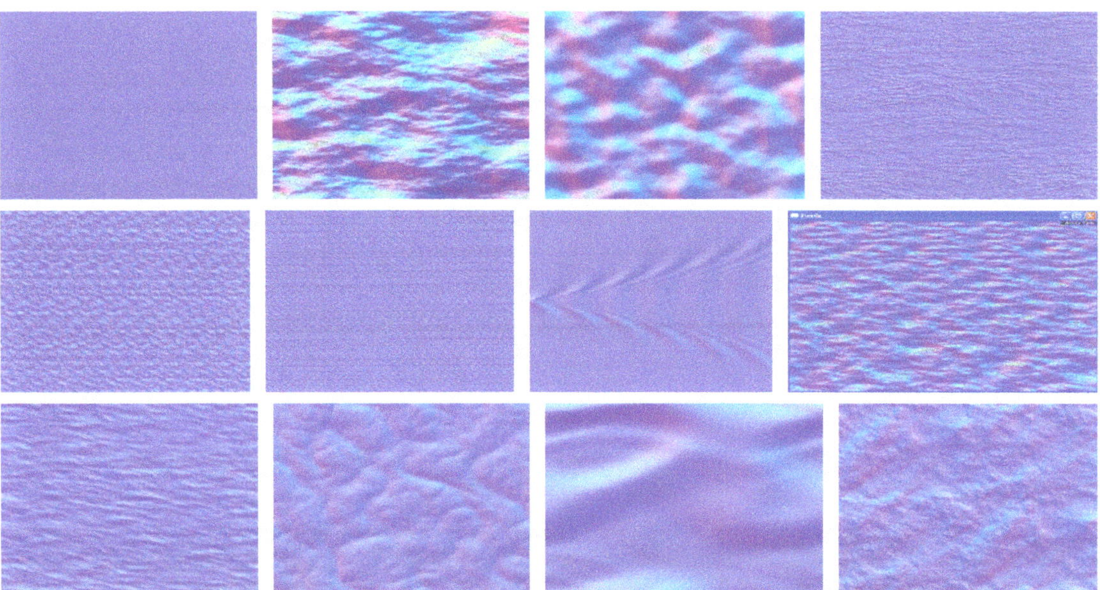

Illustration 89: Example of textures with Normal map type to create a body of water

Recipe:

1. Add a plane corresponding to the body of water (Shift + A → «Mesh» → «Plane»).
2. Go to «Edit Mode», then «U» → «Smart UV Project»

3. Add a lamp with «Hemi» type to simulate the sun (Shift + A → «Lamp» → «Hemi»).
4. Add a «Material» to the plane. Color diffuse at (1,1,1) and specular color at (0,0,0). Check «Transparency» and «Alpha»: 0.7
5. On Google images, look for «normal map water» - download a picture with a blue-violet background representing waves.
6. Open a «UV/Image editor» window and load the picture downloaded
7. Key «N», «Game properties» → Check «animated» / Start: 0 / End: 99 / X: 10 / Y: 10 (Modify next Speed to obtain the needed effect)
8. Add this picture as plane material texture. «Image sampling»: «Normal map». «Coordinates»: «UV» and select the UV Map. «Size»: (10,10,1). Uncheck «diffuse» and set «Geometry normal» at 5.0.
9. On Google images, look for «water texture» and download a picture representing waves, viewed from above (Illustration 89)
10. Add a second texture to the material and the picture downloaded. «Mapping coordinates» → «Reflection».
11. We have now an animated texture simulating the ocean (Illustration 90).

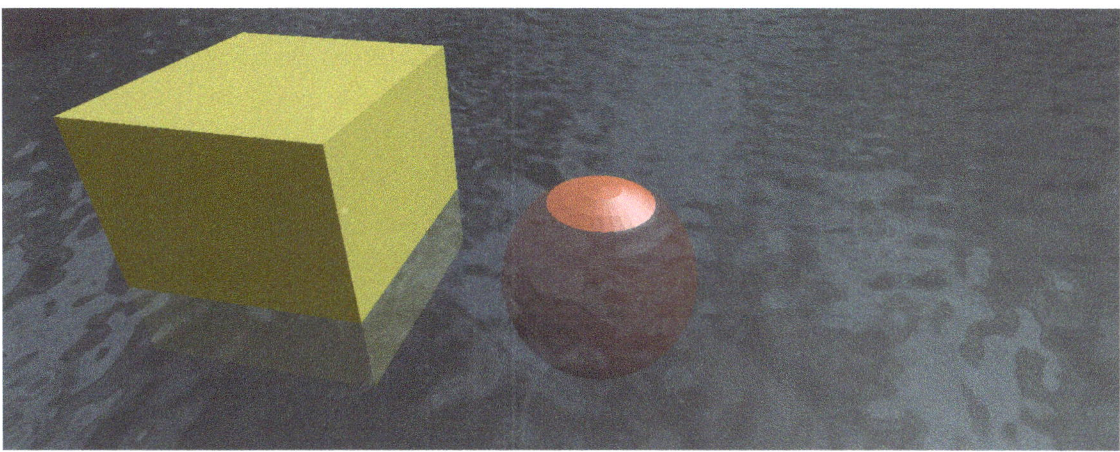

Illustration 90: effect on water requiring very little resources

Improvements:

Vary the sea level:

1. Add a new python script, name it «water.py» and copy the following lines
2. Select the body of water and go to «Logic Editor»
3. Add an «Always» sensor, check «Activate True Level Triggering», then «freq»: 10
4. Add a «Python» controller and select the precedent script.
5. Link the sensor with the controller

Script water.py:

```python
import bge, random
controller = bge.logic.getCurrentController()
obj = controller.owner
z = random.random() - 0.5
if ((z<0) and (obj.worldPosition.z>-0.3)) or
        ((z>0) and (obj.worldPosition.z<0)):
    obj.worldPosition.z += z / 10
```

Here, the plane height varies (z location) between -0.3 and 0.

It's possible to vary the sensor frequency for a more or less frequent refresh.

III.13.   OCEAN WITH VERTEX DISPLACEMENT

The precedent recipe doesn't allow relief waves effects. Viewed from above, body water approach is sufficient, but to create some waves effects, it's better to use «Vertex Displacement», that's to modify the vertex according to the wave height.

On the Illustration 91, you can see a subdivided plane modified by the «Vertex Displacement».

Recipe:

1. Repeat steps from recipe I.12
2. Select the plane, in the «Properties» window, «Modifier» panel, apply a subdivide to create a fine mesh, apply a triangulate to obtain a more elastic mesh and a decimate to «break up» the uniformity.
3. If the body of water is hidden in some places (presence of grass for example), remove all faces which never be visible. If some places will be highly visible by the player, subdivide more. The finest the mesh is, the realistic the effect is, and the more it'll take machine time.
4. In the «Text» window, create a new python script «water.py» and past the following script
5. Download the script «simplexnoise.py» written by **Eliot Eshelman** and available at the following address: http://tinyurl.com/l83pf84. This script allows us to generate some noise in a procedural way. We could use a mathematical function based on a sinus too (less realist, but faster).
6. In the «Text» window, open the new downloaded file.
7. Make sure that the plane is selected and go to «Logic Editor»
8. Add an «Always» sensor selecting «Activate on True Level Triggering» and put the frequency at 25 (2 refreshing per second at 50 FpS).
9. Add a «Python» controller, type: «module» and write: «water.update»
10. Link the sensor with the actuator

What's going on?

The waves lift more or less according to the plane size. The parameters to change are «x_scale», «y_scale» and «z_scale». The 2 firsts correspond to the noise plane. The faster we move on the map, the more brutal the variations are. It's like waves amplitude, «. z_scale» allows to modify the height of the waves.

The advantage of this technique is that we can put an object «Dynamic» or «Rigid Body» above the waves and see the waves lift the object.

Improvements:

Use «vertex shaders» to do «Vertex Displacement». It could be possible to modify the precedent script to work on the GPU in order to alleviate the CPU. A shader will be faster than a python script. A «geometry shader» allows to have not to subdivide the plane as done before but to realize it in the fly via the GPU.

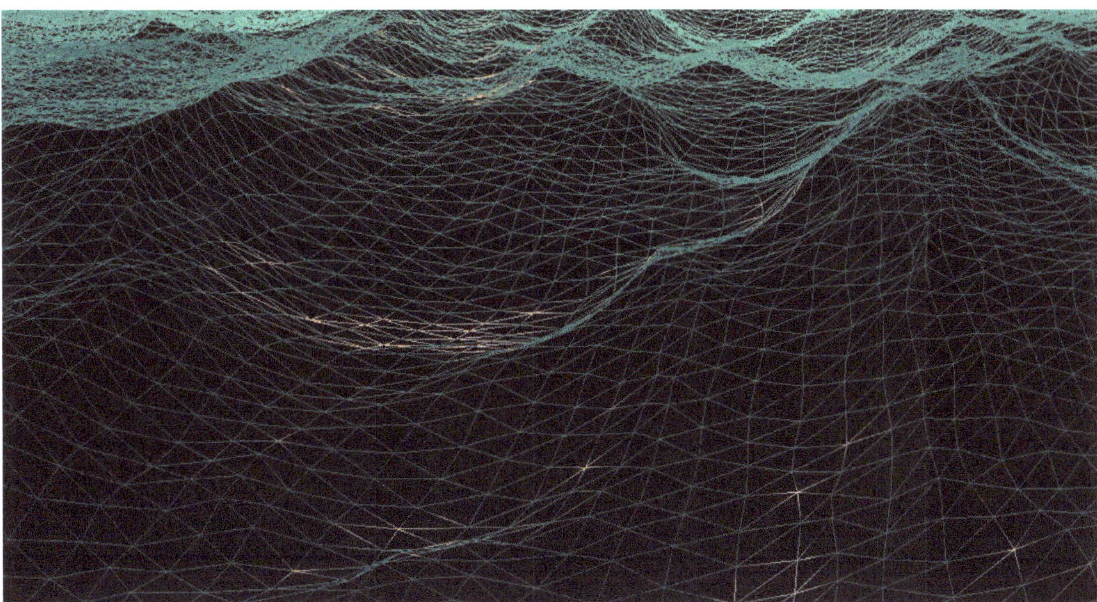

Illustration 91: Modification of a plane thanks to a «vertex displacement»

Script water.py:

```python
import math
from time import time
from simplexnoise import raw_noise_2d, raw_noise_3d

def getZ(x,y,t,x_scale=15,y_scale=10,z_scale=0.03):
    z = (raw_noise_2d( (x+t*3) * x_scale, y * y_scale) + 1) / 2
    z = (z**3) * 5
    x += t*2
    y += t*2
    z += raw_noise_2d( x * x_scale * 5, y * y_scale * 5)
    return z *z_scale

def update(py):
    t = time()
    ob = py.owner
    mesh = ob.meshes[0]

    for index in range(mesh.getVertexArrayLength(0)):
        vertex = mesh.getVertex(0, index)
        x = vertex.x
        y = vertex.y
        z = getZ(x,y,t)
        vertex.z = z

    for child in ob.children:
        x = child.worldPosition[0]
        y = child.worldPosition[1]
        z = getZ(x,y,t)
        child.worldPosition = (x, y, z)
```

III.14.   BILLBOARDS

Purpose:

To create large landscapes, the principal problem is the number of faces to display.

For the objects with a little size like grass, flowers or fruits in a tree, we use billboards, which are sprites (plane with texture like on Illustration 92) always facing the camera. Thus, the character can revolve around, he always sees the same object face. Billboards are used in the LOD management too (Level of Detail).

Illustration 92: Texture «grass» to map on a plane

Recipe:

1. Add a plane (⬆ Shift + A → «Mesh» → «Plane»)
2. Add a «Material» («Properties» Window, «Materials» Tab). In the «Game Settings» panel, «Face Orientation»: change into «Billboard»
3. Add a texture («Textures» panel) with «Image or Movie» type) and select a picture (ex: the moon).
4. Test (P) – If it's not the good direction, rotate the plane in «Edit Mode»

It's possible too to use in the «Logic Editor» the function «Edit Object» → «Track To». This method is slower.

Another approach:

To create grass, we can use some tangled planes like in the Illustration 93, then, it's not necessary to be in front of the camera. The model can be randomly instantiated on a landscape (recipe III.15) changing the angle Z.

Optimizations:

Simple forms like grass can be made from geometries, without using textures with an «alpha» canal for transparency. The process will be faster.

Illustration 93: Object «grass» made from 48 faces

III.15. RANDOMLY PLACE OBJECTS

Purpose:

To prevent positioning manually every plants, trees, stones, etc. It may be useful **to randomly generate them on the landscape**, using some rules. So, we can simulate a biotope managing height or proximity of objects to the ocean.

In this recipe, we see how to instantiate objects via a script to occupy a landscape according to some rules.

Recipe:

We determine a position randomly: on a plane with size (l,h), centered in (0,0,0), we choose randomly x between 0 and l, and between 0 and h. Then, we do a raycast downward. If the material correspond to the search, if the height correspond, etc, then, we determine the impact point and we generate an object duplicating it from another object coming from another layer. Do the same operation several times.

1. In «Text» window, create a new python script and paste the following script
2. Select the landscape to occupy (a plane or else)
3. At the end of the script, add the following command:
   scatterObject(*scenename, surfacename, objectToClone, number, name, rotation, zmin, zmax*) with:
   - **scenename:** the name of the scene in which we want to realize the operation (the most often «Scene»)
   - **surfacename:** name of the object to cover
   - **objectToClone:** name of the object to duplicate which must be in an invisible layer. It's important that any modification (location, rotation, scale) was applied before on the object which will be cloned. If we want that the object is at 1 unite above the soil, we need to place it at (0,0,1.0).
   - **number:** the number of clones to produce. Warming: if the surface is not enough large, the script could played in a loop.
   - **name:** the name of the clones (the number will be added automatically)
   - **rotation:** True = rotation on the axis Z randomly
   - **zmin:** minimal height for the object implantation
   - **zmax:** height max
4. Launch the script («Run Script»)

Example:

scatterObject("Scene","Ground","Grass",True,3000, "GrassScatter", True, -10.0, 3.0) generate 3000 objects clones of «Grass» at the surface of the object «Ground», to occupy the height of -10 to 3, doing randomly rotations on the axis Z.

The Illustration 94 give an example of the use of this function with grass.

Illustration 94: Automatic generation of grass from the model above

Script python Scatter.py:

```python
def scatterObject(scenename, surfaceName, objectToClone, number,
        name = "Clone", rotation=True, zmin=-1000.0, zmax=1000.0):

    scene = bpy.data.scenes[scenename]
    surface = bpy.data.objects[surfaceName]

    x1 = surface.location.x - surface.dimensions.x / 2
    x2 = surface.dimensions.x + x1
    y1 = surface.location.x - surface.dimensions.y / 2
    y2 = surface.dimensions.y + y1

    while (number>0):
        x = random.random() * (x2 - x1) + x1
        y = random.random() * (y2 - y1) + y1
        (result, object, matrix, location, normal) =
                        scene.ray_cast((x,y,1000),(x,y,-1000))
        if result:
            if object == surface:
                if (location.z > zmin) and (location.z < zmax):
                    clone = duplicateInstance(scene, surface, name,
                                        objectToClone, x, y, location.z)
                    number -= 1
                    if rotation:
                        clone.rotation_euler.z = random.random() * 3.14159
```

Some groups are created to allow an easier processing of the objects (ex: remove every objects from this group).

The **scatterObject**() function use another function function, **duplicateInstance**() not to duplicate object geometry, but to create a new group instance (as «⇧ Shift + A » → «Group Instance»). Indeed, we'll generate a large number of objects, and group instances allow to prevent the file becoming too big. In theory, it should be more faster, but the engine doesn't manage yet the «Hardware Geometry Instancing», performances gains are limited: smaller file and less occupied memory. Every object had the same geometry so, when you modify one geometry, you modify all object's geometry.

```python
def duplicateInstance(scene, surface, name, group, x, y, z):
    #Must be in a group
    # Create new object associated with the mesh
    ob_new = bpy.data.objects.new(name, None)

    ob_new.location = (x,y,z)

    # Link new object to the given scene and select it
    scene.objects.link(ob_new)

    ob_new.dupli_type = 'GROUP'
    ob_new.dupli_group = bpy.data.groups[group]
    ob_new.parent = surface
    return ob_new
```

To really duplicate the object geometry, you need to do some modifications. The function **duplicateObject**():

```python
def duplicateObject(scene, name, copyobj, x, y, z):
    # Create new mesh
    mesh = bpy.data.meshes.new(name)
    # Create new object associated with the mesh
    ob_new = bpy.data.objects.new(name, mesh)

    # Copy data block from the old object into the new object
    ob_new.data = copyobj.data.copy()
    ob_new.scale = copyobj.scale
    ob_new.location = (x,y,z)

    # Link new object to the given scene and select it
    scene.objects.link(ob_new)
    return ob_new
```

Improvements:

Until integration in Blender, some patches allow, by recompiling Blender, to call some «geometry shaders». With this, it's possible to make a «Hardware Geometry Instancing». There's a big performance gain when the number of objects is important.

III.16.   A LEVEL BASED ON A 3D TILESET

Purpose:

Model a complete game's level can take time when it's necessary to do it from A to Z. In 2D, a map is made by tiles (sprites). Place tiles next to each other to generate the world. Each tile is a squared picture: grass, road, sidewalk, trees, wall, etc. So, to create a level, create the basics tiles and assemble them in an array.

For 3D, we can use the same approach, **but tiles are 3D models** (Illustration 95). There are not only the objects to produce the level (barrel, lamp, box, etc.), but a dungeon can be cut into a set of elementary tiles to create complexes levels with a few elements and arrangements.

Another advantage is to easily create a level editor based on this «tileset». With a drag and drop, we can select a tile and put it on the «floor plan».

Recipe:

1. List all the necessary elements for the level creation (example after). It's possible to turn objects in every directions or use the mirror tool. To create a wall corners, one is sufficient to create all possibles combinations!

2. Duplicate some objects modifying their form and their material for more combinations.

3. Modify light atmosphere and colors to create different zones.

4. Don't place little objects in a fixed way, tilt them and use the physic to position them

5. Lacking inspiration? Use the **recipe III.15** to randomly position the flowers, stones...in the level. Then modify to not trouble the «path follow».

Example:

For a dungeon, we need: stairs (level change), an angle, a wall, a wall corner, doors, stones, a barrel, a table, potteries, a carpet, columns, a torch, a lever, a gate, a rope ladder, a tomb. From 20 elements, it's possible to do very interesting levels.

Video: **http://bit.ly/21DVh6M**

For a spacecraft inside: automatics gates (with logic BGE), floor tiles, metal tiles for walls, wires, wire with electricity (animated with electrics shocks), metal boxes, tubes for passages with bends, a teleporter, a cryogenic box, stairs, a ladder, a ventilator (animated), button, futuristic table and chairs, a barrier.

Video: http://bit.ly/1lhneko

III.17.   LARGE LANDSCAPES MANAGEMENT

Purpose:

To model vast scenes, it's possible to modify the camera **clipping** by adjusting the distance limit and the fog effects (**recipe III.5**) to decrease calculations on the graphic card. Do every optimizations like shadow clipping, decrease size of textures, etc. However, if the landscape contains a large number of objects (trees, plants, stones, etc.), to see it at a big distance, the clipping and the fog effect are not sufficient.

Before to obtain a Level Of Detail (LoD), the first thing to do is to position all the occlusion systems. In «Game Engine» mode, in the «Properties» window, «Physics» Tab, we can setup an object like «Occlude». It means that anything behind this object is not displayed. for example, if it's placed on a wall behind a window, we won't see it through the window. It's removed from the **rasterization** phase.

<u>Recipe #1</u>:

The simplest technique to obtain a LOD without code python, is to have:
- **2 scenes**: one with a high level of details, the other without.
- **2 cameras** (1 by scene): adjust the **start** and the **end** of the **clipping**.

This technique is faster, more effective... and **doesn't ask to take up too much host processing power.**

1. Import a landscape and place a camera to have a global view of the landscape. If the landscape extends over a width of 100 units.
2. Select the camera and go to the «Properties» window, «Camera» Tab, «Lens» panel and modify: «Start: 0.1» / «End: 50». In the «Display» panel, check «Limits» to see the covered zone.
3. «info» window, rename the scene in «Scene.High» and click on «+» to copy the scene «Full copy» (objects will be duplicate). Rename the copy in «Scene.Low».
4. Apply a modifier with «Decimate» type or change the models to obtain a simplified version of the scene. Divide at least by 10 the details.
5. Select the camera and go to the «Properties» window, «Camera» Tab, «Lens» panel and modify: «Start: 50» / «End: 100».
6. Go to mode camera view (0) in the 2 scenes.
7. Come back to the scene «Scene.High» and select the camera. Go to «Logic Editor»
8. Add an «Always» sensor
9. Add a «Scene» actuator, «Mode»: «Add Background Scene» and select the scene «Scene.Low»
10. Link the sensor with the actuator
11. «Text» window, add a new script «FollowCam.py» and copy the following lines.
12. Come back in the scene «Scene.Low» and select the camera. Go to «Logic Editor»
13. Add an «Always» sensor, check «Activate True Level Triggering»
14. Add a «Python» controller and select the script «FollowCam.py»
15. Link the sensor with the controller

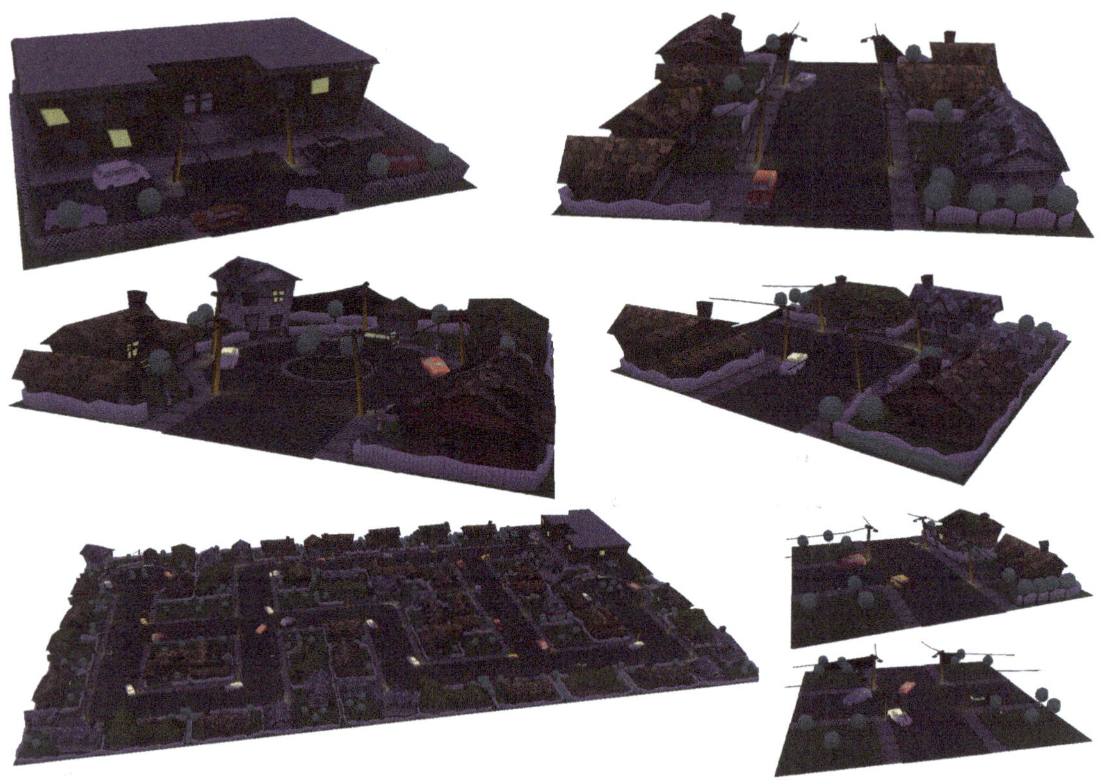

Illustration 95: 3D Tileset of a neighborhood and sewage systems made by James Marshall
http://jamesmarshall3d.com/

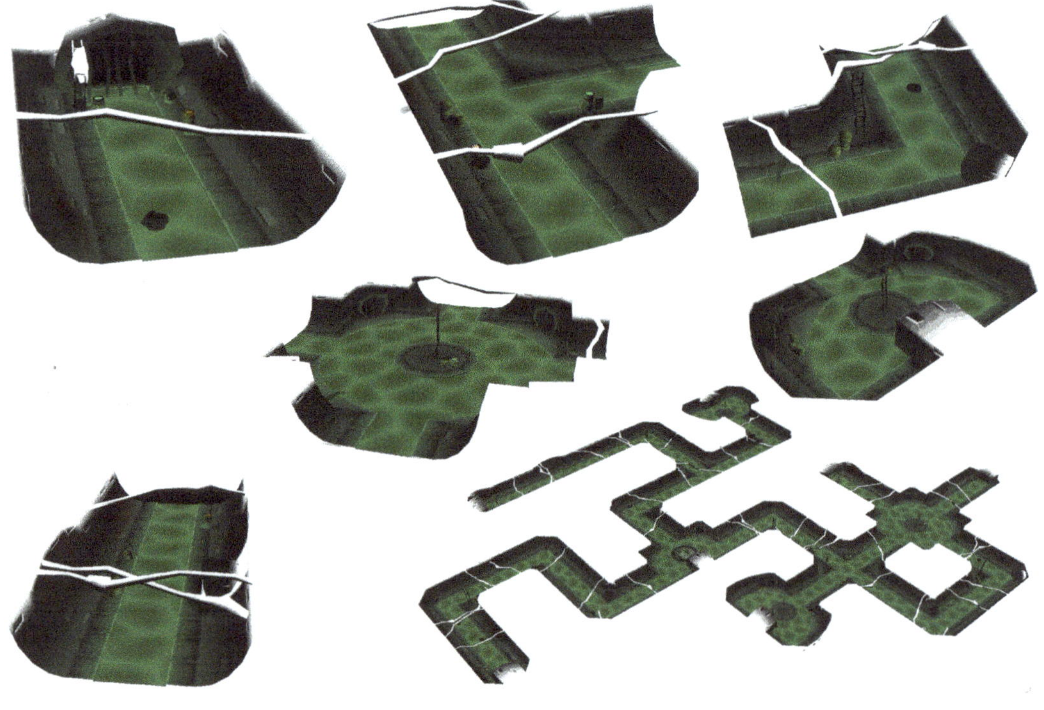

Script FollowCam.py:

```python
import bge

gl = bge.logic
scene = gl.getCurrentScene()
scene2 = gl.getSceneList()[1]
cont = gl.getCurrentController()
own = cont.owner
obs = scene2.objects

### you can replace the Camera, with the name of your camera.
own.worldPosition = obs['Camera'].worldPosition
own.worldOrientation = obs['Camera'].worldOrientation
```

Adapt the script according to the cameras name or the scenes order.

The purpose is to copy position or rotation modifications of principal view camera (Scene.High) to the second view camera (Scene.Low). A very slight offset could occur..

Disadvantages of this technique:

- do it only at the end, otherwise, you must report all the modifications from a scene to the other
- if the objects use the physique, you must manage this aspect (disable some comportment, etc.) to avoid doubling the physic management.

Recipe #2: Each game object manages its LOD

Another technique: Each game object manages its LOD. This technique is described in details in the **recipe VII.11**. It's a good solution **when we have few objects.** If there are numerous objects, the processor tales too much time to manage the phase «game logic».

Recipe #3: Use the new LOD system(version 2.70)

The LoD in the 2.70 use several meshes versions for one model – it's not entirely automatic because the Game Engine stores several object versions before its launching. The modifier «decimate» keeps the mesh UV mapping, and allows to easily generate several meshes for 1 model. The semi-automatic version use this modifier to generate simplified models, but it's possible to do it manually. We'll see the 2 methods.

Manual method:

1. Select a model on which we want to apply a LoD.
2. Copy it in a layer (**⇧ Shift**+**D**, then **M**) and apply a «modifier decimate» (Try at the most 0.5 – depending on the number of final object versions – here, we'll use 3 versions). Add «.med» (for medium) as extension of the name of the object.
3. Copy the same object in another layer and apply a decimate on this last (try at the most 0.1). Add «.low» as extension of the name of the object.
4. Add «.high» as extension of the name of the original object, then go to «Properties» window, «Object»Tab, «Level of Detail» panel, in «object to use», select the model with the extension «.med.» Specify 25 units in «distance».
5. Add a new LoD by clicking on «Add», select the model with the extension «.low». Specify 100 units in «distance».

What happens?

When the camera sees the object at a distance between 0 and 25, the «.high» model is used. Between 25 and 100, it's the model «.med». Above 100 it's the model «.low».

However, **we can't use this LoD on a ground made by only one object**. If the recipe #1 can be used in this case, this LoD will not work. With many thousands of trees, this LoD allows to manage them with a LoD on the trees.

This current LoD doesn't have python API.

→ Don't use any «Modifier» on the objects with LoD. Apply all the modifications before launching to avoid a future slowness.

The system is currently working with the mesh substitution, but there's not any python script (directly in C), it's faster and interesting in performances terms. **A real LoD integrated to BGE !**

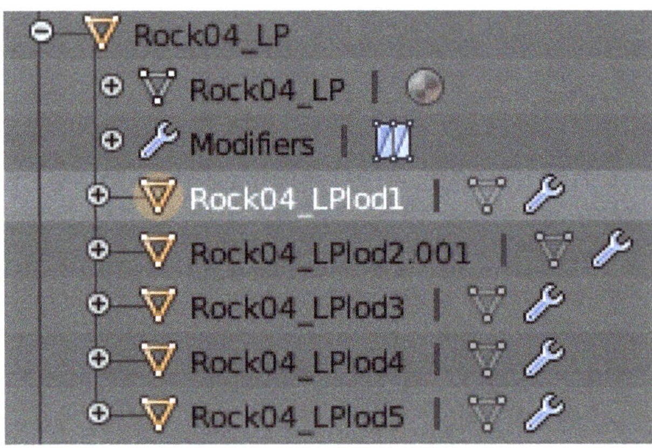

Illustration 96: Display «Package into Group» and panel

Automatic method

Illustration 97: LoD with automatic generation on 5 levels:
from the most detailed (at left) to the simplest (4% from the size max)

1. Select a model on which we want to apply a LoD.
2. «Properties» window, «Object» Tab, «Level of Detail» panel, click on the vertical arrow near «Add», select «Generate». 2 new meshes are created with «modifier»: «Triangulate» and «Decimate».
3. In «3D View» → Menu Tools (T) → modify the number of meshes (3 by default) and package the set of meshes in a group («Package into Group») to simplify the management (Illustration 96). Modify the distance parameters as you need
4. Move the generated objects in an invisible layer. Blender replaces automatically, even in edition mode in «3D View».

Improvements

Use a «**vertex and fragment shader**» like the one made by **Benjamin Vedrenne**:
http://tinyurl.com/lsb36c3.

It needs a lot settings and there are limitations. It uses «displacement mapping» in realtime, shadow maps and fog are supported. The realtime shadows (without baking) and the collisions are supported. It's an interesting work for those who want basis to write their own LoD shader.

However, the better should be to use a «Geometry Shader» (sheet #8 «Shaders») to make a model tessellation and apply a displacement mapping (Illustration 98). You must wait that the official version of Blender support the «Geometry Shaders».

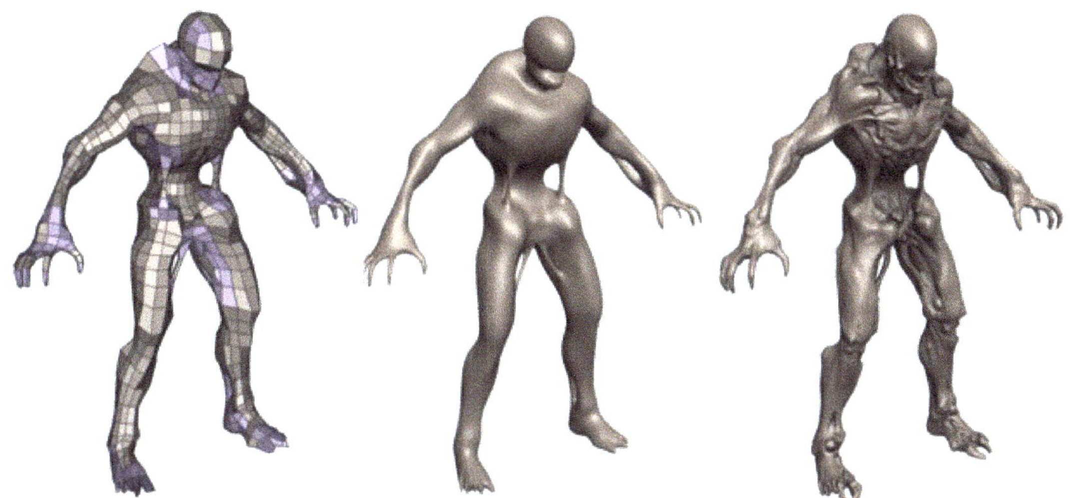

Illustration 98: When the Tessellation is applied on a model (at left), we obtain a smooth model. Application of displacement mapping (at right) © Kenneth Scott, id Software 2008

Dynamic Loading: When we walk in the world, the landscape changes. The functions bge.logic **LibLoad**() and **LibFree**() are used in this case. Create a new task (Fork) to load and unload the different elements.

In every cases, to work on vast landscapes, it's necessary to «cut» these into a number of blocks (chunks). These blocks will be used by the LoD and dynamically be loaded running according to the character moving. A game like «Plane simulator» use this technique.

III.18.   OPEN WORLDS & PROCEDURAL GENERATION

Purpose:

According to the principals game editors since 2013's E3, the next generation of games will be based on the concept of «Open Worlds» where the script is not linear in opposite to the games which have 100% scripted events. It's some kind of throwback: «Dagger Fall» was more than 1 million acres to visit, near than 750.000 NPCs, 15.000 town to explore... But the use of the 3D brings up to date this system with less Level Design but more freedom to players (**sheet #3**). Games like **GTA**, **Skyrim** or **Minecraft** use fully this type of concept.

In practice, how to create an infinite world (or almost) in Blender? The precedent recipe is not sufficient. With this method, an infinite world needs an infinite memory: the number of objects that Blender can support simultaneously is in theory very important, but in practice, it becomes unusable. We saw the basis of pseudo random distribution in the FPS game where the grass, the trees and another objects are generated in a near random way (with some rules).
What about a very vast world like for a flight simulator where one hour can correspond to million of acres traveled?

In this recipe, we learn to:
- Build dynamically a world around the player as he walks and remove the unnecessary parts of the world at the same time. It goes beyond the LoD concept where the display is the only one which is concerned – here, the object is destroyed and regenerated when it's needed.
- Build a vast landscape from a 3D TileSet (extension of the **recipe III.16**) distributed on several files blend.
- Dynamically load (background thread), all models are not in memory when game starts.

Technique:

Step #1: represent a tile model

We need to represent a model of 3D tile: it's an element with a fixed size which is a base for the landscape construction. If, for example, a landscape with 10x10 tiles is defined, each tile measure 100x100, then the landscape size obtained is 1000x1000. The landscape is made with a 2D mesh, but it's possible to adapt it for use a 3D mesh with some modifications.

These tiles can:
- Come from a model of specific tile
- Come from a specific library file (or in an invisible layer in the current file).

So, with a limited number of tiles, we can create various landscapes.

Definite an object class in python to generate a tile model:

```python
class models(object):
    def __init__(self,model):
        self.name = model[0]
        self.library = model[1]
        self.statut = ""
        self.loaded = -1 #-1 Not Loaded, 0 is loading, 1 is loaded

    def isLoaded (self):
        scene = bge.logic.getCurrentScene()
        if self.name in scene.objectsInactive:
            return True
        else:
            return False
    def load(self):
        if (self.loaded == -1) and not self.isLoaded():
            pathfile = bge.logic.expandPath('//')+self.library
            if pathfile not in bge.logic.LibList():
                self.loaded = 0
                try:
```

```python
        self.statut = bge.logic.LibLoad(pathfile,
                               'Scene',async=True)
        print ("External ",self.library," is Loaded")
    except:
        print ("Problem finding or opening ",pathfile)
        return
    self.loaded = 1
```

The model is initialized calling for example:

```python
model = models(('myobject','mylibrary.blend'))
```

To know it «model» is loaded in memory, that's to say the object represented by the model is in an invisible layer (in reality, we check if it's **inactive** because the layer concept does no more exists in running):

```python
If model.isLoaded():
```

If it's not loaded, call the function member load(). It use the function **LibLoad** in **asynchronous** mode to load the object from a referenced file. It's the only way to load in background from externals files. Create a thread in background to load doesn't deliver **acceleration** and is a source of problems. On rule to avoid problems: «never modify the game elements through a thread launched in parallel».

Step #2: represent a part of the world

We call «chunk», a part of the world based on a tile model. It has a position (x,y,0) in space, and a dimension (x,y).

The corresponding object (copy of the tile model) is or not displayed. To represent a «chunk»:

```python
class chunk(object):
    def __init__(self,model):
        self.model = models(model)
        self.position = [0.0,0.0]
        self.dimension = [0.0,0.0]
        self.alive = False
        self.obj = ""
    def draw(self,actadd):
        if not self.alive:
            self.model.load()
            if self.model.isLoaded():
                actadd.object = self.model.name
                actadd.instantAddObject()
                self.obj = actadd.objectLastCreated
                self.obj.worldPosition = (self.position[0],
                                self.position[1], 0.0)
                self.obj.worldOrientation = [0,0,0]
                self.alive = True
```

Draw() function is the most important: if the underlying object (obj) doesn't exist, it'll be generated thanks to an actuator with «Edit Object/Add Object» type. However, the copy is possible only if the model is loaded in the inactive objects list. The function call can't generate the object display, but only load the model in a first time. At the next function call, if the object was entirely loaded, it'll be added to the scene graph.

Step #3: a world of chunks

Here, a **landscape** is an array of chunks, and add it numerous functions:

- The first, **init**(), allows to generate a landscape with a randomly selection of chunks from the proposed tiles models. Of course, we could load the array with an external file and create a landscape editor.

- The second, **draw()**, ensures that all the chunks at a defined distance from the player are loaded and displayed.

- The third, **freeChunks**(), remove all the chunks situated at a superior distance given in parameters. The distance could be dynamically increased or decreased according to the available memory.

- At the last, the function **getNbrChunks**() can be used for statistical purposes to know the simultaneous number of chunks in memory.

```python
class landscape(object):
    def __init__(self, modelsName,x,y,lx,ly):
        self.x_land, self.y_land = x, y
        self.x_dim, self.y_dim = lx, ly
        self.modelsName = modelsName
        self.chunks = [""]*(self.x_land*self.y_land)

    def init(self):
        print ("Generating Landscape: ",self.x_land,"x",self.y_land)
        for y in range (0,self.y_land):
            for x in range (0,self.x_land):
                r = int(random()*len(self.modelsName))
                self.chunks[x+y*self.x_land] = chunk(self.modelsName[r])
                self.chunks[x+y*self.x_land].dimension = [self.x_dim,self.y_dim]
                self.chunks[x+y*self.x_land].position = [self.x_dim*x,self.x_dim*y]

    def draw(self,actadd,x,y,dist):
        nbcases = round(dist / 100)
        xmin = min (self.x_land,max(0,int(x) - nbcases))
        ymin = min (self.y_land, max(0,int(y) - nbcases))
        xmax = max(0,min(int(x) + nbcases, self.x_land))
        ymax = max(0,min(int(y) + nbcases, self.y_land))

        #print ("values: ",xmin,xmax,ymin,ymax)
        for xt in range (xmin,xmax):
            for yt in range (ymin,ymax):
                #print ("Draw landscape from x=",xt," and y=",yt)
                self.chunks[xt+yt*self.x_land].draw(actadd)

    def getNbrChunks(self):
        alive = 0
        for chunk in self.chunks:
            if chunk.alive:
                alive += 1
        return alive
    def freeChunks(self, distance):
        scene = bge.logic.getCurrentScene()
        cam = scene.objects["Camera"]
        for chunk in self.chunks:
            if chunk.alive:
                dist = chunk.obj.getDistanceTo(cam)
                if dist > distance:
                    #Remove chunk
                    chunk.obj.endObject()
                    chunk.alive = False
```

Recipe:

In a first time, create 5 tiles models:

1. Create a new file blend and go to the layer #2
2. Use the **recipe III.1** with the addon «ANT Landscape» to generate a landscape of 100x100. Example of setup:
   - Check «Mesh Update and «Smooth»
   - «Subdivision»: 64 and «Mes Size»: 100
   - «Random Seed»: 0, «Noise Size»: 8, «Depth»: 5, «Dimension»: 2, «Lacunarity»: 3

- «Height»: 25, «Plateau»: 20, «Falloff»: «Type 1» and«Strata»: None

3. Name «land.001» and go to the layer #1 (important, the land.001 must be inactive at the time of import, otherwise, it's copied in the current layer and it'll be impossible to generate chunks from an active model).

4. Save the file on «land1.blend»

Do the same 5 times, using a different «Random Seed» and calling the objects «land.00x» and the file «landx.blend».

Move in the landscape:

1. Create a new blend file in the same folder than the precedents files.

2. Add a file «Text» with python type, name it «dynload.py and copy the following lines and those seen in the precedent technical part (3 classes).

3. Import camera with «freeview» type (**recipe V.1**), name it «Camera» (or modify the function freeChunks).

4. Select the camera and open the «Logic Editor». Add an «Always» sensor, check «Activate on True Level Triggering» and set the frequency at 50 (a call every seconds).

5. Add a «python» controller, select «Module» and write «dynload.update». Link the controller with the precedent sensor.

6. Add a «motion» actuator, name it «Move», «type»: «simple motion», «Loc» «Z»: -1.0 and check «L». Link the actuator with the precedent controller. That allows to make a displacement in the camera direction (like a plane). The mouse movements direct the movement (thanks to «L» for local).

7. Add an «Edit Object» actuator, name it «Add», select «Add Object» don't complete anything else, the script will do. Link the actuator with the precedent controller.

8. Add a property «chunks» with «integer» type and check «i» for a display in debug mode. In the «info» window, menu «Game» → check «Show debug properties». So, in realtime, we can see the number of chunks loaded in memory.

Script python «dynload.py»:

```python
import bge, mathutils
from random import random

#insert class models, class chunks and class landscape here
modelsName = [("land.001","land1.blend"),("land.002","land2.blend"),
        ("land.003","land3.blend"),("land.004","land4.blend"),
        ("land.005","land5.blend"),
bge.land = landscape(modelsName,100,100,100,100)
bge.land.init()

def update (cont):
    own = cont.owner
    actadd = cont.actuators["Add"]
    x = own.worldPosition.x / 100
    y = own.worldPosition.y / 100
    bge.land.draw(actadd,x,y,400)
    bge.land.freeChunks(1000)

    own["chunks"] = bge.land.getNbrChunks()

    actmove = cont.actuators["Move"]
    cont.activate(actmove)
```

ModelsName contains a list of tuples (object, library) and is used by the function init() of landscape to randomly generate a landscape.

The function **update**(), called by the controller, displays all the chunks around the camera in a radius of 400 units, and the function freeChunks() remove all the objects in a radius of 1000 units.

During the tests, we don't make the elements loading. By modifying the camera clipping, choose a view from above (7) and see the camera moving and the world created or destroyed according to a define radius.

III.19.   PICTURE AS BACKGROUND

Purpose:

Games like «Alone In the Dark» use 3D models evolving in a 2D environment: like a background picture. When the character goes behind a 2D object, there's another picture which is displayed over the character (like a «Z-Buffer» picture Approach).
The character interacts with the environment but it's limited to the 3D objects of the scene. This system allows to use the design arts **without a 3D modeling.** That's a low cost way of making video games.

Illustration 99: Selection of lines for an automatic calculation of the camera

Recipe:

If the background picture chosen is placed as following: width (x), height (z), and depth (y) (Illustration 99).

1.   Add a camera to the scene, choose it as active camera («Ctrl+0»)
2.   Download the Addon «Blam» of Stuffmatic at http://tinyurl.com/noqmrgq and install it («Ctrl+Alt+U» → «Addons» Tab → «Install from file»). Version minimal: 0.0.6.
3.   Open the «Movie Clip Editor» window and open the picture to use as background
4.   Display the «Properties» panel (N) and add a new layer. Choose a «red» color(«color for all stroke in this layer») for this first layer.
5.   Draw some lines like on Illustration 99. In red, it's the lines from in front of the camera to the background of the picture. Without the deformation due to the photo, these lines should be parallels, otherwise, don't draw them. We can follow a road, a house angle, etc. To draw them, do «Ctrl+D+LMB» at the first point, keep the touch pressed and move the mouse to the second point, then drop the click.
6.   Add a new layer. Choose a «blue» color for this second layer.
7.   Draw lines like on Illustration 99. In blue, it's the verticals (case #1). Depending on the photo and the angle of vision, we could prefer the horizontals (case #2).
8.   Display the «Tools» panel (T) and go to the «Static Camera Calibration» panel.
9.   In «Line set 1»,select «y axis»

10. In «Line set 2», select «z axis» for the case #1 or «x axis» for the case #2

11. Click on «Calibrate Active Camera» - the automatic calculation is made

12. Go to «3D View», open the «Properties» panel (N) and add the photo in background: check «background image», «add image» and choose the precedent photo, «Axis»: select «Camera», «opacity»:0.50

13. Modify the values for the camera position (and not the angle) to place the mesh in such a way that it follows the soil: take the skyline and superimpose it to the end of the mesh (add some lines to the mesh if necessary in the «Display» panel of the menu «Properties»). Perspective lines must correspond if «Blam» has the goods parameters. We must obtain something like Illustration 100.

14. Add a new scene («info» window, button «+» «add a new scene by type» near «Scene») and choose the mode «Link Objects». Name «background»

15. Go into camera view (0), add a new plane and do the necessaries rotations so that it'll face the camera. Go to «Edit Mode» and get each plane «coin» to correspond to the 4 coins of the camera.

16. UV mapping (U → «Smart UV Project») and open the «UV/Image Editor» window. Load the corresponding photo and adapt the UV so that it correspond to the edges of the image.

17. Add a «Material» and check the option «Shadeless». Add a new texture and load the corresponding image. Select «Mapping: coordinates»: «UV» and select «UVMap».

18. Go to the principal scene, select the camera and open the «Logic Editor»

19. Add an «Always» sensor, rename it «RunOnce»

20. Add a controller with «Scene» type, «Mode»: «Add Background Scene» and select «background». Link the sensor with the actuator.

The background image is now composed by the chosen image and we can add some 3D objects and move them: they follow the perspective lines as if they were in the picture.

Improvements:

- Adjust light atmosphere
- Add a plane to display shadows
- Use an image retouching software to remove some objects from the picture («Clone stamp tool» from The Gimp or equivalent). These removed objects can be added in the form of 3D objects or in a scene with «overlay» type.
- Add some «invisible» objects to be «relief». In the case of the Illustration 100: stairs lining the way.

Illustration 100: The mesh follows the perspective lines on the picture

III.20.　　VIDEO AS BACKGROUND

Purpose:

It's the same principle as that for the precedent recipe, but with a video. If you film from above the Monte Carlo Automobile Rally. With the actual Mocap tools, **it's possible to deduct the camera position from the video and to add it some 3D models, like a car.** When the vehicle is moving off, it must be possible to define the video image to play. If the car reverses, you must step backward. Of course, the camera view is never modified, it's a limitation.

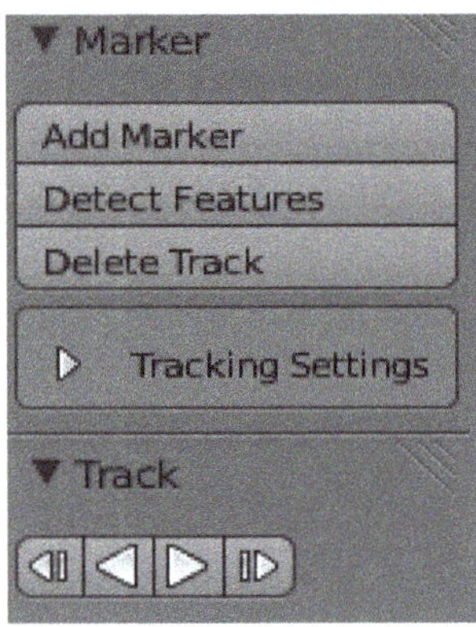

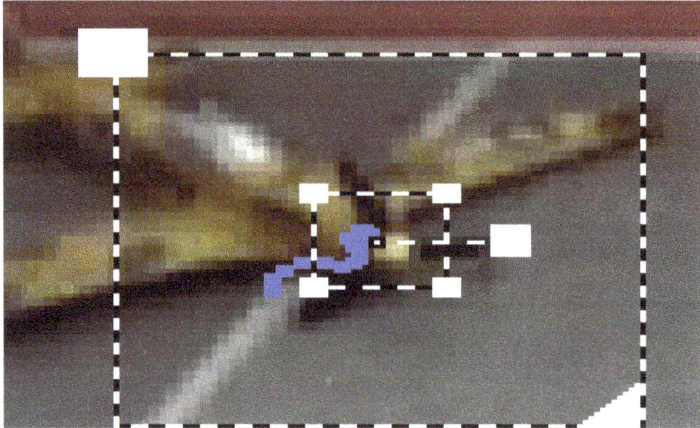

Illustration 101: Addition of a Marker (Anchor Point)

Recipe:

1. Add a camera and a lamp with «sun» type

2. «`Ctrl`+`Alt`+`U`» («User Preferences») → «System» → «memory Cache Limit» at 1024 for more edition comfort (it prevent a video lag during edition loading and unloading pictures).

3. «Movie Clip Editor» window, «Open» Tab → choose a video file corresponding to the needs. Adapt the scene parameters («Properties» Window, «Render» Tab, «Dimensions» panel) ta have the same properties as the video (size, number of FpS).

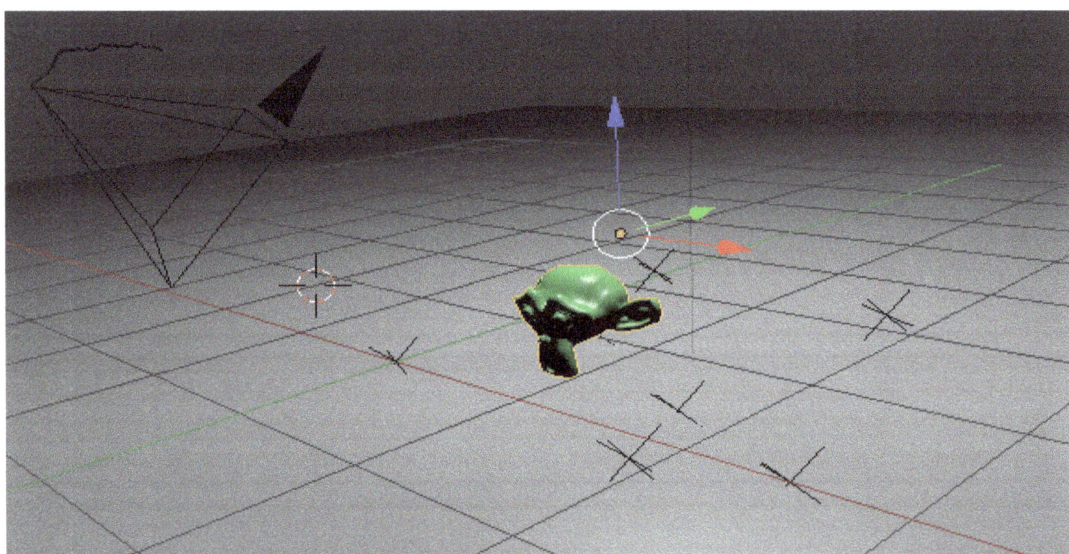

Illustration 102: Anchor points allow to position the 3D objects

4. Add 8 Tracking points. For each point, repeat the following operations (Illustration 102):
    - «Add Marker»
    - Click on an image zone where the zone remains significantly the same from the beginning to the end of the video
    - Go to the beginning of the video
    - «[Ctrl]+T» (Track) to Track the Marker.

    If this last seems to run entirely, do the next, however remove it.

5. Set «camera data» on «Blender» and adapt the parameters to those of the device which has taken the video. If the parameters are unknowns, set in the «Tools» panel → «Refine» on «Focal Length, K1, K2»

6. Launch a «Solve Camera Motion». The error rate allows to know if the points are corrects (not above 0.5). For these tests, we obtain 0.186 – it's a good result.

7. Be careful, the «rogue markers» are precalculated markers with more frames than other and which can stop the «camera motion». To find them, take one by one each marker, do a «clean» and recalculate the motion. However, the «solve» will not work.

8. Go to «reconstruction» mode

9. Select 3 points that touch «the ground» and menu «Orientation» → «Floor»

10. Go to 3D View, add «Suzanne» (mesh with «monkey» type, it'll be our model) and a plane. We can easily place Suzanne thanks to Tracking points

11. Select the plane and go to the «Properties» window, «Material» Tab, add a new «Material», then, in the «Shadow» panel: check «Receive transparent» and «Shadow Only», then «Shadow and Shading». There will be only the Suzanne's shadow on the final plane.

Illustration 103: Tracking camera: Example of integration in a video

III.21. BREAK OBJECTS

Purpose:

The physic engine «Bullet» integrated to BGE allows to play with the objects, to launch them in the sky and to observe them falling back. But we can't break an object in realtime. A way to get around that is to make several object models. With the vase example, we can have an «intact» vase, a model shattered into 3 pieces and another into 10 pieces. Each piece is a new object. Now the vase can be broken, the pieces use gravity and collision system from «Bullet» to scatter. Here is a simpler recipe.

Recipe:

1. Open the user preferences (`Ctrl`+`Alt`+`U`), «Addons» panel and activate the addon «Object: Fracture Tools», then save clicking on «Save User Settings»

2. Add a plane to make the ground (`Shift`+`A` → «Mesh» → «Plan»)

3. Add a cube and resize it so that it has a wall form (dimensions:1x10x5).

4. In front of the wall, along the X axis, add a sphere (`Shift`+`A` → «Mesh» → «Plan»).

5. «Properties» window, «Physics» panel, «Type»: «Rigid Body». Check «Collision bounds» and select «Bounds»: «Convex Hull».

6. «Material» Tab, add a new Material («+») and name it «destroy».

7. Open the «Logic Editor» and add an «Always» sensor, name it «RunOnce».

8. Add a «Motion» actuator, type: «Simple motion», «Force» «X»: -20 and uncheck «L».

9. Link the sensor with the actuator. At the outset, a force pushes the sphere on the wall.

10. Select the wall, «Physics» panel, «Type»: «Rigid Body». Check «Collision bounds» and select «Bounds»: «Convex Hull».

11. Open the «Logic Editor» and add an «Always» sensor, rename it «RunOnce».

12. Add an «Edit Object» actuator, select «Dynamics» and «Dynamic Operation»: «Suspend Dynamics». Link the sensor with the actuator. That allows to keep the wall in good repair at start and that, as long as no «Restore Dynamics» is applied.

13. Add a «Collision» sensor, «property»: enter «destroy»

14. Add an «Edit Object» actuator, select «Dynamics» and «Dynamic Operation»: «Restore Dynamics». Link the sensor and the actuator. When a piece of wall collides an object with the property «destroy», dynamics is restored, collisions and gravity work.

15. Use the fracture tool: «space»+ «Fracture Object». In the «3D View» window, display the menu «Tools» (T) - a «Fracture Object» Panel allows an additional parameter: check «Execute», «Number of shards»: 100, «crack type»: «flat»

16. Select 4 or 5 big pieces of wall «unbreakable» (example: the sides and the bottom of the wall) and transform them into static objects «Physics», «type»: «Static».

The Illustration 104 show you a wall destruction using a projectile. It's possible to combine this recipe with the one for explosions (recipe VII.17): the «invisible» object spread the pieces of wall to have a realistic scene (Illustration 105).

Illustration 104: Wall destruction using a projectile

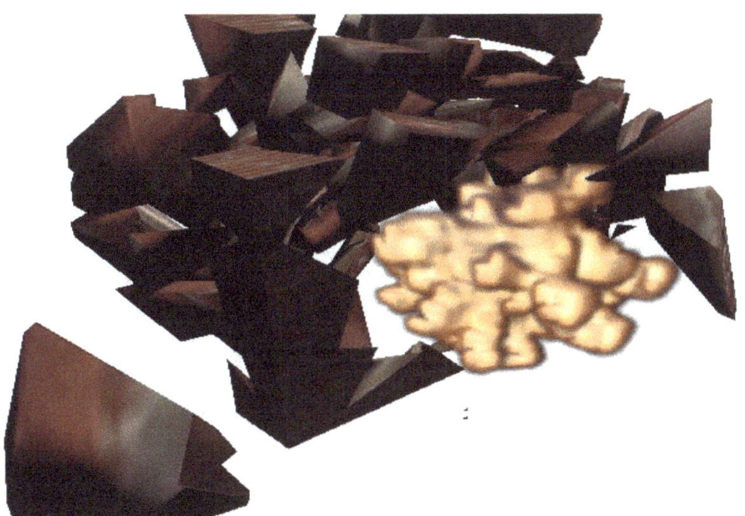

Illustration 105: Destruction combined with the «explosions» recipe

III.22. LIGHTING EFFECTS ON DECOR

Purpose:

The ambient lighting of a game is probably one of the key points for the player immersion. Shadows would not exist without light.

If the game design is done properly, any street-lamp is a refuge.

«**Contrast**», a game developed by french studios **Focus** is a game which mixes plates forms in a smart way, based on shadows. The player is a 3D little girl, who turns into a shadow to become a 2D character when she is near a wall.

Esthetic: some level designers say that illumination is the most important aspect of a game, however, this aspect is often forgotten by beginners.

Light gives a form to space, and with light, objects are visible or not. With light, atmosphere is given, light can bring joy (vibrant and bright colors), or sadness (dull colors).

We have to remember:

- Some lamps don't make shadows in BGE: lamps with «Point» and «Hemi» type

- Some lamps don't work in BGE: lamps with «areas» type (except in «**candy branch**», non-official branch of Blender). However, we can use them in «baking» mode and replace it by a plane with the same size. We can simulate them with an 180° spot too.

- «Hemi» are convenient for setup an ambient lighting (recipe III.4).

- The lamp position with «Sun» type doesn't matter: only its orientation is important.

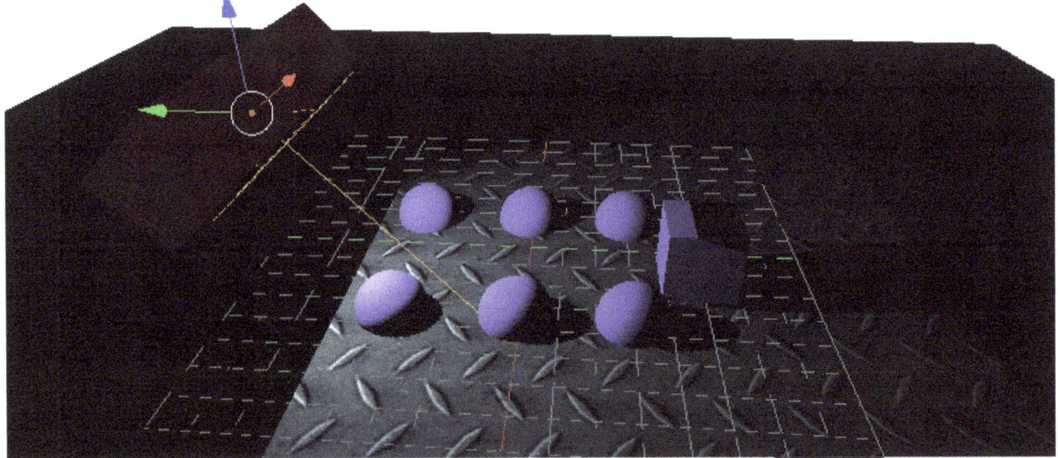

Illustration 106: Example of neon lamp made with a 120° spot . For the tube, use the recipe VII.8. Add too a «glow» effect.

- The more we use lamps, the more performances collapse. Testing configuration is easy: display the stats («info» window → «Game» → check «Show Framerate and Profile»), create a plane and add about 50 lamps with «point» type. Test (P). If the Framerate resists, double the number of lamps.

- The lamps with «spot» type can project a texture (only images presently). But we can combine that with the recipe VII.7 to project videos. The effect is particularly impressive: effect underwater, screen reflect on the movie theater, etc.

- The Material «emit» doesn't create some light, it simply makes the object brighter with BGE. There's no impact on the surrounding objects (to have an impact, do a baked radiosity simulation: recipe VII.8).

Baking:

- It allows to have «an image» of the light on the surroundings materials, but be careful to the animated objects which will not be impacted or will create some aberrations in the scene.
- This helps save resources because it's a lamp that we can deactivate and not directly managed by BGE (lightmap for that)
- Lamps which do not work in a native way with BGE can be baked, but the settings are not easy and the result is approximate
- To make a day/night cycle, or to create the idea of an alarm system with red and blue, we can use 2 different textures and activate them alternately.

Shadows:

- Complete settings for shadows with BGE is only accessible in «Game Engine» mode.
- The more important the **buffer** is, the more resources are used, but the more realistic the shadow is too. Modify the clipping to improve that (**Clip Start** and **Clip End**).
- **Soft shadows** are shadows calculated with a buffer with «variance» type on BGE: to smooth the shadows. A soft shadow can close the gaps in a too little buffer but it has a cost in time.
- «Bias» determine the gap between the object and the light. The «Bias Bleed» checks the shadow impact. There's no effect with a simple buffer.

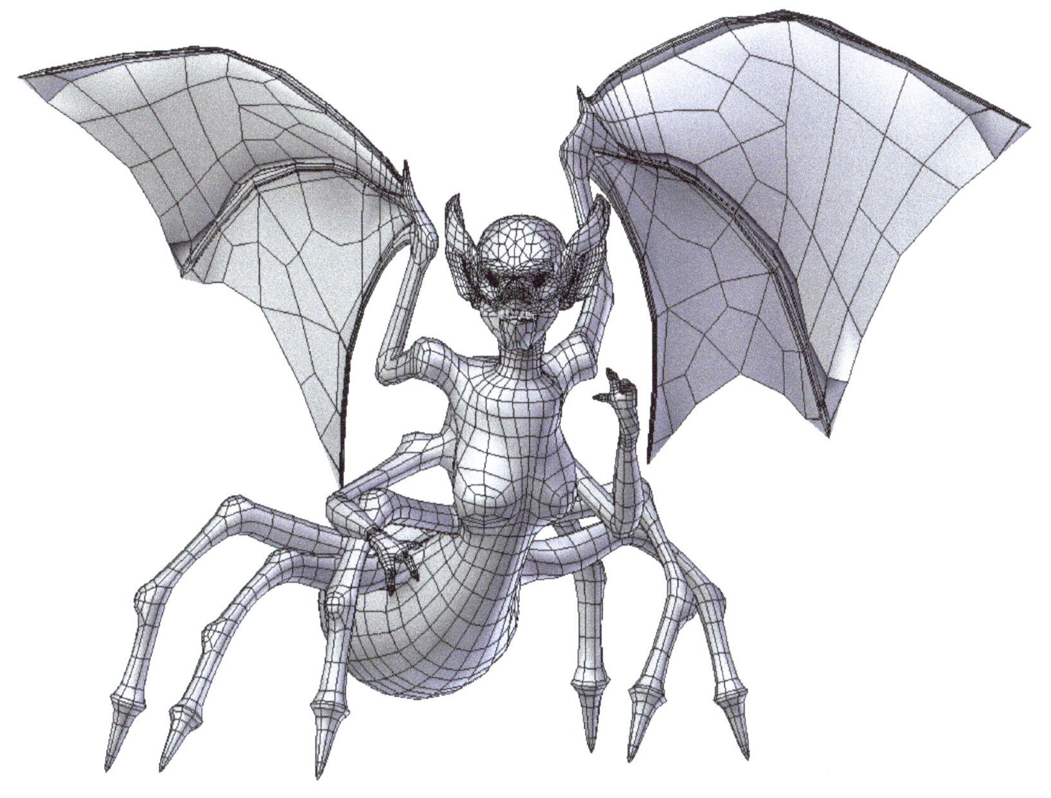

IV -   CHARACTERS RECIPES

IV.1. MODEL FOR GAMES

Purpose:

Model for games is different from model for films or computer generated image (CGI). The purpose is to obtain some models with **a little number of faces to be supporter by the graphics card in realtime**, but you must pay attention to the materials to compensate the I low resolution of the model.

Before to create a model, we make an «art design», the more often, it's a character or an object sketch. A front view is drawn, a side view too and eventually a view from above.

Recipe sketch:

1. Choose a **photo** with a front view and a side view (if it's a gif, transform it into Jpg) – There are numerous photos on http://the-blueprints.com/.

2. In the «3D View» window, go to «Object Mode» and open the «Properties» menu («N»)

3. In front view (key 1) check «background images» and add the photo. Set the **axis** in «**front**»

4. Do the same for the axis «**right**» with a side view («right view», key 3). Position the center of the mark on a same point in the 2 windows (here, the center of the robot head).

From this sketch, insert some simpler forms (cubes, sphere, etc.) in place of elements to model, then, remove or insert some vertex, extrude some parts of the object, until you obtain a model like the sketch.

Details don't need to be modeled, they can be drawn on the texture. It's possible too to add some faked reliefs applying a «normal map» (recipe IV.12). The important is to conserve a number of polygons as small as possible.

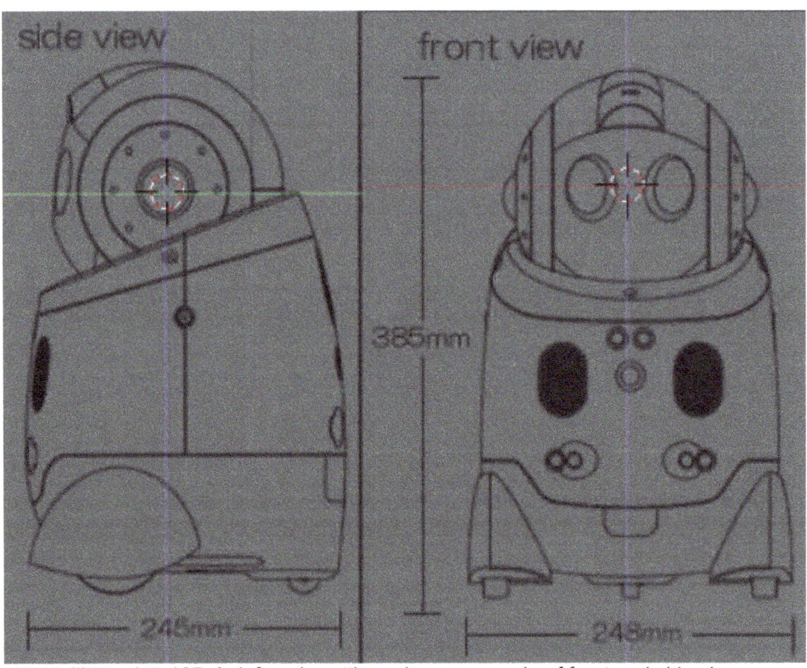

Illustration 107: At left, axis setting, above, example of front and side view

To model a symmetric object, 2 solutions:

- Work with **X Mirror:** using «mirror» of «Edit Mode («3D View», «Tools» panel («T»), «Options» Tab, check «X Mirror»). Each vertex modified is modified at the same time as another via the X axis. But the face extrude doesn't work (use a modifier with «Mirror» type).

- Remove half of the object to work only on 1 part (easier to see the remaining part). In this case, remove half of the sphere. Go to mode object, select, then «⇧Shift+D» (duplicate), «Enter», «Ctrl+M» (mirror) and «X» (axis x), «Enter». «Space» → «remove doubles» to remove the commons vertex. Use the same technique to make the other symmetrical body parts, then add the non-symmetrical parts.

When the character is modeled, do an UV mapping like for a landscape (recipe III.2). Then, it's possible to do a «Texture Painting» or to adapt the texture with a tool like «The Gimp» or «Krita». This book is not written to teach you how to model on Blender.

The modeling technique in «Lowpoly» is basic (deformation of shapes, addition of vertex, scale, extrusion, etc.). But learning requires time. The sheet #4 «modeling on Blender» show the principal used functions.

You can find numerous tutorials on internet with the key words «tutorial», «character», «lowpoly» and «Blender».

However, there are numerous model to download: some are free (with licenses).The sheet #10 «Resources for video games» gives a list of sites where you can find some models.

Illustration 108: Lowpoly modeling from Team fortress 2

IV.2. ANIMATE USING SHAPE KEYS

Purpose:

Animate a character or an object, without using an armature deformation. We modify the geometric structure between 2 keys, and let Blender calculate the intermediary frames by interpolation (morphing).

Recipe 1: simple method

Illustration 109: Shape keys

1. Create a blank scene with Suzanne (⇧Shift+A → «Mesh» → «Monkey»).

2. Add a Shape Key in the «Properties» Window, «Object Data» tab, «Shape Keys» Panel: by default, it's named «Basics», it's the model in its initial form, before eventual transformations.

3.   Then a second called «Close Right Eye»

4. Go in «Edit Mode» and zoom (⇧Shift+B) on the character's right eye.

5. In Wireframe mode («Z»), catch the low part of the Suzanne's eyelid (Illustration 110)

6. Moving the vertex («G») along the Y and Z axes, allows to simulate an eyelid which is closing to obtain the effect on the illustration 109.

7. Go to «Object Mode»: the eyelid is reopening. To modify the effect, go to «Properties» window, «Object Data» Tab, «Shape Keys» panel. Modify «Value» → result: Illustration 110 (half closed eye)

8. To animate it: go to frame 1, move the mouse cursor on «Value», choose 0.0 and press the key «I» (→ change in color).

9. Go to Frame 50, set «Value» at 1.0 and moving the mouse cursor over «Value», press the key «I». The animation from 1 to 50 is ready.

10. If we open the «Dopesheet Editor» window in «Action Mode», we see a new action named «Keyaction». This last action can be renamed and used on BGE by applying directly on the mesh, here: the object «Monkey».

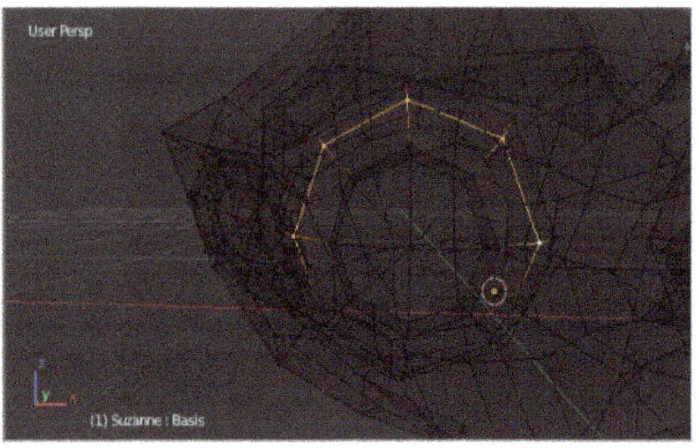

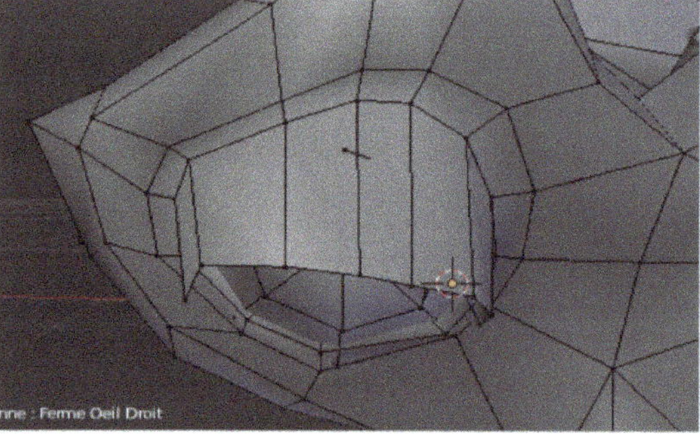

Illustration 110: Suzanne's eye modeling for a morphing in shape key

Recipe 2: Using «Driven Shape Keys»

Approach more effective for the user, it allows to use graphics objects to guide the desired movement.

1. Repeat the steps from 1 to 7 of the precedent recipe (or remove the animations keys).

2. Near the right eye, add an armature (⬆Shift+A → «Armature» → «Single Bone»). Name it «controller».

3. In an invisible layer, model an arrow «top-bottom» from a plane ZX or download a little arrow shaped object. The idea is to use this object moving it from top to bottom to control the eye opening and closing. Name it «ArrowsUD».

4. Select «Controller», then in the «Properties» window, «Bone» Tab, «Display» Panel, click on «Custom Shape» and select «ArrowsUD», then in «At», the only «Bone» available. If the replacement is not correct visually, apply a «triangulate modifier» on «ArrowsUD».

5. Resize «Controller»: it must have the same size than the eye.

6. Select «Suzanne» and go to the «Object Data» Tab, «Shape Keys» panel. Move the mouse cursor obove «Close Right Eye», choose a value of «0.0000» and Right Click → «Add Driver».

7. Open the «Graph Editor» and choose the «Drivers» mode (rather than F-Curves Editor»).

8. In the upper left-hand corner of the window, «Suzanne → Key → Value (Close Right Eye)». Select «Value» and open the menu «Properties» (N).

9. «Drivers» Panel, select «Type»: «Average Value» (you can ignore this warning message).

10. If no variable is proposed, add a variable (button «Add Variable»). Select «Variable Type»: «Transform Channel». Then, just bellow, select the object «Controller» and the bone «Bone».

11. Select «Type»: «Y Location» (for the motion top/bottom – the coordinates are modified) and «Space»: «Local Space».

12. Open «Generator» and set the polynomial coefficients in such a way that Y = «0.0000» + «-1.0000» x. Verify the settings with the Illustration 111.

13. Go to «3D View», select «Controller» (which has the form «ArrowsUD») and go to «Pose Mode». Move «Controller» from top to bottom to animate the Suzanne's eyelid.

14. Repeat the steps 8 and 9 of the precedent recipe to create a usable action with BGE, don't use the «Value» field, but use the object «Controller» to do eyelid movements.

This recipe is a real help for the animation. This is particularly valuable when a character has a lot of animations in this type. The addon Rigify works similarly with an automatic setting of the different constraints, that allows to save time.

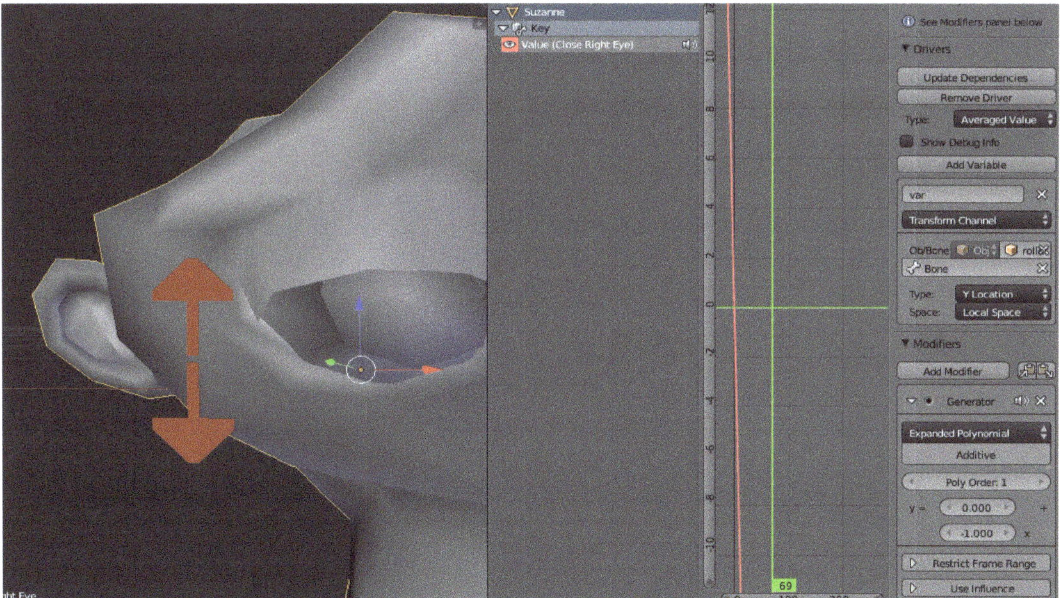

Illustration 111: Use of a driver to animate the Suzanne's eyelid

IV.3. ANIMATE USING AN ARMATURE

Purpose:

The best way to animate a character (running, jump, fight) or a tree, is to use an armature, which is a set of bones. To each bone is assigned a part of the model geometry so that moving the bone, we move the part of the model.
Coloring techniques («**weight paint**») allow to manage the bones joint deformations, when several bones share part of the model geometry. When the armature is correctly assigned to all the object geometry, we set the constraints on the bones. For example, a head doesn't rotate along the axis Z, etc.
When everything is ready, the model is «**rigged**»: very quickly, we can do numerous animations.

Recipe:

1. Create a cube (（⇧Shift+A）→ «Mesh» → «Cube»), and with some scale(«S») and extrusions («E»), create the model like in the Illustration 114

2. Add an armature: «（⇧Shift+A）»→ «Armature» → «Single Bone»

3. «Properties» Window → «Object» Tab → «Display» Panel → check «X-Ray» to make the armature visible through the object

4. Place the armature at the low center of the object, be as precise as possible

5. Go to «Edit Mode» then select the top of the Bone. With progressive extrusion (along the Z axis, then X for the head), create the armature like on Illustration 113

6. «Properties» Window → «Modifier» Tab → «Add Modifier» → «Armature», then select the armature created – don't click on «Apply»

7. Go to «Pose Mode», select the first bone, then click on the object and go to «Weight Paint» mode

8. A brush allows to color in red (progressively) around the first bone (Illustration 113). It represents the ratio given to the bone compared to the other bones in the deformation of a part of the object.

9. Click on the next bone and repeat the operation coloring only the zone around the bone. Idem, until the head.

10. Doing a rotation of one of the bones in mode pose, the object distorts to follow the movement (Illustration 117)

11. «Timeline» Window > in Frame #1 limit the animation at 30 images («End»: 30)

12. Select «LocRotScale» in «Active Keying». Imperative: Select all the object bones (to save the position of each bone

13. Go to Object mode, click on the key at the right of «LocRotScale» to create a Keyframe (or the key «I» in «3D View»). The name of the armature is displayed in orange

14. Go to Frame 10 and do a bones rotation to create a pose (Illustration 116). Select the Bones, create a new key.

15. Go to Frame 20, do a bones rotation (Illustration 115) and move everything of 1 unit on the X and Y axes (use the properties «N» then Location). Select the Bones, then create a new key.

16. Go to Frame 30, move the bones and strike a pose of origin. Select the Bones, create a new key.

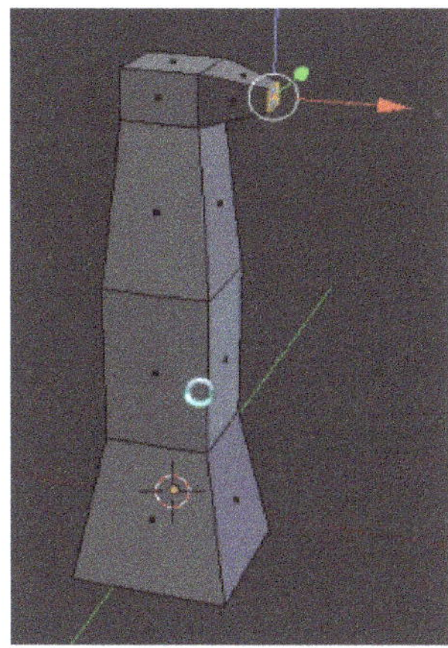

Illustration 114: simple model

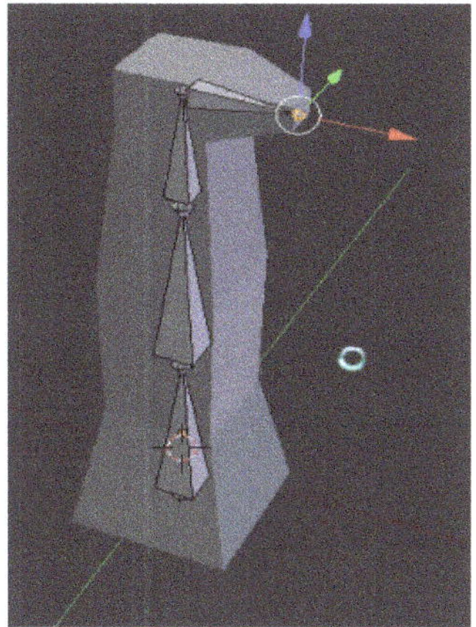

Illustration 113: structure Bones

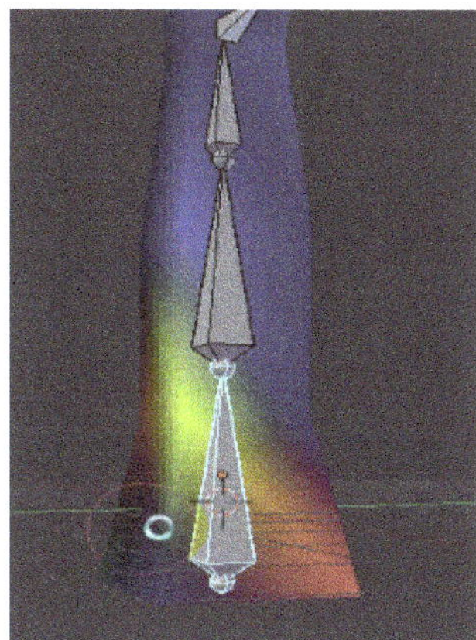

Illustration 112: Weight Painting

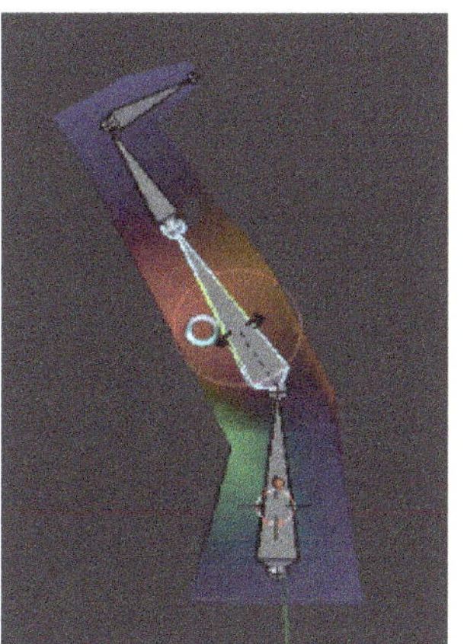

Illustration 117: Morphing using the Weight Painting

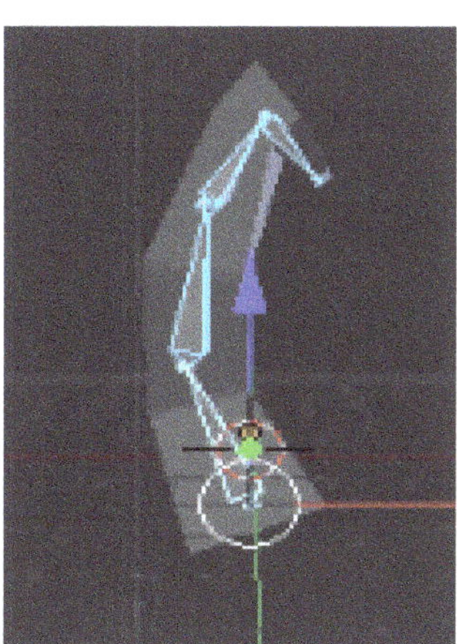

Illustration 116: Frame 10 of the animation

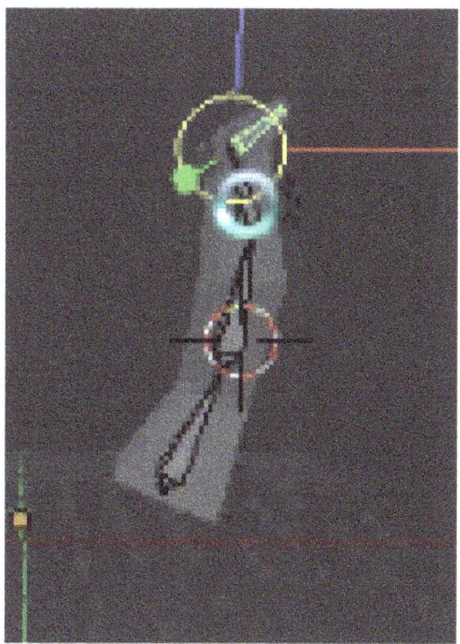

Illustration 115: Frame 20 of the animation

IV.4. ANIMATE A CHARACTER WITH RIGIFY

<u>**Purpose:**</u>

Use Rigify to obtain a character with **movement liberty axis defined**.

<u>**Recipe #1**</u>: **With Automatic Weight Paint**

1. **Activate the addon** «Rigify» by going to «User Preferences»(«`Ctrl`+`Alt`+`U`»), «Addons» Tab, «Rigging» panel, check «Rigging: Rigify».
2. **Import a** character mesh. (models in the `sheet #10` «Resources for video game»)
3. Add an **armature:** «Add» → «Armature» → «Human(meta-rig)»
4. In Edit mode, make visible the armature (check **«X-Ray»** in the «Properties» window→ «Object Data» Tab → «Display» Panel)
5. «Tools» Menu → «Armature Options» Panel → Check «X-Axis Mirror»
6. **Remove** the **useless bones** for the animation
7. **Align bones and model**. All the bones must be enclosed in the envelope. To avoid the complex movements, do some move (G) specifying the axis (x, y or z) or work with the views «above», «face» and «side», but not in free view.
8. When the bone is positioned, go to «Object Mode», select the armature «metarig»
9. «Properties» Window → «Object Data» Tab → «Rigify Buttons» Panel → «Generate». It's possible to hide «metarig» or to remove it.
10. **Link the armature «rig» to the mesh**: Select the mesh, press «`Shift`» key, then select the new armature maintaining this key, `Ctrl`+`P` → «Armature Deform with **Automatic Weight Paint**»). If there's an error message, *realign the bones and start again.* If the problem persists, *you can add a deform with Subdivision Surface type (no apply) to the model.*
11. Verify that the model is painted for each bone like in the Illustration 119: Select all the bones in mode pose and move the armature. Elements *that don't follow the armature must be painted. Select the nearest bone and paint directly the parts which are separated from the armature until they join the model.*
12. Make tests by moving only a bone to verify if the deformation is correct. We obtain a mesh to animate (Illustration 118).

<u>**Recipe #2**</u>: **With Envelop Weights**

1. Repeat the steps from 1 to 7 from the precedent recipe
2. **Link the armature with the mesh**: Select the mesh, key «`Shift`», then select the new armature and `Ctrl`+`P` → «Armature Deform with **Envelop Weights**». Group of vertex are assigned. The smoothing is not as fine as «Weight Paint», but it's easier.
3. Redefine the Group **of vertex** because the automatic mode is bad for a character. → work in mode «wire frame» and reassign the vertex to each bone (Illustration 143).
4. «Properties» Window, «Modifiers» Tab. There's the «modifier» applied to the armature. Unselect «Bone Envelops» to work with BGE. **«Preserve Volume»** allows to obtain a more suitable deformation for a character.

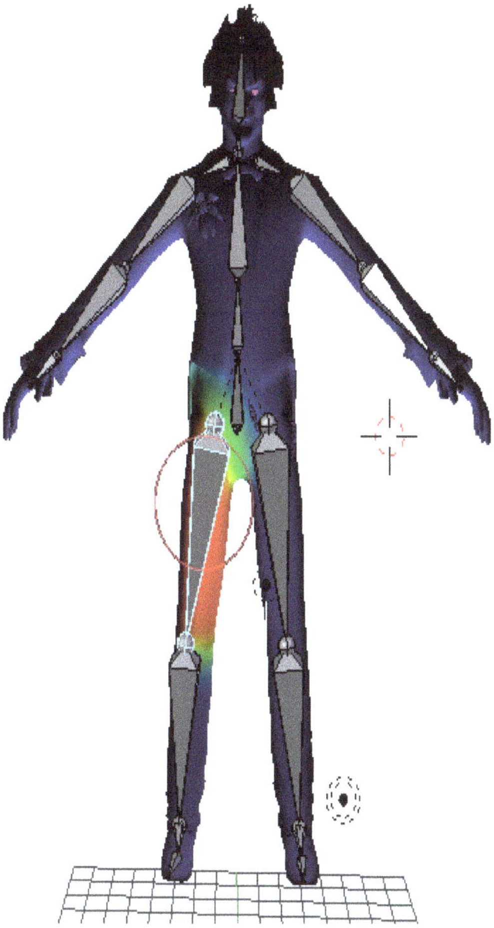

Illustration 119: Character's leg Weight Paint

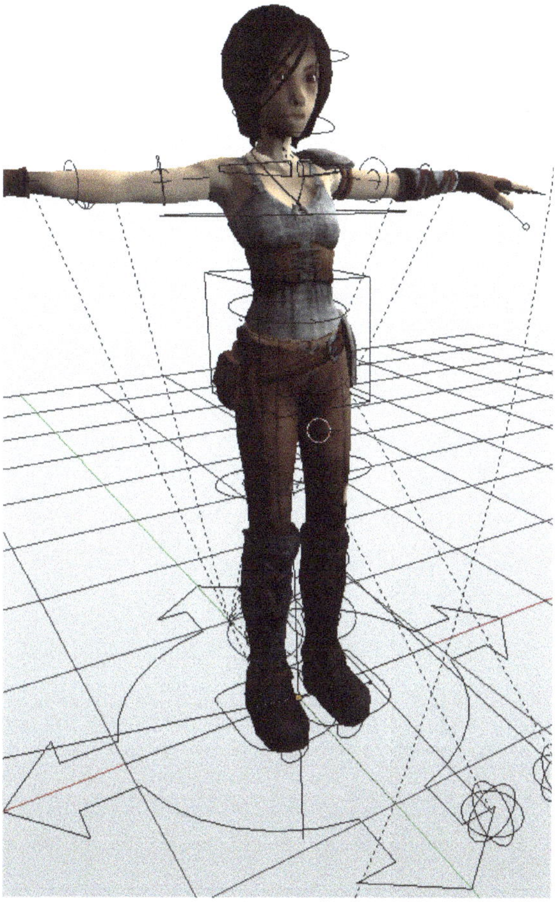

Illustration 118: Rigify in action

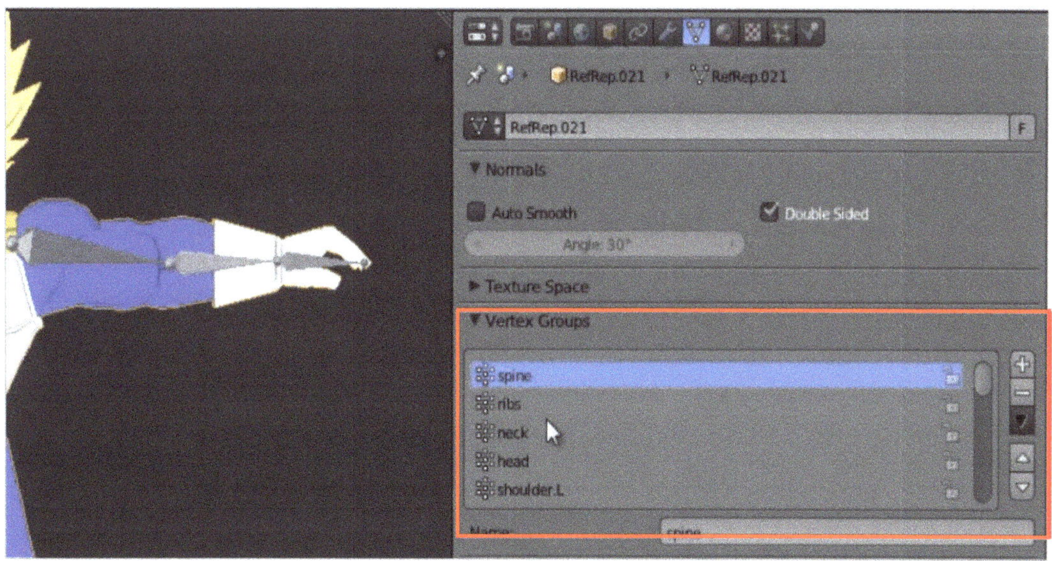

Illustration 120: mode «Envelop Weights»

IV.5. ANIMATE A CHARACTER USING ANIMATION SEQUENCE

Purpose:

When the character is correctly «rigged», how to animate it? If you don't have worked in cartoons or characters animation for video games, it's not easy to do, even with an armature correctly configured. **The using of animation sequences allows to easily obtain realistic animations.** On Google images, use key words like «animation cycle» to obtain some sequences and to begin your first animation.

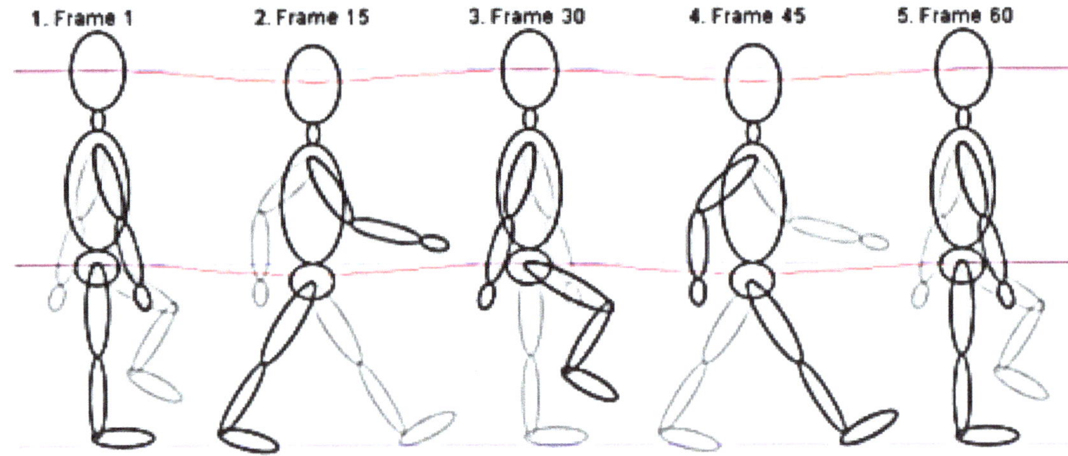

Illustration 121: Animation sequence for biped walk

Recipe:

1. **Import** a model with character type, completely «rigged».
2. Download a sequence with «Walk Cycle» type like on Illustration 121 or Illustration 122.
3. Go to «Object Mode» and open the menu «properties» (N)
4. Go to «right view», (key 3) and check «background images» then add the picture. Set the **axis** in «**right**»
5. Window Timeline → Go to Frame #1 and limit the animation at 60 images like on set of sequences (End: 60). If the set doesn't have a time indication, base on the framerate (by default: 50 FpS) and calculate the time needed for the motion, then transform it in a number of frames.
6. Select «LocRotScale» in Active Keying. Select all the object bones (to save the position for each bone)
7. Go to Objet mode, click on the key at he right of LocRotScale to create a Keyframe. The armature name is displayed in orange.
8. Go to frame 15 and do a rotation of bones to create a pose. Select the Bones, then create a new key.
9. Repeat the operation for the frames 30,45 and 60.

The «Rotoscoping» Technique:

«Rotoscoping»: **film a scene and use it to correctly parameter the animations,** doing several stop-motions and copying the different poses, like to create an animation sequence. This process was used a lot in past, like in the game «Another World» from Eric Chahi (Illustration 123).

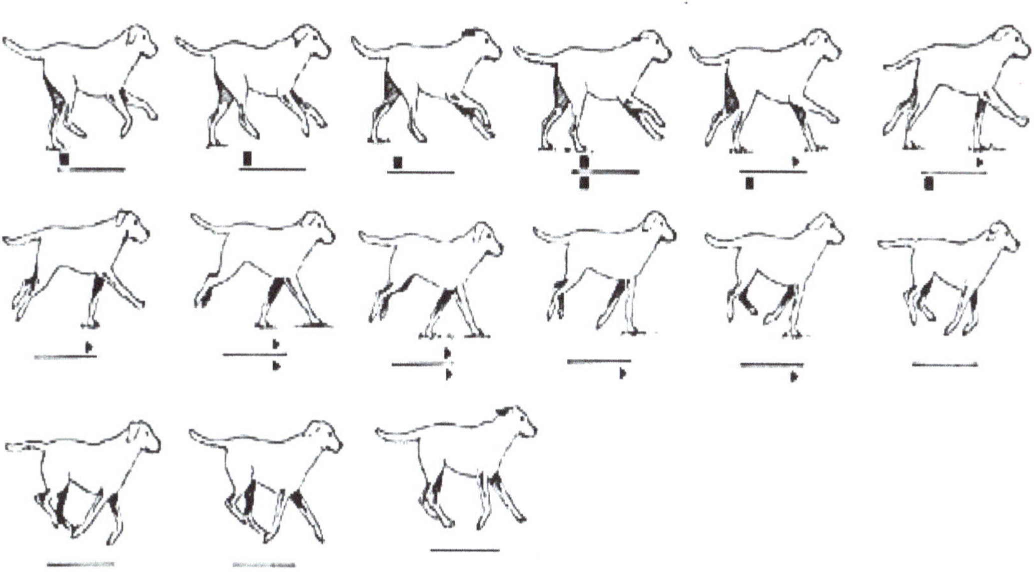

Illustration 122: Animation sequence for a dog running

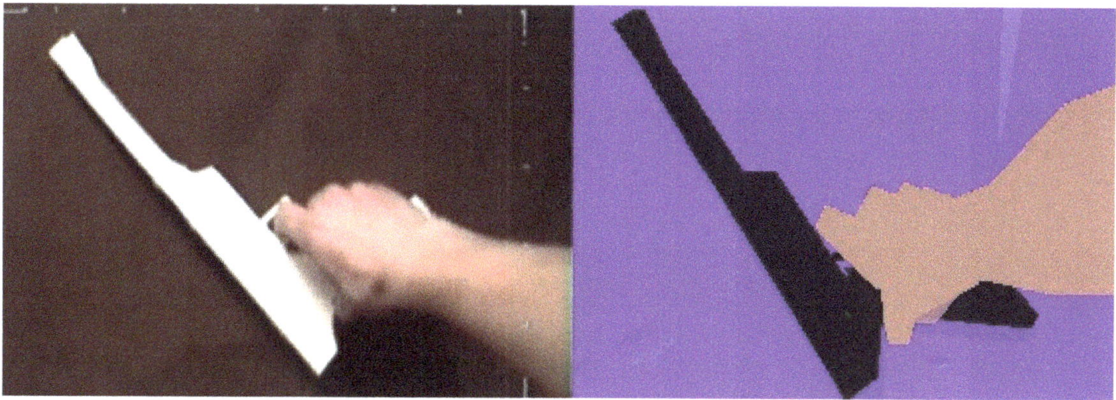

Illustration 123: Technique Rotoscoping used here for modeling and animation
(game «Another World» from Eric Chahi)

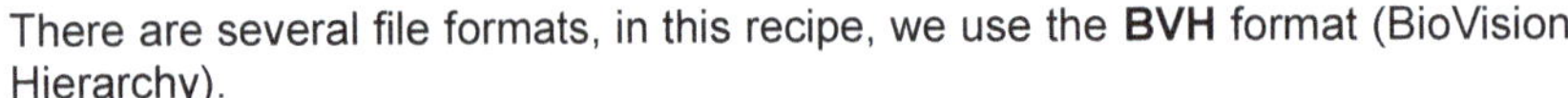

IV.6. USE A MOTION CAPTURE BANK

Purpose

A Mocap file is composed by **armature animation data for a particular movement** (example: walk, dance, shoot, etc.). There are banks with numerous Mocap files, some of these are free: **Carnegie Mellon University Motion Capture Database** (http://mocap.cs.cmu.edu/).

There are several file formats, in this recipe, we use the **BVH** format (BioVision Hierarchy).

Tools like «BVH hacker» (www.bvhacker.com) allow to modify undesired bones to reduce animation size (Illustration 125).

For the following recipes:

1. Activate the addon «Motion Capture Tools» («`Ctrl`+`Alt`+`U`» → «Addon» panel → Category «Animation»: check «Motion Capture Tools»)

2. Download the mocap file in BVH format from http://tinyurl.com/cwcclfn (*Daz friendly version*)

3. «info» window, menu «File» → «Import» → «Motion Capture BVH» → Choose a file in the downloaded bank. Choose a file corresponding to the walk («02_01» for example). When the «Scale» is known, enter it even approximately. Choose a frame from which there's no more animation, write this number in «Start Frame».

4. Select the armature and in the «Properties» window, «Object Data» Tab, «Display» panel, check «X-Ray» to make the armature visible through the character.

Illustration 124: Name of the bones in the CMU bank

The motion capture or **mocap** is a technique allowing to record the location and the orientation of objects and living persons, to control an avatar on the computer (camera, 3D model). A visual restitution of these movements in realtime is done via the 3D render engine from the interfaced application with the hardware which can store them into an animation file with a BVH format. Finally, they will be processed in a 3D software. The application extracts the raw data to use them (source: Wikipedia).

Recipe without retargeting:

It's the simplest recipe. It can be used when we don't need a particular armature (animate a face) or to use «Rigify». In this case, do a «retargeting».

1. Import a character without armature in the scene (or remove the existent armature)

2. Go to «Edit Mode». By many displacements («G»), rotations («R») and scales («S»), superimpose the BVH armature to the character. Work on each bone to align them perfectly to the model. Remove the useless bones for the animation project.

3. Repeat the **recipe IV.4** from the step 4 to rig perfectly the model.

4. Go to «Object Mode» and open the «Dope Sheet» window, mode «Action Editor», select the imported action. The action has the same name as the file BVH. Rename the action (ex: «walk») and check «F». That allows to keep the action when the armature is removed, useful to do multiples importations of BVH.

5. Each animation frame is represented by a set of keys. Each bone is represented, and each animation type: location, rotation and scale. For a game, **we won't use the character displacement** because it must be realized with **physical management**. For a walk, a jump, we need an animation with «on the spot» type. Detect the root bone («hips» in the CMU bank). Remove the keys corresponding to the hips displacement – there are 3 keys: X, Y and Z.

6. Act on all the frame keys by selecting the frame in the «Dope sheet Summary». If the frame is not available, check «Summary». In lasso mode (`Shift`+`B`), select the key «Summary» corresponding to the first animation frame we want to keep, select too the one corresponding to the last. For a walk, it's possible to select only one sample from the walk. Inverse the selection («`Ctrl`+`I`») to select all the frames remove then remove («x»).

7. Select all the keys («a») and resize the animation («S») to obtain a walk cycle as if the cycle takes 2 seconds and if the number of displayed frames per 1 second is 50, then the cycle has 100 frames. When the scale is done, move (G) all the keys to have the first which coincide with the frame 1 of the scene.

8. «Properties» Window, «Object» Tab, «Extra Mocap Tools» panel, click on «**Samples to Beziers**». The series of keys is replaced by a series of curses which stay as close to the animation and allow easier modifications. The number of keys is too smaller, alleviate the animation.

9. If the animation remains complex, use the addon «Simplify F-Curves» like in the **recipe III.11**.

The animation can be used with BGE. From there, it's easy to import new animations BVH from the same bank. Import a new file BVH, remove the new imported armature and restart at the step 4. The name of the bones est the same, so the imported action automatically works with the existent armature.

Recipe with retargeting:

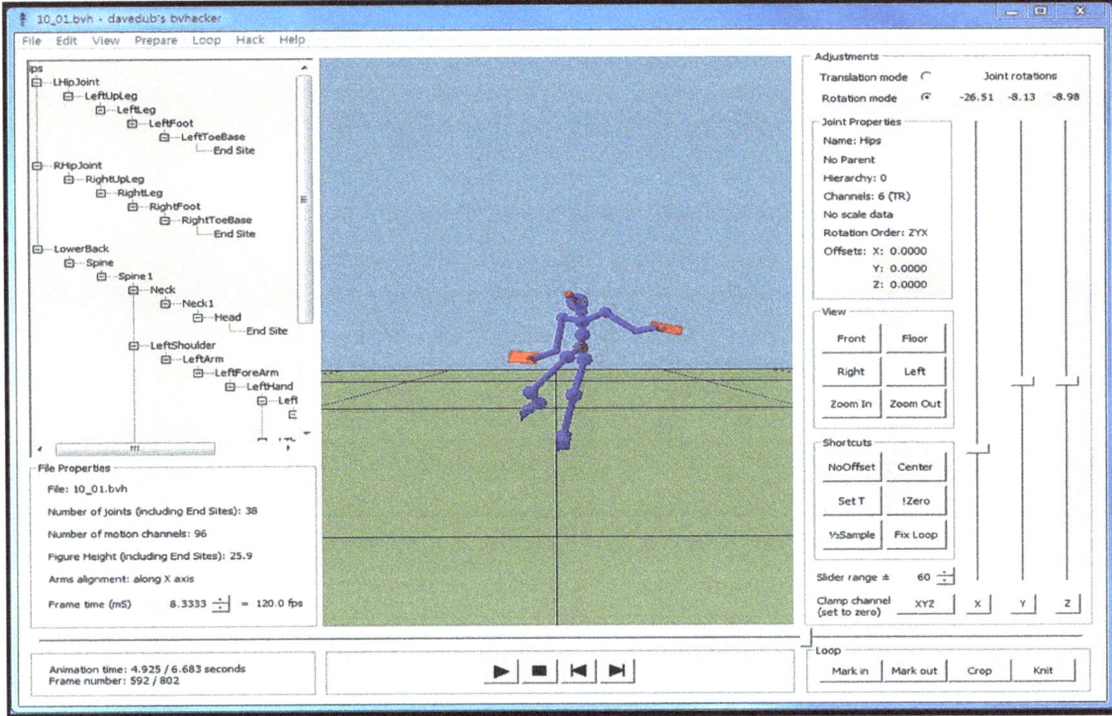

Illustration 125: BVHacker tool to modify the BVH files

1. Import a character with its armature.
2. Superimpose the 2 armatures and scale the new armature to correspond to the first one.
3. Repeat the steps from 4 to 9 of the precedent recipe.
4. In object mode, First select the simplest armature then the other (the sequence is important – if the armature has fingers, eyes, etc. – it's more complex than the armature used for the BVH → select first the BVH armature)
10. «Properties» Window, «Object» Tab, «Mocap Tools» Panel → **«Retargeting»** (Illustration 126): link each bone to its homologue.
11. Click on **«Autoscale Performer»** and «Clear Noise» if the BVH file is poor quality.
12. **«Save mapping»** to reuse this mapping with other animations.
13. Click on «retarget» (*«advanced target» must be unselected*).
14. The «retargeting» operation has created some useless actions, we can now remove them. There are «base», «auto» and «manual». In the «Dopesheet Editor», uncheck «F» and remove actions in the «NLA Editor». Actions are automatically deleted at the next file loading.

Illustration 126: Armature Retargeting

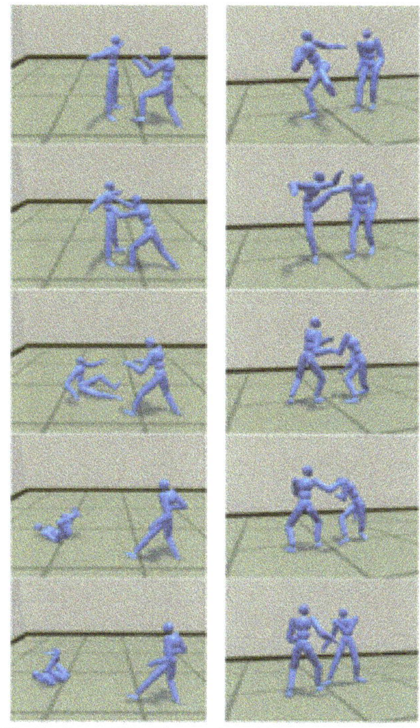

Illustration 127: Example of Mocap animation
(source: Computer Science, University of
California, Riverside

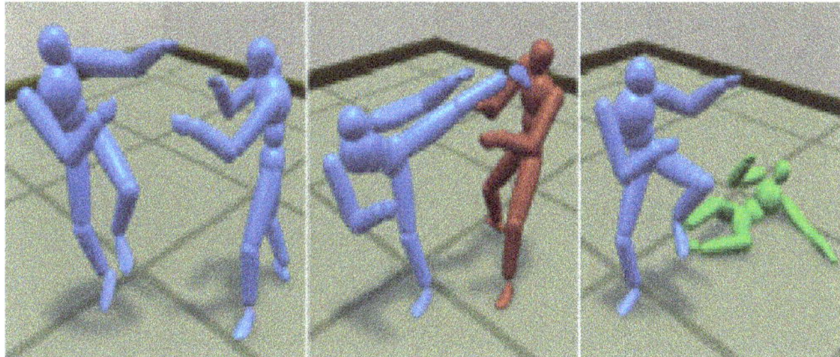

Precisions: There's «Thumb», but the other fingers are named «FingerBase» (part joined to the hand) and «HandIndex1» (fingertip, second and third part).

The illustration 128 shows the different mocap steps: sensors are placed on an actor (at the right). When the date are collected, they create a scatter plots which allow to animate an armature. The armature is the support for the animation of an avatar 3D (at left).

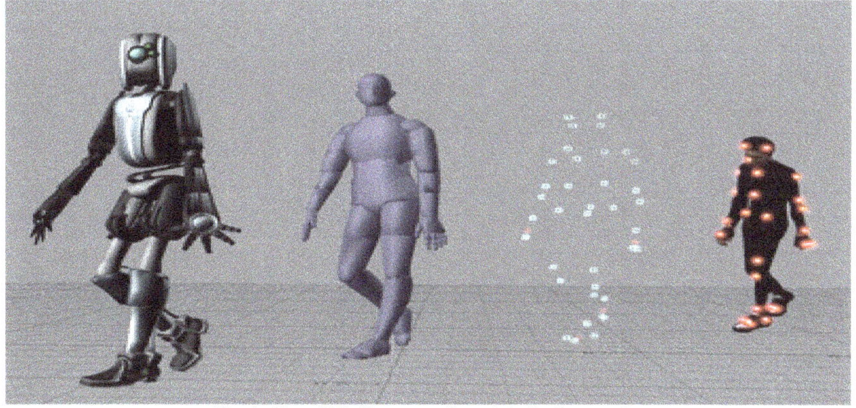

Illustration 128: From scatter plots to the avatar

Standard		Fight	
Walk	02x01	**BackKick**	87x01
Run	02x03	**FootKick**	135x11
Idle (don'thing)	77x02	**SwordFight**	02x07 à 09
Jump	02x04	**BowFire**	79x86
Pull	81x05	**GunFire**	79x96
Tract	81x05	**Die1** (Violent dead)	90x16
Climb	13x35	**Die2** (dead and fall)	90x18
Ladder	13x33	Actions	
Crouch	133x019	**Handshake**	79x06
Swim	79x02	**Wash**	02x10
Dig	79x04	**SitStandUp**	13x01
OnTheHand	85x05	**Drink**	13x07
Wheel	88x07	**Laugh**	13x14 à 16
Salto	127x24	**WashWin**	13x20
BlendLift	26x10	**SweepFloor**	13x23
WalkOverVoid	132x10	**WaitBus**	40x11
Sports		**Construction**	62x01 à 25
ModernDance	05x02 à 20	Animals	
BasketBall	06x01 à 15	**Bear**	28x11
Soccer	10x01 à 06	**Dog**	28x12
TaïChi	12x01 à 04	**Cat**	28x17
Boxing	13x17 à 18 14x01 à 03	**Snake**	28x13
Salsa	60x01 à 15	**Chicken**	28x14
Golf	64x01 à 30	**Monkey**	28x15

Tableau 1: examples of movements in the CMU bank (on 2605). Le number above, for example «90x18», means that it's the movement #18 of the subject #90.

Illustration 129: To look and download the movement, go to http://mocap.cs.cmu.edu/search.php

Recipe using the addon CMU Library Browser:

Open the user preferences («`Ctrl`+`Alt`+`U`») and activate the 3 following addons:
- «Import-Export: C3D Graphics Labs Motion Capture Files (.c3d)»,
- «Import-Export: Acclaim Motion Capture Files (.asf,.amc)»
- «Animation: Carnegie Mellon University Mocap Library Browser» (Level «Testing»).

This addon has been developed by **Daniel Monteiro Basso.** It's not entirely functional yet. However, it's more pleasant to use than the manual mode in which you must download the mocap files before import them.

Using it makes possible to automatically download BVH animations: select the subject in the «CMU Mocap Subject Browser» panel, then select the movement in «CMU Mocap Motion Browser» and click on «Import Motion Data». An animated armature is downloaded.

Before downloading the movement, we can see the **movie** clicking on «Download and Open Movie».

We can work directly with the scatter plots from the sensors by clicking on «Download and Import Marker Cloud».

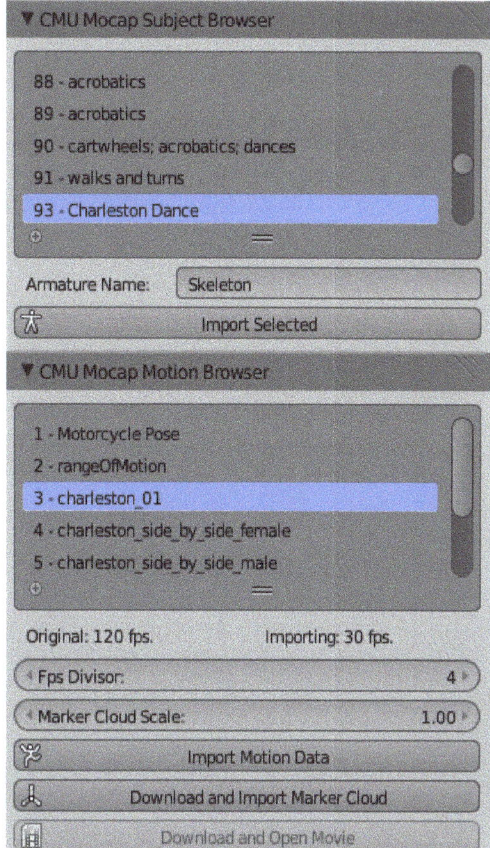

Illustration 130: Addon CMU Library Browser

IV.7. MODEL A CHARACTER WITH «MAKE HUMAN»

Purpose:

Model a human in a realistic way is not easy. If you know particularly animation or programming, you'll need some models. To customize a character, it could be hard excepted if you are a pro in modeling. A free tool and «Open Source» can help you.

MakeHuman is a **3D modeling software for human bodies.** MakeHuman has a simple interface to generate a human body based on general criteria like gender, muscles, weight, skin color or age. It allows to refine separately each part of the body with nearly 1200 modifiers and to modify the model pose with the bone system. Recent developments allow to model the faces and the clothes too.

It's a good product which rapidly evolves with time.

Among the Makehuman functionality:
- create some characters: males, female, androgynous or humanoids (aliens, mutants, etc.)
- the autoskinning allows to freely place the models from Makehuman in customized poses.
- the expression tool allows to create several expressions like angry, surprise, hate, fear, seduction, etc.
- an UV map High Definition of the entire body.
- The export to format..mhx (Blender exchange)

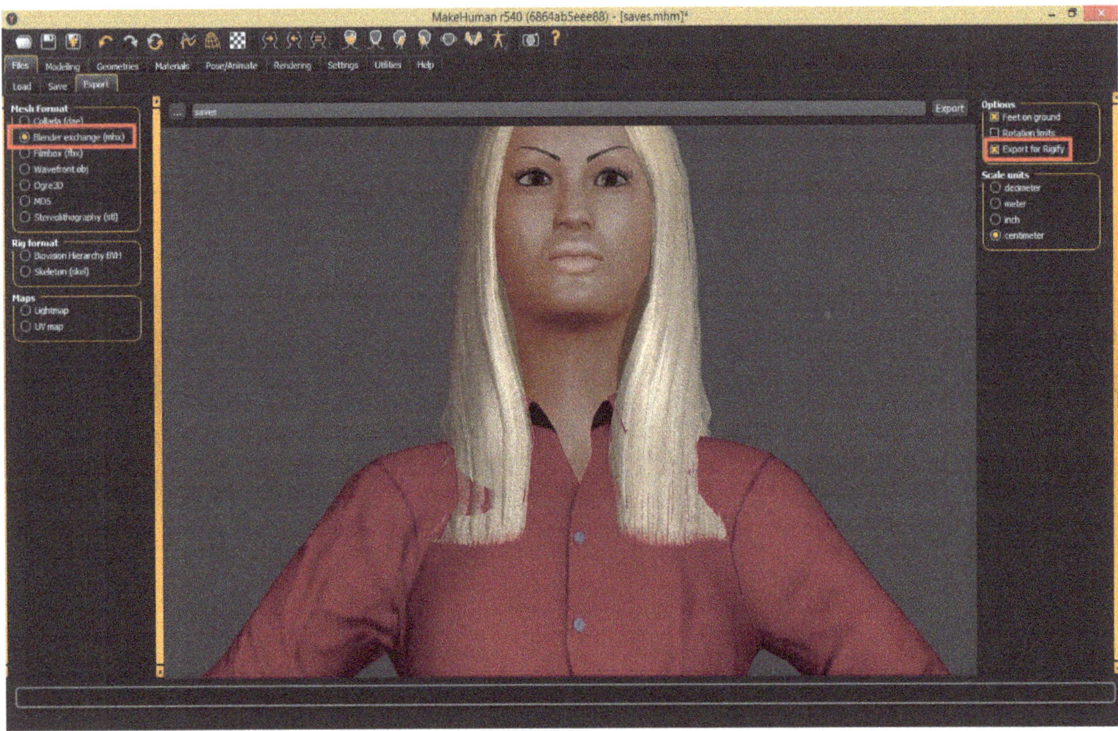

Illustration 131: MakeHuman: exportation in format mhx (with Rigify option)

Recipe:

1. Download the software «MakeHuman» from http://www.makehuman.org/. Install the software and launch it.

2. On Blender, activate the addon allowing to import projects from MakeHuman: open the user preferences «[Ctrl]+[Alt]+[U]», «Addon» Tab, «category»: «Import-Export», check the addon «Import MakeHuman (.mhx)». In the «Files» Tab, make sure that «Auto Run python script» is checked. Click on «Save User Settings» and close the window.

3. The software proposes a standard character, androgynous, which we can modify the characteristics. The different panel of the «Modeling» Tab, from «Main» to «Measure» must be looked at, they are necessary steps for model a character:
   - «Main»: genre (man, woman and the variations), size, muscles, type characteristics: African, Asiatic, Caucasian.
   - «Gender»: female characteristics like breast and male like testicles.
   - «Face»: characteristics of visage, in modeling.
   - «Torso»: torso, hips, buttocks, etc.
   - «Arms and Legs»: to modify arms and legs!
   - «Measure»: mensuration

4. Then, «Geometry» Tab (not for the color!):
   - «Cloths»: clothing the character. The bank proposed is not yet supplied, but we can imagine that the next versions will propose a lot of clothes.
   - «Eyes»: for games, use a «Lowpoly» model.
   - «Hair»: hair size and hairstyle.
   - «Teeth»: their aspect
   - «Genitals»: allows to add or not a sex
   - «Topologies»: Refine the geometry object mesh to improve the morphing.
   - «Eyebrows»: add eyebrows, with several models
   - «EyeLashes»: eyelashes more or less long
   - «Tongue»: to add a tongue

5. Go to the «Materials» Tab:
   - «Human»: Modify the skin, eyes, hair **texture** and **color** from several models,
   - «Clothes»: textures for clothes

6. Go to the «Pose/animate» panel: several armature models are proposed: the finer for complexes animations. A model «Game» with 32 bones may be useful for numerous animations. The models «second life» don't have any bone for the fingers.

7. Now, the model is ready to be animated with Blender (Illustration 143). «File» Tab, «Export» panel, select «Blender Exchange (.mhx)» in «Mesh Format» and check «Export for rigify» in Options (at right), then click on «[...]» to choose the emplacement and the name of the exported model, click on «export».

8. Go to Blender, menu «Files» → «Import» → «MakeHuman (.mhx)» and select the model realized.

9. Ensure to be in GLSL display and to have an adapted light, and test the model ([P]). There a transparency problems. If some objects (eyes for example) emerge, uncheck «Transparency» on the skin material. If the eyebrows are not good, set on «Alpha Blend» and not «Opaque». In a few minutes, the model is correct.

10. If the addon «Rigify» is activated (recipe IV.4), we obtain a manipulable model very easily like on Illustration 132. It's possible to transfer the CMU Mocap animations thanks to the addon CMU Library Browser (recipe IV.6).

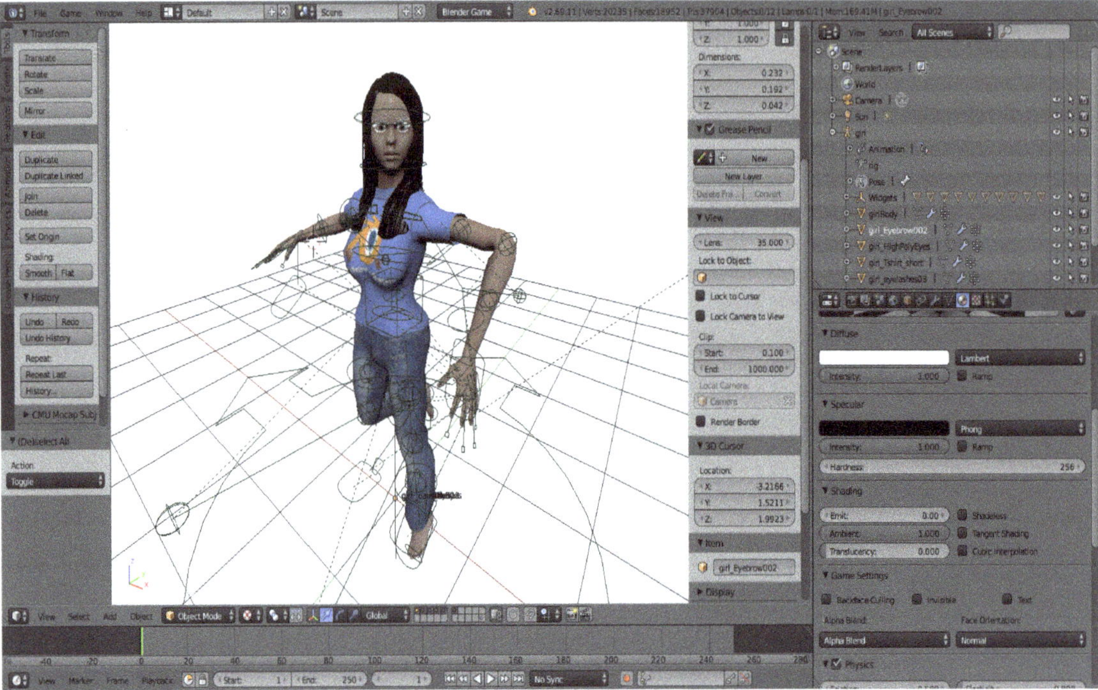

Illustration 132: The model animated with Rigify

MakeHuman is linked to Blender and propose numerous tools in the form of plugging for Blender :

MakeTarget	To create personalized morphing
MakeClothes	To create clothes
MakeWalk basic workflow	To help for retargeting mocap files (.bvh files) on a given bone
MakeWalk utilities	For actions management, t-pose, etc.

IV.8. ADD CLOTHES AND OTHER SOFT BODIES

Purpose:

Model a «Lara Croft» with a long hair plaits which can do a semicircular movement when the character turns back.

We can animate the hair plaits with some key-images and integrate it in the game logic. However, it's difficult to plan all the possibilities and it'll often be unrealistic. This first solution is a good compromise because it needs little resources.

There's another solution which allows to, for example, equip the character with a **cape which whirls around him since the fights, use some soft bodies**. The following recipe gives an example.

Recipe:

1. Add a plane (`Shift`+`A` → «Mesh» → «Plane») and subdivide it («W» → «Subdivide») 10 times, then a second time to have a mesh finer

2. Do a «triangulate» («`Ctrl`+T») to obtain some triangular faces

3. Recalculate the «Normals» («`Ctrl`+`N`»)

4. If you resize, don't forget to apply the modifications (in object mode «`Ctrl`+`A`» → «Scale»)

5. «Properties» Window → «Physic» Tab (Game Engine) → «Physics Type»: «Soft Body» / «Threshold»: 0.0015 / «Linear Stiffness»: 0.269 / «Friction»: 0.430 / «Margin» ; 0.15

6. Lean it 10 degrees and place an object bellow it (Z axis) with type «Physics»: «Static» and a «Collision Bounds» checked with «Convex Hull» type (like Suzanne)

7. We obtain a fabric which is deformed by contact with the bellow object and with the gravity like on illustration 124.

8. By applying a «**cluster collisions**», we obtain a bounce effect («rigid to soft body» and «soft to soft body»).

For hair plaits or a cape, just add some constraints.

Illustration 133: Soft-body deformation with the cluster collisions

IV.9. CONTROL THE CHARACTER'S MOVEMENTS

Purpose:

You have a character correctly rigged. Several animations are defined: walk, run, jump, shoot, Idle. How to **use directly these elements in BGE** ? And how to mix the animations?

Technique:

A character is the set of some elements:

- An invisible **physical object** («collision object») representing the object in the physics engine. It's an oversimplification of the character (sphere or cube). It's possible to use a «substitution mesh» too, invisible, representing the character more simply. Its geometry will be used for the collision calculations («collision bounds»: «triangle mesh» for example). At any time, BGE allows to substitute a mesh for another thanks to the actuator «Edit Object» with type «Replace Mesh», it distinguishes the object in its physical form from its geometrical form.

- An invisible **armature** («skeleton») is a base for the character animation and is parented to the physical object. To this armature are joined one or more **actions**.

- One or more **geometries**, parented to the armature. Based on the needs, the character can be declined with several clothes or forms, displayed or not. These geometries must be configured in «Ghost» or «No collision» in physics.

- Some invisible **anchors points** («Bone Hooks»), in most cases, «empties» parented with a particular bone. They allow for example, since the game, to give a sword to the character or to substitute it by a gun. The anchor points allow too to add some particular collision trigger (ex: on the bumper of a car or at the extremity of the cat's whiskers).

- A set of **scripts** and **logic bricks** represents the character's behavior.

When character is good, it's possible to import it in any scene: it recovers automatically all the elements above and it's directly functional.

Recipe:

1. Import in the scene a «rigged» model (**recipes IV.3 and IV.4**), and the walk, run, jump and Idle animations. To integrate more movements like crawl, tow, pull, fight, use a bow, etc., see the game project #7.

2. Add a cube (Illustration 134), name it «**Player**», center on the character and resize the cube at the character size (we create a «Bounding Box»). Then apply the modifications («`Ctrl`+`A`» → «Apply» → «Scale») so that the physics engine can receive the data.

3. **Parent the armature to «Player»** (Select the armature, then Player, and `Ctrl`+`P` →» Parent to Object»). Move the armature in the «Bounding Box» if it's not there.

4. Select the armature, go to the «Properties» Window, «Physics» Tab, «Physic Type»: Select «**No Collision**»

5. Select «Player» and in the same way, apply to it a physique «**Dynamics**» type (in the following, we explain why we don't use «Character»). Check «Actor» and «Invisible», and keep the rest like it's. Check «Collision Bounds» and for «Bounds»: Select «Box».

All the position and forces application modifications should be applied to the object «Player» and all the animations to the armature.

Illustration 134: «Bounding Box» around the character to manage the collisions

To move forward the character:

1. Select «Player» and go to «Logic Editor». Add a «Keyboard» sensor, name it «**MoveForward**», check «Activate on True Level Triggering» and set the frequency at 0. Choose a key for move forward.

2. Add a «Motion» actuator, name it «MoveForward», «Motion Type»: «Simple Motion», «Loc» «X»: 0.10 (make sure that the X axis correspond to the direction in front of the character, else, change the axis), check «L» then indicate that we use the character «local» axis, which don't change when we rotate the character.

3. Link the sensor with the 2 actuators by an «AND» controller. The character is now able to move forward, but without a walking animation.

4. Select the armature, and add the same sensor than precedent, name it too «MoveForward».

5. Add an «Action» actuator, name it «**ActionForward**», mode «Loop Stop», check «Continue» and select the action corresponding to the walk and fill «start frame» (first animation frame) and «end frame» (last frame). Set «priority» to 1 (there will be more or less priority actions, we'll see that later).

6. Link the sensor with the actuator. The character can now move forward **while walking.**

To rotate the character:

7. Select «Player» and add a «Keyboard» sensor, name it «**TurnRight**», check «Activate on True Level Triggering» and set the frequency to 0. Choose a key to turn right.

8. Add a «Motion» actuator, name it«TurnRight», «Motion Type»: «Simple Motion», «Rot» «Z»: -3°, check «L».

9. Link the sensor with the actuator. The character can **Turn Right** that it's walking or stopping.

10. Repeat the 3 last steps to turn left with «**TurnLeft**»).

So that the character seems to walk when turning, we can add the same sensors to the armature and link them to the actuator «MoveForward».

To walk up stairs:

The character can't walk up stairs, its physics collides with the one of the object «stairs». (Illustration 135)

11. Select «Player», «Properties» window, «Physics» Tab, «Collision Bounds» panel, increase «**Margin**» to 0.5. The character can now walk up stairs with 0.5 units or less.

12. Select the armature and go to the «Logic Editor». Add a «Ray» sensor, name it «**RayStairs**», «Property»: «stairs», «axis»: «-Z axis» (face down), «range»: 5.00 (don't have to be precise).

13. Add an «Action» actuator, name it «**ActionClimb**», with «Loop Stop» type, check «Continue» and select select the corresponding action while fill «frame start» and «frame end». Set «priority» at 1 (the same as for the walk), but to mix this action with the walk, use a different animation layer: «Layer»: 1 and «Layer Weight»: 0.45. Link the sensor with the actuator.

14. Select the stairs, and add them a **property «stairs»** so as they are detected by the precedent sensor.

To run:

15. Select «Player» and add a «Keyboard» sensor, name it «**Run**», check «Activate on True Level Triggering» and set the frequency at 0. Choose a key for running. It's possible to use the same key as the one to walk and add like «First Modifier» the key «⇧ Shift». So, when the player will press «⇧ Shift» the character will run.

16. Add a «Motion» actuator, name it «Run», «Motion Type»: «Simple Motion», «Loc» «X»: 0.25, check «L».

17. Link the sensor with the actuator

18. Select the armature, and add the same sensor as before, name it «Run» too.

19. Add an «Action» actuator, name it «ActionRun», mode «Loop Stop», check «Continue», select the action corresponding to the walk and fill «start frame» and «end frame», «layer»: 1 (to not have conflict with the walk animation).

20. Link the sensor with the actuator. The character can now **run**.

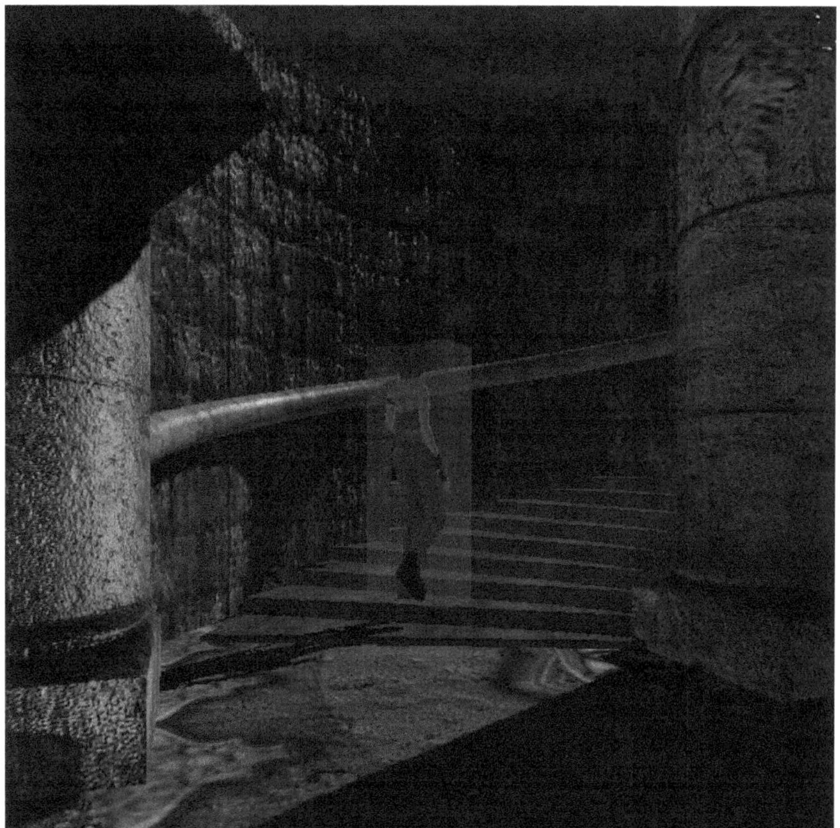

Illustration 135: Character walking up the stairs thanks to Margin of «collision Bounds» and with a posture thanks to the sensor «RayGround»

Mode «wait» (IDLE):

21. Select the armature and add an «Always» sensor, name it «AlwaysIDLE», check «Activate on True Level Triggering» ans set the frequency at 5 for example.

22. Add an «Action» actuator, name it «ActionIDLE», mode «Loop Stop», check «Continue», select the action corresponding to **mode waiting (IDLE)** and fill «start frame» and «end frame». Position «Blending» at 10 (the transition between a walk action and this will take 10 images – there will be morphing) and set «Priority» at 3. So, the walk gets always priority over the waiting mode, we reserve 2 intermediates levels for the needs.

23. Link the sensor with the actuator. The character, from the beginning, is waiting. When the player press «move forward» key, the character walks immediately. When the character stops, it takes 10 frames to be in Idle mode.

To jump:

24. Select «Player» and add a «Keyboard» sensor, name it «**Jump**», check «Activate on True Level Triggering» and set the frequency at 50 to avoid that this key's taken into account for each frame. It needs 50 frames before the key is tested again.

25. Add a «Ray» sensor, name it «**RayGround**», axis «-Z axis», «range»: -4. The distance «range» begins with the object. The idea is to allow to manage the jump impulsion, more or less strong

according to the time while the key is pressed. Then, with a distance superior at the one with the ground, it's possible to modulate this impulsion.

26. Add a «Motion» actuator, type: «Simple Motion», «force»: (100,0,350), check «L». The force depends on the character mass, here, it's a jump particularly strong for a character with a mass 1.00 ! But the game often needs we exaggerate the reality for fun. Later, we'll choose a less strong force to lower jump...

27. Add a «Message» actuator, name it «ActionJump», «To»: Select the armature, «Subject»: write «jump». Use this message to avoid to use a sensor with «ray» type, like the precedent. When the armature recipe the message, the animation is induced.

28. Link the sensors with the actuators using an «And» controller.

29. Select the armature and add a «Message» sensor, name it «ActionJump», «Subject»: «jump».

30. Add an «Action» actuator, name it «ActionJump», mode «Loop End», select the action corresponding to the jump and fill «start frame» and «end frame». Position «Blending» at 5 and set «Priority» at 0 (jump is a priority). «Layer»: 1 and «Layer Weight»: 0.50. So, if the character walks during its jump, the 2 animations are mixed equally.

31. Link the sensor with the actuator.

For a character which fall back more quickly:

32. We could modify the gravity in the physic engine but this gravity would be applied to all the objects. When a character does big jumps, we want he fall back more quickly, for fun. To do that, apply to it an artificial force. However, be careful to not conflict with the physique that allow to walk up stairs by successive collisions.

33. Select «Player» and add an «Always» sensor, name it «**Gravity**», check «Activate on True Level Triggering» and set the frequency at 10.

34. Add a «Ray» sensor, name it «**RayStairs**», «Property»: «stairs», «axis»: «-Z axis» (points down), «range»: 5.00 (like the armature)

35. Add an «Expression» controller and enter «Gravity AND NOT RayStairs»

36. Link the 2 sensors with the controller.

37. Add a «Motion» actuator, name it «Gravity», «Type»:«Simple Motion», «Force» «Z»: «-50.0». Uncheck «L».

38. Link the precedent controller with the actuator.

39. Add an «AND» controller, link it with the «RayStairs» sensor.

40. Add a «Message» actuator, name it «ActionClimb», «To»: select the armature and «Subject»: fill «climb».

41. Link the controller with the actuator.

42. Select the armature and modify the sensor with «Ray» type «RayStairs» in «Message», name it «ActionClimb», «subject»: «climb».Select «Player» and add an «Always» sensor, name it «**Gravity**», check «Activate on True Level Triggering» and set a frequency at 10.

43. Add a «Ray» sensor, name it «**RayStairs**», «Property»: «stairs», «axis»: «-Z axis» (points down), «range»: 5.00 (like the armature)

44. Add an «Expression» controller and set «Gravity AND NOT RayStairs»

45. Link the 2 sensors with the controller.

46. Add a «Motion» actuator, name it «Gravity», «Type»:«Simple Motion», «Force» «Z»: «-50.0». Uncheck «L».

47. Link the precedent controller to the actuator.

48. Add a controller with «AND» type, link it to the sensor «RayStairs».

49. Add a «Message» actuator, name it «ActionClimb», «To»: select l'armature and «Subject»: enter «climb».

50. Link the controller with the actuator.

51. Select the armature and modify the sensor with «Ray» type «RayStairs» in «Message», name it «ActionClimb», «subject»: «climb».

To crouch:

To allow the character to crouch and to walk in this position, we need to define a key to crouch and a key to get up.

52. Add the following script lines to the script «character.py»

53. Select «Player» and add a property «**crouching**» with «boolean» type, unchecked (False).

54. Add a «Keyboard» sensor, name it «**CrouchON**», check «Activate on True Level Triggering» and choose a frequency: 50. Choose a key to crouch.

55. Add a «Property» actuator, name it «CrouchON», «Mode»: «Assign», «Property»: Select «crouching», «Value»: «True».

56. Add an «Action» actuator, name it «ActionCrouch», mode «Loop Stop», check «Continue», select the corresponding action and specify «start» and «end». The action gets priority, keep everything else at 0. This actuator is called when the player wants the character crouches, when the key is pressed.

57. Link the sensor with the actuators by an «AND» controller.

58. Repeat the steps for the sensor and the actuator «**CrouchOFF**». The only difference is that the property is «False» and the controller is not joined to an «Action» actuator.

59. Add a «Property» sensor, name it «**CrouchToggle**», «Evaluation Type»: «Changed», «Property»: Select «crouching». When the crouching value change, the sensor is activated.

60. Add a «Python» controller, select «Module» and enter «character.crouch». Link the sensor with the controller.

Script python «character.py»:

```python
import bge

def crouch(cont):
    own = cont.owner
    scene = bge.logic.getCurrentScene()

    if own["crouching"]:
        scene.objects["Player"].position.z -= 0.1
        scene.objects["Player"].worldScale = [4,1.1,0.4]
        own.worldScale = [1,1,1]
    else:
        scene.objects["Player"].position.z += 1
        scene.objects["Player"].worldScale = [1,1,1]
        own.worldScale = [1,1,1]
```

This script allows to **change the «Player» form**, (character bulk) when there are collisions (Illustration 136).

The position modification allow to the character to reposition itself in space without going through the ground due to the scale.

To valid the sate «crouch»:

61. Transform the controller joined to the sensor «AlwaysIDLE» in «expression» and enter «AlwaysIDLE AND NOT crouching»

62. Idem for walk and run: «Run AND NOT Crouching», «MoveForward AND NOT Crouching».

63. Add a controller with «expression» type and enter «MoveForward AND crouching», then, link it with the sensor «MoveForward» and to the actuator «ActionCrouch». The character can now move in a «crouch way».

The state «crouch» is managed thanks to a variable and some conditions, using the controller «Expression». We could create a state «crouch» through a logic layer.

Illustration 136: Character squatting in a tunnel, its bounding box is adapted

Differences between «Blending/Priority» and «animation Layer»:

It's very important to understand the difference between these 2 elements:

- **«Blending/Priority»** correspond to the number of necessary images for the **transition of an action into another**. The higher the «priority» value is, the less priority the action is. The precedent example corresponds to the phase «IDLE», less important than the other animations. As the action is launched by an «Always» sensor, it's important to clarify that it's not the priority, otherwise, the other animations will not work.

- **«Layer»** is the animation layer. It allows to use **simultaneously several animations**: like «walk» and «raise arm». If we use the «Blending», we can only go from one to the other, we can't do they work simultaneously. «Layer Weight» allows to manage the cases when the same elements are asked by the 2 animations working simultaneously. If we precise «0.50», the 2 animations influence the movement in the same way (50%). This influence is always defined from a layer N-1 to a layer N: it's the influence percentage from the precedent layer on the precedent.

<u>Type «Character» vs «Dynamic»</u>

This recipe uses the physique **«Dynamics»** type. We could to take the **«Character»** type.

The advantage of this type is:
- the character walks up the stairs automatically according to the defined setting («step height», the height max of the stairs)
- and the jump only requires 2 parameters («Jump Force», and «Fall Speed Max» the speed on which the character falls). There's a button **«Jump»** in the actuator «Motion». For simpler games, this type is sufficient, but it's not enough configurable in Python (only 3 functions: «onGround()» returns «True» if the character is on the ground, «gravity», a modifiable value to accelerate the fall of the character and «jump()» to...jump!!!!).

Now, this type is **not enough accomplished**, but you must monitor it, it's an interesting shortcut. Instead, we use the «Dynamic» type in which we add some logic bricks to obtain the same result, but more configurable.

IV.10. POINT, CLICK AND MOVE

Purpose:

To realize an adventure game in «point & click», we need to be able to displace the character by clicking anywhere in the scene.

Recipe:

The `recipe V.12` allows to move a character towards an object looking for the shortest route with a Navigation Mesh. This recipe has all the ingredients to move the character.

The `recipe VI.8` allows to display the mouse cursor and to select objects with the mouse. We need principally to determine the exact point where the mouse is in contact with an object, and if this point correspond to a zone where the character can go.

1. Repeat the `recipe V.12` («simple decor»): project to reuse entirety
2. Remove the «green sphere» and add an «Empty» (with «Sphere» type for example), name it «Waypoint», its position is no important (place in [0,0,0] for example).
3. Repeat the `recipe VI.8` to add a graphic cursor («MouseCursor») and a camera.
4. Select the «red sphere», name it «player» and go to «Logic Editor»
5. Add a property «useWaypoint» with Boolean type, unchecked. This variable will help us to determine if the player must move towards the selected object.
6. Modify the actuator with «Steering» type: for «Target Object», select «Waypoint»
7. Add a «Property» sensor, «Evaluation type»: «Equal», select «useWaypoint» and «Value»: 1. Link the sensor with the controller «And». So, the «Steering» mode only takes place when the «useWaypoint» value is positive.
8. Select «CursorMouse» and add a «Mouse» sensor, name it «MouseClick», «Mouse Event»: Select «Left Button».
9. Add a «Mouse» sensor, name it «MouseFloor», «Mouse Event»: «Move Over Any».
10. Add a «Python» controller, select «Module» and «Value»: «character.moveTo»
11. Link the 2 sensors with the controller.
12. Add a new file text, name it «character.py» and paste the following script lines.
13. Add a property «floor» with «boolean» type, check it, at each objects in the decor and on which we can walk. here, there's only the «plane».

Script python «character.py»:

```python
import bge

def moveTo(cont):
    mouseclick = cont.sensors["MouseClick"]
    mousefloor = cont.sensors["MouseFloor"]

    if mouseclick.positive and mousefloor.positive:
        hitobj = mousefloor.hitObject
        if not "floor" in hitobj:
            return
        hitpos = mousefloor.hitPosition
        scene = bge.logic.getCurrentScene()
        player = scene.objects["Player"]
        waypoint = scene.objects["Waypoint"]
        waypoint.worldPosition = hitpos
        print (hitpos)
        player["useWaypoint"] = True
```

IV.11.   NPC BEHAVIOR

Purpose:

The No-Player Characters (NPC) are characters that the player can't control. According to the game type, these characters stay in IDLE (mode waiting), run over the player to kill him, to help him, or go about one's business. You choose and program this behavior!! The BGE provides only several functions as for a tracking mission, an escape mode and a capacity to move from a point to another using the shortest way.

Example:

Example: the `recipe V.9` allows to define some navigation node for a Path Follow. With this technique, it's possible to create a patrol path. When it gets to the last control point, the guard takes a break before to take a new watch tour. Thanks to another sensor, the «Radar» sensor (`recipe V.7`), this guard can be alerted by the player presence. We can add a «ray» sensor in front of the player's character too. With this, the character will not be seen if it's hidden behind an object. When the guard detects the player, he can alert the other guards (with a «Message» actuator for example). The guard state goes from «patrol» to «chase the player». The other guards can use the «Path Finding» of the `recipe V.13` to join the point from where the alert was launched and to be in «vigilant» state. After a given time period, it returns to patrol mode. The guard which follows the player can, at a certain distance (sensor «Near»), take the «ranged attack» state and shoot at the player. When the guard life is bellow a certain value, the guard turns in escape mode and go in the opposed direction. Etc.

This behavior is named characters A.I.(Artificial Intelligence). That's an overused word in this case, but some games need some complex behaviors, like Sims for example.

This behavior is represented by the Illustration 137. Each arrow corresponds to a transition from a state to another. These transitions are managed by rules.

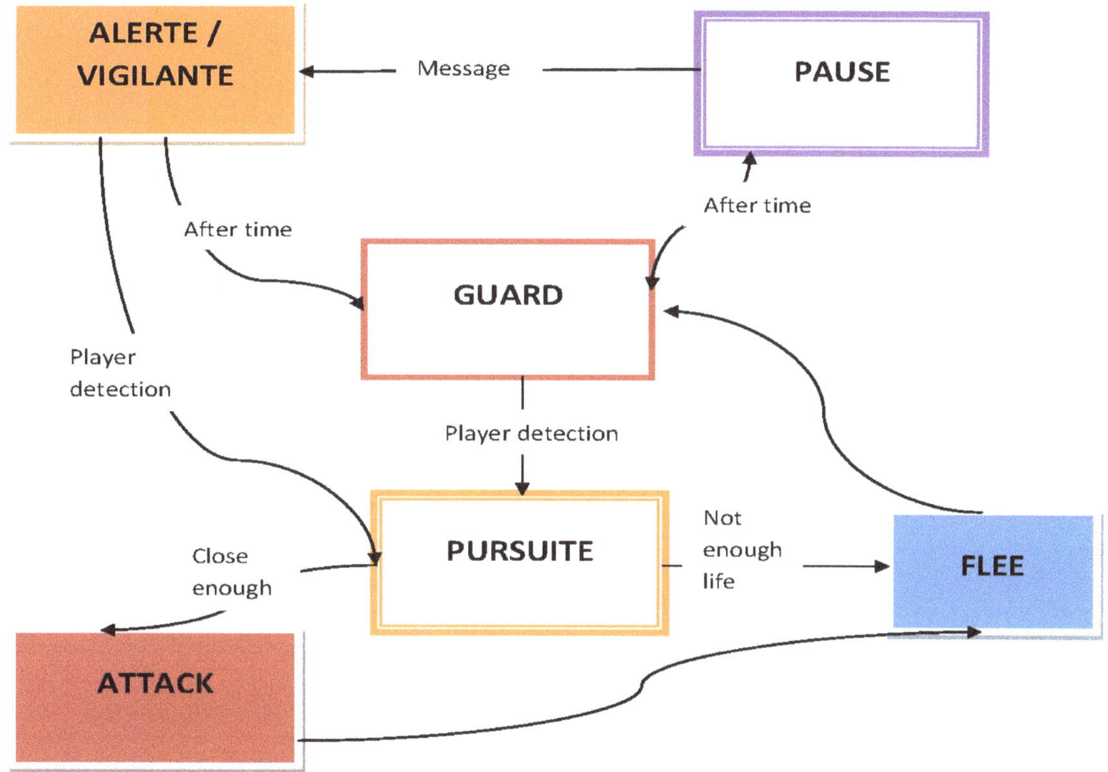

Illustration 137: Example of NPC guard behavior

Script vs Logic Bricks:

Thanks to **logic bricks**, it's possible to program the characters A.I. Each layer can correspond to a particular state («wait», «patrol», «fight», «chase», «escape»). Each rule consists in using sensors, controllers and actuators. However, it's quickly becoming an intricate project when the number of rules increases. At this point, best in using a script.

Using bricks is always quicker than developing a python script, but scripting allows to:
- create some different **behaviors for a same character model**, and dynamically change the scripts (according to the difficulty or to adapt to the player level, or using random).
- Let to players have the opportunity **to write their own scripts** and adapt the game functionality. It's very much welcome in the case of RPG: the players can program their own team A.I. for example.

With a script, simply:
- add a «property» to describe the NPC state
- use an «Always» sensor with «Activate On True Level Triggering» checked and a frequency to determinate when to launch the python script which manages the NPC behavior.
- Add all the necessary sensors to different detections (Message, Ray, Radar, Near, Collision, etc.)
- add all the necessary actuators to different actions (Message, motion, action, etc.)

Example of transition rule:

```
If (state == patrol):
        if (NEAR_PLAYER):
                state = purchase
        else
                move_to_next_navigation_node
```

The sensors and actuators names, and every developed functions, represent an API you can open to the players. Then, they'll be able to develop their own A.I., or use several behaviors developed by others.

For more complexes behaviors (as NPC capacity to learn), we can use the library **pyBrain** at the address: http://pybrain.org.

IV.12.   FROM HIGHPOLY TO LOWPOLY

Purpose:

Modeling for video games is not so easy because you must obtain a compromise between the object resolution (level of details) and the final report quality. **Modeling in Lowpoly is a solution**, but it's an artistic impoverishment. For exzample, you can't use the Blender tools like the famous «**Sculpt Mode**» studied in the **recipe III.1**.

Another solution: **directly model the character in High Resolution** (Highpoly), **extract a «normal map»** (reliefs texture) and **apply it to a simplified model of the same character** (Lowpoly). So, we obtain an object with numerous details and with an inferior geometry resolution. It's a good compromise, especially to use the Level of Details (**recipe III.17** and **VII.10**).

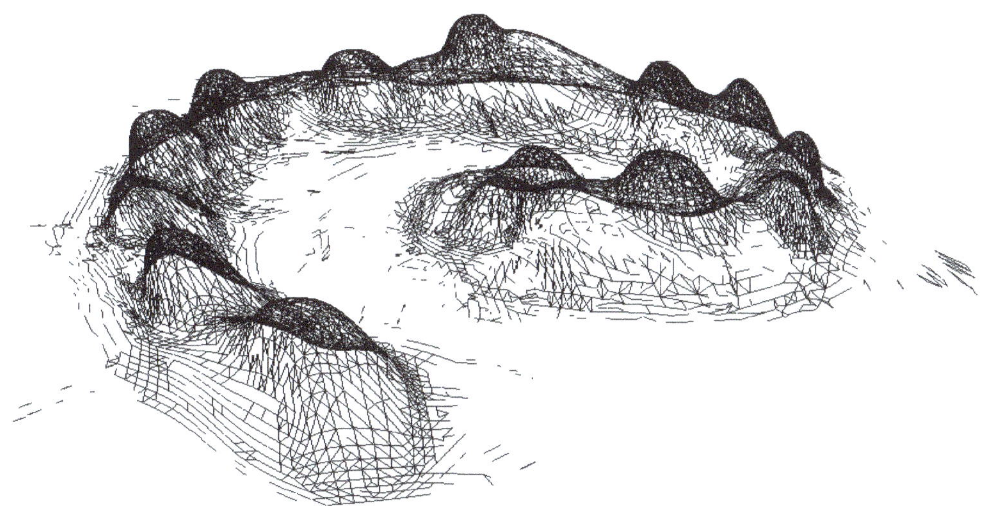

Illustration 138: Relief creation on a plane in «Sculpt Mode»

<u>Recipe:</u>

1.   Add a plane (**⬆ Shift**+**A** → «Mesh» → «Plane»)

2.   In the «3D View» window, go to «Sculpt Mode» and activate the dynamic topology («Tools» Menu, «Topology» Panel, check «Enable Dynamic»). It allows to distort the object by adding dynamically mesh.

3.   Create some relief like on Illustration 138. To use the different brushes, see the **recipe III.1**.

4.   Go to view top view mode («7»), then in «Edit Mode» (**Tab**) do an UV mapping («u» → «Project form View»).

5.   Open the «UV/Image Editor» window and add a new picture (resolution: 4096x4096), name it «NormalMap».

6.   «Properties» Window, «Render» Tab, «Bake» panel, select «Bake Mode»: «Normals» and «Normal Space»: «Object», click on the button «Bake». The picture «NormalMap» will be colored to take account the relief.

7.   Add a new plane with the same size

8.   «Properties» Window, «Materials» Tab, add a new «Material» («+»)

9.   «Textures» Tab, add a new texture with «Image or Movie» type. «Image Sampling» Panel, check «Normal Map» and select bellow «space»: «Object».

10.   «Influence» Panel, uncheck «Color». In «Geometry», check «Normal» and precise the value1.0.

The Illustration 139 shows the 2 planes viewed from above. The resemblance is uncanny, according to the different settings. For the plane which we have assign the «NormalMap», changing the angle of view, the light and the shadows seem moving, as for a real relief.

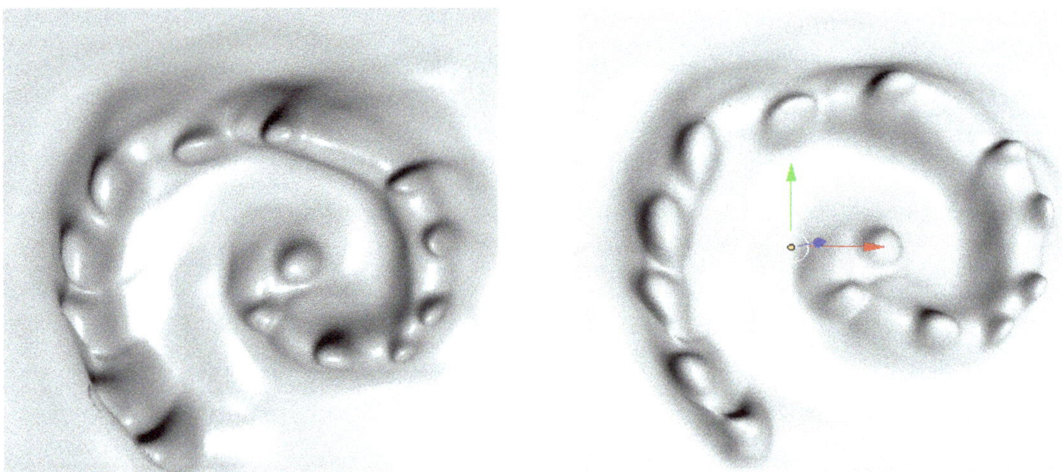

Illustration 139: At left, a simple plane (1 face) and a normal map, at right, the high resolution model

However, illusion disappears when we take a side view because object geometry has not been modified (Illustration 140). It's only a shadow effect!

Application to a character:
The example developed in this recipe is not representative of the work on a character: we can't simplify object from **50.000 faces to only 1** as in this case. But the same principle is applicable. For a character mesh, we don't use UV mapping. The assumption here is that the High Resolution Model UV coordinates are already correctly mapped. Apply « intelligently» a «modifier decimate» and make a few corrections in «Edit Mode». Fortunately, this «modifier» can work on the UV coordinates too, so the normal map generated works with the new object.

Another approach is to add some details to the «Lowpoly» model textures with this system. In that case, we directly work in the «UV/Image Editor» window in «Paint» mode. Now, it's possible to add some details with the brush.

Numerous details don't need geometry to create some realism. The most important case is the one of the **recipe VII.3**: we don't create the wall by placing brick or by digging joints in a plane! A normal map is sufficient to give the relief illusion.

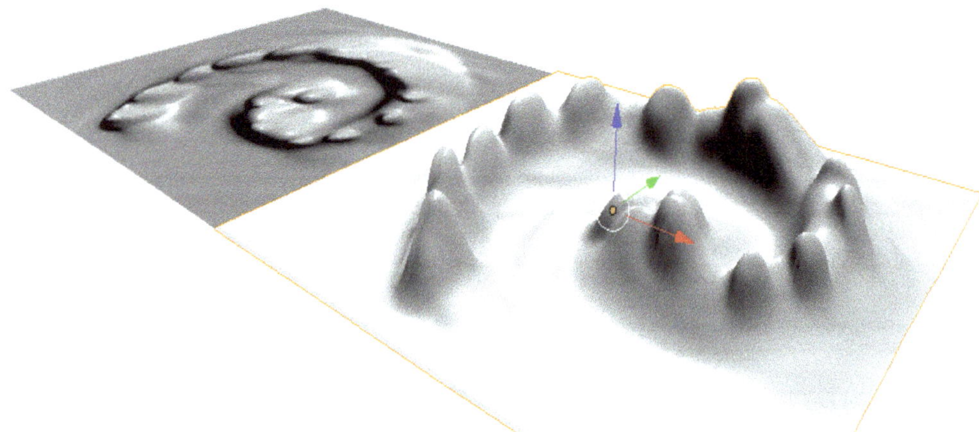

Illustration 140:The illusion disappears when we changes the point of view

However, the Illustration 140 is disappointing: in several conditions, the result is not good. If we use a normal map for an armature relief, viewed from a certain distance, it'll be good, but when the camera will be near the mesh... not as good. We know that the **object mesh is not modified**, it's only a variation of the light at each point of the texture. But it's also possible to use a **«Geometry Shader»** to modify the object mesh (Tessellation). This geometry shader increases the object resolution and use the normal map to modify the coordinates of each point of the object (not vertex). The graphics card makes all the work! And when we'll have several hundreds of units which process in parallel these modifications, the saving of time is important.

For «Geometry Shader» (sheet #8), we can have an idea by using the «Geometry/**displace»** option in the «Influence» panel for the texture. It doesn't work in GLSL, only with the Blender render. Maybe the functionality will be add to BGE through this option (precise the mesh subdivision too for the shader), when the «Geometry Shaders» will be added to BGE.

Illustration 141: Tesselation by Jacob Nielsen, these available: http://tinyurl.com/m8yz245

Create your own 3D games like pros with Blender Game Engine

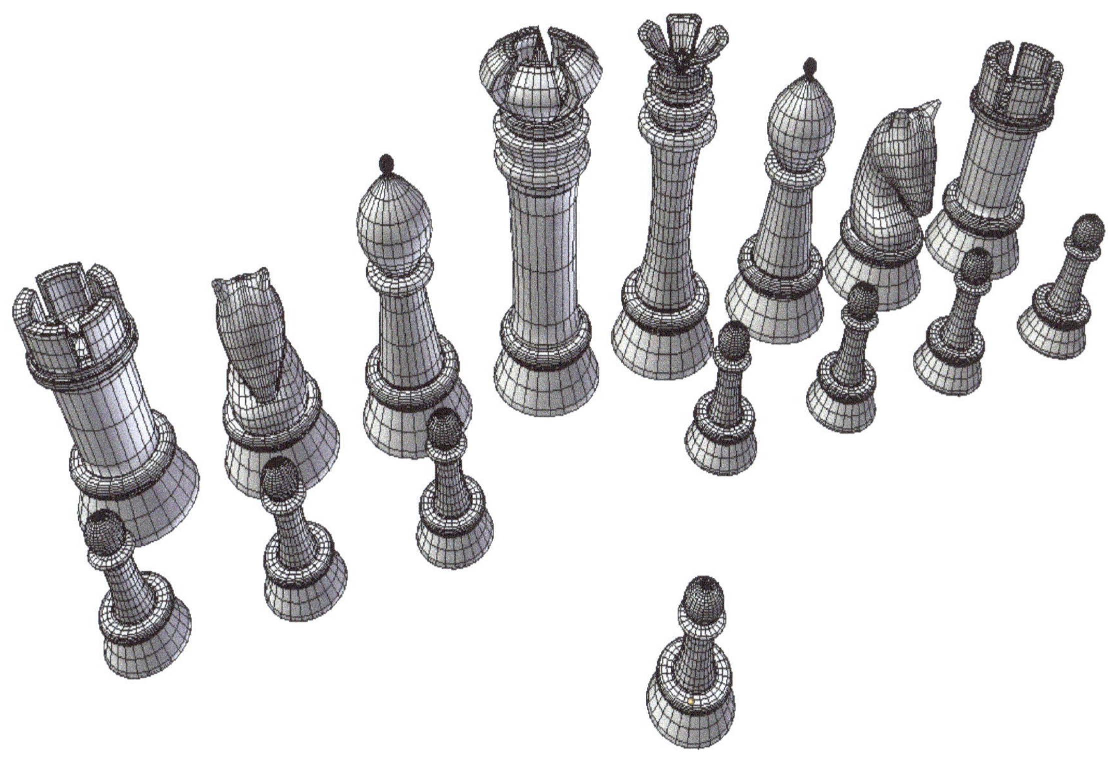

V -   GAME LOGIC RECIPES

V.1. CREATE A FREEVIEW CAMERA

Purpose:

Create a camera with a free angle like in a flight simulator.

Rotate the view in all directions with the mouse and move it with the keyboard.

Recipe (before the version 2.72):

1. Add a light, a camera (`⇧ Shift`+`A` → «Camera»), and do a 90° rotation on the X axis.
2. Add an object (ex: «Suzanne») to test the script walking around.
3. Open the «Text Editor» and create a new script, name it «mouselook.py» and copy the following script lines.
4. Select the camera and open the «Logic Editor».
5. Add a «Mouse» sensor, name it **«MouseLook»**, «Mouse Event»: «Movement».
6. Add a «Python» controller, select «Module»: and enter «mouselook.move». Link the sensor with the controller.
7. Add a «Motion» actuator, «Motion Type»:«Simple Motion» and name it **«LeftRight»**. Don't set anything, it's the script which do it.
8. Add to «Camera» (important, the only operation to do on the camera with the «Logic Editor») a «Motion» actuator, «Motion Type»: «Simple Motion», name it **«UpDown»**. Link the actuators to the precedent controller «python».
9. Add a «Keyboard» sensor, name it «Forward» and choose a key to «move forward» (ex: «Up Arrow» (key «↑»).
10. Add a «Motion» actuator, name it «Move Forward», «Motion Type»: «Simple Motion», «Loc»: «Z»: -0.10 and check «L». Link the actuator with the precedent sensor.
11. Add a «Keyboard» sensor, name it «Backward» and choose a key to «move back» (ex: «Down Arrow» (key «↓»).
12. Add a «Motion» actuator, name it «Move Backward», «Motion Type»: «Simple Motion», «Loc»: «Z»: 0.10 and check «L». Link the actuator with the precedent sensor.
13. Add a «Keyboard» sensor, name it «Left» and choose a key to «take a step to the left» (ex: «Left Arrow» (key «←»).
14. Add a «Motion» actuator, name it «Move Left», «Motion Type»: «Simple Motion», «Loc»: «X»: -0.10 and check «L». Link the actuator with the precedent sensor.
15. Add a sensor with «Keyboard»type, name it «Right» and choose a key to «take a step at right» (ex: «Right Arrow» (key «→»).
16. Add a «Motion» actuator, name it «Move Right», «Motion Type»: «Simple Motion», «Loc»: «X»: 0.10 and check «L». Link the actuator with the precedent sensor.

For the displacement axes with the keyboard, it's important to verify the camera axes. In the Illustration 142, to move forward, you must apply a positive value to Z for example.

Attention: respect the different names or adapt the script (Sensor «MouseLook», Actuator «UpDown», «LeftRight»).

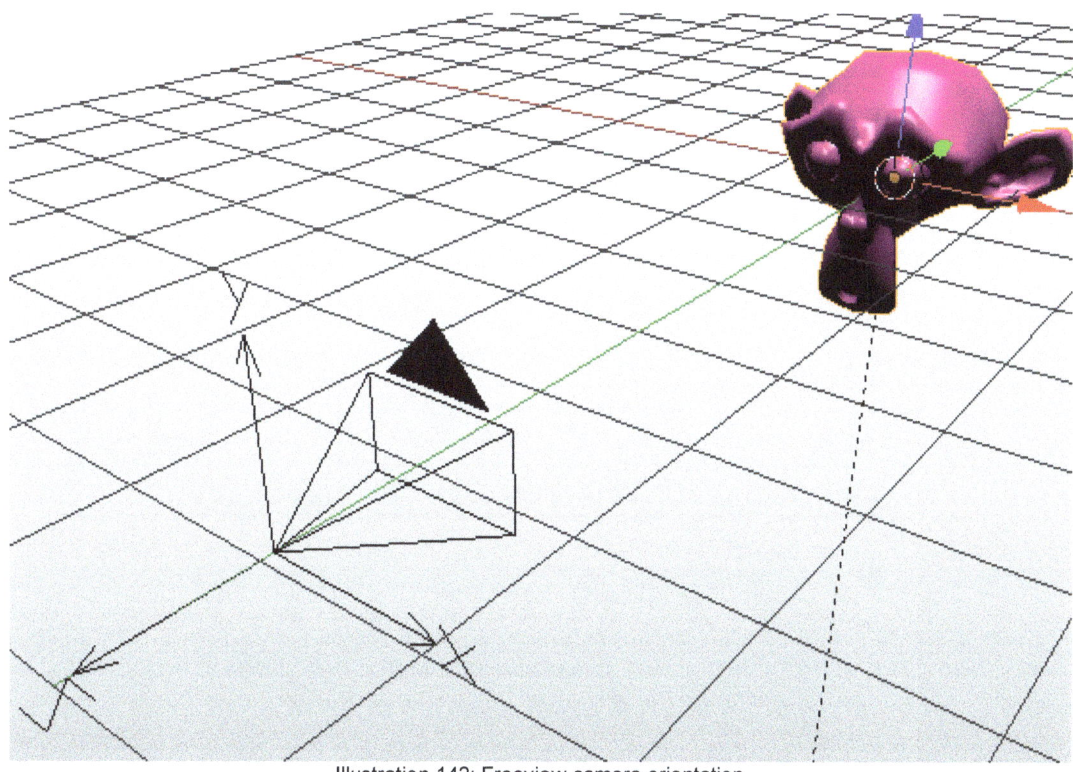

Illustration 142: Freeview camera orientation

script «Mouselook.py»:

```python
import bge

def move(cont):
    cont = bge.logic.getCurrentController()
    mouse = cont.sensors["MouseLook"]
    if (not mouse.positive):
        return

    #Default values, may be changed
    sensitivity = 0.0005
    invert = 1 # -1 to invert

    own = cont.owner
    width,height = bge.render.getWindowWidth(), bge.render.getWindowHeight()

    # distance moved from screen center
    x,y = width/2 – mouse.position[0], height/2 - mouse.position[1]
    # initialize mouse so it doesn't jerk first time
    if 'mouseInit' in own == False:
        obj['mouseInit'] = True
        x,y = 0,0
    if not mouse.positive:
        x,y = 0,0

    upDown = y * sensitivity * invert
    leftRight = x * sensitivity * invert
    act_LeftRight = cont.actuators["LeftRight"]
    act_UpDown = cont.actuators["UpDown"]
    act_LeftRight.dRot = [ 0.0, 0.0, leftRight]
    act_LeftRight.useLocalDRot = False
    act_UpDown.dRot = [ upDown, 0.0, 0.0]
    act_UpDown.useLocalDRot = True
    cont.activate(act_LeftRight)
    cont.activate(act_UpDown)

    # if cursor needs to be centered
```

```
if [x,y] != [int(width/2), int(height/2)]:
    bge.render.setMousePosition(int(width/2),int(height/2))
else:
    cont.deactivate(act_LeftRight)
    cont.deactivate(act_UpDown)
```

So, it's possible to turn around the object using the mouse or the keyboard arrows.

Recipe (version 2.72+):

This recipe is based on a script which is not needed yet because the version 2.72 introduces the notion of « mouse look » in its actuator «mouse». However, this script allows you to understand the mouse management through Python.

To obtain the same effect by using this new actuator, delete the reference to the python script link the sensor «MouseLook» to the actuator with «Mouse» type.

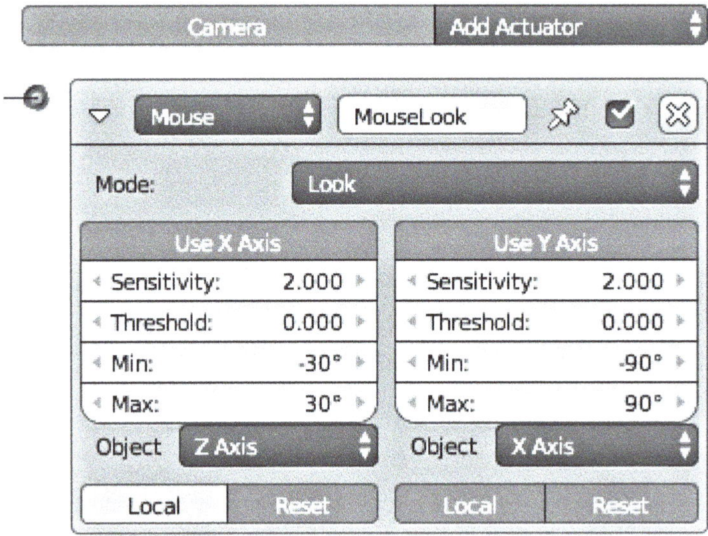

Illustration 143: Actuator "Mouse" (v2.72+)

V.2. FPS CAMERA

Purpose:

Create a «FPS» camera (First-Person Shooter) or **subjective camera** which moves with the key and is oriented with the mouse. The physique management is integrated. By using this recipe on a decor or a simple plan, it's possible to move in as well as if we were the hero in «Doom».

Recipe:

We modify the precedent recipe, but we keep the same script.

1. **Model the player** in the form of a cube (name it «player»), resize this cube to obtain the following sizes: X: 1,0 / Y: 0,5 / Z: 1,80 (medium bulk for a man, *change for an armature or a character with a different size*).

2. Add a **camera** facing cube +X, like on Illustration 144.

3. Select the camera and the object «player» and parent them (Ctrl + P → «set parent to object»).

4. Add a **plane** bellow (for dynamics tests, it'll be the ground).

5. Select the «player» object, «Properties» window, «Physics» Tab (mode «Blender Game»), «Physics Type»: Select **«Rigid Body»**, check «Invisible», then check «Lock Rotation» for X,Y, and «Lock Translation» for X,Y too.

6. Check «Collision Bounds», «Bounds»: «Box» with Margin at «0.060»

7. For keyboard, repeat steps 9 to 16 from the precedent recipe, except that we apply to the Player and not to the camera, and that the axes are modified.
   - «Move Forward» → «Loc»: «X»: 0.10
   - «Move Backward» → «Loc»: «X»: -0.10
   - «Move Left» → «Loc»: «Y»: 0.10
   - «Move Right» → «Loc»: «Y»: -0.10

8. For the other part of the logic programming, it's the same as the steps 2 to 8 of the precedent recipe– apply on the «player» object <u>excepted</u> for the actuator «UpDown» applied to the camera (it's the one) !

Improvements:

We could add the actions: to jump, to duck, to run.

We can climb a ladder or to lean on an element decor to jump higher too. As you need, you can use the «Physics: Character» type (game project #7).

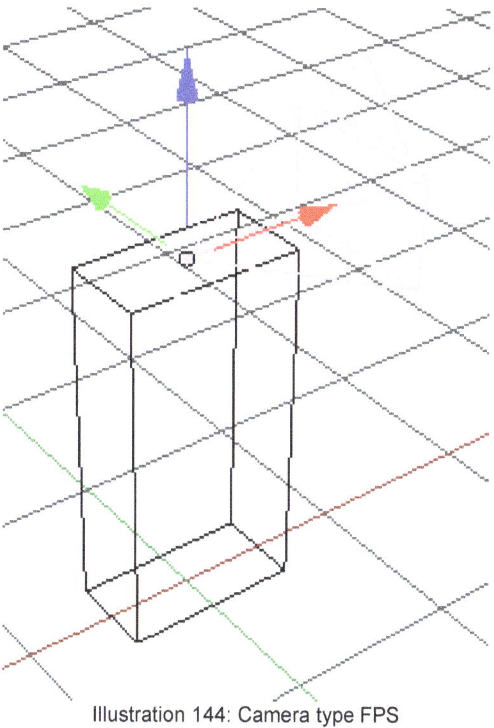

Illustration 144: Camera type FPS

V.3. DISPLAY THE MOUSE CURSOR

Purpose:

Use an image to represent **the mouse at a screen** position and follow its displacement.

Recipe(before 2.72):

1. Open the «Text Editor» window and add a new script, name it: «mouse.py»
2. Add the following lines:

```
import Rasterizer
Rasterizer.showMouse(1)
```

3. Select one of the objects in the scene (the camera for example), and go to the «Logic Editor» Window
4. Add an «Always» sensor
5. Add a «Python» controller and select thee script «mouse.py». Link the sensor with the controller

Recipe (2.72+):

Use the «mouse» actuator, mode «Visibility».

To use a configurable graphic cursor, use the recipe VI.8.

Illustration 145: Recipe VI.8 – use a graphic mouse cursor

V.4. TPS CAMERA

Purpose:

Create a camera type «TPS» (Third Personal Shooter) or objective camera. The most common example is the camera which follows the character to keep it at the view center.

Recipe #1:

The simplest way is to parent the camera to the character:

1. Create a cube (⇧ Shift + A → «Mesh» → «Cube») en (0,0,0)

2. Add a camera (⇧ Shift + A → «Camera») in (-5,0,25). Rotation (20,0,-90)

3. Select the camera and the cube, then parent them (Ctrl + P → «Set Parent to Object»

4. Select the camera, in the «Properties» window, «Object» Tab, «Relations extra» panel, check «Slow Parent» and enter offset: «200»

5. Add a displacement control to the cube object (recipe V.5)

So, the camera follows the cube with a delay (200 frames) and turn with it. If the camera is parented to only one cube vertex, **it won't follow the object rotation anymore.**

Recipe #2:

Using the «Tracking» mode:

1. Repeat the steps 1 and 2 of the precedent recipe.
2. Select the camera and go to the «Logic Editor» Window
3. Add an «Always» sensor
4. Add an «Edit Object» actuator, «Track To» and select the character or the object to follow. Set «Time» at 50 and check the option «3D» for adapt to space. Keep the default axes. Then, link the sensor with the actuator.

Recipe#3:

Using an actuator with «camera» type:

1. Repeat steps 1 and 2 of the first recipe.
2. Select the camera and go to the «Logic Editor» Window
3. Add an «Always» sensor
4. Add a «Camera» actuator, name it «FollowPlayer», «Camera Object»: «cube», «Height»: 25, «Axis»: «+X», «Min»: 15, «Max»: 30, «Damping»: 1. This last parameter correspond to the maximum number of frames for allow the camera to catch up the camera delay on the object.
5. Link the sensor with the actuator

So, the camera is placed 25 units above the character (cube), try to place along the object axis +X, and maintains a distance of between 15 and 30 max with the object.

This actuator permits finer points, but you choose the recipe according to the desired effect.

Recipe #4: To get around the obstacles with the camera

1. Open the «Text Editor» and add a new script «cam.py», paste the following script lines.

2. Setup a camera as seen in the **recipe V.3** with the actuator name: «FollowPlayer», it'll be used in the script.

3. Select the character, place the cursor on its head, add an Empty with «Cube» type, name it «camTarget».

4. Select «camTarget», then the character and go to «Edit Mode». Select 1 point situated at the top of the character skull, parent them (`Ctrl`+`P` → «Parent to Vertex»). With this mode, the empty will follow all the character displacements, but not its rotations.

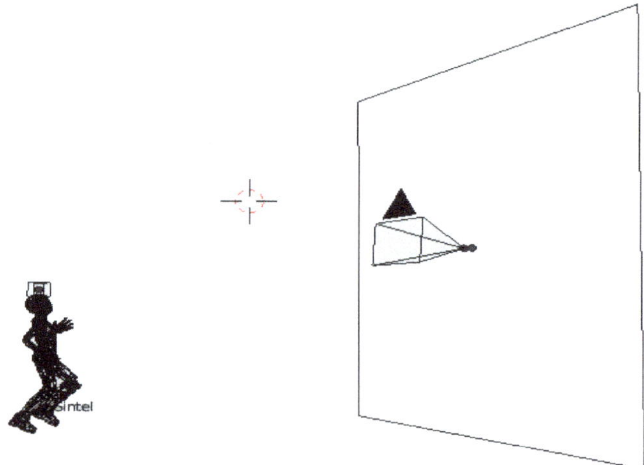

Illustration 146: System to detect the obstacles between the camera and the character

5. Go to «Object Mode». Select the camera, then «space» → «Snap cursor to Selected» to be positioned at the camera level. Add a plane, name it «camPlan» and do a rotation to have a vertical plane like in the Illustration 146.

6. Parent the plane plan to the camera by selecting the plane then the camera, `Ctrl`+`P` → «Parent to Object».

7. Select «camTarget» and open the «Logic Editor»

8. Add an «Always» sensor, check «Activate on True Level Triggering» and set the frequency at 5.

9. Add an «Edit Object» actuator, type: «Track To» and select «camPlane», «Time»: 0; check «3D». Keep the default axes.

10. Link the sensor with the actuator. «camTarget» automatically turns towards the plan.

11. Add a «Ray» sensor, name it «RayForward», «Axis»: «+Y axis», «Range»: 10000. Check «Activate on True Level Triggering» and set the frequency at 5 too.

12. Add a «python» controller, select «module» and enter «cam.obstacle»

Script «cam.py»:

```python
import bge

def obstacle(cont):
    scene = bge.logic.getCurrentScene()
    ray = cont.sensors["RayForward"]

    if ray.positive:
        hitObj = ray.hitObject
        cam = scene.objects["CameraFree"]

        if hitObj.name != "CamPlane":
            cam.worldPosition = ray.hitPosition
```

V.5. INTERACT WITH AN OBJECT USING KEYBOARD

Purpose:

Allow to the player to move an object (or the principal character) with the keyboard. The recipe is similar to those for a joystick. To use the mouse, use the **recipe V.14.**

Recipe:

1. Select the object to interact with the keyboard and go to the «Logic Editor» Window
2. Add a «Keyboard» sensor, name it «KeyLeft», key «←»
3. Repeat for «KeyRight», key «→», then «KeyForward», key «↑»
4. Add a «motion» actuator, name it «Turnleft» and specify «Rot» «Z»: «5°». Repeat for «Turnright» and specify «Rot» «Z»: «-5°»
5. Add a «motion» actuator, name it «MoveForward» and specify «Loc» «X»: «1.0»
6. Link the sensor «KeyRight» with the actuator «Turnright», the sensor «KeyLeft» with the actuator «Turnleft», and the sensor «KeyForward» with the actuator «MoveForward».

Illustration 147: Gamer's keyboards

V.6. DOORS AND TELEPORTERS

Purpose:

A character walks and arrives near of a door. He opens the door and enters...change of scenery, we are now in a cave! To optimize the speed of execution, we subdivide the decor as much as possible. In our example, the scenery and the cave are 2 distinct scenes. When you came through this door, scene is changing. This recipe explains how to manage this change of scene, position and angle.

Recipe:

1. Create a new file «Text», name it «teleport.py» and add the following script lines. Remove the comments if necessary: if we change the scene, replace «level02» by the name of the scene.

2. Add a teleporter or a door and move it into the decor. Name it «Teleport»

3. Add an «Single Arrow» Empty, name it «zone1» and move it on the decor. Ensure the empty axes correspond to the moved object axes: «player».

4. Open the «Logic Editor» and select the «Teleport» object. Add a property with «boolean» type, name «Teleport», checked. Add a second property «target», with «string» type and enter «zone1» (the name of the precedent empty)

5. Select the «player» object and add a «Collision» sensor (we could use a «ray», or a «near» also). Name it «Teleport», «Property»: «Teleport».

6. Add a «python» controller, select «Module» and enter «teleport.teleportTo»

7. To change the scene, add a «scene» actuator, «mode»: «Set Scene» and select the scene in which the object must be teleported.

8. Link the sensor with the controller, and the controller with the actuator if necessary.

9.

Script teleport.py (addition):

```python
import bge

def teleportTo(cont):
    senstelep = cont.sensors["Teleport"]
    if not senstelep.positive:
        return
    own = cont.owner
    teleport = senstelep.hitObject
    zone = teleport["target"]

    #if no scene changing uncomment below
    #scene = bge.logic.getCurrentScene()

    #if change scene to «level02» uncomment below
    # scenes = bge.logic.getSceneList()
    # scene = [scene for scene in scenes if scene.name == "level02"][0]
    zoneObj = scene.objects[zone]
    own.position = zoneObj.position
    own.worldOrientation = zoneObj.worldOrientation
```

For the doors opening when the player approaches, see the following recipe.

V.7. MANAGE THE PROXIMITY SENSORS

Purpose:

When the character is moving in the scene, some mechanisms can be triggered (open a door, light a lamp,...). These interactions make the game interesting and more realistic. They are many ways to trigger a mechanism: by touching it, by walking past it (with a certain detection angle). There is one recipe to manage each case.

To use the following recipes, model a character with a ball form and add it a keyboard interface for the displacement. It'll be our test «framework».

Recipe #0: Prepare the character and its environment

1. Add a plane named «floor» for the ground, resize it with a ratio 10 (S 10).
2. Add a «sun» light
3. Add a sphere named «Player» for the player, move it in (0.0,0.0,1.0), add it a «Material» with red diffuse color.
4. In the «Properties» window, «Physics» Tab, select «Rigid Body».
5. Open the «Logic Editor»
6. Add a property «Player» with «boolean» type and check
7. Like for the **recipe V.5**, add the following «Keyboard» sensors and the following «Motion» actuators:
     - key «↑»: «Torque» «X»: -3.0 don't check «L»
     - key «↓»: «Torque» «X»: 3.0 don't check «L»
     - key «←»: «Torque» «Y»: -3.0 don't check «L»
     - key «→»: «Torque» «Y»: 3.0 don't check «L»
8. Add a «Keyboard» sensor, and select the key «Space»
9. Add a «Scene» actuator, «Mode»: «Restart» and link the actuator with the sensor.
10. Go to «3D View» and test (P). With the keyboard keys, we can move the «player» on the plane. At each time, it's possible to come back at the center by pressing the «space» key.

Recipe #1: By touching it

1. Repeat the recipe #0 to obtain the test «framework».
2. We need a mechanism which is activated when an object touches it. Symbolize it with a plane or download the following object designed by Danimal: http://www.blendswap.com/blends/view/66754. Import (Append) the objects «main body», rename them «Trap» and «Spikes».
3. Move «Trap» to (-7.0, -7.0, 0.0) and «Spikes» to (-7.0, -7.0, -1.5)
4. Select «Trap» and «Spikes» and open the «Logic Editor»
5. Add to «Trap» a «Collision» sensor, «property»: «player», check «Activate on True Level Triggering» and precise a frequency of 2000 (we don't want the mechanism always work during the collision)
6. Add to «Spikes» an «And» controller
7. Add to «Spikes» a «Motion» actuator, «Loc» «Z»: 0.20 (to bring the spikes out).
8. Link the sensor with the controller, and the controller with the actuator.
9. Go to «3D View» and test (P). By touching «trap», the spikes emerge and repel the player.

Rather than a collision, use a «Ray» sensor on the «Z» axis, the same «property» and a range: «0.5». The advantage is the trap is triggered only when the «player» touches the object's center and automatically stops when the object is ejected from its position.

<u>**Recipe #2**</u>**: Near from**

Add a door which is automatically opened when the object is near from it:

1. Repeat the recipe#0 to have the «Framework» for test, or repeat the recipe#1 to have the 2 types of mechanisms.
2. Create a door by adding a cube, resize (1.0, 0.2, 2.0) and move inn (0.0, 7,0, 0.0).
3. Modify the rotation center: Select the hinge door side face in Edit mode and do «⇧ Shift + S» → «Snap cursor to selected», go to «Object Mode» and menu «Object» → «Transform» –> «Origin to 3D Cursor».
4. Add an action for the door opening: select the door, go to frame 1, and add a rotation key («i» → Rotation). Go to frame 50, do a rotation on the Z axis (90°) and add a new rotation key. Go to frame 1 and limit the number of frames at 50.
5. Open the «Logic Editor» and add a «Near» sensor, «Property»: «player», «distance»: 1.0, «reset distance»: 2.0
6. Add an «Action» actuator, select the action «cubeAction» (or the door name), «start»: 1, «end»: 50. Link the sensor with the actuator.

When we approach the object «Player», the door is automatically opened. To make the door closing:

1. Add to the door object a property «frame» with «Integer» type
2. Add to the precedent actuator: «Frame property»: Select «frame»
3. Add a «Near» sensor, copy out the same info as in the precedent, but check «Invert»
4. Add a «Property» sensor, «Evalutation type»: «Equal», select the property «frame» and «Value»: 50.
5. Add an «And» controller and link it with the 2 precedent sensors.
6. Add an «Action» actuator, select the action «cubeAction» (or the door name), «start»: 50, «end»: 1. Link the actuator with the controller.

When the «player» object moves away from the door, the door is closed, without coding. We could use the «reset distance» to sent a «negative» impulsion to the controller, but in this case, you need to manage the actuator via a python script.

<u>**Recipe #3**</u>**: By moving past it (with a certain detection angle).**

Take the tank cannon and orient it in the player direction if this last one is in an axis of 45°:

1. Repeat the recipe #0 to have the «Framework» test, or repeat the recipe #2 to have the trap and the door.
2. Download the Mutte's object from: http://www.blendswap.com/blends/view/70285. Import (Append) all the «cannon.*», the «roda.*» and the «suspencao.*». Resize x 0.5 and move in the lower right corner plane (Illustration 148). Do an «cannon.002» object (turret) rotation of 180° on the Z axis and apply the following modifications («Ctrl + A» → «Apply» → «Rotation»).
3. Select the «cannon.002» object and open the «Logic Editor»
4. Add a «radar» sensor, «property»: «player», «Axis»: «+Y Axis) (if the cannon doesn't turn towards the Player object, do a new rotation on the Z axis and apply the modifications), «Angle»: 45°, «Distance»: 7.5
5. Add an «Edit Object» actuator, «Track To» type, «Object»: select the «Player» object and «Time»: 50 (the cannon needs 50 frames to have the object direction). Keep the default axes. Link the sensor with the actuator.
6. Go to «3D View» and test (P). Until «Player» is staying away from the cannon, he is okay, but if the player enters in the 7.5 units around the cannon center zone, and in the detection angle (-45° → +45°), the cannon is turned towards him.

By adding a «ray» sensor with axis +Y, we can activate the shoot.

V.8. USE COUNTERS

Purpose:

With this receipt, you can **count several events**: the number of objects to collect, the number of lives, the number of munitions,...

We'll collect objects when we pass closed to them.

Recipe:

1. Create an object with «Empty» type
2. Select the object to collect, go to «Logic Editor» and add a «Near» sensor. Distance: 0.5 / Reset Distance: 2.0
3. Add an «actuator» with «message» type-To: «Empty» / Subject: «pickup» (to indicate that we collect).
4. Link the sensor with the actuator.
5. Select the Empty, add a property «Item» to contain the number of collected objects
6. Add a «Message» sensor / Subject: «pickup»
7. Add a «Property» actuator/ Mode: «Add» / Property: «item» / Value: 1 (pour +1). Link the sensor with the actuator.

Improvements:

To remove the collected object, add an «Edit Object» actuator to it: «End Object» and link it with the precedent sensor (Near).

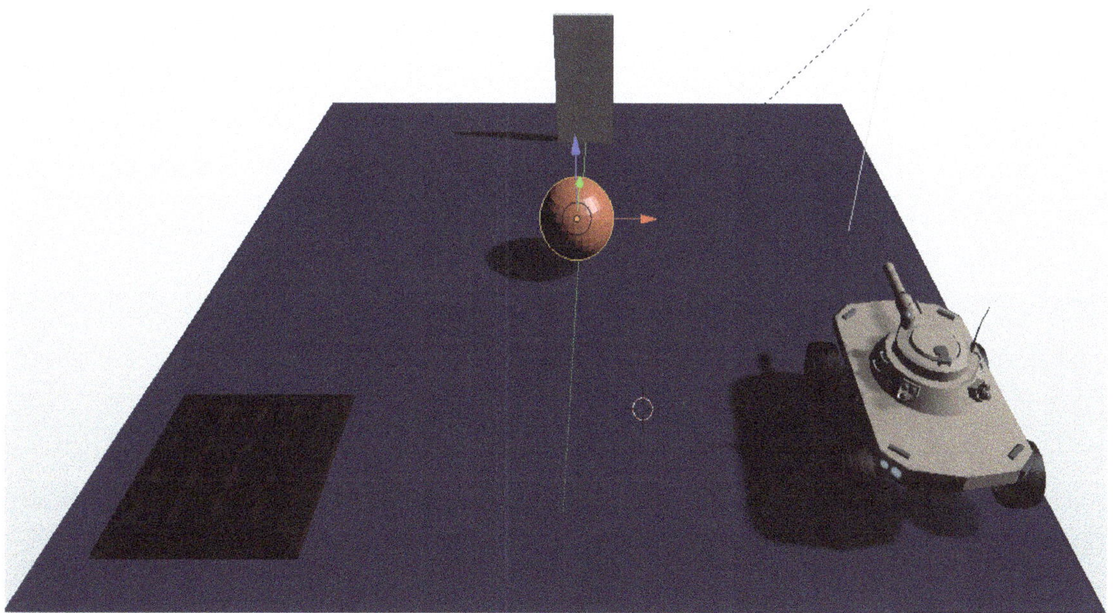

Illustration 148: Scene for tests for the 3 types of interaction

V.9. PATH FOLLOWING

Purpose:

To have an object which follows a path before to come back to its starting point, or goes throw different positions (or «nodes»), it's possible to use a simple method with or without «Navigation Mesh» (nodes technique).

Recipe using a Path:

Use a curse as path for the object displacement:

1. Add a cube to the scene (⇧ Shift + A → «Mesh» → «Cube»). It's the object in movement.

2. Add a curse (⇧ Shift + A → «Curve» → «Bezier»). Go to «Edit Mode» and with successive extrusions (E), create a mesh to follow (Illustration 149). The curse can be closed by selecting the first and the last point and pressing «F».

3. Select the cube and in the «Properties» window, «Constraints» Tab, **add a constraint with type «Path Follow»**: «Curve»: Select the precedent curse.

    - «Follow Curves»: allows to do a cube rotation along the curse.

    - «Forward»: if it's an object with an orientation, select the corresponding axis. Example: for a car, take the axis from the car center to the front of the vehicle.

    - «Offset»: to change the animation point of departure on the curse.

    - «Influence»: to «resize» the path. At «0.5», the object follows a curse (curse path) that's half of the one we have selected.

4. Select the curse, and in the «Properties» window, «Object Data» Tab, «Path animation» panel, check, define the number of frames necessary to do the movement.

5. Test with the editor (Alt + A) – The cube must follow the path. If we test with BGE (P), it doesn't work: the curses are not managed yet by BGE.

6. **«Bake» the animation**: In «3D View», select the cube, then menu «Object» → «Animation» → «Bake Action». Enter the first picture («Start Frame») and the last picture («End Frame»). The «Frame Step» allows to define the using frequency for an animation key. The higher the frequency is, (Frame Step little – minimum=1) the more the animation is like the original, but heavier too. For simpler animations, increase «Frame Step». We can use «Simplify Curves» too (see later). Check «Clear Constraints» to remove the constraints on the object. In «Bake Data», select «Object» and click on «Ok». See Illustration 149.

7. Now, remove the curse because the constraints have been transformed into animation keys, and an action has been generated.

8. Open the «Logic Editor», add an «Always» sensor.

9. Add an «Action» actuator, type: «Loop End», select the generated action («Action») and set «Start Frame» and «End Frame» like above.

10. Link the sensor with the actuator.

11. Go to «3D View» and test (P)

Illustration 149: Path and action curse simplification

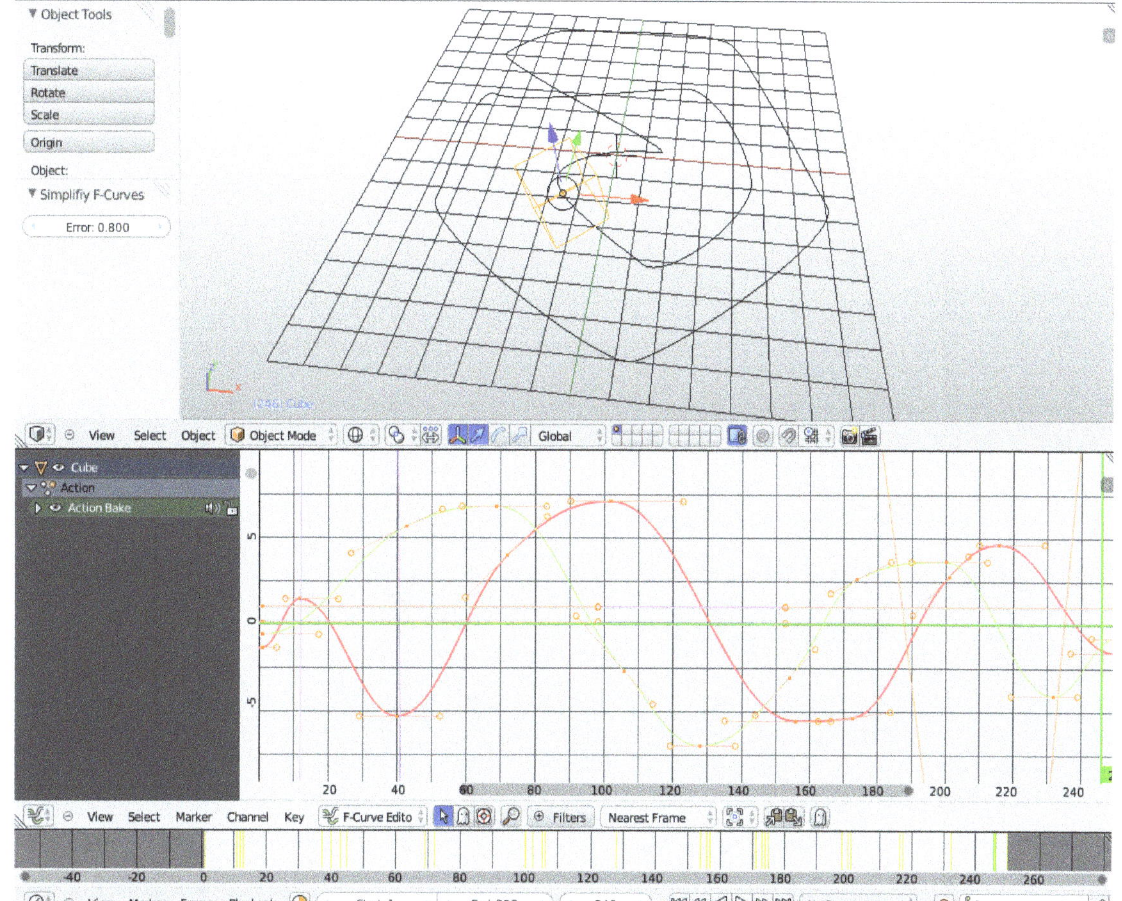

Simplify Curves: the `recipe III.11` give an example for an animation simplification. This Addon can be used here to obtain a lightest animation, while obtain the needed result.

Recipe «mesh node system»:

1. Add a cube to the scene (`Shift`+`A` → «Mesh» → «Cube»). It's the object in movement. At the same place, add an «Empty» (`Shift`+`A` → «Empty» → «Sphere»). Name it «Cube.body». Select the cube, then the empty and parent (`Ctrl`+`P` → Parent to Object).

2. To represent the positions that the cube must alternatively take, position some «empty» (`Shift`+`A` → «Empty» → «Sphere» for example). Each «empty» is a mesh node system. Name each empty: mesh-name-step.node-number. For example: route-step.5 is the 5th step in the mesh.

3. Open the «Text Editor» and add the following script «navigation.py».

4. Select «Cube.body», «Properties» Window, panel «Physics», set with «No collision» and check «Invisible». No matter the cube «Physics» type, it'll follow its parent.

5. Open the «Logic Editor» and add 2 properties to Cube:
    - «step» with «Integer» type containing the number of the step precedent the first node to reach (if 3 then first move towards the node#4). By default: 0 to reach the first node.

- ○ «path» with «String» type containing the mesh system name, here «trajet»
6. Add an «Always» sensor, check «Activate on True Level Triggering» and select a frequency of 20 for example (change as you need).
7. Add a «Steering» actuator, «behaviour»: «seek», «Dist»: 0.0 (to reach exactly the destination).
8. Add an «Edit Object» actuator, «Track To» and check «3D». Keep the default axes.
9. Add a «Python» controller, select «Module» and enter «navigation.selectNode2D»
10. Link the sensor, the controller and the actuators.

script navigation.py:

```python
import bge
gdvel = 5

def selectNode2D(cont):
    own = cont.owner
    step = own["step"]

    scene  = bge.logic.getCurrentScene()
    act = cont.actuators[0] # seek
    track = cont.actuators[1] # track to

    try:
        target = scene.objects[own["path"]+
                         "-step."+str(step+1)]
    except: # no other step
        target = scene.objects[own["path"]+"-step.1"]
        own["step"] = 0

    act.target = target
    track.object = target

    dist = (target.position - own.position).length

    distmin = act.velocity / gdvel

    if dist < distmin: # step reached
        own["step"] += 1 # next step

    cont.activate(act)
    cont.activate(track)
```

gdvel (velocity gradient) is an arbitrary parameter. It's used when the object can reach the arrival in a frame or less. So, the higher the velocity is, the less the destination precision is.

Limitations: The «Steering» functions work in 3D space, with a mesh support. **We always consider that we lean on something**. It's the functioning of the «navigation mesh». However, to realize a space game, we need to find one's way in 3D. It's necessary to add a «track to» for the object to move towards this point. However, it doesn't work directly with «Rigid Body» - You must take an «Empty» and parent the real object to the empty. It's only necessary for displacements in 3D space.

This solution doesn't take into account the physics of the object. In reality, if the object is heavy and fast, it can't stop short like the empty.

Another approach (to conserve a «Rigid Body»):
This script modification allows to use directly a «Rigid Body». Be careful to the mass: with a gravity at 9.80, the mass must not exceed 100 Units (limit for compensating force: 1000). To develop a space game, decrease the gravity to keep the objects kinetic and use high masses.

1. Repeat the precedent recipe, but **remove the actuator «Edit Object»**, and the empty for the cube.
2. Add to the cube a new actuator with «Motion» type and link it to the existing controller. Set «Damping Frames» to 100.
3. Change the controller name into «navigation.selectNode2».
4. Go to «3D View» and test (⌨P)

script navigation.py (addition):

```python
zstep = 21.0
gdvel = 5.0

def selectNode2(cont):
   own = cont.owner
   step = own["step"]
   scene  = bge.logic.getCurrentScene()
   act = cont.actuators["seek"]

   try:
      target = scene.objects[own["path"]+
                           "-step."+str(step+1)]
   except: # no other step
      target = scene.objects[own["path"]+"-step.1"]
      own["step"] = 0

   act.target = target
   dist = (target.position - own.position).length

   distmin = act.velocity / gdvel

   if  dist < distmin: # step reached
      own["step"] += 1 # next step
   mot = cont.actuators["Motion"]

   if abs(target.position.z - own.position.z) < 1.0:
      own.position.z = target.position.z
   else:
      mot.dLoc = [0,0,((target.position.z -
                   own.position.z) / dist)/(zstep/act.velocity)]

   #Max force is 1000
   mot.force = [0.0,0.0,-scene.gravity[2] * own.mass]
   cont.activate(act)
   cont.activate(mot)
```

Note: The parameter **zstep** (gradient Z) is arbitrary. According to masses and distances, refine it. This solution is not perfect, but allows to manage this scenario.

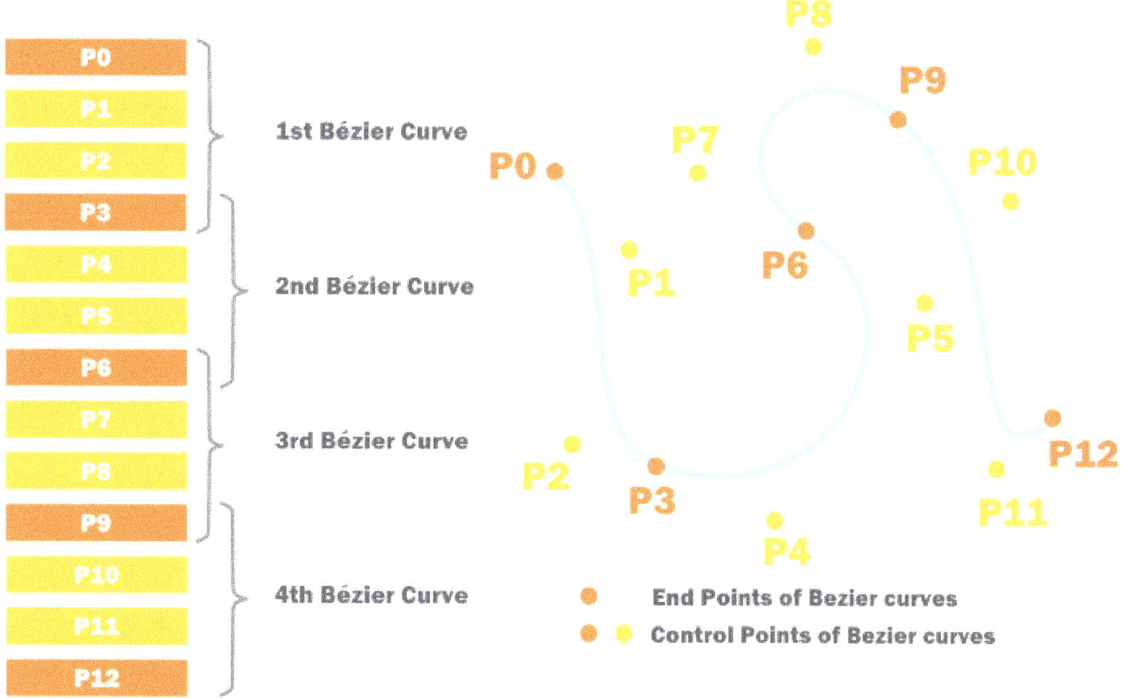

Illustration 150: Using Bezier curves – explanations on devmag.org.za: http://bit.ly/1SH4B40

V.10. OBJECTS IN CONTACT WITH THE GROUND

Purpose:

Since the character jumps, he can't do a new jump because he can't touch the ground. If he could do that, he would be a superhero which flies. When **we do a jump by pressing a key, you must control that the character is in touch with ground.** If we launch a projectile and we want that it explodes when it's at 10 meters in high, you must know the distance between the object and ground.

Recipe #1: Using a vertical ray

1. Add to ground a «floor» property with boolean type, checked
2. Select the character or the object and go to the «Logic Editor» Window
3. Under the sensor managing the event «jump» (ex: keyboard key), add another sensor with «Ray» type. Set: «Property»: «floor» and «Z axis»: «range:0.5»
4. Then, link this sensor with the controller managing the event «jump» as supplementary condition.

Recipe #2: Using collisions

1. To the object or the character which jumps, add a variable «IsJumping», boolean, False
2. Add a «Collision» sensor and select the material corresponding to the ground (or a property like in the precedent recipe)
3. Add an actuator with «property» type / Mode: Assign / Property: «IsJumping» / Value: 0
4. Test this value for the jump and do the jump only if the value =0, then move it to 1.

Recipe #3: Distance

To calculate the distance between 2 objects, we use the function python **getDistanceTo**().

Ex: own.getDistanceTo(object) gives the distance between the object «own» and «object».

V.11. SIMPLY ANIMATE AN OBJECT

Purpose:

BGE can do **simple animations without create some actions.** In this recipe, we rotating the blades mill (simple rotation). Other animations in the recipes IV.2 and IV.3.

Recipe:

1. Create an object with mill type (name the blades mill «mill_arbor» - rotation axis «Z») or download on http://www.blendswap.com/blends/view/71393 the **bshop's model.**

2. Select the object «mill_arbor» and open the «Logic Editor»

3. Add an «Always» sensor, check «Activate on True Level Triggering», and set the frequency at 10

4. Add a «Motion» actuator, «Motion type»: «Simple Motion» and «Rot» «Z»: «0.2», check «L»

5. Link the sensor with the actuator.

It's possible to rotate and move without needing actions for this recipe. The blades mill are simply animated.

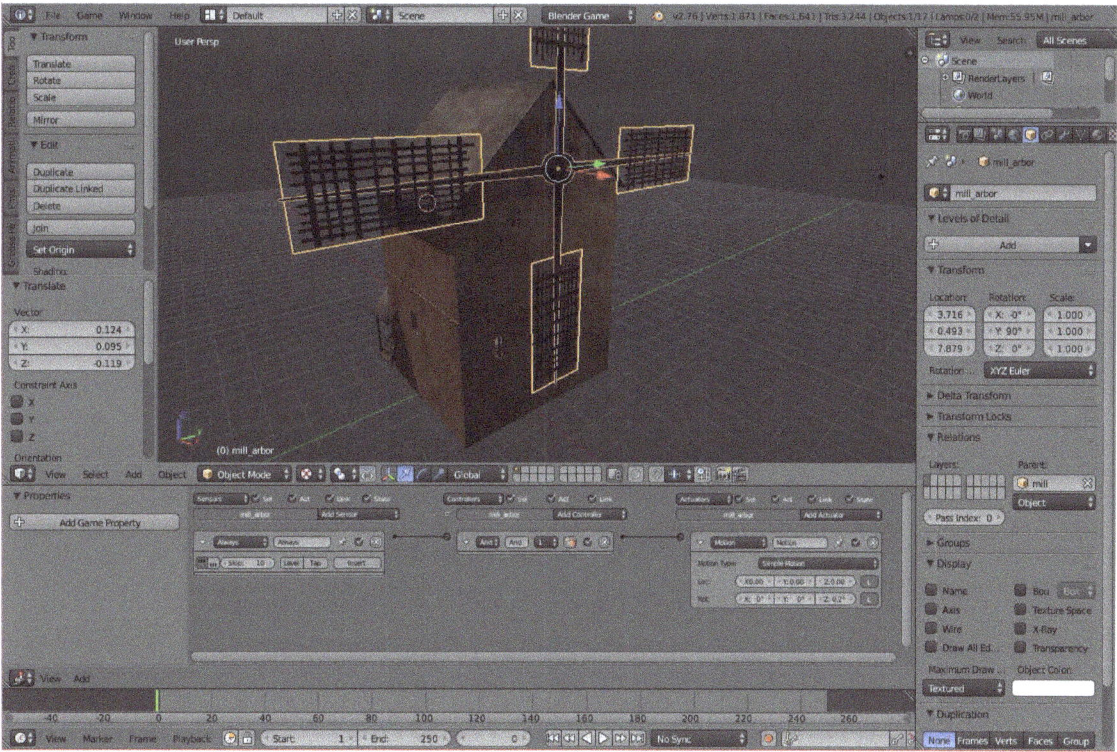

Illustration 151: How to simply animate a mill

V.12. GENERATE BULLETS DECALS

Purpose:

When a character shoots, there are some bullets marks on the walls. These marks are some «objects» made by a plane and a texture with «hole» type displayed superimposed on the wall, in place of the impact. The problem is when there are 2000 cartridges, there are 2000 supplementary objects. The more often, we limit the lifetime for these objects to avoid this problem. In this recipe, we'll see **how determinate this impact point and how generate this object**.

Recipe:

Use 3 objects: the character («player»), a gun and a bullet:

1. Place the object Bullet in an invisible layer

2. Select «Bullet», «Properties» window, «Physics» Tab, «Physics Type»: «Dynamic». Set the «radius» at 0,05 m. Keep a mass of 2 pounds (1Kg) because the bullet speed will be limited (and its kinetic energy) to see the bullet. In reality, we never see the bullet. With a higher speed, we can set a lower mass keeping an impact on the objects.

3. Parent the object «gun» to the character's hand (Select the first, then the second, and `Ctrl`+`P` → «Set Parent to Object»).

4. Add an Empty (`Shift`+`A` → «Empty» → «Plain axis») of which the X axis is directed forward and placed at the end of the barrel. Name it «Raycast».

5. Parent it in a way that it always stays at the end of the barrel.

6. Select the «Raycast» object, go to the Logic Editor

7. Add a «Mouse» sensor, «Mouse Event»: Select «Left Button»

8. Add an «Edit Object» actuator: «Add Object», «Object»: «Bullet» setting a speed like «Linear Velocity»: 50.0 (according to the needed effect and to the world size. Use 1 Unit Blender = 1 meter). Limit «Time» at 200, to allow the bullet to be no longer managed by the system after 200 frames.

9. Link the sensor with the actuator. The generated object by «add object» at the place of the empty «Raycast», has a velocity of 5 on the X axis.

10. To avoid the bullet be subject to the gravity, apply to it an inverse force (on the Z axis) with the same intensity (physique setting: Gravity, normally at 9.80): Select Bullet and go to the Logic Editor, then add an «Always» sensor.

11. Add a «Motion» actuator / «Force: Z: 9.80». Link the sensor with the actuator.

12. So that the bullet collides with other objects: Select Bullet, in the «Properties» window, «Physics» Tab, check «Collision Bounds», «Bounds»: «Sphere» (faster than «Box»).

Then, draw in an invisible layer a bullet impact (texture on a plane). Name it «impact». Then, use a Raycast to determinate the impact surface, from an empty, parented to the player or camera object (if FPS), and on which we add the following logic:

13. Select the «raycast» object, go to the «Logic Editor»

14. Add a sensor with «Ray» ttype / Select «Property»: «solide» / Select «+X axis» / Range «100»

15. Add a sensor with «Mouseclick» type, «Mouse Event»: Select «Left Button»

16. Add a «Python» controller and call the following script

17. Add an «Edit Object» actuator / Type «Add Object» / Select the «impact» object, «Time»: 2000

In this case, we do a raycast forward the camera. If the ray touches an object with the property «solid» (we could use too the «Material»), then it executes the python script and generate an «impact» object instance with a lifetime of 2000 frames. Range = 100 can be changed to define the maximal length for shooting.

The Property using on the ray allow to differentiate the different targets, so we can use different scripts and sounds according to the target.

Be careful to Raycast: it collides the «collision bounds» and not the real object. If a window is in a wall, and if a wall «collision bounds» is a box, it's the wall which collides and not the window. You must move it to «Convex Hull», or cut the wall into 4 sections.

python script:

```python
from bge import logic as GameLogic
from mathutils import Vector
c = GameLogic.getCurrentController()
own = c.owner
space = 0.003

mouseclick = c.sensors["mouseclick"]
ray = c.sensors["Ray.V"]
spawn = c.actuators["Spawn.V"]
if mouseclick.positive and ray.positive:
        pos_vec = Vector(ray.hitPosition)
        normal_vec = Vector(ray.hitNormal)

# make object
spawn.instantAddObject()
bullet_hole = spawn.objectLastCreated

# position hole
bullet_hole.alignAxisToVect(normal_vec.xyz, 2, 1)
normal_vec.magnitude = space
bullet_hole.worldPosition = (pos_vec + normal_vec).xyz
```

This script allows to position the plane according to the impact normal and the impact position.

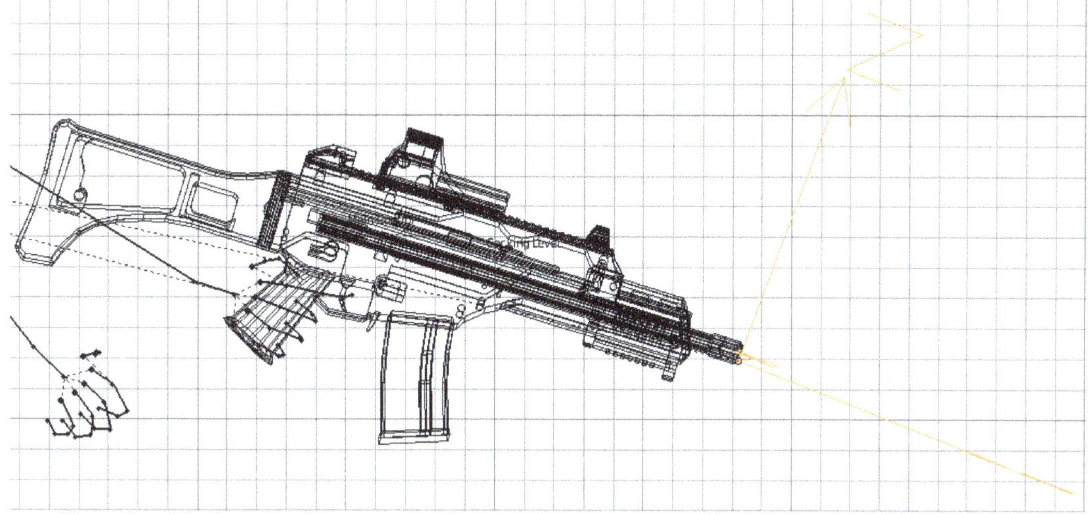

Illustration 152: Example of the empty positioning in the shooting axis for the Z axis and parented to the gun

If we want to do some «bounces», we must manage the impacts differently. The **game project #6** shows this scenario.

V.13. PATH FINDING

Purpose:

The «Path Finding» consists in finding a path between a starting point and an arrival by taking account different constraints, while a «Follow Path» only follows a defined way.

Blender allows to automatically **manage a displacement zone** («Navigation Mesh») for the non players characters (NPC) moves.

«Steering» functions are available to reach a target (or to escape it) with these constraints. For programmers, it's a path in A* (**shortest paths research**). This technique works with any decor on which a character can walk. It doesn't work in 3D space (example: a space ship), for this case, we must use hybrid techniques with nodes (recipe V.9) or write a calculation function for the shortest path.

Simple decor – Recipe #1:

1. Add a «plan» ([Shift]+[A] → «Mesh» → «Plan»). Resize (S) 20X. Subdivide 10X («Edit Mode», «W» → «Subdivide», then menu «Tools» → «Cuts») like the Illustration 153.

2. Select a set of boxes (in «Edit Mode», selecting by faces) and extrude (E) these last on the Z axis at a height of 2 in a schema type labyrinth like the Illustration 154.

3. «properties» Window, «scene» Tab, «**Navigation mesh**» panel: set «cell size» at 0.10 and click on «Build navigation mesh». A path is drawn like on the illustration 155. The path corresponds to the zone in which the characters will evolve.

4. Add a **red sphere** ([Shift]+[A] → «Mesh» → «UV Sphere») in a corner of the labyrinth, name it «monster».

5. «properties» Window, «Physics» Tab, «Physic Type»: «Dynamic».

6. Add a **green sphere** in another corner, name it «player»

7. «properties» Window, «Physics» Tab, «Physic Type»: «Rigid Body»

8. Select «monster» and go to the **Logic Editor** and add a «Always» sensor

9. Add a **«Steering»** Actuator / Behavior: «path following» / Target Object: «player», «Navigation mesh»: «Navmesh». Link the sensor with the actuator.

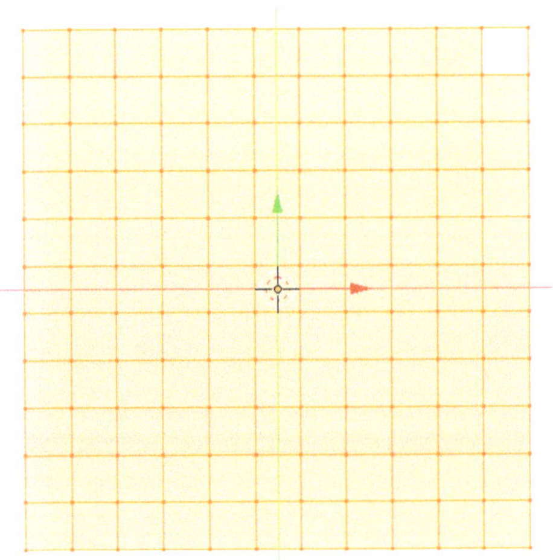

Illustration 153: Plan subdivide 10 times

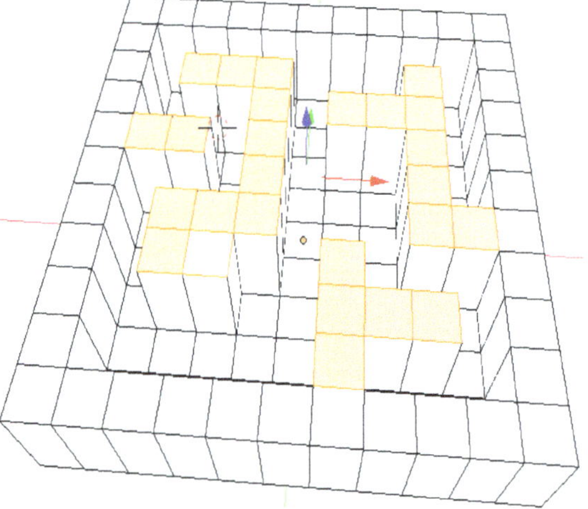

Illustration 154: Extrude labyrinth type

The monster charges at the player. With keys, move the «player», the monster calculates in realtime its moves.

Illustration 155: Navigation mesh automatically created

«Navigation Mesh» details panel:

- **Cell Size**: channel width. The higher the value is and the wider the way must be.
- **Cell Height:** height to allow the passage. Example: use 0.20 (axis Z), and everything smaller is not an obstacle, but anything bigger is an obstacle.
- **Agent Height:** Height minimal allowing the character to pass.
- **Agent radius:** the character radius. At 0.60, in every directions (X,Y), he goes in the zones with a width maximal of 0.60.
- **Agent Max Slop:** angle maximal for the character when he changes direction (here, set at 45°).
- **Agent Max Climb:** Walls height maximal on which the player can climb (Precise 0.9)
- **Min region size**: The smaller zones are removed from the path, considered as impracticable.
- **Merged region size**: The smaller zones are combined not to have different paths.
- **Max edge length:** Size maximal for the zone edge (if the number is decreased, the navigation mesh is made with smaller polygons, so more numerous)
- **Max edge error:** maximal error admissible for the calculation of the max distance
- **Verts per poly**: number maximal of used polygon points to model the zones in the navigation mesh (6 by default).

In most cases, set only the first 4 parameters, the rest is used for calculation optimizations.

«Steering» Actuator details:

«Seek» type allows to move forward the target, but without trying to flee from the obstacles → often a blockage situation.

«Flee» type allows to flee from the target, without trying to flee from the obstacles.

«Path Following» type allows to take the shortest path to reach the target while respecting the navigation mesh.

Complex decor- recipe #2:

If we place some objects on the decor, the «navigation mesh» takes them into account for the calculation only if they are a part of the object geometry. To avoid to merge the objects, add, **without applying,** a «modifier» property with «boolean» type on the decor object by adding to it the objects (obstacles futures). It's the best when there are too many obstacles.

Another solution: modify the «Navigation Mesh» geometry:

1. Select the «Navmesh» obtained with the precedent recipe and go to «Edit Mode»
2. Key «W» → «Subdivide»: apply as many times as necessary to have a fine enough mesh (around the objects) to select the zone below the object.
3. Go to top view («7») and in «Lasso» mode («Ctrl+LMB»), select one by one the zones bellow the objects, then remove them («x»).
4. Repeat these steps for every zones where the monster can go (water bodies, etc.). A «Navigation Mesh» good setting avoid to have too much work.
5. Go to «Object Mode» and apply a «decimate modifier» to simplify the new navigation mesh. 3 subdivisions is the equivalent of increasing the number of faces with a factor of $4^3 = 64$. To get back to the same level, we need a «decimate» of 1/64 = 0,016. Use a higher coefficient. Check the box «Triangulate». Check by visual inspection in «Object Mode» before to apply the «modifier».
6. «Physics» Tab, «Navmesh Clear Data», then «Navmesh Reset Index Values» to recaculate everything

«obstacle» mode details:

There is another possibility but this doesn't allow monsters to avoid the obstacles.

To activate the «obstacles» mode:

1. «Properties» Window, «World» Tab, «Obstacle Simulation» panel, choose 1 of the 2 methods («ray» or «cell»).
2. For each obstacle object (character and monster included), in the «Physics» Tab, check «create obstacle» and set the radius, the radius from the center of the obstacle (for a cube of 1 U side, the radius will be $\sqrt{2}/2=0.71$, for a circle with dimension 3, the radius will be 3/2=1.5).
1. The «steering» actuator configuration is very important. Some modifications for «Velocity», «Turn Speed» and «Acceleration» allows or not the monster to avoid the obstacles. When the speed is high, it's difficult to turn...
2. The «obstacle» mode can't be used for a game with an important size (with complexes decors). The time for calculation is too important and the number of Frames per second is not enough. In this case, the better solution is the precedent recipe.

V.14. GRAB AN OBJECT

Purpose:

In an adventure game, we can have to click on an object to select it and move it into the inventory for example. In «Half Life 2», the hero can use a gravity cannon and grab the objects to launch them in a direction. In the 2 cases, it's like **a drag and drop.**

This technique is a basis for the **level editor creation**. You only have to use an inventory like in the **recipe VI.6**, to store in it different models for objects or tiles (**recipe III.16**) and to position the objects, using or not a magnetic mesh. This mesh allows a more precise positioning, aligning on a defined mesh customizable by the user.

We can too use this recipe to create a bowling for example, or a chess game.

Recipe:

Repeat the **recipe VI.8** for the mouse cursor but modify the way to move.

1. Create a scene with some objects: a cube, a sphere and a «Suzanne» (monkey), all installed on a plane. In «Properties» window, «Physics» Tab, select the «Rigid Body» type for the 3 first and keep «static» for the plane. For «Suzanne», in «Physics», set a «collision bounds» with «Convex Hull» type.

2. Use the **recipe V.1** to create a camera with «freeview» type to easily displace the camera in the scene.

3. Add a plane in front of the camera and close to the camera to prohibit something can be between camera and the plane. Name it «MouseCursor». Resize the plane and place it at the center of the camera view.

4. Do an UV mapping of the plane («Mode Edit», «U» → «Unwrap»).

5. «Properties» Window, «Materials» Tab, add a Material, name it «MaterialMouse», check «Shadeless», check «Transparency», «Z Transparency» and set «Alpha» at 0.0

6. «Textures» Tab, add a Texture, with «Image or Movie» type. «Mapping» panel, «Coordinates»: «UV» and «Map»: «Uvmap». «Diffuse» panel, check «Alpha» and set at 1.0, to exploit the image transparency (canal alpha).

7. «Physics» Tab, select the «No collision» type.

8. Parent to the camera (select the plane, then the camera and `Ctrl`+`P` → «Parent to Object»).

9. Select «MouseCursor» and «`Shift`+`S`» → «Snap cursor to selected».

10. Add an Empty, name it «grabber» and move it on the Y axis in such a way that it represents the distance needed to catch an object. Then, modify this distance to catch objects farther or less.

11. In «Physics», select the «Dynamic» type and check «actor» and «ghost».

12. Parent «grabber» to the camera too.

13. Add to «MouseLook.py» (**recipe V.1**) the following script lines.

14. Select «grabber» and open the «Logic Editor». Add an «Always» sensor, name it «RunOnce» (will be executed once, at first)

15. Add a «Mouse» sensor, name it «MouseClick», «Mouse Event»: «Left Button»

16. Add a «Collision» sensor, name it «MouseCol», check «Activate one True Level Triggering», and set the frequency at 0. «Property»: «select»

17. Add a «Python» controller, Select «Module» and enter «MouseLook.grab». Link the 3 sensors with the controller.

18. Find 3 textures with a canal alpha (transparent background) representing: the standard cursor (cursor.png), the cursor when an object can be grabbed (grab-off.png) and the cursor when an object is grabbed (grab-on.png) and put the images in the project root directory (the same as the file «.blend»).

19. Add a property «select» to all objects that can be dragged and dropped. For these objects, in the «Material» Tab, «Options» Panel, by checking «Object Color», the script can temporarily change the object color.

Addition to the Script «MouseLook.py»:

```python
def grab(cont):
    col = cont.sensors["MouseCol"]
    click = cont.sensors["MouseClick"]

    scene = bge.logic.getCurrentScene()
    obj = scene.objects["MouseCursor"]
    matID = VideoTexture.materialID(obj, "MAMaterialMouse")
    texture = VideoTexture.Texture(obj, matID, 0)

    if not "texon" in obj:
        obj["texon"] = VideoTexture.ImageFFmpeg("grab-on.png")

    if not "texoff" in obj:
        obj["texoff"] = VideoTexture.ImageFFmpeg("grab-off.png")

    if not "tex" in obj:
        obj["tex"] = VideoTexture.ImageFFmpeg("cursor.png")

    if click.positive and col.positive:
        hit = col.hitObject
        texture.source = obj["texon"]
        obj["texture1"] = texture
        hit.worldPosition = cont.owner.worldPosition
        hit.applyForce((0,0,9.8),False)
        hit.color = [1,0.9,0.1,1]

    elif col.positive:
        hit = ray.hitObject
        texture.source = obj["texoff"]
        obj["texture2"] = texture
        hit.color = [1,1,1,1]
    else:
        texture.source = obj["tex"]
        obj["grabobj"] = ""
        obj["texture3"] = texture

    texture.refresh(False)
```

We use 3 properties «text», «texon» and «texoff» to store the texture image and to not load it every time. Note «MA» before the «Material» name, the function VideoTexture.materialID() use the 2 first letters to know the data type to look for («MA»for Material).

When we drag an object, we apply to it an inverse force to gravity to move it freely, (so we don't change the «Collision» sensor frequency) on we copy the «grabber» object coordinates to move it with the camera.

Note the use of the 3 properties «texture1», «texture2» and «texture3»: they are **essential** because the textureis not really joined to the object and will be removed during the following cycle. By storing it in a property, the system can't remove it.

V.15. CAMERA SWAP

Purpose:

According to the player position, for a race game or an adventure games, we can activate different cameras. That allows to have different points of view. In the following recipe, we use a «Near» sensor, but we could use a radar to refine the management too (angle for example).

Recipe:

1. Open the «Text Editor» and create a new python script «tools.py». Add the following script lines.
2. Select the player and open the «Logic Editor».
3. Add a property «player» with Boolean type, checked. Add a property «cam» with string type containing the active camera type too (before the change of camera)
4. Add a new camera and place it at a precise location in the decor. Go to the «Logic Editor»
5. If the camera must automatically follow the player (angle only): Add an «Always» sensor. Check «Activate on True Level Triggering» and set a frequency (10 for example). Add an «Edit Object» actuator, select «Track To» and the object representing the player. Check «3D». Keep the default axes. Link the sensor with the actuator.
6. Add a «Near» sensor, «property»: «player» and enter «Distance», the distance from which the camera must be activated (there's a «positive» impulsion) and «Reset Distance», the distance from which we want the camera deactivated (there's a «négative» impulsion). The 2 values can be the same.
7. Add a «Python» controller, select «Module» and enter «tools.setCamera».
8. Add a «Scene» actuator, «Mode»: «Set Camera», the field «Camera Object» is to be left empty.
9. Link the sensor with the controller, then the controller with the actuator.

Script python «tools.py»:

```python
import bge
def setCamera(cont):
    own = cont.owner
    act = cont.actuators[0]
    sen = cont.sensors[0]
    if sen.positive:
        act.camera = own
    else:
        scene = bge.logic.getCurrentScene()
        player = scene.objects["player"]
        cam = player["cam"]
        act.camera = scene.objects[cam]
```

V.16. SPLIT SCREEN

Purpose:

The «multiplayer» mode doesn't mean «LAN» or «internet or WAN» - it's possible to play on the same screen too. The players doesn't have necessarily the same camera view. For a race car for example, each player has a view from hits own cockpit. We cut the screen in 2, and so, each player can follow its own vehicle.

In many games, **it's possible to play until 4 players with 2, 3 or 4 viewports**.

Recipe with 2 viewports, horizontal split:

1.   Add a first camera (**Shift**+**A** → «Camera»), name it «camera1». Repeat the operation for «camera2».
2.   Open «Text Editor» and add a new python script «viewports.py». Copy the following lines.
3.   Add an «Always» sensor
4.   Add a «Python» controller and select the script «viewports.py»

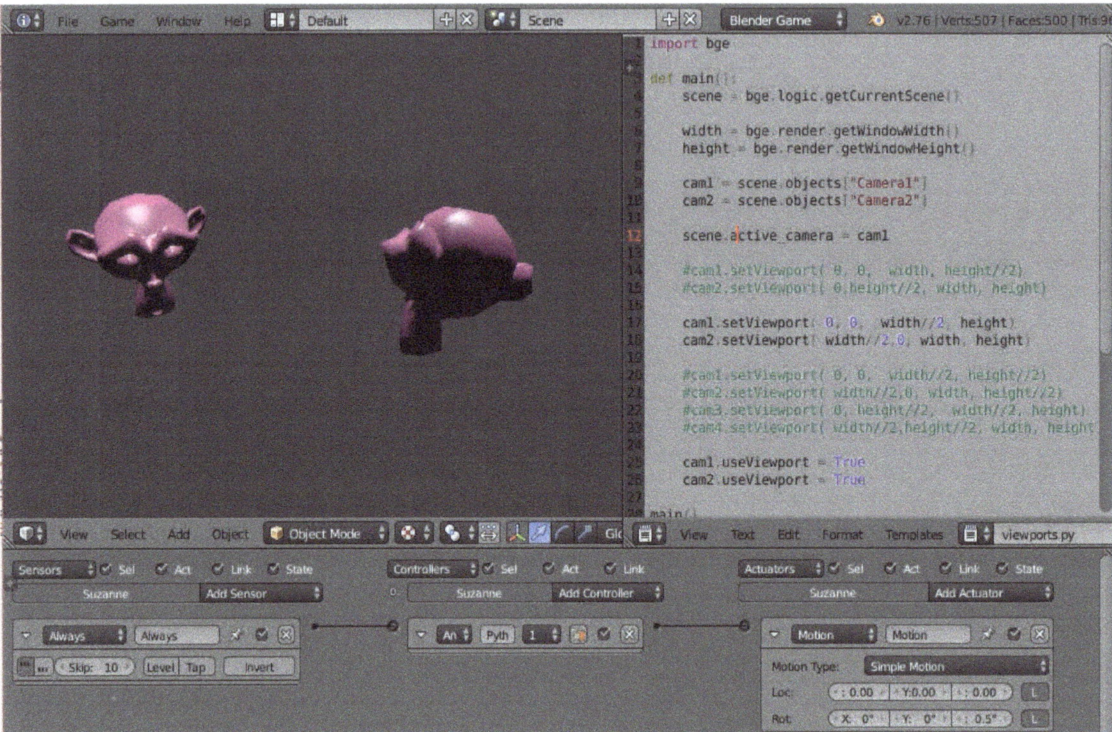

Script python «viewports.py»:

```python
import bge

def main():
    scene = bge.logic.getCurrentScene()

    width, height = bge.render.getWindowWidth(), bge.render.getWindowHeight()

    cam1, cam2 = scene.objects["Camera1"], scene.objects["Camera2"]

    scene.active_camera = cam1
```

```
    cam1.setViewport(0, 0,  width, height//2)
    cam2.setViewport(0,height//2, width, height)
    cam1.useViewport, cam2.useViewport = True, True

main()
```

The **setViewport**(x1,y1,x2,y2) function defines the screen portion which will be managed by the camera. The camera has the following parameters:

- •   (x1,y1): the lowest point at left of the screen
- •   (x2,y2): the highest point at right of the screen
- •

To obtain a **vertical split:**

```
cam1.setViewport(0, 0, width//2, height)
cam2.setViewport(width//2,0, width, height)
```

To obtain **4 cameras**:

```
cam1.setViewport(0, 0, width//2, height//2)
cam2.setViewport(width//2,0, width, height//2)
cam3.setViewport(0, height//2, width//2, height)
cam4.setViewport(width//2,height//2, width, height)
```

Illustration 156: Revolt Race Game - Download the game: http://bit.ly/1Il1AvJ

V.17. PLAY ON LAN OR INTERNET (WAN)

Purpose:

To play with others, it's necessary to establish a communication between computers.

Theory:

A **socket** is a communication channel between 2 computers that permits information transmission. This channel is identified by a number, which is the **port**. The computer is identified by an address (the **IP address**). A client is connected to a server using a channel, and a server communicates with its x clients by x channels. The way in which the communication is accomplished is called a **protocol**. It's a language convention, in a certain manner.

In a network game using LAN (Local Area Network) or WAN (internet), there are 2 sockets types: UDP and TCP. **TCP** encapsulates UDP by adding to it a good reception control. So, UDP is quickly, but the data sent is not necessarily received or correctly received. When speed is more important than data quality, we use UDP.

The Multicast allows to diffuse and collect data between all connected computers. It allows clients and servers to connect using the same IP address and the same port: most routers support this system. In IPV4, the addresses between 224.0.0.9 and 224.0.0.255 are reserved to Multicast. However, it's usable only on a LAN, so we won't present this system.

Recipe: synchronize an object from a server

This recipe allows to create a client and a simple server. When we move an object on the Server, it affects the client.

1er file: server.blend

1. Add an object to the scene (ex: Suzanne: «⇧ Shift + A» → «Mesh» → «Monkey») and open the «Logic Editor».
2. Add a «Keyboard» sensor, name it «KeyUp», Select la key «↑»
3. Add a «Motion» actuator, name it «GoUp», «type»: «Simple Motion», «Loc» «Z»: 0.5
4. Link the sensor with the actuator. We can now raise the cube to the top.
5. Repeat the 2 to 4 for the key «↓», name it «KeyDown» and the actuator «GoDown» with «Loc» «Z» -0.5. We can now move down the cube.
6. Repeat the operation for the keys «←» and «→», «KeyLeft» and «KeyRight» with respectively the actuators «TurnLeft» («Rot» «Z»: -1) and «TurnRight» ((«Rot» «Z»: 1). The cube can turn around thanks to the left and right arrows.

For the network part:

7. Add a new file «Text», name it «server.py» and copy the following script lines.
8. Add an «Always» sensor, name it «RunOnce»
9. Add a «Python» controller, select «Module» and enter «server.init».
10. Link the sensor with the controller. The server is initialized.
11. Add an «Always» sensor, check «Activate On True Level Triggering» and set the frequency at 0.
12. Add a «Python» controller, select «Module» and enter «server.update».
13. Link the sensor with the controller. For each cycle, the server will send the object position and the orientation to the client.

Script server.py:

```python
import bge, socket, pickle

ClientHost = 'localhost'
ClientPort = 10001

def init(cont):
    # Set UDP socket
    bge.server = socket.socket(socket.AF_INET, socket.SOCK_DGRAM)

def update(cont):
        own = cont.owner
        # Get Position and Orientation
        pos, ori = own.worldPosition, own.worldOrientation
        info = (pos[0], pos[1], pos[2],
                    ori[0][0], ori[0][1], ori[0][2], ori[1][0],
                    ori[1][1], ori[1][2],    ori[2][0], ori[2][1],
                    ori[2][2])
        data = pickle.dumps(info)

        # Send Data to client
        bge.server.sendto(data, (ClientHost, ClientPort))
```

The function **init**() creates the socket.

The function **update**() will get back the object information, package them in data container thanks to pickle and send to the client (sendto).

2nd file: client.blend

1. Add an object to the scene (ex: Suzanne: «⬆ Shift+Ⓐ» → «Mesh» → «Monkey»)
2. Add a new file «Text», name it «client.py» and copy the following script lines.
3. Select the object and open the «Logic Editor», then add an «Always» sensor, name it «RunOnce»
4. Add a «Python» controller, select «Module» and enter «client.init». Link the sensor with the controller. Le client is initialized.
5. Add an «Always» sensor, check «Activate On True Level Triggering» and set the frequency at 0.
6. Add a «Python» controller, select «Module» and enter «client.update». Link the sensor and the controller. For each cycle, the client receives the object position and orientation.

Script client.py:

```python
import bge, mathutils, socket, pickle

ServerHost = "localhost"
ClientPort = 10001

def init(cont):
    # Set UDP socket
    bge.socketClient = socket.socket(socket.AF_INET,socket.SOCK_DGRAM)
    bge.socketClient.bind((ServerHost, ClientPort))

def update(cont):
    own = cont.owner
    try:
        # Get data in buffer
        data, SRIP = bge.socketClient.recvfrom(1024)
        info = pickle.loads(data)

        # Set Position and orientation
        own.worldPosition = (info[0], info[1], info[2])

        # Orientation must be a matrix
        ori = mathutils.Matrix(((info[3], info[4], info[5]),
            (info[6], info[7], info[8]), (info[9], info[10], info[11])))
        own.worldOrientation = ori
    except:
        pass
```

The **init**() function creates a socket, waits and is in «non-blocking» mode: if it sends data (sendto) or waits for data (recvfrom), it doesn't wait for an answer.

The **update**() function receives a datagram and the un-package thanks to pickle, then apply the object position and orientation information. Everything is secured by a bloc «try/except» to avoid the errors in case of non-reception, or corrupted data. SRIP which is not exploited correspond to the transmitter IP address and the used communication port (that has nothing to do with ClientPort).

In use: on a local computer, we launch the server in first Blender instance then, we launch the client. In the server window, with the keys, we move and rotate the object, simultaneously, we see the result on the client. To do tests thought the LAN, give different addresses for ClientHost and ServerHost (ex: 192.168.1.10 for the server and 192.168.1.20 for the client – it depends on the LAN configuration).

With internet, it's harder when we are using a router. The computer has a local address (LAN), and the router an internet address (WAN) and a LAN too. You must give the WAN address, but the router must know that if it receives data on such port (ClientPort), then it must «reroute» the information towards an identified (with its LAN address) computer (and eventually, another port). The thread is done through the NAT protocol (Network Address Translation). To configure the NAT, you must access to the router in administrator mode. To know its WAN address, see: http://whatismyipaddress.com/

This recipe gives a simple solution for the socket use – it's pedagogic, but can't meet the synchronization real needs for a multiplayer game.

To do that, use a system with a process managing the network part, working in parallel of the game. Why do we use a process instead of a thread? What is the difference? See the **sheet # 7** on Python, section «Create a thread or a process in background mode».

It's necessary to use a control system to preface the messages sent on the network. The basics controls are: «send updates» and «here are my updates», while specifying the corresponding object.

During a position synchronization between the server and a client, which has the «true» updated information? If the object was moved by the client, it's probably the client, excepted if a collision has created the same movement on the server. When the information is received, isn't outdated yet ?

To send some information through network (to create a chat for example) is relatively simple, but when you must **synchronize the 3D game entities using a physical engine**, it's more complex.

Illustration 157: Image taken on a server with a 200ms lag 200 ms. There's a lag between that the player see and the physic reality of the phenomenon (c) Valve Corporation

V.18. OCULUS RIFT: A STEP TOWARDS VIRTUAL REALITY

Purpose:

Almost everyone heard about **Oculus Rift**, this headset with a **stereoscopic** vision to explore 3D worlds with an impressive immersion. This recipe gives you some ideas to integrate this system to BGE.

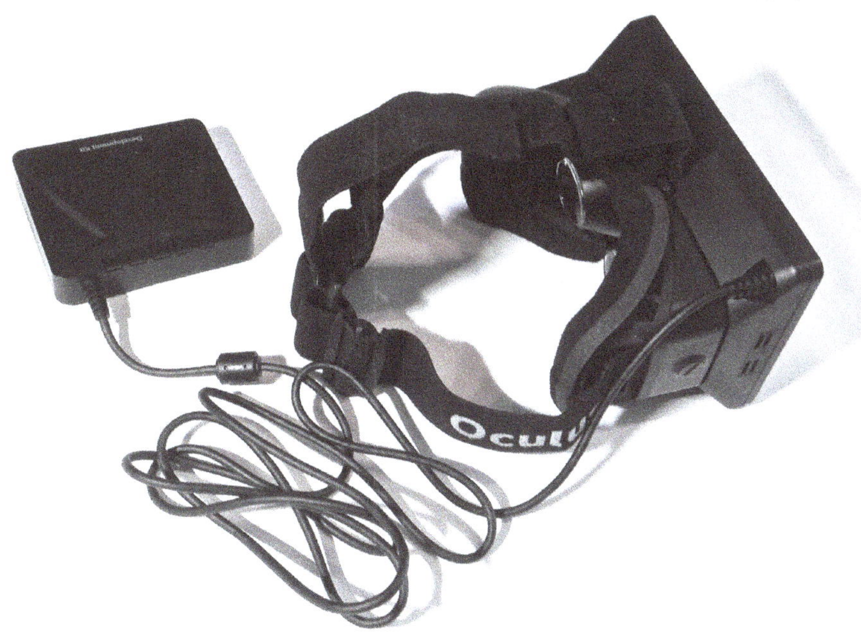

Illustration 158: 3D virtual reality headset Occulus Rift

SDK Description:

Oculus Rift will be soon accessible to general public. It's yet possible to buy a development kit (about 350$ for DK2).

The precedent development kit (DK1) has a 7 inch screen with 1280 × 800 pixels (or 640 × 800 pixels per eye). The movements recognition is at 1 KHz on 3 axes thanks to a gyroscope, an accelerometer and a magnetometer. It weighs less than 1 lbs. DK2 is available since July 2014. This version integrates the last developments on vibration reduction motion blur, on motion detection and the new screen resolution: full HD 1080p.

Games must be designed specifically to work with Oculus Rift. The development Kit (SDK) available for developers allows to integrate Oculus in their games. SDK includes code, examples and documentation. The Unreal Engine and Unity already integrate this technology.

Recipe:

Officially, there's not yet OR support with Blender. However, programers adapts several scripts to support this technology.

A script allows to display a camera view in a texture, this script can be used with 2 cameras and 2 different angles and to project their view into 2 textures. But OR is not only a stereoscopic display. How to use it with Blender?

There are 3 ways to use this technology:

- the **official Kit** uses C and Linux by NSB, but it has a proprietary license, so it's not very interesting. To find the kit: http://bit.ly/1Rklpzb
- An interesting project is **libvr** by thib, under license BSD-2. It works with Linux too.
- **OpenHMD** under license Boost. The library is available at: http://bit.ly/1MVoFOI. You need a wrapper python, you can find one at: http://bit.ly/21sXEcz

Illustration 159: Example using the Lubosz's work

Source Codes, example and explanations files: http://bit.ly/17NzIcd

Next?

The commercial version should be near 200€ or 220$, but there will be copies soon. It's not a hardware but a technology. It'll flood the market in the next years.

Games like Team Fortress 2, Doom 3, Half-Life 2, Left 4 Dead, Skyrim, Portal 2, BioShock. or Hawken give an idea of the capacities of this technology.

We are far away from the virtual reality device from «The Lawnmower Man » from Brett Leonard, a Stephen King's novel, but it's coming.

VI -   MENU RECIPES

Image made by **Maxime Karam**. Modified by the author. Blender sources are available at:
http://www.blendswap.com/blends/view/56763

VI.1. CREATE THE GAME MENU

Purpose:

Give a **menu** to allow the player to launch the game, to pause it, to resume, to choose the character, etc. It's like to create some objects on which we can click and that are displayed in overprinting on the screen (overlay).

Blender don't have, for GLSL display, a set of graphics elements (**widgets**) like checking boxes, simple buttons or radio buttons, window, selection boxes, etc. However, we can do without them.

Simple recipe (button use):

1. Add a new scene or rename the current scene «Menu» in the «info» window
2. Use the **recipe VI.8** to make the mouse cursor visible
3. Add a plane, name it «background». Add a «Material» to this plane, check «Shadeless» to be independent from a light source and check «Transparency». Set «Alpha» at 0.5 to see behind the plane.
4. Add a camera with the axis pointing below (-Z) above the plane, so that this plane takes 80% of the camera view.
5. Add a new plane with a button form, between the camera and the background, name it «Launchgame». Configure the «Material» like «Background», modify the diffuse color for example.
6. Add a text (`↑ Shift`+`A` → «Text»), place it above «Launchgame» and go to «Edit Mode» to enter the phrasing «Launch the game», go to «Object Mode». Resize to be in the button frame. Then `Alt`+`C` → «Convert to Mesh from Text» to transform it into geometry («Mesh»).
7. Add a «Material» to the text to change the color (black for example) and check «Shadeless».
8. Then, merge it with the button «LaunchGame» («`Ctrl`+`J`»).
9. Select «Launchgame», open the Logic Editor and add a first sensor with «Mouse» type: «Mouse Over» and a second with «Mouse» type: «Left Button»
10. Add a «Scene» actuator: Mode: «Set Scene» and select the corresponding scene.
11. Add a controller with «AND» type and link the sensors with the controller and the controller with the actuator

Improvements:

When the mouse cursor is over a button, we can grow it, we can change its color, then give it its first state when the mouse is not yet over the object. We can add also a sound when there's a click.

Other menu elements:

It's possible to emulate other widgets using some planes and substituting some images to others. The Illustration 160 gives a texture example with some widgets to use in the game.

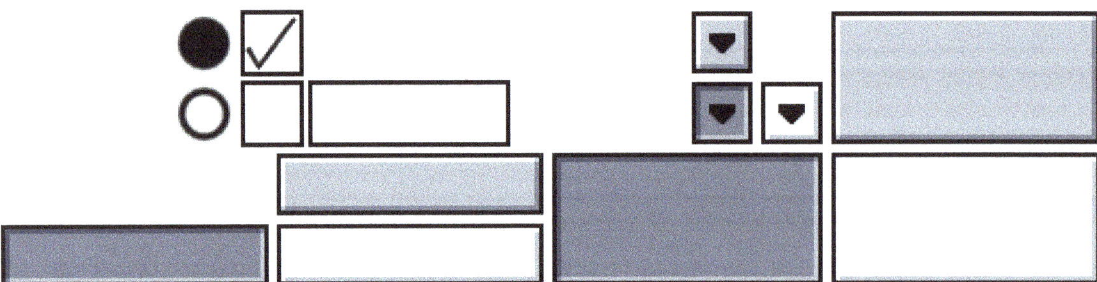

Illustration 160: Widgets example made by SolarLune for BlenderArtists

VI.2. CONFIGURATION MENU

Purpose:

When we launch the game with the external launcher («BlenderPlayer»), sometimes it's helpful to propose to the player **a full-screen mode**, a possibility to **change the game resolution graphic,** to activate or not the antialiasing, to adjust the sound and the musics. These configuration elements can be stored in a file and reloaded at each launch. The external launcher accepts a certain number of factors at launch.

Recipe:

The script is not complex but is large, download the «BlendSling» project by SolarLune.

1. Download the archive from: **http://tinyurl.com/p3paevx**
2. Unpack BlendSlingV0.2_Blend and open the Blend file with blender.
3. Launch the game mode «P», set some elements, then click on «Play Game».
4. A file «launcher.cfg» is created and contains the configuration set.
5. Reloading the game play, the configuration is automatically reloaded.
6. For BlendSling to launch the game, name the game «Game.blend» and place BlendSling in the game directory. The first scene to launch must named «LaunchHook».

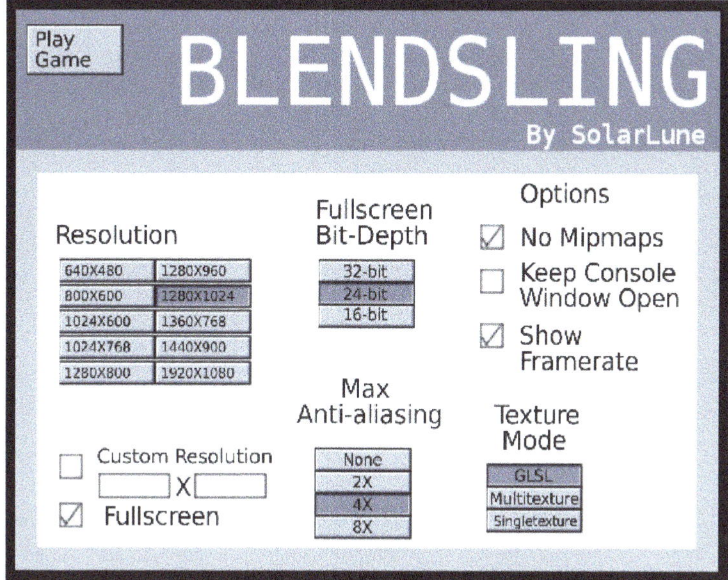

Illustration 161: «BlendSling» launcher made by SolarLune

BlendSling allows to add a file **encryption** thanks to the function base64.b64encode. It's automatic and done at each launch if there's the Blendfile. To give the game, you must remove the Blendfile, BlendSling will start the crypted file «game.bgdata». The file is decrypted only in memory (using LibLoad), so all is secured.

VI.3. SAVE AND LOAD A GAME

Purpose:

A play can be seen as the modification (position, rotation, properties) of each game object. The following script allows to **store these information in a file and reload them when needed**.

If the decor never changes and contains numerous objects, it's possible to exclude it from the saved objects list, adapt this script as you need.

Recipe:

To load, call the function **load**() and save the function **save**(). Thanks to «raco» from «BlenderArtists» for his script.

Script game.py:

```python
from bge import logic
import pickle, sys

file_name = sys.argv[1] #if launched with blender/blenderplayer file.blend
if len(file_name)=0:
        file_name = 'save'

#objects_names = ['objname1', 'Objname2', 'Objname3']

def save(cont):
   def getObjects(cont):
      scene_objects = cont.owner.scene.objects
      #return [scene_objects[name] for name in objects_names]
      return (scene_objects)
   def getDict(objects):
      dict = {}
      for ob in objects:
         properties = {prop: ob[prop] for prop in ob.getPropertyNames()}
         transform = [list(vector) for vector in ob.worldTransform]
         velocity = list(ob.worldLinearVelocity) if ob.getPhysicsId() else None
         dict[ob.name] = properties, transform, velocity
      return dict
   def store(dict):
      file = logic.expandPath('//' + file_name + '.sav')
      file_write = open(file, 'wb')
      file_write.close()

   for sensor in cont.sensors:
      if not sensor.positive:
         return

   objects = getObjects(cont)
   dict = getDict(objects)
   store(dict)
   print (logic.PrintMemInfo())

def load(cont):
   def loadDict():
      file = logic.expandPath('//' + file_name + '.sav')
      file_read = open(file, 'rb')
      dict = pickle.load(file_read)
      file_read.close()
      return dict
   def update(objects, dict):
      for key, value in dict.items():
         ob = objects[key]
         properties, transform, velocity = value
         if properties:
            for prop_name, prop_value in properties.items():
               ob[prop_name] = prop_value
         ob.worldTransform = transform
         if velocity: ob.worldLinearVelocity = velocity
   for sensor in cont.sensors:
      if not sensor.positive:
         return
   try:
      data = loadDict()
```

```
    objects = cont.owner.scene.objects
    update(objects, data)
except FileNotFoundError:
    return
```

The **pickle** module is used to create a dictionary with the properties, transformations and velocities for each object of a scene. We can only save some chosen objects with their names (comments in the code) or add a property «save» to each object we want to save. Save by doing a filter in the function **getObjects**().

We can improve the function by adding some verifications: existence of the object, to store the object mesh, etc.

The pickle module don't support matrix or vectors. A simple conversion is sufficient to resolve this problem.

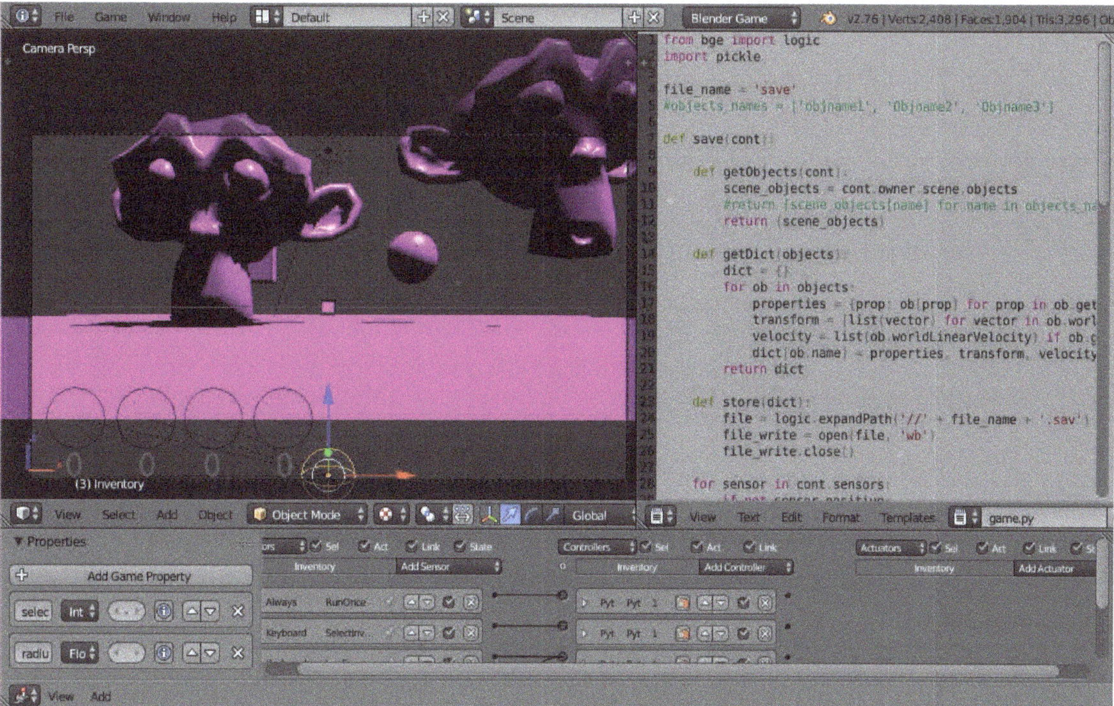

Illustration 162: Save all the objects location and orientation

VI.4. INTERFACE CREATION WITH BLENDER

Purpose:

When we develop some tools for the game, like scripts, to set some elements «designer side», it's possible to **call them through the Blender interface**, taking advantage of the windowing system: check boxes, select boxes, input fields, buttons, rules, etc.

General recipe:

To add an element into the Blender menu, we create a script. It'll be launched from the interface (not in BGE).

```python
import bpy

class MyExample(bpy.types.Panel):
    #...
    bl_space_type, bl_region_type = 'PROPERTIES', 'WINDOW'
    bl_context = "object"

    def draw(self, context):
        layout = self.layout
        #...
def register():
    bpy.utils.register_class(MyExample)

def unregister():
    bpy.utils.unregister_class(MyExample)

if __name__ == "__main__":
    register()
```

MyExample is the new menu element created.

At the minimum, it must:
- come from an existing graphic class (here: bpy.types.Panel)
- have the functions register() and unregister() to become integrated into the interface
- a display function: draw()

In the precedent example, we create a panel in the «Properties» Window (bl_space_type), «Object» Tab (bl_context).

To use the following recipes, add the functions **register**(), **unregister**() and **main**() seen before and include the BPY.

Recipe for a panel:

```python
class HelloWorldPanel(bpy.types.Panel):
    bl_label = "Hello World Panel"
    bl_idname = "OBJECT_PT_hello"
    bl_space_type = 'PROPERTIES'
    bl_region_type = 'WINDOW'
    bl_context = "object"

    def draw(self, context):
        layout = self.layout
        obj = context.object
        row = layout.row() #Line 1
        row.label(text=
                    "Hello world!",
                    icon='WORLD_DATA')

        row = layout.row() #Line 2
        row.label(text=
                    "Active object is: " +
                    obj.name)

        row = layout.row() #Line 3
        row.prop(obj, "name")

        row = layout.row() #Line 4
        row.operator("mesh.primitive_cube_add")
```

This example allows to add 4 lines to the panel (Illustration 163):
- display a text and its icon
- recuperate the object context (to allow the «object» is available, an object must be selected) and display it
- add an input box with the object name (modifiable)
- add a button with a primitive creation function with «Cube» type (mesh.primitive_cube_add)

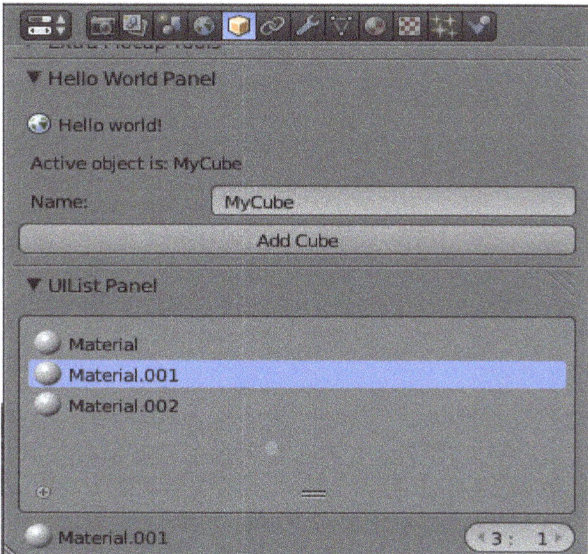

Illustration 163:Simple panel and panel with list type examples

Graphical elements

The display is organized by lines and each line can be cut in columns (Illustration 164):
- to add a new line: row = layout.row()
- if we add some elements without to create a new line, they all will be on a same line
- if we indicate row = layout.row(align=True), the elements will be aligned without separation
- To create columns, recover the split = layout.split(), add the column: col = split.column(). Launch again col = split.column() to create a second column, then a third, etc.
- Xe can change the line name by adding layout.label(text="mon texte") before to create it
- We can use 3 lines for only one element by adding after the line creation: row.scale_y = 3.0
- to obtain an element taking 2 columns in the line, use sub = row.row() then sub.scale_x = 2.0, use row for elements with normal size and sub for the elements with double size.

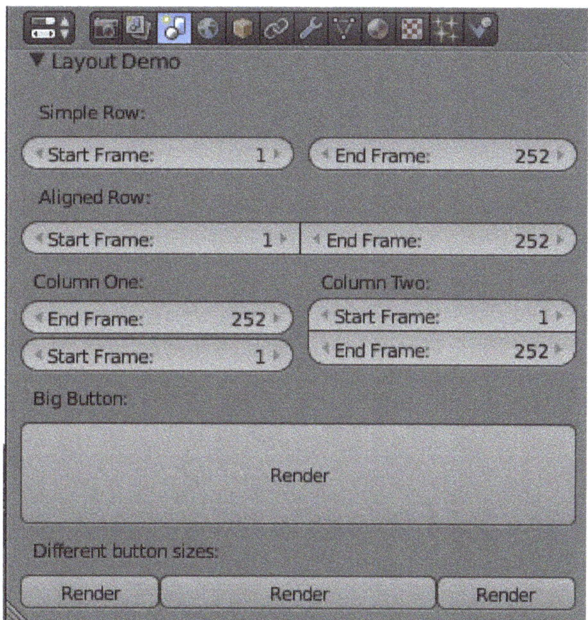

Illustration 164: Example of display in columns and other properties

<u>Manage a list</u>:

```python
class MATERIAL_UL_matslots_example(bpy.types.UIList):
    def draw_item(self, context, layout, data, item, icon,          active_data,
            active_propname):
        ob = data
        slot = item
        ma = slot.material
        if self.layout_type in {'DEFAULT', 'COMPACT'}:
            if ma:
                layout.prop(ma, "name", text="", emboss=False, icon_value=icon)
            else:
                layout.label(text="", translate=False, icon_value=icon)
            if ma and
                                not context.scene.render.use_shading_nodes:
                manode = ma.active_node_material
                if manode:
                    layout.label(text="Node %s" % manode.name,translate=False,
                                    icon_value=layout.icon(manode))
                elif ma.use_nodes:
                    layout.label(text="Node <none>", translate=False)
                else:
                    layout.label(text="")
        elif self.layout_type in {'GRID'}:
            layout.alignment = 'CENTER'
            layout.label(text="", icon_value=icon)
```

This example lists the materials associated to the selected object. There are 2 opening modes (Illustration 163).

<u>Important</u>: you have to register this class before using it in a Panel.

To call it from the panel (for all graphic elements, in draw):

```python
layout.template_list ("MATERIAL_UL_matslots_example"," ", obj, "material_slots", obj, "active_material_index")
```

We can precise the option type='COMPACT' to have a condensed version of the list.

<u>Recipe for contextual menu</u>:

To create a menu providing a choice (as when we do «⇧ Shift + A» to add an object):

```python
class SimpleCustomMenu(bpy.types.Menu):
    bl_label = "Simple Custom Menu"
    bl_idname = "OBJECT_MT_simple_custom_menu"

    def draw(self, context):
        layout = self.layout
        layout.operator("wm.open_mainfile")
        layout.operator("wm.save_as_mainfile")
```

This example contains a menu with 2 choices:
- open (open_mainfile)
- save the current file (save_as_mainfile)

This menu can be called in a script through the following call:

```python
bpy.ops.wm.call_menu(name=SimpleCustomMenu.bl_idname)
```

To list some elements from a submenu, use the following function:

```python
layout.operator_menu_enum("object.select_by_type", property="type", text="Select All by Type...",)
```

This example selects the elements according to their type.

VI.5. SHARE THE INTERFACE BY CREATING AN ADDON

Purpose:

To add permanently a level editor, or a landscape generator or a function for Blender, we can create an **Addon**. It's a plugin that can be easily integrated in Blender and shared with the Blender community.

If you want to use it, you must register the **addon**. To share the addon, use the following recipe.

To List the Addons, go to preferences («`Ctrl`+`Alt`+`U`») «Addons» panel. We can activate or deactivate an Addon, or install it from a zip file.

Recipe:

Set up an objects import/export to create levels. It as accessible in «export» and «import» of the «info» window, menu «File».

You need:

- the file must be in the directory: scripts/addons
- the addon must be activated in the users preferences
- to respect a minimal structure like this (in the same order) – In italic, the variable parts. In bold, the non essentials parts.

```
bl_info = {
    "name": "Export Game Level Format(.lvl)",
    "author": "Gossellin Gregory",
    "version": (1, 1),
    "blender": (2, 7, 0),
    "location": "File > Export > Game Level Format(.lvl)",
    "description": "Export Game Level Format(.lvl)",
    "warning": "",
    "wiki_url": "",
    "tracker_url": "http://www.benicourt.com/blender/Scripts/exportLevel/",
    "category": "Import-Export"}
```

These elements contain the information indicated in the users preferences.

Wiki_url is used if the script is registered with Blender and if there's a reserved space on the wiki. Tracker_url appears to report an error.

The category can be seen at left in the addons list.

```
import bpy
from bpy.props import *
import mathutils, math, struct
from os import remove
import time
from bpy_extras.io_utils import ExportHelper
"wb")
    #file.write(...)
def do_export(context, props, filepath):
    file = open(filepath, "wb")
    #file.write(...)

    file.flush()
    file.close()
    return True
```

This is the code for the exporter. It's empty, but if you use the script like that, it'll ask a file name and save the file with nothing. You must complete this part.

```
###### EXPORT OPERATOR ######
class Export_lvl(bpy.types.Operator, ExportHelper):
    bl_idname = "level.lvl"
    bl_label = "Game Level (.lvl)"
    filename_ext = ".lvl"

    select_obj = BoolProperty(name="Selected Object Only",
        description="Export only selected objects for level",default=False,
    apply_modifiers = BoolProperty(name="Apply Modifiers",
        description="Applies the      Modifiers",default=True,)

    def execute(self, context):
```

```python
        start_time = time.time()
        print('\n______START______')
        props = self.properties
        filepath = self.filepath
        filepath = bpy.path.ensure_ext(filepath, self.filename_ext)
        exported = do_export(context, props, filepath)

        if exported:
            print('finished export in %s seconds' %
                                ((time.time() - start_time)))
            print(filepath)
        return {'FINISHED'}
    def invoke(self, context, event):
        wm = context.window_manager
        if True:
            # File selector
            wm.fileselect_add(self) # will run self.execute()
            return {'RUNNING_MODAL'}
        elif True:
            # search the enum
            wm.invoke_search_popup(self)
            return {'RUNNING_MODAL'}
        elif False:
            # Redo popup
            return wm.invoke_props_popup(self, event)
        elif False:
            return self.execute(context)
```

This code contains all the graphic elements which will be seen at left after a click on export/import, when we select the file name.

```python
### REGISTER ###
def menu_func(self, context):
    self.layout.operator(Export_lvl.bl_idname, text="Game Level (.lvl)")
def register():
    bpy.utils.register_module(__name__)
    bpy.types.INFO_MT_file_export.append(menu_func)
def unregister():
    bpy.utils.unregister_module(__name__)
    bpy.types.INFO_MT_file_export.remove(menu_func)

if __name__ == "__main__":
    register()
```

For the export function, it can contains the following information:

ob in bpy.data.objects and

- ob.type: {'MESH','ARMATURE','LAMP','CAMERA','EMPTY'}
- ob.parent.name: parent object name (filtrate "_proxy" if the object is from another file)
- ob.rotation_euler.x, ob.rotation_euler.y, ob.rotation_euler.z (to be multiplied by 180.0 / math.pi to be in degrees
- ob.location.x, ob.location.y, ob.location.z: position
- ob.scale.x, ob.scale.y, ob.scale.z: scale

See all the objects in the datablocks (or in the python: dir(ob) window) to recover the properties, everything is here, also the physic caracteristics.

VI.6. MANAGE AN INVENTORY

Purpose:

In most games, the player collects some objects. They are placed in an inventory either directly available on the screen, or in another screen via a key. In this recipe, we see an example with an inventory at the bottom of the screen, with an opportunity to:

- collect some objects with a particular property
- store objects by classifying them by type to store several objects in an emplacement with the number of objects displayed
- manage some storage units (cells) graphically and to place them where we need
- select an active object
- extract an active object from the inventory
- be visible or not

Recipe:

As it's impossible to transfer an object from a scene to another without using the Python function **LibLoad**, so prefer not using an overlay for the inventory displaying. The only way to duplicate an object is to store a copy permanently in an invisible layer.

Similary, it's impossible, in run mode, to move an object in an inactive layer.

So, objects stay in the current scene and are just hidden and in «Ghost» mode (no collision).

1st step: Implementation

1. Repeat the **recipe V.14.**

2. To each object, add a «String» property named «type» and complete with: «monkey» for Suzanne, «box» for the cube and «ball» for the sphere. This property allows to stack the objects with different names.

3. Duplicate the different objects to do collect tests and to verify the parameters.

4. Add an Empty (**⇧ Shift**+**A** → «Empty» → «Sphere»), name it «Inventory». This object is the inventory.

5. Parent the «Inventory» to the object «CameraFreeview» and place it at the bottom, at the center of the camera view, closest to the camera. Add a «property» «radius» with float type and enter a value (ex: «0.1»).

6. To represent the object storage unit (cell), use a circle. This circle has a radius equal to the precedent radius. Add a circle (**⇧ Shift**+**A** → «Mesh» → «Circle») and do the necessary displacement (G), rotations (R) and scale (S) to have a circle placed in camera mode (0), at the place we display the first inventory object (ex: at the bottom at left of the screen). The Illustration 165 shows a version with 4 cells.

7. In the «Properties» window, «Physics» Tab, select «Physic Type»: «No Collision».

8. Rename the circle «cell0» and parent to the «Inventory» object (Select «cell0», then «inventory» («⇧ Shift»), and **Ctrl**+**P** → «Parent to Object»)

9. Add a text, name it «Cell0Text» and parent too to the object «Inventory». Position the text just bellow of «Cell0». This object is used to display the number (if >1) of the object occurrences.

10. In the «Properties» window, «Physics» Tab, select «Physic Type»: «No Collision» too.

11. The text resolution is not sufficient for a text so close of the camera, and the camera can be modified only in Python (in run mode), you need to add a script.

12. Select «Cell0Text» and open the «Logic Editor». Add an «Always» sensor, name it «RunOnce».

13. Add a «Python» controller, select «Module» and enter «inventory.initText» in«Value». Link the sensor with the controller.

14. Add a new script file «inventory.py» and copy the following lines.

15. Duplicate the couples «Cell0» and «Cell0Text» (⬆ Shift + D) in several objects: «Cell1/Cell1Text» … ««Cell3/Cell3Text» like on Illustration 165.

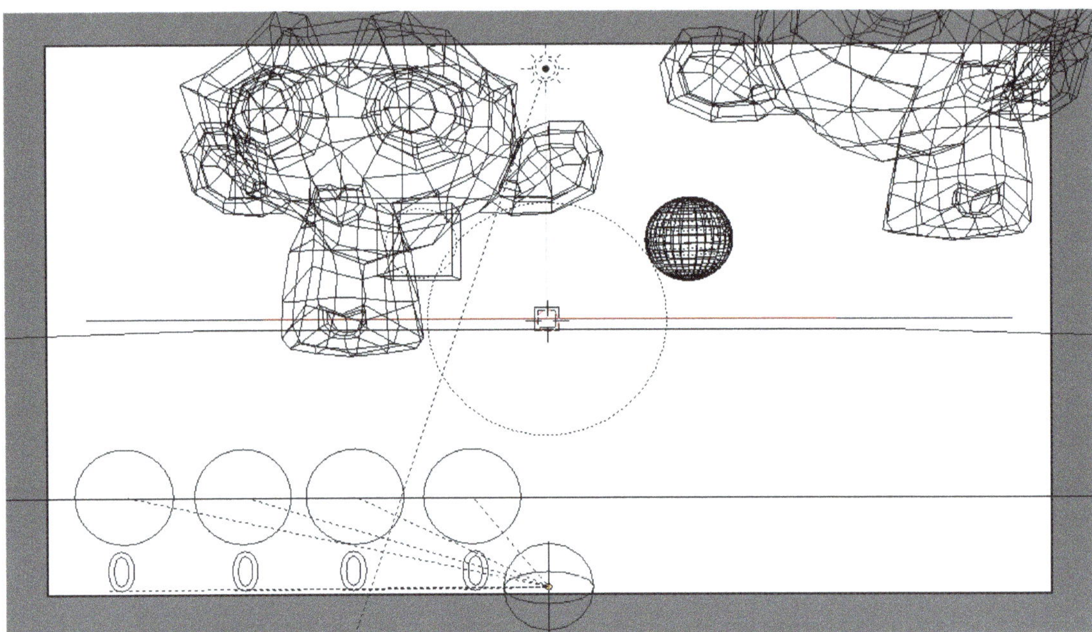

Illustration 165: Inventory positioning example, at the bottom left, in camera view

Script python «inventory.py»:

```python
def initText(cont):
    cont.owner.resolution = 10 #default is 1
    cont.owner["Text"] = ""
```

Step 2: collect some objects

1. Modify the script «MouseLook.py» - repeat the lines #1 and #2 in the following script and insert the corresponding code.

2. Select the «grabber» object and go to the «Logic Editor». Add a «Mouse» sensor, name it «MousePick», Select «Mouse Event»: «Right Button». Link the sensor with the existing controller.

Script «MouseLook.py» modification:

```python
#   click = cont.sensors["MouseClick"] #1
    pick = cont.sensors["MousePick"]

#if click.positive and ray.positive: #2
    elif pick.positive and ray.positive:
        #Picking Object
        hit = ray.hitObject
        bge.inventory.add(hit)
#   elif ray.positive: click = cont.sensors["MouseClick"]
```

3. Create a new script «tools.py» file and paste the following script lines. This script allows to determinate an object size scrolling through all the objects points. We obtain the «bounding box» measures, a box around the object. (Script made by solarLune on «BlenderArtists»).

Script «tools.py»:

```python
from mathutils import Vector

def getDimensions(object = None, roundit = 3, offset = 1, meshnum = 0):
   #from solarLune module BGHelper
        if object == None:
                object = logic.getCurrentController().owner
        s = object.worldScale
        mesh = object.meshes[meshnum]
        verts = [[], [], []]
        originpos = [0, 0, 0]
        for mat in range(len(mesh.materials)):
                for v in range(mesh.getVertexArrayLength(mat)):
                        vert, pos = mesh.getVertex(mat, v), vert.getXYZ()
                        verts[0].append(pos[0])
                        verts[1].append(pos[1])
                        verts[2].append(pos[2])
        verts[0].sort(), verts[1].sort(), verts[2].sort()

        if offset != 0:
                offsetpos = [
                        (verts[0][len(verts[0])-1] + verts[0][0]) / 2,
                        (verts[1][len(verts[1])-1] + verts[1][0]) / 2,
                        (verts[2][len(verts[2])-1] + verts[2][0]) / 2,
                        ]

        if roundit >= 0:
                size = [
                round((verts[0][len(verts[0])-1]-verts[0][0])*s[0], roundit),
                round((verts[1][len(verts[0])-1]-verts[1][0])*s[1], roundit),
                round((verts[2][len(verts[0])-1]-verts[2][0])*s[2], roundit)]
        else:
                size = [(verts[0][len(verts[0]) - 1] - verts[0][0]) * s[0],
                (verts[1][len(verts[0]) - 1] - verts[1][0]) * s[1],
                (verts[2][len(verts[0]) - 1] - verts[2][0]) * s[2]]
        if offset:
                return (Vector(size), Vector(offsetpos))
        else:
                return (mathutils.Vector(size), None)
```

4.   Add an «Always» sensor, name it «RunOnce».

5.   Add a «Python» controller, select «Module», enter «inventory.init» in the «Value» field.

6.   Link the sensor with the controller. The «inventory» object is initialized with the corresponding cells and stored into BGE to be available from the other functions.

Addition to Script «inventory.py»

```python
import bge
from tools import getDimensions
from mathutils import Vector

class cell(object):
   def __init__(self):
     self.position = Vector()
     self.scale = Vector()
     self.obj = ""
     self.objPick = []
     self.type, self.total, self.text = "", 0, ""

   def updateText(self):
     if self.total > 1:
        self.text["Text"] = self.total
     else:
        self.text["Text"] = ""

class inventory(object):
   def __init__(self,gameobj):
     self.cells = []
     self.obj = gameobj
     self.visibility = True
     self.radius = gameobj["radius"]

   def set(self,ob):
     self.cells.append(ob)

   def add(self,hit):
     print("Add ",hit," to inventory")
     if not "type" in hit:
        hit["type"] = hit.name
     cell = self.getCell(hit["type"])
     hit.worldPosition = cell.obj.worldPosition
     hit.setParent(cell.obj) #gost auto
```

```python
        dimhit = getDimensions(hit)[0]
        cell.scale = Vector(hit.worldScale) #copy, not pointer
        hit.worldScale = [hit.worldScale[0]*self.radius/dimhit[0],
            hit.worldScale[1]*self.radius/dimhit[1],
            hit.worldScale[2]*self.radius/dimhit[2]]
        cell.objPick.append(hit)

        if cell.total > 0:
            hit.visible = False

        cell.type = hit["type"]
        cell.total +=1
        cell.updateText()

    def getCell(self,type):
        c = 0
        for cell in self.cells:
            if cell.type == type:
                c = cell
                break
        if c == 0: #not found
            for cell in self.cells:
                if cell.total == 0:
                    c = cell
                    break
        return c

def init(cont):
    scene = bge.logic.getCurrentScene()
    own = cont.owner
    inv = inventory(own)

    cellnames = ['Cell0','Cell1','Cell2','Cell3'] #Here to select Cells
    for i in cellnames:
        x = cell()
        x.obj = scene.objects[i]
        x.text = scene.objects[x.obj.name+"Text"]
        inv.set(x)

    bge.inventory = inv #add bge
```

The init() function has a «**cellnames**» variable in which we store the cells name. We can add as many cells as we need. The «Text» objects, with the number of occurrences of stored objects, have the same name than the cell object, we add «Text» to the name. Example: «Cell45» with «Cell45Text».

The **updateText**() function from the cell class allows to update the number of collected objects by the cell. The text is only displayed if there are 2 or more objects.

The **getCell**() function from the inventory class allows to choose the cell for store an object. A first search in the cells is done and if the type is found, the cell is selected. If there's no cell, the first empty cell is selected.

The **add**() function from the inventory class allows to add the object to the inventory. The object is resized and parented to the cell. If there's already an object in the cell, we hide the last collected object

Step 3: Selection menu of an inventory menu

A selected object rotates ans its color is modified. The key «Tab» allows to go from one to another.

1. Select the «Inventory» object and go to the «Logic Editor».
2. Add a Property «select» with «Integer» type, and initialized to «-1» (= no selection)
3. Add a sensor with «keyboard» type, and select a key to change the selected object in the inventory (example: «Tab»).
4. Add a «Python» controller, select «Module» and enter «inventory.selectNext» in «Value». Link the sensor with the controller
5. Select «Cell0» and add a property «active» with «boolean» type, unchecked (value «False»).
6. Add an «Always» sensor, check «Activate On True Level Triggering» and enter «50» as frequency.
7. Add a «Property» sensor, «Evaluation Type»: «Equal», «Property»: Select «active» and «Value»: «true»
8. Add an «And» controller and link it to the 2 precedents sensors.

9. Add a «Motion» actuator, select «Simple Motion», and enter «Rot» «Z»: 1.0. Link the actuator with the precedent controller. Now, when the property is «active» and positive, the cell object turns with the objects parented to it.
10. Repeat the operation for all the cells (or duplicate the cells)
11. Add to script «inventory.py» the following lines.

Addition to script «inventory.py»:

```python
def selectNext(cont):
  if cont.sensors[0].positive:
    own = cont.owner
    select = own["select"]

    if select >= 0:
      bge.inventory.cells[select].obj["active"] = False
      bge.inventory.cells[select].objPick[0].color = [1,1,1,1]
    select += 1
    while select < (len(bge.inventory.cells)) and
                    bge.inventory.cells[select].total == 0:
      select += 1

    select %= len (bge.inventory.cells)
    bge.inventory.cells[select].obj["active"] = True
    bge.inventory.cells[select].objPick[0].color = [1,0.9,0.1,1]
    own["select"] = select
```

Step 4: Drop a selected object

1. Select the «Inventory» object and go to «Logic Editor».
2. Add a «Keyboard» sensor, name it «keydrop» and select a key to drop an object (example: «D» pour «drop»)
3. Add a «Mouse» sensor, name it «mouseOver» and select «Mouse Event»: **«Mouse over Any»**.
4. Add a «Python» controller, select «Module» and enter «inventory.dropActiveObject» in «value». Link the 2 sensors with the controller.
5. Add to the script «inventory.py» the following lines. The class name is in commentary, add the functions in the correct classes (the function dropActiveObject is not linked to a class).

Addition to the script «inventory.py»:

```python
#class cell(object):
  def drop(self,fromObj,position):
    if self.total <= 0:
      return

    self.total -= 1
    if self.total == 0:
      fromObj["select"] = -1
    self.updateText()

    obj = self.objPick.pop()
    print ("Drop ",obj.name," from inventory")
    obj.removeParent()
    obj.worldScale = self.scale
    obj.color = [1,1,1,1]

    obj.worldPosition = position+Vector([0,0,2])

    if self.total >= 0:
      obj.visible = True


#class inventory(object):

  def drop(self,position):
    if self.obj["select"] >= 0:
      self.cells[self.obj["select"]].drop(self.obj,position)
```

```python
def dropActiveObject(cont):
    mouseover = cont.sensors["mouseOver"]
    if cont.sensors["keyDrop"].positive and mouseover.positive:
        pos = mouseover.hitPosition
        bge.inventory.drop(pos)
```

The sensor «mouseOver» allows to determinate the object position dropped. Add 2 units to Z to make the object falling back to the floor.

Step 5: to hide the inventory

1. Select the «Inventory» object and go to the «Logic Editor».
2. Add a «Keyboard» sensor and select a key to display and hide the inventory (example: «I»)
3. Add a «Python» controller, select «Module» and enter «inventory.showHide» in «value». Link the sensor with the controller.
4. Add to script «inventory.py» the following script.

Addition to the script «inventory.py»:

```python
def showHide(cont):
    if cont.sensors[0].positive:
        bge.inventory.visibility = not (bge.inventory.visibility)
        bge.inventory.obj.setVisible(bge.inventory.visibility, True)
```

The setVisible() function is used with the recursive parameter, to hide or display all the object «Inventory» children.

VI.7. DISPLAY TEXT

Purpose:

For an adventure game or a FPS, it's often useful to display **dialogues at screen, to display the book interior or to tell a story**.

Recipe True Type:

1. Add an object with «Text» type (**Shift**+**A** → «Text»)

2. Go to «Edit Mode» (**Tab**) and modify the text by «Waiting...»

3. «Properties» window, «Data Object» Tab, «Font» panel, font «Regular», click on «Load a new font from file» and choose a font TrueType file(ext. TTF).

4. To change the **color**, go to «Object» Tab, «Display» panel and modify «Object Color». The material application don't allow to change the color like for other objects.

5. Open the «Logic Editor», display the menu «Properties» (N). A new option is available: click on «Add a Text Game Property». By default, it's a character string (String), but it's possible to use another types. By clicking on the button, we give to logic bricks the possibility to use the property «Text» of these objects. With python, the property is used like any property.

6. Add a «Delay» sensor, set «Delay»: 200

7. Add a «Property» actuator, «Mode»: «Assign», select the property «Text» and enter «"First Move"» in the field «value» (don't forget the « «). Joint he sensor with the actuator.

8. Add a second sensor with «Delay» type, set «Delay»: 400

9. Add a «Property» actuator, «Mode»: «Assign», select the property «Text» and enter «"Second Move"» in the field «value». Link the sensor with the actuator.

10. Test (**P**): The text will be «Waiting...», then a few seconds later, «First Move», and a few seconds later «Second Move».

Numerous options don't work with BGE, like extrusion, «Shear», the «textbox», etc. Of course, we can convert the «Text» object into «Mesh» («**Alt**+**C**» → «Convert Mesh from Text»), but you'll can't change the text.

Recipe Font Bitmap:

Before «Text» type works with BGE, this recipe allows to use an **image as font model.** A part of the image corresponds to a letter. Using a plane with the coordinates UV, this plane displays a letter. By duplicating this plane and modifying the UV coordinates, the planes displays another letter. Repeat the operation and align the different planes to make words, then phrases.

The system **is automatic.** It's used to make its own fonts or tout add particular colors.

1. Download a font texture: http://tinyurl.com/pgz7y8y

2. Add a plane (**Shift**+**A** → «Mesh» → «Plane»).

3. Go to «Edit Mode» and an UV mapping («U» → «Unwrap»).

4. «Properties» window, «Material» Tab, add a new material («+»). «Shading» Panel, check «Shadeless». «Game Settings» panel, «Alpha Blend»: selection «Alpha Blend» and check the option «Text». «Transparency» panel, check to activate, select «Z Transparency» and set «Alpha» at 0.

5. «Texture» panel, add a new texture with «Image or Movie» type. Open the downloaded image file. «Mapping» panel, «Coordinates»: «UV», «Map»: «uvmap». «Influence» Panel, «diffuse»: check «Alpha» and set at 1.

6. Make sure to be in «Edit Mode» and open the «UV/Image Editor». Select the image and resize (S) the UV mapping ta have only the size of 1 letter, then move (G) the mapping on the 1st letter at the

top left of the picture.

7. Open the «Logic Editor» and add a property «Text» with «String» type, then enter the value «Automatic Writing with Bitmap Font».

8. Test (): the plane is replaced by the precedent text.

Working: On the texture (Illustration 166), there's a line at the top, it's a code that associate letters to locations (UV coordinates). With this code, the system knows where are the letters to display from a string.

How to create its owns fonts?

There's a tool to transform fonts «True Type» into images exploitable (coding line).

FTBlender can be downloaded from: http://tinyurl.com/qzurl2g

```
ftblender.exe -o KGA.tga -x 512 -y 512 -r 53 ppem KGAllofMe.ttf
```

This command line open a window with the next texture («F2» to save, «q» to quit). In the precedent example, we create an image «KGA.tga» (don't use a loosy compression because the coding line will be modified) with resolution 512x512 and 53 dpi.

Download some free fonts (to transform with ftblender or to use directly with the first recipe) at the following address: http://www.1001fonts.com/

To create a bitmap font, modify an existing texture and keep the same letters disposition and size without modify the coding line.

Illustration 166: Colored font example from a TTF – source: www.blendenzo.com

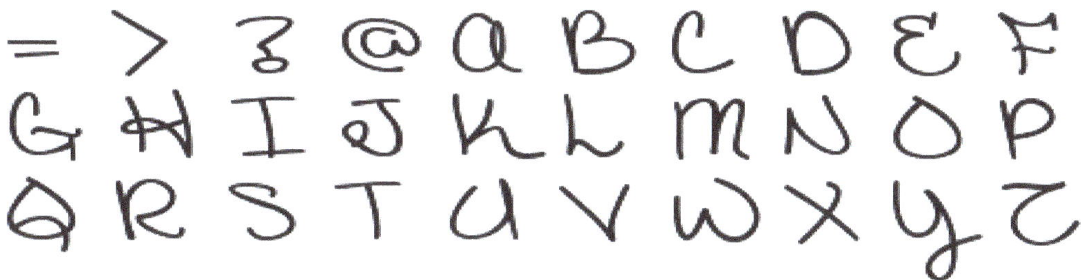

Illustration 167: Another TFF example : CatholicSchoolGirls

VI.8. A MOUSE GRAPHIC CURSOR

Purpose:

Sometimes, we need to display the mouse cursor to click on a menu. To change the cursor, we can hide it.

The **recipe V.3** allows to display the mouse cursor. So, to hide it, call: Rasterizer.showMouse(0)
To know where the chosen cursor must be displayed, follow the mouse cursor position hidden.

In this example, use a scene with «overlay» scene, with a fixed camera like in the **recipe VI.1.** The cursor is a plane moving on the axes X and Y according to the mouse movements:

1. To the script «mouse.py», add the following script lines.

2. Add a plane for the cursor, name it «MouseCursor», move it on a Z coordinate so that nothing can be between the camera and the cursor.

3. In «Edit Mode», do an UV mapping («U» → «Unwrap»).

4. Go to «Object Mode», then, in the «Properties» window, «Materials» Tab, add a new «Material» («+»). «Shading» Panel, check «Shadeless». «Transparency» Panel, check to activate, select «Z Transparency» and set «Alpha» at 0.

5. «Textures» Panel, add a texture («+») with «Image or Movie» type, select an image representing the cursor with an alpha canal for transparency (check «show alpha» to verify). «Mapping» Panel, «Coordinates»: Select «UV», «Map»: «UVMap».

6. «Diffuse» Panel, check «alpha» and set at 1. So, the texture transparency is done. If it not, the selected image doesn't contain alpha canal («Show alpha» must show a checkerboard).

7. «Physics» Tab, «Type»: Select «no collision». The sensor «Mouse Over» use a «Ray» to know the object that the mouse fly over. Position the graphic cursor in «No collision» to allow this last to be not an obstacle between the real cursor and the object.

8. Open the «Logic Editor» and add a «Mouse» sensor, name it «MouseMove», «Mouse Event»: «Movement»

9. Add a «Python» controller, select «Module» and enter «mouse.move». Link the sensor with the controller.

10. Add a property «xfactor» with «float» type and with a value: 1.2. Add a property «yfactor» with «float» type and value: 1.1.

11. Keep the cursor displayed and do a test. The graphic mouse cursor must follow the real mouse cursor «mouse.show». If there's a lag on the X axis, increase the xfactor value. Otherwise, decrease the value. Do the same for «yfactor».

Addition to the script «mouse.py»:

```python
from bge import render

def move(cont):
    mouse = cont.sensors["MouseMove"]
    cursor = cont.owner
    width, height = render.getWindowWidth(), render.getWindowHeight()
    x,y = ( width / 2 – mouse.position[0]),( height / 2 - mouse.position[1])
    cursx = -x / (width / 2)*cursor["xfactor"]
    cursy = y / (width / 2)*cursor["yfactor"]

    cursor.position.x, cursor.position.y = cursx, cursy
```

To move the camera, parent «MouseCursor» to the camera.

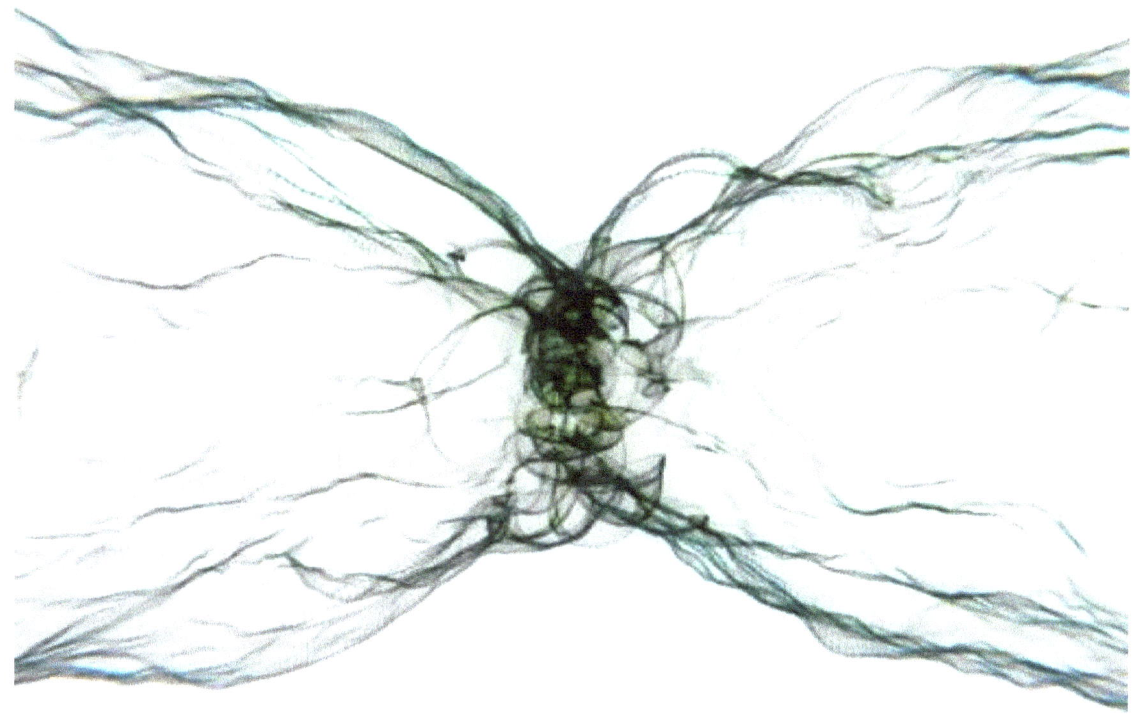

VII -   IMPROVEMENTS AND FX RECIPES

VII.1. BAKED SHADOWS (LIGHTMAPS)

Purpose:

The rendering with **ray-tracing** type allows to calculate the **shadows effects in a scene.** The realtime rendering, the **GLSL display**, is less realistic because you need to display between 25 and 60 images per second and calculations are simplified. If we add too much lights in a scene, we obtain a jerkily rendering. **Lamps with «point» type don't create shadow with BGE (actually).** You can use the advantages of the ray tracing without its inconvenient via the **Lightmaps** (sheet #1 «3D glossary»), with set of «objects-lamps» which are not in movement.

Recipe:

Choose a scene already designed with 1 or more light points, and some objects.

Verify that there's some shadows in rendering mode and not in GLSL Mode.

1. Select non-dynamic objects decor where you want to see shadows and go to «Edit Mode» (key «Tab»)

2. Contextual menu UV Mapping (Key «U») → **«Smart UV Project»** – Select «All Faces» and Image Size at 1024 – button «Ok». Image Size correspond to the shadow resolution, the higher it's, the more resources he needs, but the clearer the shadow is.

3. «UV Image Editor» Panel, near the UV, button «+ New» to add a new image (size: 1024), name it «TextureLightmap».

4. Select the «Lightmap» in «Active UV Map» (choice not available if we are not in *«edit Mode»* in the 3D View):

5. «Properties» window → «Texture» panel → Add New Texture («+») with «Image or Movie» type

6. «Image» Panel → select «TextureLightMap» by clicking on the Image icon («Browse Image to be linked»)

7. «mapping» Panel → Select «Coordinates»: «UV» and «Map»: «Lightmap».

8. «Influence» Panel → Select «Blend: Overlay» (for soft shadow) or select «Blend: Mix» (hard shadow), and uncheck «RGB to Intensity».

9. «Render» Panel → «Bake» Panel, «Bake mode»: Select «Shadow», click on the button «Bake».

Illustration 168: Scene without Lightmap

VII.2. AMBIENT OCCLUSION WITH BGE

Purpose:

Ambient Occlusion is a visual effect that was originally developed by Industrial Light and Magic (ILM) and used in the 2001 film Pearl Harbor.

The «**Ambient occlusion**» mechanism is normally reserved to ray-tracing rendering. It allows to calculate the shadow made by an object on itself, independently of any light source. Specifically, it **simulates a global illumination with the sky luminosity view from a given point.**

Ambient occlusion is a lighting model that calculates the brightness of a pixel in relation to nearby objects in the scene. More specifically, it determines when certain pixels are blocked from the environmental light by nearby geometry, in which case, its brightness value is reduced. It accounts for the general dimming effect when two evenly lit objects are brought close to each other.

The scene is more realistic. Fortunately, we can use bake this effect if we want to use it with BGE.

Illustration 169: Scene with Lightmap (Shadow Baking)

Recipe:

1. Repeat the recipe VII-1 changing the «bake mode: Ambient Occlusion».
2. Activate it: «Properties» Window → «World» panel → Check «Ambient Occlusion» (available in mode «Blender Render»). Factor allow to amplify the darkening effects.
3. Refine the result using more samples: «Properties» Panel → «World» panel → «Gather» → «Sampling»: set Samples at 15. The number of occlusion rays is the square of this number (here: 15x15 = 225). By default, the value is 5, just sufficient for a previsualization.
4. «Distance» = length of rays – the bigger this value is, the more the distant geometries have an impact on the shadows.

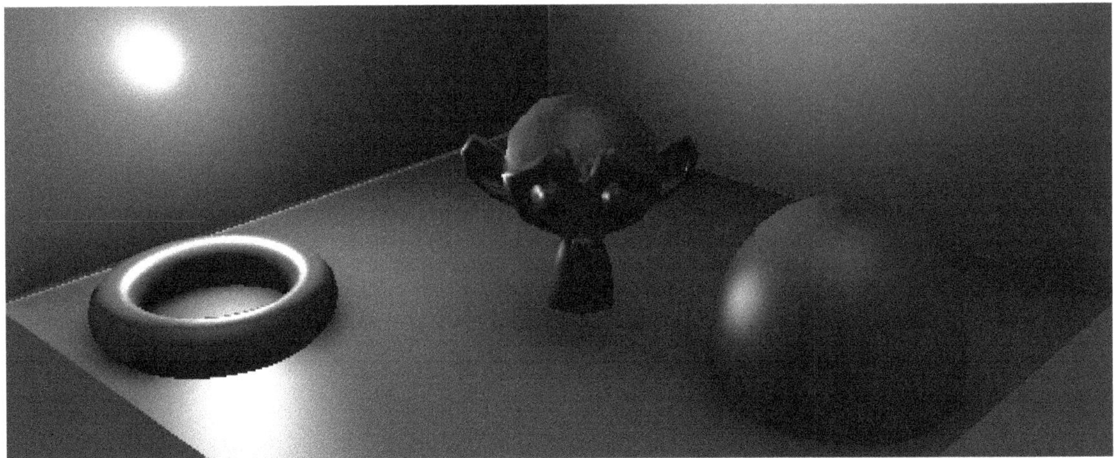

Illustration 170: Scene with Ambient Occlusion

Illustration 171: With a more complex scene...

VII.3. BUMP AND NORMAL MAPPING

Purpose:

The Bump and the normal mapping consist in **using a texture to give the impression of granularity to a surface**. The example type is the brick. According to the displacement of the light, the joints create different shadows.

The Bumpmap images are often in black and white, they are used to simulate a relief on a plane surface. **Normal Map** record the normals direction (object faces orientation), coding it into colors. So we have a more precise rendering.

Recipe #1:

With a bump map (black and white) and a texture with «Specular» type like in the Illustration 172 (3 images at the top):

1. Select the object, and add a «Material» in the «properties» window, «Material» Tab
2. In «Properties», «Texture» panel, add a first texture, named «Texcolor» set in «diffuse intensity»: 1.0 and «color»: 1.0
3. Add a second texture, named «Texnormal»: uncheck all you find in «diffuse», check «geometry»: «normal» (play on the normal value to increase the effect).
4. Add a last texture named «Texspecular», uncheck «diffuse», and set «specular intensity» at 1.0
5. Add a lamp with «point» type above the object and move it to see the effect (in GLSL display) Illustration 172 (image at the bottom).

Recipe #2:

With a colored normal map (blue variations) like the Illustration 173:

1. Repeat the steps 1, 2, 3 and 5 of the precedent recipe.
2. For «TexNormal», «image sampling» Panel, check«Normal map»: «Tangent».

If the Normal map is made of a multitude of colors like on image in the upper right of the Illustration 173: «Bump» effect using a «normal map», it's probably a Normal map calculated in mode «object space». In this case, in the «image sampling» panel, check «Normal map»: «Object». A texture with this type is used in the recipe IV.12.

Recipe #3:

Implementation of its own Bump map

As seen on the Illustration 173: «Bump» effect using a «normal map», take the left image to obtain the image on the middle.

1. Open the picture in any image editor software (The Gimp or Paint.NET).
2. Transform the image in black and white, increase the contrast,
3. Invert the colors

If it's possible to create a Bump map effect from any texture, we can't create a real Normal map from a simple texture. We can do a false Normal map, but we often need spatial information to do that. Otherwise, we can do a normal map from high resolution objects to apply it on an object with a lower resolution (recipe V.12).

Illustration 172: Result of the operation with the combination of the 3 textures

color

normal (tangent space)

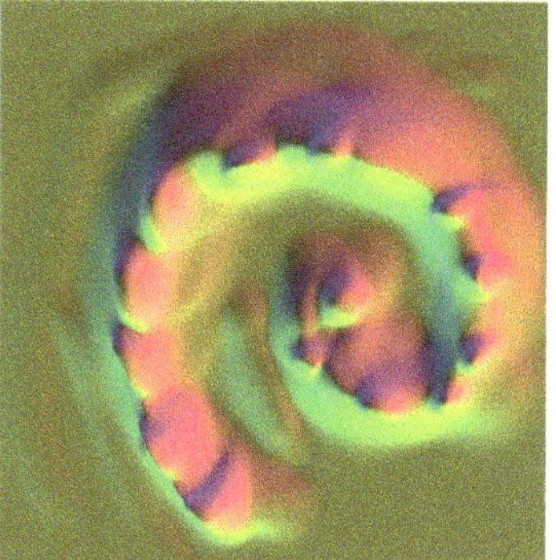

Normal (object space)

Illustration 173: «Bump» effect using a «normal map»

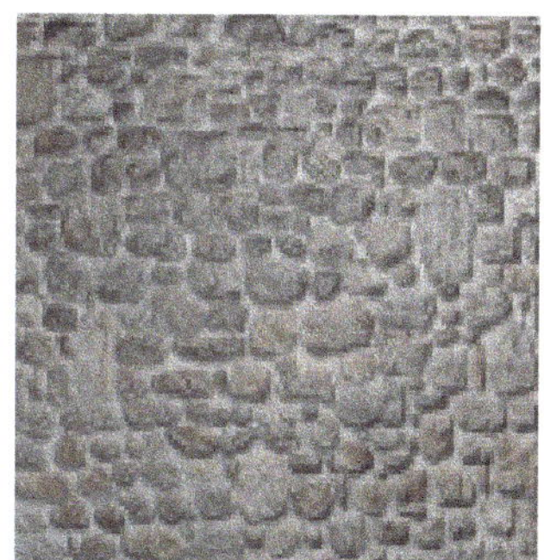

Illustration 174: at left the initial image, in the middle, the image revised
and at right, the final image with «Bump» effect

VII.4. ALL TEXTURES IN ONE

Purpose: Reduce graphic card work

The more we have textures, the more the graphic card has work to do. According to the graphic card, we can store more or less textures. However, as soon as the limit's reached, exchange mechanisms operate between the central memory (RAM) and the graphic card memory (VRAM). Performances drop.

When we model a mesh, we often use a bank of materials that we apply on the different parts of an object. We have several textures per object.

The following recipe allows to:

- **combine every object textures in only one**, easier to manipulate with the graphic card, keeping the materials characteristics.

- **Use the Blender procedural textures** normally inaccessible via BGE.

Recipe:

Create an object that contains several procedural textures, (the same recipe for textures with «images» type) and merge them into only one, using several materials.

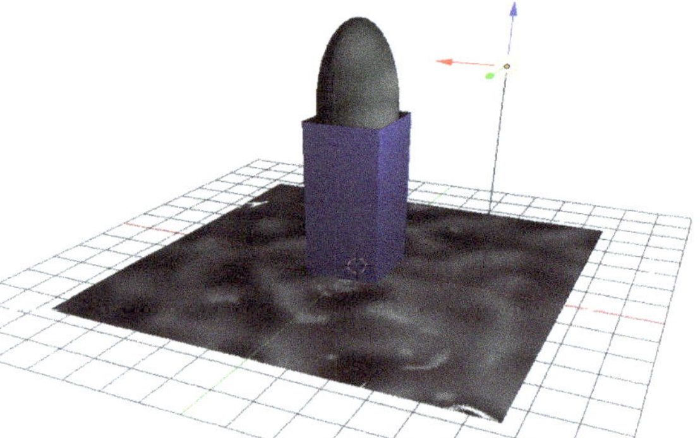

Illustration 175: Example of the recipe for baking multi-textures

1. **Create a simple scene** made with a cube, a sphere (with a scale on Z) and one plane like the Illustration 175.

2. **Add a «Material» for each object,** then assign a texture for example:
   - with «Stucci» type for the plane, with a normal geometry at 10 (change the color too)
   - with «Noise» type for the cube
   - with «Voronoi» type for the sphere («Material»: «Specular Intensity» at 0)

3. At this level, we don't have texture, F12 displays the rendering.

4. Go to object mode, select the 3 objects, go to «Edit Mode», do an **UV mapping** («U» → «Lightmap Pack», «Selection»: «Selected Mesh Objects», check «Share Tex Space», «New UV Map», and «New Image», then click on «Ok».

5. Display the UV Image Editor, and **select the new created image** (lightmap)

6. Go to object mode, «Render» Tab → «Bake» Panel → select «Bake mode: Textures», then click on the button«Bake».

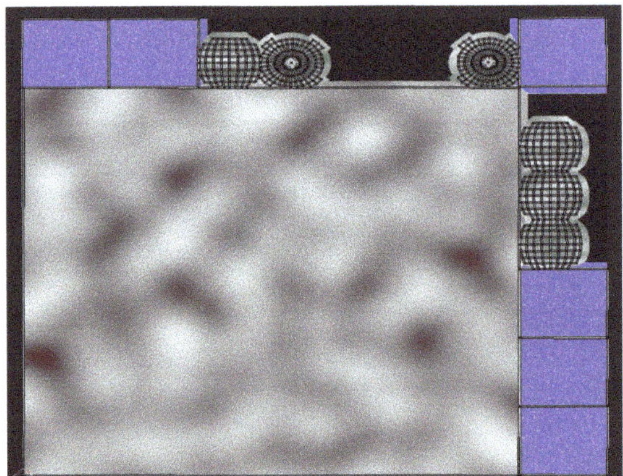

Illustration 176: Final Texture

We obtain the texture like on Illustration 176 (save it: «Image» → «Pack as PNG»).

7. For each object, replace the existing texture by «lightmap» and in the «Textures» Tab, «Image Mapping»Panel: set «Coordinates»: «UV» and select «UVMap» that represents the object UV coordinates in the texture containing several objects.

8. The unified texture is usable in BGE (so in GLSL display) with the possibility of apply the needed effects at the «Material» level (Bumpmap, etc.)

VII.5. ANIMATED TEXTURES

Purpose:

Some special effects need too much resources: explosion, flame, smoke, etc. Sometimes, it's easier to **simulate this effect by using a film made by several images.**

Recipe to use an animated texture:

1. **Add a plane** which will be the projection screen for the animated texture (`⇧ Shift` + `A` → «Plane»). Be in front of the camera to for easy observation.
2. «Properties» Window, «Object Data» Tab, «UV Maps» Panel, **add a new UV map** (button «+»), name it «CandleFlameUV»
3. Add a «Material»: «Properties» Window, «Material» Tab, button «+»
4. Check «Shadeless» or set «Emit» at 1
5. «Game Settings» Panel, position «Alpha Blend» on «Alpha sort»
6. Check «Transparency», select «Z Transparency» and set «Alpha» at 0.
7. Add a texture to this «Material»: panel «Texture», button «+»
8. **Create or download an animation tiled** image (multi-columns/lines like the Illustration 177: Texture made by a flame animation , not an «animated gif») and use it as texture.
9. «mapping» Panel: «coordinates»: select «UV» and «CandleFlameUV»
10. Go to «Edit Mode», then do an UV mapping («U» → «Unwrap»)
11. Open «UV/Image Editor» and select the corresponding image
12. In «3D View»: display the «Properties» menu («N»), «Game properties» Panel:
    - Check «Animated»
    - «Start»: 0, «End»: 9, «Speed»: 15
    - Check «Tiled»
    - «X»: 5 and «Y»: 2
    Here, set 10 images at 15 FpS, and the image is made by a sequence of 5 columns by 2 lines.

Illustration 177: Texture made by a flame animation

Recipe to create an animated texture:

Blender can generate an animation in the form of images but it can't generate directly a «tiled» image.

We need to use the tool «The Gimp»: http://bit.ly/1XGc44o

A texture take place in memory when it's unpacked.

The following table give animation size examples according to several parameters:

8 bits Bitmap	16 sprites (4x4)	36 sprites (6x6)	64 sprites (8x8)	100 sprites (10x10)
1024x1024 1Mo	256	170	128	102
2048x2048 4Mo	512	341	256	204
4096x4096 16Mo	1024	682	512	409
8192x8192 64Mo	2048	1365	1024	819

If we want an animation with 64 sprites and not texture superior to 4MB (when it's unpacked in memory), the maximal size for the images to use is 256x256. A 16 bits image takes twice memory than in 8 bits.

The precedent recipe can't work with DDS textures, so we can't benefit of data compression.

So, for an example, we have 64 images with a size of 256x256. The purpose is to obtain a «tiled» texture of 4MB.

1. Go to: http://tinyurl.com/nyvosls **and copy the** script in a text file, save in the scripts directory of «The Gimp» and name the files «layers-to-sl-animation.scm». Initially, this script was made for «Second Life».

2. Launch «The Gimp», menu «file» → «Open as Layer» and select the 64 corresponding images keeping «⇧ Shift» pressed (be careful to the alphabetical filing), then click on «Open». An image made by 64 layers is created.

3. Menu «Script-fu» → «Second Life» → «Frames to Texture». Precise 8 in horizontal and 8 in vertical, uncheck «Generate LSL Script», then click on «Ok». There's an error if the number of layers doesn't correspond pas to 8x8, 64.

4. A texture made by 64 «tiled» images is generated. However, return vertically this image to use it with Blender: menu «Image» → «Transform» → «Flip vertically».

Recipe to control the animated texture

When we use a cycling animation, we don't need to control the animation to ensure it begin at 1. If the problem occurs, use an Addon and do the animation in another way.

1. **Download** the «UV Scroll» addon available at: http://tinyurl.com/ppzydax

2. Open the users preferences («Ctrl + Alt + U»), «Addons» panel, click on «Install from file» and select the downloading file, then valid. Check the addon «Game Engine: UV Scroll» and click on «Save User Settings»

3. **Add a plane** which will be the projection screen for the animated texture («⇧ Shift + A» → «Plane»). Be in front of the camera to for easy observation

4. Select the plane.

5. «Space» → enter «UV Scroll». A configuration window appears. Click on «+» near «UV Map», select the UVs in the field at left. In «Cells»: «X» and «Y» correspond to the number of images in width and in high. «Step» allows to skip some images: a step of 2, for example, skip 1 image on 2.

6. «Loop»:
    - -1: we repeat the animation
    - 0: the animation is played once
    - n (>0): the animation is repeated n times.

7. «Ping Pong»: if activated, when a loop, the animation is played one time in one direction, then in the other direction.

8. In «Sequence», enter a sequence such as:
    - «n1-n2» (ex: «0-64»): to go from the image n1 to the n2 through all the intermediates values
    - «n1,n2,n3»: ex: «0,32,64» to go from the image 0 to 32 then 64
    - «n*t» (ex: 0*60): to repeat t times the image n
    - all combinations are possibles. Ex: «0*60,1,-63,64*60» to display 60 times the first image, go to the second to the last but one, then 60 time the last.

9. Add a «Material»: «properties» window, «Materials» Tab, button «+»

10. Check «Shadeless» or set «Emit» at 1. «Properties» Tab→ Material» Panel →Game Settings, position «Alpha Blend» on «Alpha sort».

11. Check «Transparency», select «Z Transparency» and set «Alpha» at 0.

12. Add a texture to this «Material»: «Texture» panel, button «+»

13. **Create or download a tiled animation image** (multi-columns/lines like after, not an «animated gif») and use it as texture.

14. «Mapping» Panel: «Coordinates»: Select «UV» and «UVmap»

15. «Diffuse» Panel, check«Alpha» and set at 1.

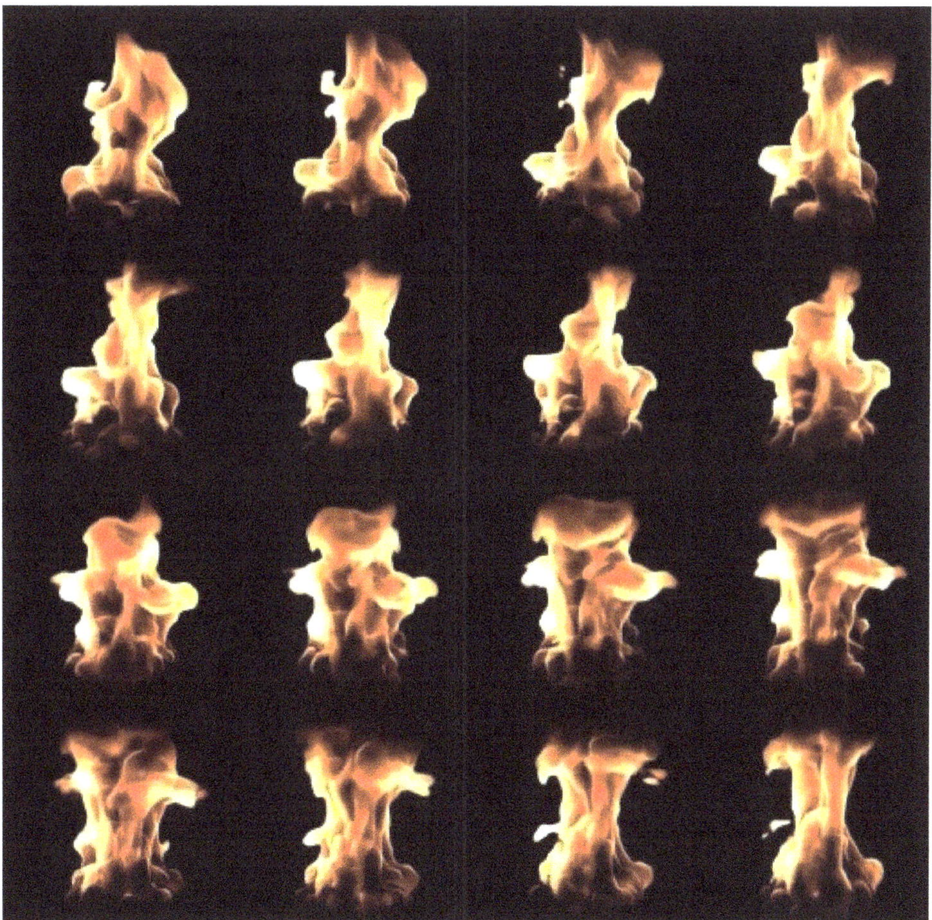

Illustration 178: Another Example: http://bit.ly/1INDP4k

VII.6. MIRROR AND REFLEXION

Purpose:

Create a mirror using the function RenderToTexture from python API (Illustration 179).

It's a false reflexion, we don't use the ray-cast to do the scene rendering, we do a render in realtime using a camera. The illusion is good. However, we can't bring the 2 mirrors face each other to obtain a redundancy effect.

Illustration 179: Creation of a realtime mirror (without additional camera)

Recipe:

1. **Create a plane** (`Shift`+`A` → «Mesh» → «Plane»). Name it «mirror»
2. «Properties» Window → «Materials» Tab → Button «+», name it «Reflect». In «Shading», check «Shadeless»
3. On Google Images, look for «Texture Text» and **download an image with a readable text** (used to direct the UVs).
4. In «Edit Mode»: do an UV mapping («U» → «Unwrap Cube Projection»)
5. «Properties» Window → «Textures» panel → Button «+», with «Image or Movie» type, **select the texture** downloaded before. «Mapping» Panel: «Coordinates»: «UV», select «Map»: «UVmap».
6. Open «Image/UV Editor» and open the image downloaded before («`Alt`+`O`»)
7. **Split the window in 2** to see the 3D View at the same time.
8. «Image/UV Editor» Window, do an UV mirror («`Ctrl`+`M`» - choose X or Y) to obtain in the «Mirror» object (window alongside) the text like it was read in a mirror.

9.   Open the «Text» window and **create a new script** «mirror.py». Copy the following lines.

10. Select the «Mirror» object and go to «Logic Editor». Add a new sensor with «Always» and check «Activate True Level Triggering»

11. Add a new controller with «Python» type and select the script «mirror.py». Link the sensor with the controller.

Script «Mirror.py» (source: www.tutorialsforblender3d.com, license Common creative 3.0):

```python
import bge

controller = bge.logic.getCurrentController()
obj = controller.owner
if "Mirror" in obj:
   obj["Mirror"].refresh(True)
else:
   scene = bge.logic.getCurrentScene()
   matID = bge.texture.materialID(obj, "MA" + obj['material'])
   cam = scene.active_camera

   if 'channel' in obj:
     texChannel = obj['channel']
   else:
       texChannel = 0
   mirror = bge.texture.Texture(obj, matID, texChannel)
   mirror.source = bge.texture.ImageMirror(scene, cam, obj, matID)

   obj["Mirror"] = mirror # save mirror as an object variable
```

We can add a property «channel» to specify the level of texture we want to apply to the mirror.

VII.7.PLAY VIDEOS

Purpose:

Launch a video in an object texture to **simulate a TV or a movie screen** (Illustration 180)

Recipe:

1. Add a plane (⇧ Shift + A → «Mesh» → «Plane»). Name it «Screen».
2. Go to «Edit Mode» and do an UV mapping («U» → «Unwrap» → «Smart UV Project»)
3. Select the plane, add a «Material» («Properties» Window, «Materials» Tab, «+»). Name it «Screen» too. In Shading → Check «Shadeless»
4. Add a new texture (panel «Textures», «+») with «Image or Movie» type. Add the video file (images → Open). Resize the UVs if necessary.
5. Add a new script («Text» window → «+ New»). Name «movie.py», and copy the following code lines.
6. Go to «Logic Editor» and add some properties to the plane: «material» with «String» type and with value «Screen», «movie» with «String» type and value «video.avi» (replace by the video to display name) and «loop» with «boolean» type and check (to read a video in loop, uncheck to read the video once).
7. Add an «Always» sensor (or any other trigger to launch the video)
8. Add a «Python» controller, select «movie.py». Link the sensor with the controller.

Illustration 180: Video in a texture with BGE

Script movie.py (source: www.tutorialsforblender3d.com, license: Common creative 3.0):

```python
import bge
controller = bge.logic.getCurrentController()
obj = controller.owner
if "Video" in obj: # check to see variable Video has been created
    video = obj["Video"]
    video.refresh(True)
else:
    scene = bge.logic.getCurrentScene()
    matID = bge.texture.materialID(obj,"MA" + obj["material"])
    video = bge.texture.Texture(obj, matID) # get the texture
    movieName = obj['movie'] # get the name of the movie
    movie = bge.logic.expandPath('//' + movieName) # get movie path
    video.source = bge.texture.VideoFFmpeg(movie) # get movie
    video.source.scale = True
    obj["Video"] = video
    if "loop" in obj:
        if obj['loop']:
            video.source.repeat = -1
        else:
            video.source.repeat = 0
    video.source.play() # start the video
```

Illustration 181: Model your own theater and display movies

VII.8. RADIOSITY SIMULATION

Purpose:

Do you remember the clothes in the film «Tron» or the television series «Automan»? There are light strips («Glow effect»). The function «Emit» of a «Material» gives to the object the capacity to emit light, but without transmitting the light in realtime.

We can use the capacity of the **internal rendering engine** of Blender to use radiosity while BGE can't do it. Radiosity is a global illumination algorithm in the sense that the illumination arriving on a surface comes not just directly from the light sources, but also from other surfaces reflecting light. It uses the light radiative physical transfer between the different elementary surfaces of the scene.

Recipe:

1. Model a simple scene like on Illustration 182 (a plane and 4 simple forms with different colors)
2. To each form (except the plane), modify the «Material»: «Shading» panel, set «Emit» at 8.0 and «Specular Intensity» at 0. Be careful, according to the plane color, the effect can be minimized. Here the blue prevents the red to manifest. So if it's possible, keep the plane in white.
3. «Properties» Window → «World» panel → check «indirect»
4. «Lighting» Panel, set «Bounces» at 12 and click on «Approximate» instead of «Raytrace ».
5. Add a texture named «Emit» to the plane, with image type. Create a new image named «EmitImage» with size 1024x1024.
6. In «Edit Mode», do an UV mapping of the plane («U» → «Unwrap»)
7. In the «UV/Image Editor» window, link the UV to the new image «EmitImage»
8. Remove the light (or check «negative»)
9. Make sure that «EmitImage» is not activated to avoid the problems from «Loopback» (error of cyclic redundancy generated by Blender because it tries to use the texture in the calculation of the texture).
10. «Properties» Window, «Render» Tab, «Bake» Panel: select «full render», then click on «Bake»
11. Link the texture to the «Material», then set «Emit» at 1.0 – we obtains the third Illustration 182 photo after the application of a texture for example.

→ Calculate the radiosity with its original textures instead of working with colored materials.

Improvements possibles:

For a better effect, use 2D filters with «**bloom**» type + **HDR** (High Dynamic Range) in the recipe VII.13

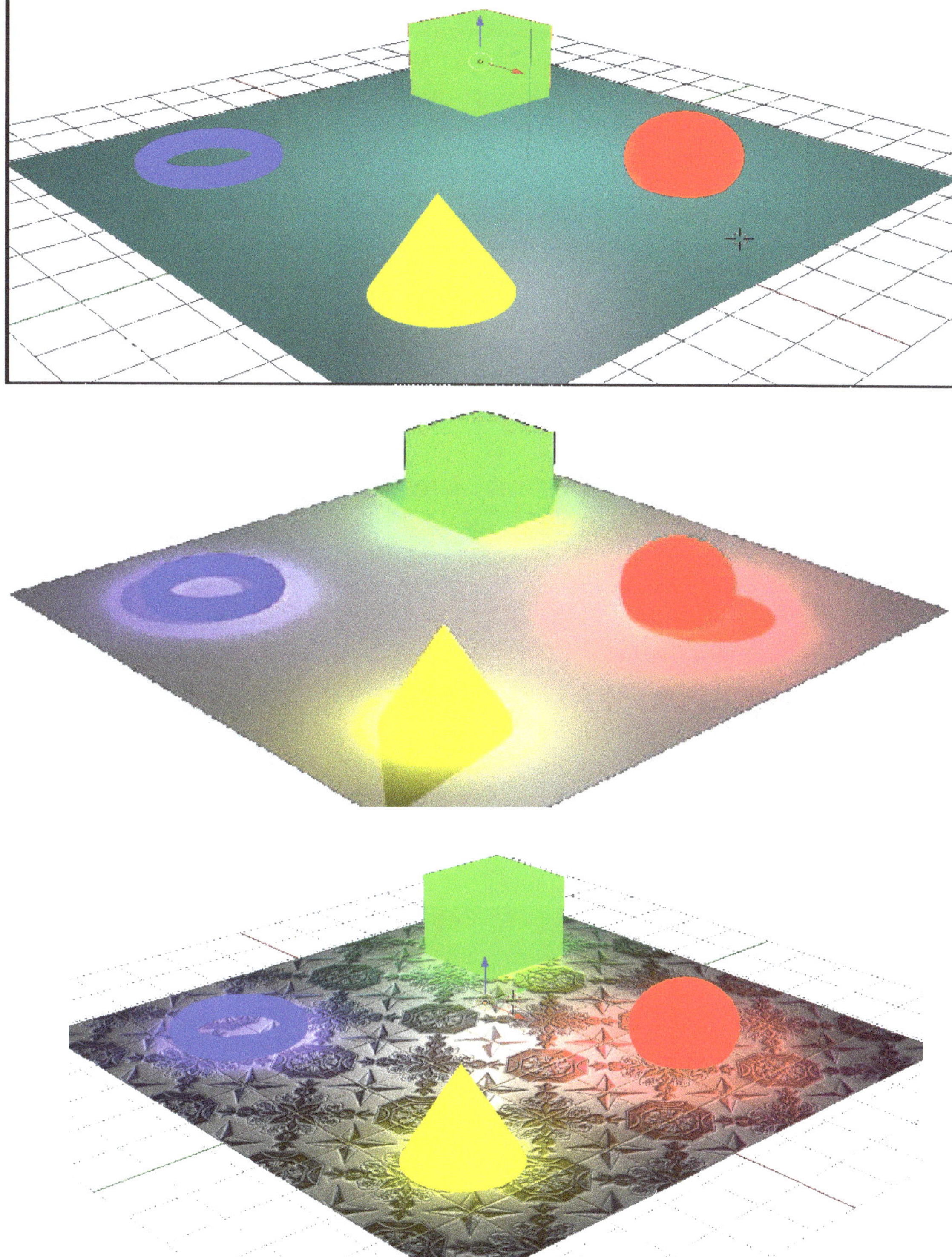

Illustration 182: Radiosity simulation which a precalculation of the result in a texture

VII.9. 2D FILTERS (FX)

<u>Purpose:</u>

The BGE offers some «2D» effects that we can apply directly on screen. The Illustration 183: Native special effects with BGE shows the principal effects.

<u>Recipe:</u>

1.   Go to Logic Editor and add an «Always» sensor
2.   Add an actuator with «Filter 2D» type, select the type wanted in the list. Link the sensor with the actuator

We can accumulate their effects by choosing the pass at which we want to apply it (from 0 to 99).

It's possible to create its own effects by writing some GLSL programs and using «Custom Filter» into the actuator «Filter 2D». Several are presented in this book (HDR, Godray, thumbnail, etc.). In the sheet #8 «The GLSL shaders», you can see the basis for these programs.

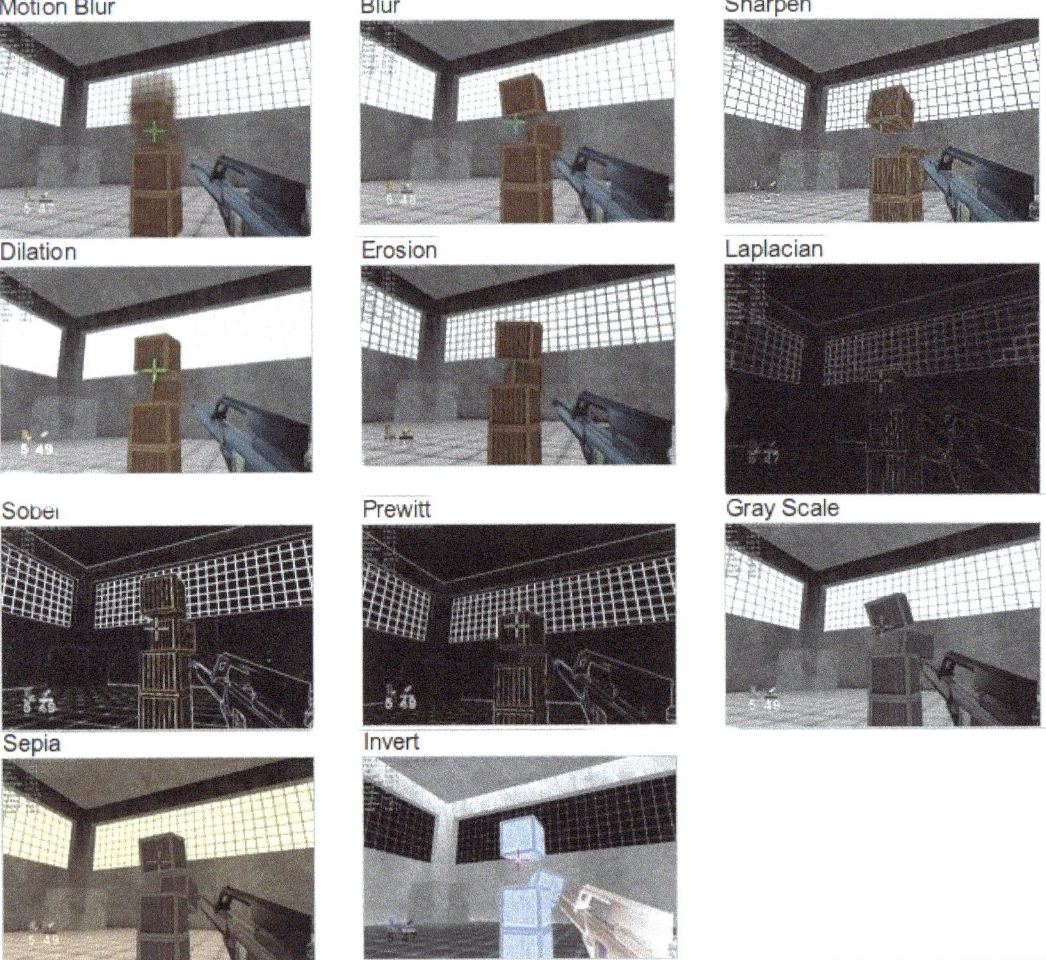

Illustration 183: Native special effects with BGE

VII.10. MANAGE THE LOD OF A MESH

Purpose:

This technique consists in managing several geometries for one object. **The farther the object is, the less we can see details**. We can use a simplified model with less vertex. The reverse is true. We use this technique to save **resources, computer time and to display bigger scenes.** The LOD is very important to display large landscapes.

The version 2.70 of Blender gives **a semi-automatic approach** of this system. The advantage is that all is coded in C and not in python like here: so prefer the 2,70 approach. The **recipe III.17** explains how to activate it. However, this recipe explains the internal working of the LOD of the version 2.70.

Recipe:

1. Model an object with 4 levels of details, name each object with the same name, but with a number from 1 to 4 according the level of detail (1is the max level of details) – Illustration 184
2. Place the **4 object versions** in an **invisible layer** and copy the first in the current layer, remove the number of its name.
3. In the text editor, add a new Python script, name it «LoD.py» and copy the following lines
4. Select the object in the visible layer and go to the Logic Editor
5. Add a property «LoD» with «Integer» type, initialized at 1, and «meshname» with «String» type and containing the object name.
6. Add an «Always» sensor
7. Add a «Python» controller and select the script «LoD.py»
8. Add an «Edit Object» actuator→ «Replace Mesh», activate «Gfx» and deactivate «Phys». Link the sensor with the controller, and the controller with the actuator.

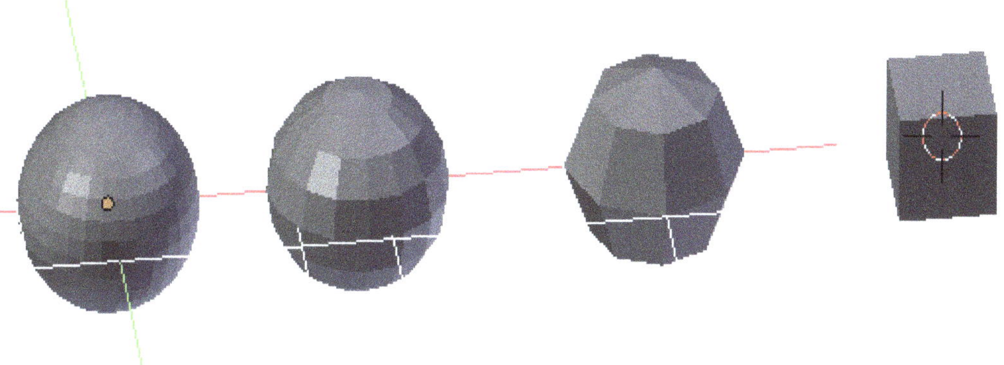

Illustration 184: 4 level of detail for one object,
the most detailed (at left) the simplest (at right)

Script LoD.py:

```python
import bge
g = bge.logic
cont = g.getCurrentController()
replace = cont.actuators['replace']
ob = cont.owner #Load in the current Object
scene = g.getCurrentScene() #Loads in the current scene
obs = scene.objects #Loads in a list of objects in scene
cam = scene.active_camera #Loads in the current camera
dist = cam.getDistanceTo(ob) #Gets distance to object
cont.deactivate(replace)
if dist < 1000: #If object is closer than 1000 units
```

```
    replace.mesh = str(ob['meshname']) + "4"
    cont.activate(replace)
if dist < 60:
  10 replace.mesh = str(ob['meshname']) + "3"
    cont.activate(replace)
if dist < 30:
    replace.mesh = str(ob['meshname']) + "2"
    cont.activate(replace)
if dist < 10:
    replace.mesh = str(ob['meshname'])
    cont.activate(replace)
```

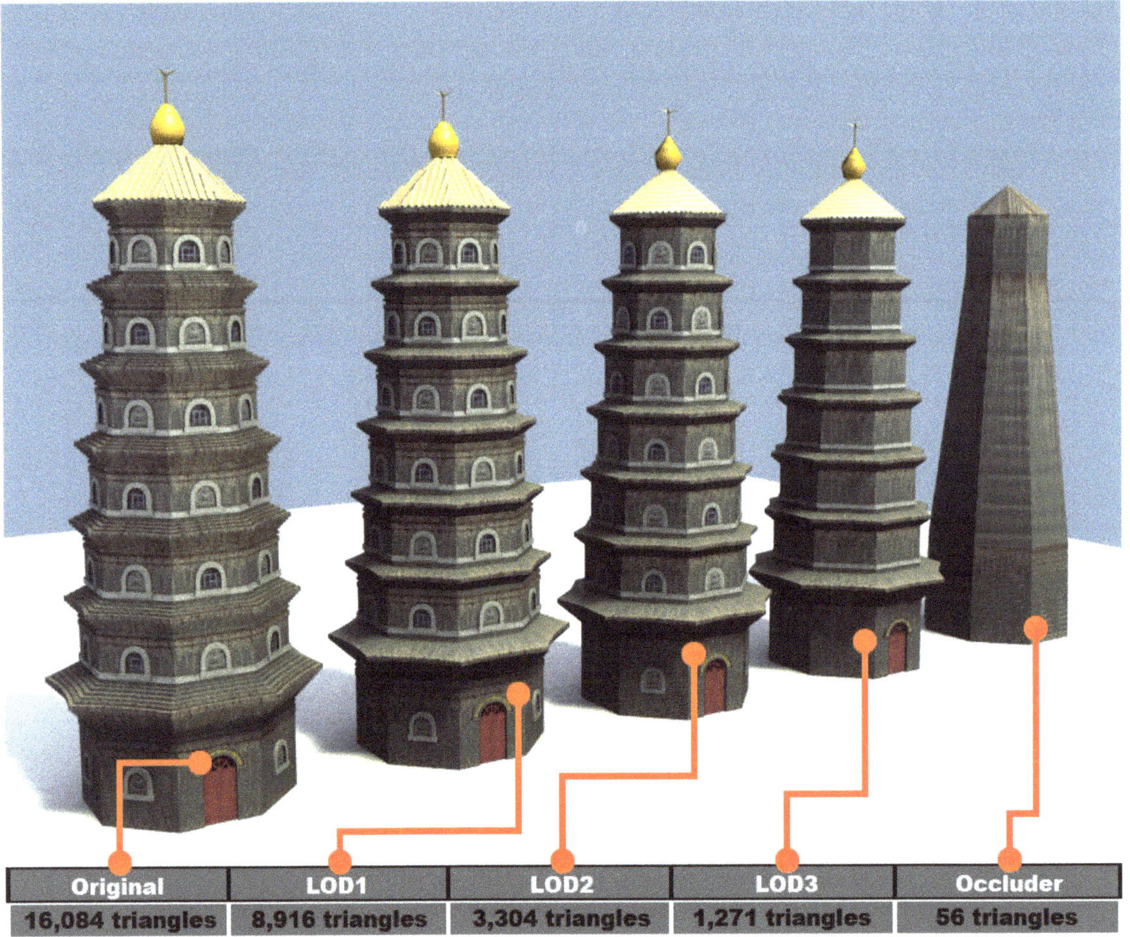

Illustration 185: Lod of a tower - Check out more of his fantastic work in www.clement-melendez.com

VII.11.   CATHEDRAL EFFECT (RAYLIGHT OR GODRAY)

Purpose:

When we are in front of a stain-glass windows or when there's a smog or dust or when we look at vehicle lights, the light propagates along a visible cone, **tracing light rays** (Illustration 186). This effect is not native on BGE, but it's possible to do it thanks to a **GLSL shader.**

Illustration 186: Cathedral effect on a stain-glass

Recipe:

1. **Add a plane** (`Shift`+`A` → «Mesh» → «Plan»), name it «Vitrail» (stain-glass)

2. **Copy this plane** (`Shift`+`D`), place it higher than the precedent (Z+1). Name it «Lux»

3. **Rotate «Vitrail» on 180°** along the X axis

4. **Add a camera**, place it in Z-10 and turn it towards the stain-glass (rotation X of 180°)

5. Select «Lux», add a «Material» («Properties» window, «Materials» Tab, «+»). In «Shading», check «Shadeless».

6. Select «Vitrail», add a «Material». «Shading» Panel, «Emit:»: 0.7, «Ambient»: 0.5 and «Translucency»: 0.5

7. Go to Google images, search **«texture stained-glass»** and download an image representing the church window for example

8. **Add a texture** («Properties» window, «Textures» panel, «+»). Type: «Image or Movie». Image → Open, Select the dowloaded image.

9. Open the «Text Editor» window, button «+ New». Name it «godray» and paste the following **script**.

10. Select «Lux» and go to «Logic Editor»

11. **Add an «Always» sensor**
12. **Add an actuator** with «Filter 2D» type, «Type»: «custom filter» and «Script»: Select «godray». **Link the sensor with the actuator.**

Shader godray:

```glsl
uniform sampler2D bgl_RenderedTexture;
uniform sampler2D bgl_DepthTexture;

const float dens = 0.6; // Density
const float dec = 0.95; // Decay
const float weight = 0.2;
float exp = 0.25; // Exposure
// Light Screen (Origin if effect is not working Play with XY)
uniform float xPos = 0.5; // 0.0 - 1.0
uniform float yPos = 0.8; // 0.0 - 1.0
uniform vec2 lightScreenPos;

// Number of Ray Samples (Quality 1 - 128)
const int raySamples = 64;

void main() {
  vec4 origin = vec4(0);
  vec4 sample = vec4(0);
  vec4 mask = vec4(0);
  vec2 lightScreenPos = vec2(xPos,yPos);
  vec2 deltaTexCoord = vec2(gl_TexCoord[3]) - lightScreenPos;
        vec2 texCoo = gl_TexCoord[0].st;
        deltaTexCoord *= 1.0 / float(raySamples) * dens;
        float illumDecay = 1.0;
  for(int i=0; i < raySamples ; i++)  {
    texCoo -= deltaTexCoord;
    if (texture2D(bgl_DepthTexture, texCoo).r > 0.9)
      sample += texture2D(bgl_RenderedTexture, texCoo);
    sample *= illumDecay * weight;
    origin += sample;
    illumDecay *= dec;
  }
  vec2 texcoord = vec2(gl_TexCoord[0]);
  gl_FragColor = texture2D(bgl_RenderedTexture, texcoord) + (origin*exp);
}
```

The value «0.9» is parametrized according to the object size and the proximity of the camera. Increase it if the object is more important. Modify too xpos and ypos to obtain rays with different angles.

Illustration 187: Godrays in real life

VII.12. THUMBNAIL EFFECT

Purpose:

The «thumbnail » effect allows to **simulate the torch use** (Illustration 188). We could do the same thing with a spot but the scene lighting will be modified. With this GLSL Shader, we can rapidly change the size, the color of the zone and do some «psychedelic» effects to simulate a fever vision.

Recipe:

Apply the `recipe VII.9` and specify «Filter 2D Type»: «Custom Filter» and the name of the GLSL Shader in «Script». Don't forget «Pass Number» if there are several filters to avoid to add up the effects.

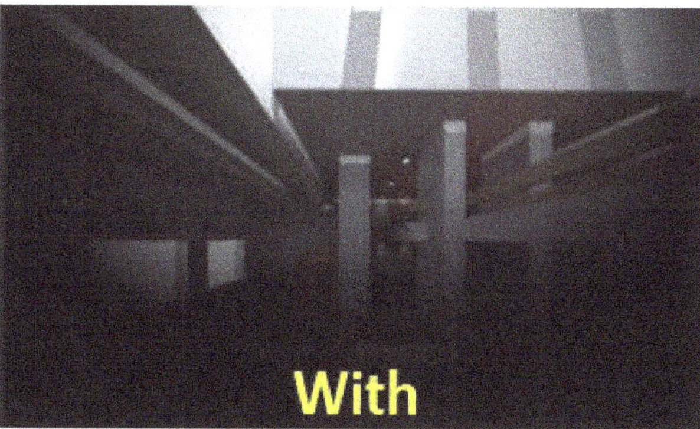

Illustration 188: «thumbnail » effect with a GLSL

GLSL Shader «Sticker»:

```
uniform sampler2D bgl_RenderedTexture;
uniform float thumbnail_size;
const float tolerance = 0.2;
void main(void){
 vec2 powers = pow(abs(gl_TexCoord[3].st - 0.5),vec2(2.0));
 float radiusSqrd = pow(thumbnail_size,2.0);
 float gradient = smoothstep(radiusSqrd-tolerance, radiusSqrd+tolerance,
   powers.x+powers.y);
 gl_FragColor = mix(texture2D(bgl_RenderedTexture, gl_TexCoord[0].st), vec4(0.0),
   gradient);
 gl_FragColor.a = 1.0;
}
```

VII.13. HDR EFFECT (HIGH DYNAMIC RANGE)

Purpose:

The **HDR** is an advanced brightness effect used in 3D realtime to **simulate the retina**.

It's a technique used in imaging and photography to reproduce a greater dynamic range of luminosity than is possible with standard digital imaging or photographic techniques. The aim is to present the human eye with a similar range of luminance as that which, through the visual system, is familiar in everyday life. The human eye, through adaptation of the iris (and other methods) adjusts constantly to the broad dynamic changes ubiquitous in our environment. The brain continuously interprets this information so that most of us can see in a wide range of light conditions.

It allows a highlighting and color accenting (Illustration 189)

Illustration 189: «HDR» effect with a GLSL Shader

Recipe:

Apply the `recipe VII.9` and specify «Filter 2D Type: Custom Filter» and the name of the GLSL Shader in «Script». Don't forget «Pass Number» if there are several filters.

GLSL Shader «HDR»:

```
uniform sampler2D bgl_LuminanceTexture;
uniform sampler2D bgl_RenderedTexture;
float avgL = 0.4;
float HDRamount = 0.5;
vec2 texcoord = vec2(gl_TexCoord[0]).st;
void main(void) {
        float contrast = avgL;
        float brightness = avgL * HDRamount;
        vec4 value = texture2D(bgl_RenderedTexture, texcoord);
        gl_FragColor = (value/contrast)-brightness;
}
```

VII.14.   CARTOON EFFECT

Purpose:

The «Cartoon» effect («Toon Shading») refers to the cartoons where **the characters are simply drawn with unrefined contours**. In 3D, it's the «Cell Shading» (celluloid shading, Illustration 190). The game video «XIII» was one of the firsts to illustrate this technique in games.

Illustration 190: Celluloid shading example in 3 steps:
contours, base texture, then thresholding of shadows

To do this effect, we use a **pixel shader** (sheet #8): the technique needs many calculations: thresholding and outlining need calculations for each image pixel. The methods without shaders work only on the objects vertex, less numerous. However, the modeling is more simplistic with little texturing.

Recipe:

Apply the recipe VII.9 and specify «Filter 2D Type: Custom Filter» and the GLSL Shader name in «Script». Don't forget «Pass Number» if you use several filters to accumulate the effects. A filter with «Dilation» type in 0 reinforces little details.

GLSL Shader «cartoon #1» (Illustration 191):

The following code was developed by **Jose I. Romera**, based on the filter «Prewitt». It's under license GNU GPL and was modified by **Martinsh** from BlenderArtists.org

```glsl
uniform sampler2D bgl_RenderedTexture;
uniform sampler2D bgl_DepthTexture;
uniform vec2 bgl_TextureCoordinateOffset[9];
const float near = 0.1;
const float far  = 30.0;

float depth(in vec2 coo) {
        vec4 depth = texture2D(bgl_DepthTexture, coo);
        return -near / (-1.0+float(depth) * ((far-near)/far));
}

void main(void) {
   vec4 sample[9];
   vec4 border;
   vec4 texcol = texture2D(bgl_RenderedTexture,
           gl_TexCoord[0].st);
   for (int i = 0; i < 9; i++) {
     sample[i] = vec4(depth(gl_TexCoord[0].st +
                 bgl_TextureCoordinateOffset[i]));
   }
   vec4 horizEdge = sample[2] + sample[5] + sample[8] -
           (sample[0] + sample[3] + sample[6]);
   vec4 vertEdge = sample[0] + sample[1] + sample[2] -
           (sample[6] + sample[7] + sample[8]);
   border.rgb = sqrt((horizEdge.rgb * horizEdge.rgb) +
```

```
                (vertEdge.rgb * vertEdge.rgb));
   if (border.r > 0.8||border.g > 0.8||border.b > 0.8){
       gl_FragColor = vec4(0.0, 0.0, 0.0, 1.0);
   } else {
           gl_FragColor.rgb = texcol.rgb; gl_FragColor.a = 1.0;
   }
}
```

Illustration 191: recipe cartoon #1

Illustration 192: recipe cartoon #2

GLSL Shader «cartoon #2» (Illustration 192):

The following code was developed by **Jose I. Romera**, based on the filter «Prewitt». It's under license GNU GPL and was modified by **Endre Barath** for the game «Dead Cyborg».

```
uniform sampler2D bgl_RenderedTexture;
uniform vec2 bgl_TextureCoordinateOffset[9];
void main(void){
        vec4 sample[9];
        vec4 border;
        vec4 texcol = texture2D(bgl_RenderedTexture,
                gl_TexCoord[0].st);
        for (int i = 0; i < 9; i++){
                sample[i] = texture2D(bgl_RenderedTexture,
                gl_TexCoord[0].st +
                bgl_TextureCoordinateOffset[i]);
        }

        vec4 horizEdge = sample[3] - sample[4];
        vec4 vertEdge = sample[1] - sample[4];
        border.rgb = sqrt((horizEdge.rgb * horizEdge.rgb) +
         (vertEdge.rgb * vertEdge.rgb));

        if (border.r > 0.03||border.g >0.05||border.b > 0.05) {
                gl_FragColor.rgb = 0.1; gl_FragColor.a = 1;
        } else {
                gl_FragColor.rgb = texcol.rgb; gl_FragColor.a = 1;
        }
}
```

Illustration 193: progressive application progressive of a toon shading from left to right
Credits: The Metal Master with KeyShot

VII.15.   TRANSPARENCY AND FADING EFFECTS

<u>Purpose</u>:

To display a tree leaf, a grid, or a bit dirty window, we use a **plane and its transparency.** In every case, the image need to support transparency, i.e. to have an **alpha canal**. The formats image **PNG** (Portable Network Graphics) or **DDS** (DirectDraw Surface) are perfect for that. There are many ways to use a texture transparency, but the fade effects with BGE doesn't work with all techniques.

To remove an object, we can use the actuator «Edit Object»: «End Object». But a **fade effec**t is more attractive. Likewise to make the objects visible.

2 recipes in one, to have a good fade effect, you must setup the transparency.

<u>Recipe «transparency»</u>:

1. Select the object, go to «Edit Mode» and apply an UV mapping («U» → «Unwrap» according to the object)
2. «Properties» window, «Materials» Tab, add a new «Material» («+»)
3. «Textures» Panel, add a new texture, with «Image or Movie» type. Load the image with an alpha canal and check **«Show Alpha»** to control (a little checkerboard appears in place of the transparent zone)
4. «Mapping» Panel, «coordinates»: «UV» and select l'UVMap.
5. «Influence» Panel: check **«Alpha»** and«color».
6. «Materials» Tab, «Game Settings» panel, «Alpha Blend»: Select «Alpha Sort». Eventually, uncheck the **«Backface Culling»** to see the back of the object when there's transparency.
7. «Options» Panel: check «Face Texture» and «Object Color»
8. **«Transparency»** Panel: Check to activate and select «Z Transparency» then Alpha: 0.0.

<u>Recipe «fade in & out»</u>:

We'll do a **dissolution, i.e. an increasing disappearance** (without remove it): a «fade out».

To do the opposite, exchange the 2 values of the alpha in the recipe.

1. Select the object, go to «Properties» window, «Object» Tab, «Display» panel, click on the color («Object Color») and set «Alpha» (A) at 1.0, then valid.
2. Position the mouse cursor on this color and press «I». A frame is around the color because a **keyframe was created**.
3. Change of Frame, with steps for example of 100 and modify the color alpha at 0.0
4. Position the mouse cursor on this color and press «I» to create a new key
5. Go to «Logic Editor» and add an «Always» sensor
6. Add an «Action» actuator, «Mode»: «Play», «Start»:1, «End»:1. Link the sensor with the actuator
7. Add a sensor to launch the «fade out» (ex: «Keyboard»: «All Keys»).
8. Add an «Action» actuator, «Mode»: «Play», «Start»:1, «End»:100. Link the sensor with the actuator

VII.16.   GENERATE OBJECTS VIA PYTHON

<u>Purpose</u>:

When we work directly with OpenGL or DirectX, we can create some objects from an array of points, joined to form faces, these faces forming a geometry. Blender is a modeler tool, so all theses operations are made without programing. Otherwise, everything can be also done in command line, from the interpreter available in the «Python» window.

In this recipe, we'll see how to use this potential in games, to, for example, create a level editor.

<u>Recipe</u>:

At first, we generate a cube «Mesh» (Illustration 194), i.e. its geometry. To do that, we need 2 things: the points list (vertex) and the faces list. The vertex are expressed in 3D coordinates (x,y,z) and the faces, in a vertex list (vertex0, vertex1, vertex2, vertex3). The order in which we define these faces determine the face visible side. If we reverse, the mesh will be visible only from the interior (except if «flip normals»). With these elements, we can manage the object and its geometry, then link it to the current scene.

Then, we generate a «**Material**» (or use an existing «Material») and a **texture**. The texture normally use UV coordinates with BGE to be correctly applied to an object. We need to define the UV coordinates for each face (not Blender Renderer)

An **UV coordinate** is expressed in: ([0-1],[0-1]). So, if the size of the image is 256x256 and its UV coordinate is (0.25, 0.75), the position in the image will be (64,196) from the bottom left corner.

In the following script, the bottom left corner and the size of the image part (width, height) chosen are used in function parameters.

Example: *createCube('ground','ground.png',0,0,1,1)*

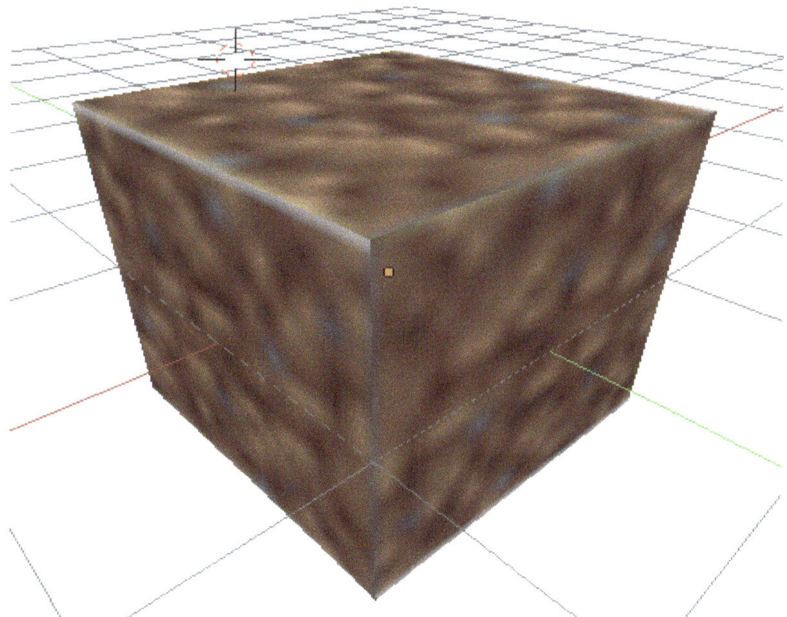

Illustration 194: Cube generated by Python with a texture application

Script python:

```python
def createCube(name,imgFilename,xt,yt,width,height,transp=False):
    verts = [(1.0, 1.0, -1.0),(1.0, -1.0, -1.0),
             (-1.0, -1.0, -1.0),(-1.0, 1.0, -1.0),
             (1.0, 1.0, 1.0), (1.0, -1.0, 1.0),
             (-1.0, -1.0, 1.0), (-1.0, 1.0, 1.0)]
    faces = [(0, 1, 2, 3), (4, 7, 6, 5),(0, 4, 5, 1),
             (1, 5, 6, 2),(2, 6, 7, 3), (4, 0, 3, 7)]

    me = bpy.data.meshes.new(name+'Mesh')
    ob = bpy.data.objects.new(name, me)
    ob.location = (0.0,0.0,0.0)

    # Link object to scene
    scn = bpy.context.scene
    scn.objects.link(ob)
    scn.objects.active = ob
    scn.update()

    # Create mesh from given verts, edges, faces
    me.from_pydata(verts, [], faces)
    me.update(calc_edges=True)

    # Create UV's and Texture Layer
    uvtex = me.uv_textures.new()
    uvtex.name = 'UVMain'
    uv_layer = me.uv_layers.active.data

    uverror = 0.005 #modify pbs with texturing
    for x in range (6):
        uv_layer[x*4+0].uv= ((xt+uverror),(yt+uverror))
        uv_layer[x*4+1].uv= ((xt+uverror),(yt+height-uverror))
        uv_layer[x*4+2].uv= ((xt+width-uverror),(yt+height-uverror))
        uv_layer[x*4+3].uv=((xt+width-uverror),(yt+uverror))

    realpath = os.path.expanduser(imgFilename)
    tex = bpy.data.textures.new('ColorTex', type = 'IMAGE')
    tex.image = bpy.data.images.load(realpath)

    # Create material MTex
    mat = bpy.data.materials.new('TexMat')
    mtex = mat.texture_slots.add()
    mtex.texture = tex
    mtex.texture_coords = 'UV'
    mtex.use_map_color_diffuse = True
    if transp:
        mat.game_settings.alpha_blend = 'ALPHA'
        mat.use_transparency = True
        mat.transparency_method = 'Z_TRANSPARENCY'
        mat.alpha = 0.0
        mat.texture_slots[0].use_map_alpha = True
        mat.texture_slots[0].alpha_factor = 1.0

    ob.data.materials.append(mat)
```

The transparency management (transp: last parameter) allows to use the «alpha» layer from a texture. By default, we don't use the transparency.

VII.17. SIMULATE AN EXPLOSION

Purpose:

To create an explosion with BGE, it's possible to use a set of billboards like on following recipe. However, we use the Blender capacities to create this type of explosion and recover the animation created in the form of a «tiled» texture.

Recipe to generate an explosion:

1. Add a sphere to the scene (⬆ Shift + A → «Mesh» → «Uvsphere») en (0,0,0)

2. Add a camera (⬆ Shift + A → «Camera», displace (G) in (20,-18,10), rotation (64,0,47). «Properties» Window, «Object Data» Tab, «Lens» Panel, set «Focal Length»: 26.

3. Select the sphere and «Object» → «Quick Effect» → **«Quick Explode»**. Setup: «Explode Style»: «Explode», «Amount of Pieces»: 50 (number of pieces), «Duration»: 100, «Start Frame»: 1, «End Frame»: 100, «Outwards velocity»: 10 (it's the explosion intensity) and check «Fade». It's possible to test the animation created (Alt + A)

4. Select the sphere and go to «Object» → «Quick Effect» → **«Quick Smoke»**. An object «Smoke Domain» is created. Resize it with a factor 10.

5. Ensure to be in the render: «info» window, select «Blender Render»like Engine. Select «Smoke Domain», then «Properties» window, «Physics» Tab, «Smoke» panel: «Divisions»: 24, check «dissolve», «time»: 5

6. Select the sphere, «Physics» Tab, «Smoke» panel: «Flow Type»: «Fire+Smoke», uncheck «Absolute Density», «Surface»: 1.

7. «Render» Tab, «Dimension» Panel, «Resolution» «X»: 256, «Y»: 256, «100 %», «End Frame»: 64.

8. «Shading» Panel, select «Alpha»: «Transparent» (under «Cycles», in the panel «Film» there's a check box «Transparent»).

9. «Output» Panel, check «RGBA» and «Color Depth»: 8

10. «Render» Panel, click on «Animation» to launch the creation of the 64 images that will be stored in the directory specified in the «Output» panel.

11. Use the `recipe VII.5` (creation recipe, then with the addon «UV Scroll») to create an animated plane from a texture «Tiled» (Illustration 195: Texture «Tiled» made by 64 images to make an explosion)

12. Use the `recipe VII.15` to create an animation of «fade in» so that at the end of the explosion (Illustration 196: Example: boxes projected), the alpha is at 0.

13. Select the plane, name it «explode» and open the «Logic Editor». Add a sensor with «always» type, name it «RunOnce».

14. Add an «Action» actuator, type «Play», «Start»: 1, «End»: 64.

15. Link the sensor with the actuator. Now, when the «explode» object is created, the animation is on 64 images more and more transparent.

To use the explosion:

Create the object with an actuator «Edit Object/Add» limiting the time at 64. To deflect objects away from the explosion point, add an invisible cube with «static» type with a «collision bound» and «box» type. The cube must be generated like the animated plane corresponding to the explosion. At the time of the generation, it must be large enough to collide all the objects in the explosion zone. Limiting its time life at 5 and applying to it an angular velocity and an upward linear velocity, we simulate an explosion.

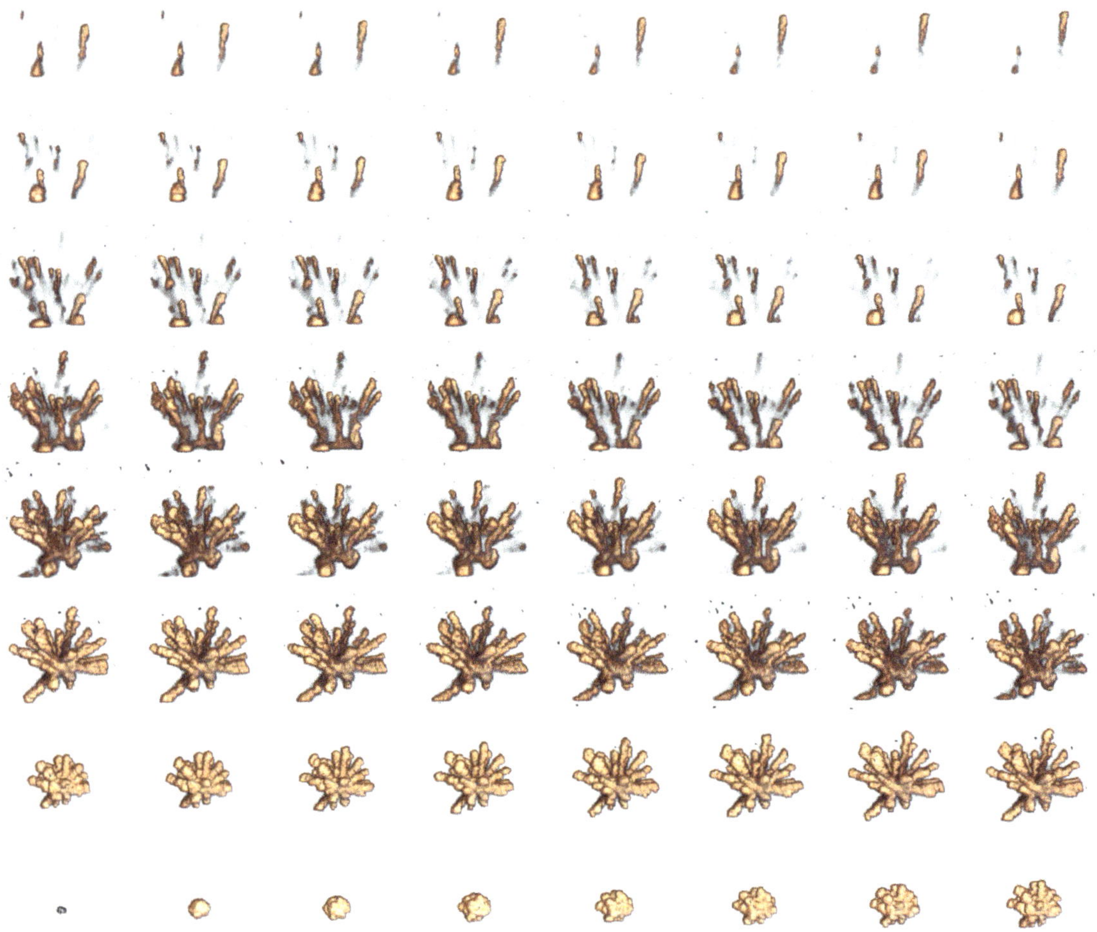

Illustration 195: Texture «Tiled» made by 64 images to make an explosion

Illustration 196: Example: boxes projected

VII.18. SIMULATE A FIRE

Purpose:

With the billboards and the actuator «Edit Object/ Add», it's possible to easily simulate fire or smoke. In this recipe, we'll use another approach: a GLSL Shader to have a more interesting effect.

Illustration 197: Flame texture for the fire

Recipe:

1. Download flame picture or o fire on black background (Illustration 197: Flame texture for the fire). It'll be the texture for the flame.

2. Download a smoke picture (Google images: «texture Smoke»). According to the picture, the results will be different, so, it'll be possible to setup several fire types. This image is not used to create smoke but to generate a distortion for the fire animation.

3. Add a plane (`Shift`+`A` → «Mesh» → «Plane»). Name it «Fire». Do an UV mapping in «Edit Mode» («U» → «Unwrap»).

4. Add a lamp with «point» type (`Shift`+`A` → «Lamp» → «Point»), parent it to the plane (select the lamp, the plane and `Ctrl`+`P` → «Parent to Object»). Name it «FireLight».

5. «Properties» window → «Materials» Tab → add a new «Material» («+»). Name it «Fire». «Shading» Panel → Check «Shadeless».

6. In the «Game Settings» Panel, «Alpha Blend»: select «Add» for the black background transparency and «Face Orientation»: «Billboard» so that the plane is always in front of the camera (so the position at the beginning is important). Panel «Shadow», uncheck every all.

7. «Textures» Panel, add a new texture («+») with «Image or movie» type. Name it «Fire». Select the first downloaded image (flame). In the «Mapping» panel, select «coordinates»: «UV» and «Map»: «uvmap».

8. Add a second texture with «Image or movie» type. Name it «Distorsion». Select the second image downloaded (smoke). In the «Mapping» panel, select «coordinates»: «UV» and «Map»: «uvmap».

9. Open the «Logic Editor» and add an «Always» sensor, check «Activate on True Level Triggering»

and set the frequency at 1.

10. Add a «Python» controller, select «Module» and enter «fire.action». Link the sensor with the controller.

11. Go to «3D View» and test (P). We obtain an interesting effect like on Illustration 198 (for the smoke effect, see the following recipe).

Illustration 198: Final render animated with smoke

Script python «fire.py»:

```
import bge

VertexShader = """
varying vec3 view, normal;

void main() {
        gl_Position = ftransform();
        gl_TexCoord[0] = gl_TextureMatrix[0] * gl_MultiTexCoord0;
        normal = (gl_NormalMatrix * gl_Normal);
        view = (gl_ModelViewMatrix * gl_Vertex).xyz;
}
"""
FragmentShader = """
uniform sampler2D distortion;
uniform sampler2D flame;
uniform float time;
varying vec3 view, normal;

vec2 TexCoord0, TexCoord1, TexCoord2, TexCoord3;
vec4 bx2(vec4 x) {
  return 2.0 * x - 1.0;
}
```

```glsl
void main (void) {
        vec2 texCoord = gl_TexCoord[0].st;
        vec4 layer_speed = vec4(0.7, 0.9, 0.9, 1.0);

        TexCoord0 = texCoord.st;
        TexCoord1.x = texCoord.x + time * 0.3;
        TexCoord1.y = texCoord.y - layer_speed.x * time;
        TexCoord2.x = texCoord.x + time * 0.2;
        TexCoord2.y = texCoord.y - layer_speed.y * time;
        TexCoord3.x = texCoord.x+ time * 0.1;
        TexCoord3.y = texCoord.y - layer_speed.z * time;

        float gradient; // our base 'stripe color'
        gradient = float(mod(gl_TexCoord[0].t, 1.0));
        gradient = clamp(gradient, 0.0, 1.0);

        float distortion_amount0  = gradient*gradient*0.2;
        float distortion_amount1  = gradient*0.2;
        float distortion_amount2  = gradient*gradient*0.5;
        vec4 height_attenuation = vec4(0.2, 0.2, 0.0, 1.0);
        vec4 noise0 = texture2D(distortion, TexCoord1*0.5);
        vec4 noise1 = texture2D(distortion, TexCoord2*2.0);
        vec4 noise2 = texture2D(distortion, TexCoord3*2.5);
        vec2 noiseSum = (bx2(noise0) * distortion_amount0 +
                bx2(noise1) * distortion_amount1 +
                bx2(noise2) * distortion_amount2).xy;
        vec2 perturbedBaseCoords = TexCoord0.xy + noiseSum * (TexCoord0.y * height_attenuation.x +
                height_attenuation.y);
        vec4 flame = texture2D(flame, perturbedBaseCoords );
        float fresnel = abs(dot(normalize(view),normalize(normal)));
        gl_FragColor = flame * fresnel;
}
"""
def action (cont):
        own = cont.owner
        time = own['time']

        MaterialIndexList = [0] # material index
        GlobalAmbient = [0.39,0.35,0.32,1]
        AmbF = 0.5

        mat = own.meshes[0].materials[0]
        shader = mat.getShader()
        if shader != None:
                if not shader.isValid():
                        shader.setSource(VertexShader, FragmentShader,1)
                shader.setSampler('distortion',1)
                shader.setSampler('flame',0)
                shader.setUniform1f('time',time)
```

Normally, the light from a fire is not constant. To simulate the variations, we add a function to randomly vary the «FireLight» intensity:

1. Open «Fire.py» and add the following script lines
2. Select «FireLight» and open the «Logic Editor». Add an «Always» sensor, check «Activate on True Level Triggering» and set the frequency at 5.
3. Add a «Python» controller, select «Module» and enter «fire.light». Link the sensor with the controller.

Addition to script «fire.py»:

```python
import random

def light(cont):
   light = cont.owner
   light.energy = random.random() * 0.3 + 0.8
```

To enhance the effect, add some embers. The embers pop thank to the particles system, like for the following smoke recipe. A sound that «loops end» in 3D mode is appreciable too.

VII.19.   SIMULATE SMOKE

Purpose:

To make smoke (campfire, exhaust pipe, reactor rocket.....), we can't use the physique simulation engine of Blender, like for fire. Use the billboards and the actuator «Edit Object/Add» to generate objects on the fly.

To make a realistic smoke, **the parameters must be precise**. A minor difference in the parameters causes an important difference in the render. So try the following recipe, before to modify the parameters to make it yours.

Recipe:

1. Add an Empty at the place of the smoke (`⬆ Shift`+`A` → «Empty» → «Sphere»). Name it «SmokeEmitter». Make sure that a plane or an object with collision is bellow (at 1,5 units on the Z axis): the smoke will be projected downward and the collision with the ground or this object will create «dispersion».

2. In «3D View», press the key «N» to display the «Properties» menu.

3. In an invisible layer, create a plane (`⬆ Shift`+`A` → «Mesh» → «Plane») in coordinates (0,0,0). Name it «SmokeParticule».

4. Do a rotation on the axes X and Z de 90°, and a scale of 0.6 («S»). Then apply the modifications (`Ctrl`+`A` → «Apply» → «Rotation and Scale»). This orientation is taken by the next Billboard. If there's no smoke, do a rotation of this plane of 90° on the Z axis then, apply the rotation and do the test.

5. In «Edit Mode», do an UV mapping («U» → «Unwrap»), then go to «Objet Mode» (`Tab`).

6. In the «Properties» window, «Materials» Tab, add a new «Material» («+»). «Diffuse» Panel: «Intensity»: 0.01

7. «Shading» Panel, «**Emit**»: «0.003». It's just enough to see the smoke in black sky. Increase this value to have a more important smoke. The value is low, so a lamp must light this smoke like in the precedent recipe.

8. «Game Settings» Panel, uncheck «**Backface Culling**», position «Alpha Blend» on «Add» - use a texture with black background to avoid the transparency calculations which need time.

9. Position «Face Orientation» on «**Billboard**». So, whatever the view angle used, the plane is always in front of the camera. Uncheck «Physics» and anything in linked to «Shadows».

10. «Options» Panel, check «Object Color»: to realize an animation on the object color.

11. Download a texture with «cloud» type round on black background. This cloud simulate the smoke (ex: on «Google Images»: «Texture Cloud Smoke».

12. «Texture» Panel, add a new texture («+») with «Image or Movie» type). Open the downloaded image. In the panel «Mapping», Sslect «coordinates»: «UV» and «Map»: «uvmap».

13. «Physics» Tab, select «Physics Type»: «Rigid Body». We want that each cloud has its own dynamic, and its collisions to create interesting effects. Panel «Attributes», set «Mass» at 2, «radius» at «0.05» and «Form Factor» at 1.0. Check «Collision Bounds» and select «Bounds»: «Sphere», set «Margin» at 0.

14. Create an animation to do the object scale on 200 frames environ. To do that, go to Frame 1. Do a scale of 0.1. Inset a key with «Scale» type (if it's difficult, see the `recipe IV.5`). Go to frame 200, do a scale of 5 and insert a new key with «Scale» type.

15. Change the cloud color: go to frame 1, «Object» Tab, «Display» panel, move the mouse above the color under «Object Color» and insert a key («I»). Go to frame 200, click on the color under «Object Color», choose a dark color, then under «Object Color» insert a new key.

16. Open the «Logic Editor», add an «Always» sensor, name it «RunOnce» (launched once at the particle origin).

17. Add a «Motion» actuator, «Motion Type»: «Simple Motion», and precise «Force» «Z»: 21 (just

enough to escape the gravity because the mass: 2).

18. Add an «Action» actuator, type: «Play», select «SmokeParticuleAction» (name by default created when we have done the shape keys). Enter «Start»: 1 and «End»: 200. Link the 2 actuators to the sensor with a controller with «And».

19. Select the «Smoke Emitter» object. Add an «Always» sensor, check «Activate on True Level Triggering» and choose a frequency of 2 (higher = less smoke, because we generate less particles).

20. Add an «Edit Object» actuator, select «Add Object», then the Object: «Smoke Particle». Indicate a lifetime («Time») of 400 (more, if we want that the smoke persists, but be careful to the slowdown if there are too much particles).

21. To disperse the smoke in the fireplace, indicate a «Linear Velocity» in «X» at 0.05 and to touch the soil at first, in «Z» at -1.5. Link the sensor with the actuator.

22. Go to «3D View» and test (P). The smoke emerges of the fireplace after several seconds like in the Illustration 198.

To apply a **lateral wind to the smoke**:

1. Select «SmokeParticule» and open the «Logic Editor»

2. Add a «Random» sensor, check «Activate on True Level Triggering» and choose a frequency of 50 (lower for a regular wind).

3. Add a «Motion» actuator, «Motion Type»: «Simple Motion», and enter a «Force» «X» (here, the wind is along the X axis, but we can combine several axes): 1.0. Link the sensor with the actuator.

VII.20.   SIMULATE RAIN AND SNOW

Purpose:

To obtain a realistic rain effect, we can use numerous raindrops (particles). However, this operation need too much computer time.

The following recipe is a hybrid method: use billboards to generate continuous rain and add some raindrops to have bouncy effects and which run down the objects.

To obtain snow, use the same method, but with a snowball texture.

<u>**Recipe:**</u>

1. Add a new text file «rain.py» and copy the following script lines. Replace «CameraFreeview» with the character.

2. In an invisible layer, create a plane (⬆Shift+A → «Mesh» → «Plane») in coordinates (0,0,0). Name it «Rain».

3. Do a rotation on the axes X and Z of 90°, and a scale of 15 («S»). Then apply the modifications (Ctrl+A → «Apply» → «Rotation and Scale»). This orientation is taken by the next **Billboard**. If there's no rain, do a rotation on this plane of 90° on the Z axis, then apply the rotation and do the test.

4. In «Edit Mode», do an UV mapping (U → Unwrap), then go to «Objet Mode» (Tab). Do a new scale on the Z axis of 2 and apply the scale to vertically deform the plane.

5. In «Properties» window, «Material» Tab, add a new «Material» («+»). «Diffuse» Panel: «Intensity»: 0.01

6. «Shading» Panel, «Emit»: «0.05». According to the image, modify this parameter to have a rain more or less visible.

7. «Game Settings» Panel, uncheck «**Backface Culling**», position «Alpha Blend» on «Add» - use a texture with black background to avoid the transparency calculation.

8. Position «Face Orientation» on «Billboard». So, whatever the used view angle, the plane will always be in front of the camera. Uncheck «Physics» and anything linked to «Shadows».

9. Download an image corresponding to rain on black background (ex: Google images: «texture rain»). Choose a rain in the form of vertical features, dense.

10. «Textures» Tab, add a new texture («+») with «Image or Movie» type). Open the downloaded image. In the «Mapping» panel, select «coordinates»: «UV» and «Map»: «uvmap».

11. «Physics» Tab, select «Physics Type»: «No Collision»

12. Open the «Logic Editor» and add an «Always» sensor.

13. Add a «Motion» actuator, «Motion Type»: «Simple Motion» and enter a value of «Loc» «Z»: -0.25. Now it's raining. Link the sensor with the actuator.

14. Add an Empty (⬆Shift+A → «Empty» → «Sphere»), name it «RainEmitter» and parent it to the camera (or to the player): Select the empty, then the camera and Ctrl+P → «Parent to Object». Position the empty above its parent, at 20 units.

15. Open the «Logic Editor» and add an «Always» sensor. Check «Activate on True Level Triggering» and set the frequency at 0. To have a rain less dense, use a higher frequency. To have a more intense rain, duplicate «RainEmitter».

16. Add a property «zone» with «Float» type, value«50.0». It's the size of the square centered on the camera or the character and representing the zone where it's raining.

17. Add a property «z», with «Float» type, value «20.0». It's the height from which the rain begin. If we want to use a higher rain, increase the object «Rain» lifetime generated on the fly.

18. Add a «Python» controller, select «Module» and enter «rain.moveAround».

19. Add an «Edit Object» actuator, name it «AddRain», select «Add Object» and «Object»: «Rain»,

    and enter a lifetime («time») at 50.

20. Link the sensor, the controller and the actuator.

Script «rain.py»:

```python
def moveAround(cont):
  own = cont.owner
  zone = own["zone"]

  own.localPosition.x = (random.random() - 0.5) * zone
  own.localPosition.y = (random.random() - 0.5) * zone
  own.localPosition.z = own["z"]

  for act in cont.actuators:
    cont.activate (act)
```


To add several raindrop:

1. In an invisible layer, add a «cube» (**⇧ Shift**+**A** → «Mesh» → «Cube»). Name «RainDrop». Modiffy the dimensions (0.02, 0.02, 0.1) and apply the scale (**Ctrl**+**A** → «Apply» → «Scale»)

2. In the «Properties» window, «Materials» Tab, add a new «Material» («+»). Choose a diffuse grey color (RVB = 0.25, 0.25, 0.25). «Shading» Panel, check «Shadeless». «Physics» Tab, set **«Friction»** and **«Elasticity»** at 1.0.

3. «Physics» Tab, select «Physics Type»: «Rigid Body». Change the «radius» at 0.020 and «Form Factor» at 1.0. Check «Collision Bounds» and choose «Sphere» type.

4. Select the «RainEmitter» object and open the «Logic Editor».

5. Add an actuator with «Edit Object», name it «AddDrop» and select «Add Object» and «Object»: «rainDrop». Limit its timelife («Time») to 200 and apply «Linear Velocity» «Z» of «-6».

6. Link the actuator with the controller linked to the actuator «AddRain».

To have a rain deflected by wind, use a texture with an inclined rain and apply the corresponding force for the fall.

Add a collisions management for the RainDrop on some objects to generate a splash with finer particles, removing the original particles.

VII.21.　　LENS FLARE EFFECT

Purpose:

When we use a camera and there's a powerful light (sun), a particular effect occurs, created by a diffusion of light in the lens. We see halos made by stars and circles. In video games, it's a «Lens Flare». Most of drawing software can simulate a Lens Flare, but for a game, we need a realtime animated effect.

When we look at the sun, the pupils retract, so we see with more contrast and less intensity for other objects. To do that, we use the filter HDR (High Dynamic Range) of the recipe VII.13.

Recipe:

3 steps:

1. make the required content to create a «Lens Flare» with BGE. Rather than download external images, we use a tool to create this kind of objects: the **Blender Render**.

2. Create the logic for all the contents.

3. Create a progressive dazzle using the HDR.

Step #1: content creation

Create 6 effect samples. Modify progressively the elements and see each effect with a rendering («F12»). These effects are created to held in a texture of 512x512. Be careful, if this size is modified, the texture can be rectangular instead of circular because of the color gradation toward the alpha out of the texture.

1. Create a new file blend. This file is used to create the textures used in the next step. In the «info» window, go to «Blender Render» mode.

2. «Properties» window, «Render» Tab, «Dimension» panel, set the rendering size at 512x512 (100%). Check «Antialiasing» and «Full Sample».

3. Create a plane, go to top view («7»). Go to «Edit Mode» («⇥») and remove 3 of 4 vertex. Go to «Object Mode» (⇥) and «Object» → «Transform» → «Geometry to Origin». **The object created is made with one point centered in (0,0,0)**.

4. «Properties» window, «Materials» Tab, add a Material («+»), check «Halo»

5. **1st Texture:** «Halo» Panel, «Alpha»: 1.0, «Size»: 2.0, «Diffuse color»: RGB = (0.8, 0.7, 0.05), «Hardness»: 10.0, «seed»: 0, «Add»: 0.0, «Lines»: 30 with a «Diffuse Color»: RGB = (1.0, 1.0, 1.0). «Star Tips»: 8.

6. Check «Flare», «Size»: 1.5, «subflares»: 1, «Boost»: 2.0, «Subsize»: 0.8, «Seed»: 6.0.

7. Do a rendering («F12») and save the picture («F3») in «lensflare01.png». The created effect is a star which sparkle by turning.

8. **2nd Texture: in another layer,** repeat the operations 3 and 4.

9. «Halo» Panel, «Alpha»: 0.8, «Size»: 5.0, «Diffuse color»: RGB = (0.8, 0.67, 0.2), «Hardness»: 40.0, «seed»: 5, «Add»: 0.1.

10. Check «Flare», «Size»: 1.0, «subflares»: 1, «Boost»: 3.0, «Subsize»: 1.0, «Seed»: 6.0.

11. Do a rendering («F12») and save the picture («F3») in «lensflare02.png». The effect is a yellow halo around the light source (here, the sun).

12. **3rd Texture: in another layer,** repeat the operations 3 and 4.

13. «Halo» Panel, «Alpha»: 0.9, «Size»: 4.5, «Diffuse color»: RGB = (0.8, 0.24, 0.03), «Hardness»: 50.0, «seed»: 0, «Add»: 0.0, «Rings»: 5 with a «Diffuse Color»: RGB = (1.0, 0,53, 0,57).

14. Check «Flare», «Size»: 1.2, «subflares»: 1, «Boost»: 2.0, «Subsize»: 1.0, «Seed»: 3.0.

15. Do a rendering («F12») and save the picture «lensflare03.png». It's a particular Lens Flare, made by reddish concentric circles.

16. **4th Texture: in another layer,** repeat the operations 3 and 4.

17. «Halo» Panel, «Alpha»: 1.0, «Size»: 7.0, «Diffuse color»: RGB = (0.8, 0.2, 0.2), «Hardness»: 80.0,

«seed»: 0, «Add»: 0.0, «Rings»: 5 with a «Diffuse Color»: RGB = (1.0, 0.97, 0.57).

18. Do a rendering («F12») and save the picture «lensflare04.png». The created effect is another star which sparkle by turning in the opposite sens than the 1st texture.

19. **5th Texture: in another layer,** repeat the operations 3 and 4

20. «Halo» Panel, «Alpha»: 1.0, «Size»: 7.0, «Diffuse color»: RGB = (0.8, 0.8, 0.2), «Hardness»: 80.0, «seed»: 0, «Add»: 0.0, «Rings»: 5 with a «Diffuse Color»: RGB = (1.0, 0.97, 0.57). Check «Extreme Alpha».

21. Do a rendering («F12») and save the picture («F3») in «lensflare05.png». The created effect seems to the reddish «Lens flare», but can be used placed before and after with more intensity.

22. **6th Texture: in another layer,** repeat the operations 3 and 4

23. «Halo» Panel, «Alpha»: 0.6, «Size»: 5.0, «Diffuse color»: RGB = (0.67, 0.7, 0.8), «Hardness»: 50.0, «seed»: 2, «Add»: 0.0, «Rings»: 8 with a «Diffuse Color»: RGB = (0.1, 0.08, 1.0).

24. Do a rendering («F12») and save the picture («F3») in «lensflare06.png». The created effect is a series of concentric circles with a blue halo.

In the Illustration 199, you see these 6 textures. Try different parameters to see the effects. The parameter «Seed» allows to modify the element luck used.

Illustration 199: 6 Textures to create different Lens Flare

Before the «logical» phase, setup the different objects:

1. Create a new file blend and import a camera with «Freeview» type (**recipe V.1**) for the test (or adapt the principal camera). Place the camera in (0,0,0).

2. Add a plane (**Shift**+**A** → «Mesh» → «Plane»), name it «camPlane» and parent it to the camera. Setup in the menu «properties» of the «3D View» a rotation of (180,0,0), and a size (10,10,0). In the «Physics» Tab of the «Properties» window, check «Ghost» and «Invisible». Place this plane just behind the camera. This plane will be used for the tests, to see if there's nothing between the light and the camera.

3. Add a second plane, name it «lensPlane» and repeat the precedent operation with this plane behind the camera at 25 units. The plane allows to adjust the lag between the different planes used to display the «lens flare». The farther it's from the camera, the more important the angle between the concentric circles is.

4. Illustration 200: top view of the system modeling.

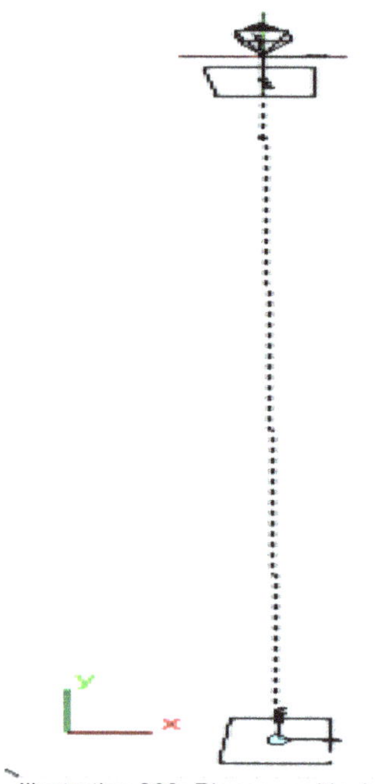

Illustration 200: Planes positioning

5. Create an Empty (**Shift**+**A** → «Empty» → «Cube»), name it «Lens» and create a series of planes parented to this «Empty», along the +Y axis like on Illustration 201. The distance of the farthest plane is 75 on the Y axis.

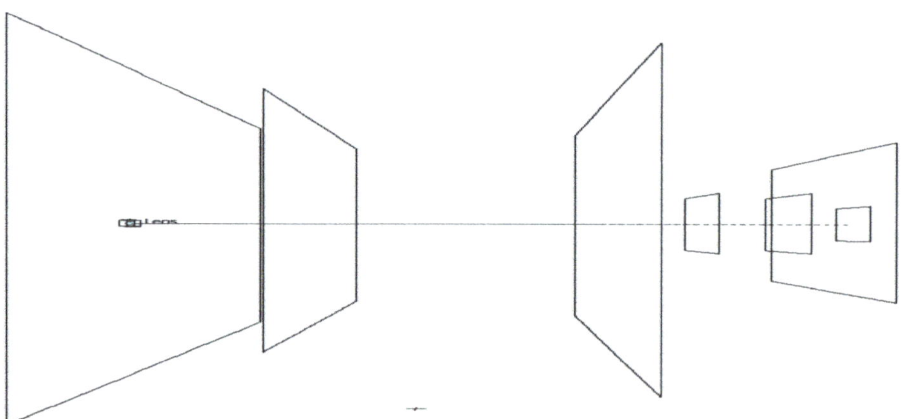

Illustration 201: Sequence of planes to create the «Lens Flare»

6. **For each plane**, setup like this:

    • «Materials» Tab, add a new «Material» («+»). «Shading» Panel, «Emit»: 1.00. «Game Settings» Panel, select «Alpha Blend» for the alpha. «options» Panel, uncheck «Use Mist». «Shadow» Panel: uncheck everything. Check «Transparency», «Z Transparency» and set «Alpha» at 0.0.

    • «Textures» Tab, add a new texture («+») with «Image or Movie» type. Open one of the textures created since the precedent step. «Influence» Panel, check «Alpha» and enter the value proposed hereafter:

Sequence of planes example (from the closer to «Lens» to the farthest, or from left to right on the precedent illustration:

- Plan 1 (600x600): Texture #1 – Alpha 0.2
- Plan 2 (450x450): Texture #2 – Alpha 1.0
- Plan 3 (550x550): Texture #5 – Alpha 0.2
- Plan 4 (120x120): Texture #6 – Alpha 0.1
- Plan 5 (120x120): Texture #6 – Alpha 0.1
- Plan 6 (300x300): Texture #4 – Alpha 0.05
- Plan 7 (80x80): Texture #3 – Alpha 0.1

Main objects are ready to be programmed, but before, we need to setup the scene. Use a scene with «Overlay» type which display the effects without being troubled by the objects of the current scene.

7. Add a new scene «Lens» and join the current objects: «info» panel, button «+» near «scene» → «Link Objects».

8. In the main scene, add a plane for the ground, an object representing a tower and eventually a skydome (size 1000x1000x500) (**recipe III.3**).

9. Place a lamp (**⇧ Shift**+**A** → «Lamp» → «Sun»), name it «Sun», and place it (-150,-300,350). Displace «Lens» to superimpose it to the sun. Displace the camera in (70,70,10) and orient the sun rays rayon toward the camera (rotation: 30, -30, 30).

10. Add an Empty in (-150,-300,350), name it «ToCamPlan» and parent it to «Sun»

11. Remove from the current scene the 7 textured planes. There will be always available in the «Lens» scene.

At first, the «Lens Flare» must orient towards the camera, but **with a lag**, that's why we need the «lensPlane»:

12. Select the «Lens» object and open the «Logic Editor» add an «Always» sensor, name it «RunOnce».

13. Add a «Scene» actuator, «Mode»: «Add Overlay Scene» and select the «Lens» scene.

14. Link the sensor with the actuator. This sequence allows to display the «Lens» scene in superimposition to the current scene.

15. Add an «Always» sensor, check «Activate on True Level Triggering» and enter a frequency between 0 and 10.

16. Add an «Edit Object» actuator, select «Track to» and the «lensPlane» object, «Time»: 0 and check «3D». Keep the default axes.

17. Link the sensor with the actuator. The planes are always oriented toward «lensPlane» and as the camera is near, **the textured planes farthest from «Lens» are displayed with a lag compared to the nearest**, that create the needed effect.

18. To rotate the textured stars planes (planes 1 and 6), use an «Always» sensor, «Activate On True Level Triggering» with frequency 0 joined to a «Motion» actuator, «rotation», «Z» at 0.05 for one and -0.05 for the other. So we have a sparkling effect. We can too realize an animation of the plane #2 (simple scale on dozens of images) to give an impression of cold dilatation.

The effect is functional. By directing the camera to the light source, we see the effect. Through the back of the tower object which hide the sun, there's the effect too, that's normal at this programming step.

We want launch a ray on the camera to know if there's nothing between the camera and the light source.

We can't use «Lens» differently oriented... So we use «ToCamPlan»:

1. Select the «camPlan» object and go to «Logic Editor».

2. Add a property «cam» with «boolean» type, checked.

3. Select the «ToCamPlan object and add an «Always» sensor, check «Activate on True Level Triggering» and set the frequency at 0.

1. Add an actuator with «Editor Object» type, select «Track To» and the «camPlane» object, «Time»:0 and check «3D». Keep the default axes.
2. Link the sensor with the actuator. The «ToCamPlan» object orients its +Y axis towards the camera.
3. Add a «Ray» sensor, name it «RayCam», select «property», in «value» enter «cam», select «+Y Axis», «Range»: 10.000.
4. Add a «Message» actuator, don't precise any recipient and «Subject»: «LENS-ON».
5. Link the sensor with the actuator. As long as the ray reaches the planes just behind the camera, it's that no object is placed between the camera and the light source, so we maintains the effect.
6. Add an «Expression» controller and enter the expression «NOT RayCam».
7. Link the controller with the sensor «RayCam».
8. Add a «Message» actuator, don't precise the recipient, «Subject»: «LENS-OFF».
9. Link the controller «expression» to this actuator. If we can't see the camera, a message «LENS-OFF» is sent!
10. Select the «Lens» object and add a «Message» sensor, «Subject»: «LENS-ON».
11. Add an actuator with «Visibility» type, name it «VisibilityON», check «Visible» and «Children». Link the sensor with the actuator.
12. Add a «Message» sensor, «subject»: «LENS-OFF».
1. Add an actuator with «Visibility» type, name it «VisibilityOFF», keep «Visible» unchecked and check «Children». Link the sensor with the actuator.

Now, when we are behind the tower, we stop the effect.

Step #3: Effect HDR for a better dazzle !

The «Lens Flare» effect is realist but there's not the dazzle to give life. The combination of the 2 effects gives good results:

1. Import the GLSL «HDR» program of the recipe VII.13 and do the following modifications:

```
uniform float avgL;
float HDRamount = 0.30;
```

     Instead of fix avgL in the script, it'll be in a «Property», so we use the word «uniform».

2. Add a new python script «hdrlens.py» and add the following script lines.
3. Select the «camPlane» object and open the «Logic Editor». Add a property «avgL» with «float» type initialized at 0.95.
4. Add a property «HDR» with «boolean» type, checked.
5. Add an «Always» sensor, name it «runOnce».
6. Add an actuator with «Filter 2D» type, «Type»: «Custom Filter», «Pass Number»: 0 and select the program «**HDR**»
7. Link the sensor with the actuator. The filter is activated at the beginning, but the parameters «avgL» and «HDR» modify its functioning.
8. Add an «Always» sensor, check «Activate on True Level Triggering» and set the frequency at 5 (more or less as you need).
9. Add a «Python» controller, select «Module» and enter «hdrlens.modify». Link the sensor with the controller.
10. Add a «Message» sensor, «Subject»: «LENS-ON».
11. Add a «Property» actuator, «mode»: «Assign», select the properties «HDR» and «value»: «true». Link the sensor with the actuator.
12. Repeat the steps 11 to 13 for the message «LENS-OFF» that position «HDR» at «false».

Script python «hdrlens.py»:

```python
import bge
from mathutils import Vector

def modify(cont):
  scene = bge.logic.getCurrentScene()
  try:
    sun = scene.objects["Sun"]
  except:
    return #Not good scene

  own = cont.owner
  if own["HDR"]:
    vectSun = own.getVectTo(sun)
    vectZ = own.getAxisVect( [0.0, 0.0, 1.0])
    angle = vectSun[1].angle(vectZ)

    hdr = 0.85+abs(angle/5)
    if hdr > 0.90:
      hdr = 0.90
    own["avgL"] = hdr
  else:
    own["avgL"] = 0.95
```

The effect intensity is modulated by the angle calculated from the Z axis orientation of «camPlane» (forwardly camera orientation) and the sun direction. When the angle is small, the effect is intense: to do that, decrease the value of avgL. The effect produced is the Illustration 202.

Illustration 202: «Lens Flare» effect + HDR at left and effect stopped at right

VII.22.   BULLET TIME EFFECT

Purpose:

The **bullet time** is a visual effect obtained through a series of cameras around the action. They are triggered simultaneously or with a short lag so, after montage, we can **create the illusion of a camera freely moving around the fixed action or slowed down significantly.**

The term had first been used within the original script of the 1999 film **The Matrix**, and later in reference to the slow motion effects in the 2001 video game **Max Payne**. In the years since the introduction of the term during The Matrix films it has become a vastly applied expression in popular culture.

Recipe:

To make a «slow motion», we could slow down the game «framerate» (*bge.logic.setLogicTicRate(ticrate)*). However, the effect would not necessarily good bellow 25 Frames per second.

1. Create a scene with a cube type Physic:«Rigid Body», duplicate it (Alt + D) 10 times and dispose a plane with Physic type:«Static» bellow.
2. Tester («P»): the cubes fall on the plane and scatter with normal speed.
3. Add a script «ticRate.py» and copy the follwoing script.
4. Select the plane (for example) and open the «Logic Editor» window
5. Add a property «rate» with «Float» type and value 3000
6. Add an «Always» sensor
7. Add a «python» controller, select «Module» and enter «ticRate.set». Link the sensor with the controller

Test: the cubes speed is 120 times lower (=3000/50)

8. Add a «Keyboard» sensor, key «+». Check «Activate True Level Triggering»to manage the event «key pressed».
9. Add a «Property» actuator/ «Mode»: «Add» / Select «rate» / Value: 10
10. Link the sensor with the actuator. Link the sensor with the controller managing the script «tricrate.py»
11. Repeat the operation with the key «-» and the value «-10» for «rate».

Test: now, you can freeze time, slow down, etc.

This recipe can be used to **«debug» a game.** Many problems are difficult to see with a normal speed. If we add a «freeview» camera like on recipe V.1, we can study it in all directions, like **William Murdoch** in The Murdoch Mysteries.

If we increase the Ticrate Logic», the physique is slow down. But moving an object with a «simple motion» - it moves quickly! So use variables style «acceleration factor» to apply to this kind of displacements to be coherent.

Script «TicRate.py»:

```python
import bge
c = bge.logic.getCurrentController()
own = c.owner
def set():
    if own["rate"] > 0:
        bge.logic.setLogicTicRate(own["rate"])
    else:
        own["rate"] = 0
```

It's possible to work with bge.logic.setPhysicsTicRate().

Improvements:

The «Bullet Time» effect can be exacerbated using a camera centered on an object and which rotate around the object since the «slow motion». It's the real Matrix effect.

Illustration 203: Making this effect in real life is a bit more difficult...

VII.23.   WEB CAM

Purpose:

Capture images via a **web cam** and use them into a **texture**.

Recipe:

1. Add an object (example: a cube) and on one of its faces, attribute a Material named «VideoMat». Add a texture to this Material (displayed before the video start)

2. Open the «Text» window, create a new python script «webcam.py» and paste the following script

3. Select the object and go to «Logic Editor»

4. Add a «Keyboard» sensor, assign to it the key «Enter»

5. Add a «Python» controller, select «type»:«Module» and enter: «webcam.init». Link the sensor with the controller

6. Add an «Always» sensor, select «Activate on True Level Triggering» and keep «Freq» at 0 (modify to obtain a slower refreshing)

7. Add a «Python» controller, select «type»:«Module» and enter: «webcam.refresh». Link the sensor with the controller

8. Go to 3DView and do a test (⊞). By pressing the key «Enter», the web cam appears on the chosen surface: Surprise, it's not Brad, not Angelina at screen...

Script «webcam.py»:

```python
import bge
import sys
from bge import texture

def init():
    contr = bge.logic.getCurrentController()
    obj = contr.owner

    if not hasattr(bge.logic, 'video'):
        if sys.platform in ['win32', 'cygwin']:
            pathCam = ""
        elif sys.platform in ['linux', 'linux2']:
            pathCam = "/dev/video0"
        matID = texture.materialID(obj, 'MAVideoMat')
        bge.logic.video = texture.Texture(obj, matID)
        bge.logic.vidSrc = texture.VideoFFmpeg(pathCam, 0, 25, 640, 480)
        bge.logic.vidSrc.scale = True

    if contr.sensors[0].positive:
        bge.logic.video.source = bge.logic.vidSrc
        bge.logic.vidSrc.play()
def refresh():
    if hasattr(bge.logic, 'video'):
        bge.logic.video.refresh(True)
```

VII.24.   THE GAME IS TOO SLOW ?

Purpose:

A game must have a speed between 25 to 50 FpS. With a lower speed, the game is not pleasant with jerks.

Recipes:

Modeling

1. Ensure that the models are «Lowpoly». Remove points and faces in duplicate («Remove doubles»). Do some «decimate» (modifier) where it's possible. Remove the objects parts we'll never see.

2. Deactivate the «Backface Culling» (Game settings in «Materials» Tab) instead of adding more faces with the modifier «Solidify» (for billboards and other plans)

3. Put together some objects (Ctrl+J) to have a smaller scene graph and to use fewer resources.

4. Use copies with link (Alt+D) rather than simple copies (Shift+D) because they share the same geometry and use less resources. That allows futures optimizations too (when the «Hardware Geometry Instancing» will be possible). Use also «Group Instances».

Materials and textures

1. In materials properties, use «Lambert diffuse» and «Phong Specular» which are faster.

2. For textures, use Blending «mix, add, subtract or multiply» which are faster too.

3. Reduce the texture size, respecting a power of 2 (16, 32, 64, 128, 256, 512, 1024, 2048). Merge the textures when it's possible (Baking – recipe VII.4)

4. Use **DDS** textures (Direct Draw Surface) – They will be compacted in the graphic card memory. So, as the memory saturates less often, there are fewer exchanges between the central memory and the GPU. To convert a texture into DDS:
   - Gimp: http://registry.gimp.org/node/70
   - Photoshop: http://tinyurl.com/paz97yz
   - (Windows), The «Compressonator» d'AMD: http://tinyurl.com/qc8476d

5. Use transparency sparingly

6. Reduce the «Bump Mapping Method» («textures» Tab using «Geometry Normal»)

7. For large landscapes using big textures, use the «Texture Splatting» texture in the recipe V.2. It can be also applied when a texture is often used, but modified by added imperfections, marks, blood, etc.: a stencil can be a solution to keep a HD texture, and add some modifications.

Scene management

1. Reduce the «Occlusion Culling» resolution in the «World» Tab, «Physics» panel

2. Reduce the camera clipping

3. Split large objects to allow the operations of clipping and Culling.

4. Split scenes and use «teleporters» or doors to go from one to the next

5. Set up a LoD everywhere you can (recipes III.17 and VII.11) – combine the homemade LoD using 2 cameras with the automatic one from the version 2.7. Deactivate the «Normal Map» and the specular light on the farthest objects, and anything which is not useful (script, physique, etc.).

Lights Management

1. Reduce the number of lamps, deactivate the lamps «Specular» when it's not used or when there are too many lamps. Replace the statics lamps without impact on the objects in movement by «ambient occlusion» (recipe VII.2)

2. Reduce the lamps shadows buffers – remove the shadow on the objects in movement and replace static ones by Lightmaps (recipe VII.1)

Post-treatment

1. Deactivate the 2D filters and others non essentials shaders
2. Deactivate fog (as long as you don't need to increase the camera clipping)
3. **Bake everything you can**
4. Deactivate antialiasing
5. Use a smaller screen resolution

Physics

1. Use first «Collisions Bounds» as spheres (faster), boxes (faster too), capsules, cylinders, cones. The «Convex Hull» is slow and the «Triangle Mesh», slower.
2. Remove useless collisions on objects
3. Use objects with «Rigid Bodies» and «Dynamics» type sparingly. Remove them or generate them via scripting or «brick from Logic Editor» when they are no needed. Avoid the «no sleep»
4. Avoid the sensors with «Always» type with «True Pulse mode» and a «Freq» at 0
5. Reduce the number of sensors using frequency as «radar» and «near» (they need too much resources)
6. Transform some physics simulations (cap, dress or braid) in animations with the `recipe III.11`.
7. In «World» Tab, «Physics» panel, reduce the Time of «Physics Deactivation».
8. Use «Occluders» (physics) (`recipe III.17`) when it's possible.
9. Replace the number of sensors «Near» and «Radar» by simple form using «Sensors» physic type objects.

Animations

1. Be careful to IK (Inverse Kinematics) on bones. The are calculated hundred of times per bone and per frame. Do an armature with IK for the animations and another without IK on which the animation is «baked»
2. «Constraints» take resources too. Remove the constraints which are not needed.
3. Reduce the number of character bones: do we need the fingers bones?
4. Use the addon «Simplify Curves» to simplify complex animations (`recipe III.11`)

Sounds

1. Transform all the sound files with a little file and which are compressed (MP3, OGG, etc.) into WAV files, especially for those which are often called. They are bigger in memory but faster (5 to 6 time faster)

Scripting

1. Use modules rather than scripts. All module global variables will be executed once.
2. Never do «bpy» import in a script executed during the game (multiply the logic cycles)
3. Deactivate characters A.I. (artificial intelligence) which are away from player (IDLE mode).
4. Replace all scripts working on the vertex, or on the object geometry, or doing 2D graphic process by appropriate GPU shaders to help CPU (verify GPU Latency before).
5. Replace all scripts by their sensors or actuators equivalents when it's possible. The logic bricks with «actuator» type can be 3 time faster and the «sensors» can be 6 time faster[1].

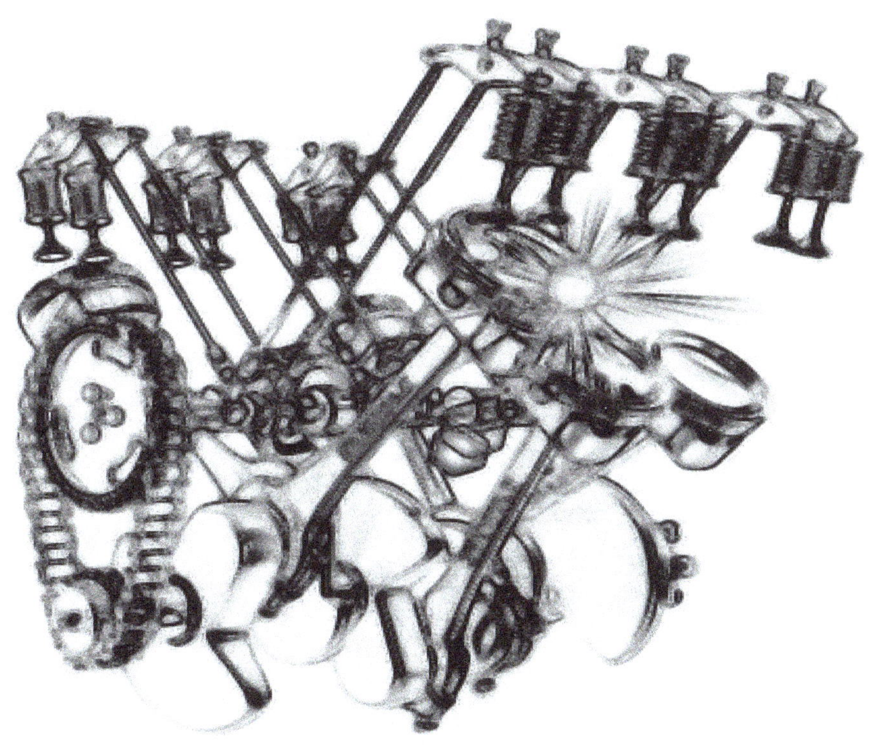

VIII - MEMO SHEETS

Image made from a **squibblejack's model**: http://www.blendswap.com/blends/view/71080

SHEET #1: 3D AND GAME GLOSSARY

3D Isometric: In the 2D games times, we feel that we were in 3D thanks to a bird's eye view (45°). In 3D, the **isometric perspective** is a representation method in which the 3 directions are represented with the same importance.

3D Engine: Program or library which allows realtime 3D rendering. If it manages other things like sound or inputs, it's a game engine.

3DS max: 3D animation, rendering and modeling software for games and cinema creation. It's a Blender equivalent but with a commercial license (Autodesk).

3D Tileset: Set of bricks made of several 3D objects. We can create level with these bricks like Lego™.

Addon (module, plug-in): Blender extension (Official or not) that we can activate in the users preferences ($\boxed{Ctrl}$+$\boxed{Alt}$+$\boxed{U}$).

A.I. (Artificial Intelligence): characterize any decision from a NPC (or group of) managed by the game. It's a set of routines and scripts to find the shortest path between 2 given points, or to adapt NPC's behavior to the player's experience, etc. The A.I. concept can be used for all the game logic.

Alpha Blending: technique used to create transparency in games. It use a Z-Buffer or a layer.

Ambient occlusion (AO): to bring more realism to a scene. Closer the faces are, lower the light is between the faces. The AO can be baked in a texture.

Anti-aliasing: A bitmap image is made of pixels. The edges of the forms with a particular angle look like stairs: it's the aliasing. The anti-aliasing smooths these forms to remove this stairs effect.

API (Application Programming Interface)*:* Software Functions opened for programmers. The Blender API is made by a set of objects and functions usable thanks to the python modules BPY and BGE.

Armature: skeletal structure made of bones, which allows to animate a character or another object by distorting its geometry mesh. The armature is animated with the Blender «Pose Mode» and animation key frames are created.

Art design: sketch or 2D illustrations made to be a model for the 3D model maker.

Asset: models, textures, materials, scripts, sounds... library. With Blender, an Asset is a Blend file in which we take resources through an «Append».

Backface Culling: hide object internal faces. Displayed faces are those with a normal vector pointing at the camera. So, when we look a cube from the inside, we don't see anything. In the same way, a plane is only visible from one side, except if the Backface Culling Is deactivated.

Baking: calculate in advance several elements needing a lot of resources, to use only their «finished» form. Example: ambient occlusion for a scene calculation (it can take several minutes) and the result is stored in a texture in superimposition on the scene in realtime.

Blend4Web: Blend4Web is a tool for interactive 3D visualization on the Internet. Blend4Web-powered apps work in common web browsers including mobile ones, completely eliminating the need to install plug-ins. Content is authored in Blender. A scene can be exported to a browser with a single click, even as a standalone web page. This makes creating and sharing your 3D content extremely easy. Blend4Web is open source software and does not depend on any non-free components or cloud services.

Billboard: Sprite always facing the camera.

Bitmap: Image made by colored points (pixels), as opposed to scalable vector graphic made by primitives.

Brick (logic): Alternative visual programming system complimentary to scripting. We put basic bricks together to create a program.

Blockbuster: video game with a big success and often characterized by next chapters.

Bullet: physic engine name in Blender, it's an independent, free and open-source library too.

Bump Mapping: A bumpmap is a rough texture. This is achieved by perturbing the surface normals of the object and using the perturbed normal during lighting calculations. The result is an apparently bumpy surface rather than a smooth surface although the surface of the underlying object is not actually changed. This process needs a lot of resources but provides realism to the object material.

Burster: Extension to run a Blender file directly in an Internet navigator (requires an installation) – there is also Blend4Web, a best alternative.

BVH (BioVision Hierarchy): animation file used for Motion Capture.

Capture the flag: Multiplayer game. 2 teams are opposed to capture the enemy flag and to preserve its own.

Cinematic (Cut Scene): Like a movie, player can't do anything. It allows to make the transition from a game step to another or to present important elements of the game. In past, it was videos (pre-calculated 3D scenes), now it's rendered in realtime.

Clipping (camera): determine the maximal distance beyond which the objects are not rendered by the camera. It's an optimization technique.

Compression: reduce the image or audio size (or another file) using an algorithm. 'AAAAAABBBB' (10 characters) can be compressed into '6A4B' (4 characters), the compression rate is here: 40%. It's a loss-less **compression** because unpacking it, we obtain a data strictly identical to the original. However, several compression formats admit losses (like MP3, JPG, DivX, etc.) and smooth details. Ex: 'AAAAABAAAA' (10 characters) is near '10A', the compression rate is 30% and the error rate is 10%.

Crowd-funding: Funding a project or venture by raising monetary contributions from a large number of people, typically via the internet. You have to present the idea or the prototype. According to the engagements taken, you'll have to reverse a part of the benefices or offer the product to participants.

CryEngine: game development kit developed by Crytek, specialized in FPS. One of the principal concurrent of UE4 (Unreal Engine 4). It can export to PC, PS4, Xbox One, PS3, Xbox 360, Wii U, iOS or Android. Since may 2014, the game engine is available for leasing for 9,90 € per month, and without obligation to give a percentage of the game recipes. Le free SDK is available for downloading. Crytek offers commercial developers full source code license for larger and longer term projects that benefit from a real partnership with Crytek.

Crystal Space: open source and free game engine for Windows, Linux and OSX. The Crystal Entity Layer (CEL) offer an abstraction layer to Crystal Space to make it easier to use in games. The CELstart application allows to create a game with Python.

Debug: bug-hunting activity – correcting errors and everything that can reduce a scene realism (a character which pass through a wall for example).

Diffuse (color): color reflected by the object when it's enlighten.

DirectX: Libraries for multimedia applications programming, games or programs on plates forms Microsoft (Xbox and Windows). It's an OpenGL's rival.

Displacement mapping: Technique similar to Bump mapping, normal mapping, and to parallax mapping. The difference is the use of a texture (which can be procedural) called «height map». The texture modifies the position of each points of the surface on which we apply this «displacement map». To use with the tessellation.

Drag & drop: the more often with the mouse. We drag an object and we drop it at another place.

Level editor (or map): Application, integrated or not to a video game, to design, load, save and test the levels. The editor is used by the Level designer. It can be too given with the game to allow the players to create their own maps and share them on the Internet.

Floor plan: ensemble of a level elements (ground and any surface on which the character can walk). From the Floor plan we make a navigation mesh and we do some test for the character and the movements. It's the level map.

Fog of War: fog to hide a part of the game map, such that the player can't see enemies moves, activities or to hide an unexplored land.

Font: it's a graphic text representation made with the vectorial matrix of each letter.

FpS (Frames per Second): number of images displayed in 1 second by the rendering engine, calculated in realtime. 25 fps are sufficient to give the impression of a fluid movement. 60 fps is a good goal.

Freeview: Camera in free view, not linked to a particular object. We can move it in all directions.

FSM (Finite State Machine): It's a behavior model made by states, transitions and actions. A state stores information on the past and reflects the changes. A transition is subject to a condition. An action is the description of an activity which has to be executed at the right time. We use them to describe the state of a game entity (Character, animated element of the decor) and the conditions of transition from one state to another.

Game Design: Video game conception (theoretical). The game designer imagines a game and transcribes it on paper: game type, story, game-play...

Game Engine: with a rendering engine (3D or not), managing devices (keyboard, joystick, mouse, etc.), the audio output device and eventually a physic engine. It's the root component of a game creation kit.

Game Pad: Joypad, Pad or Paddle.

Game-play: *"the way that the game is played"*. Quality of playing, coherence in the actions, handling, fluidity.

Geometry Instancing: Process that allows the batch processing of identical objects via the graphic card.

Gimp: Image editor like Photoshop but free and open source.

GLSL (OpenGL Shading Language): programming language of shaders for OpenGL (sheet #8).

GPU (Graphics Processing Unit): on the graphic card, it allows the computing functions for displaying.

HDR (High Dynamic Range): Effect applied on an image to enhancing the contrast and create a glare effect by simulating the retina functioning.

Heightmap: image representing a map of the heights (topography) used to generate a ground in relief. Each pixel can deform a 3D grid and give it a height. Generally, the heightmaps are in grey level, and if a pixel is near white, the corresponding point is in an elevated location. So, with a random generation (noise, Voronoï diagram) or painting, we create a realistic ground.

Highpoly: as opposed to Lowpoly, it's a model (mesh) represented in High Resolution, i.e. made by a fine mesh points to represent an objects and its details.

IDLE: literally «do nothing». When a character don't receive any order, it takes a waiting position to not remain static at screen.

Idtech: Game engine developed by ID Software, used for example by «Doom».

Indie (studio): little and independent studio with or not subcontracts for creating video games. Budgets are lowers than in the big studios, so, the indies are often very creative and innovative.

Instance (object or group): An object instance is an object and a model with 1 geometry (mesh). So, any modification on the model mesh lead to a modification on every instances of this model. However, each instance has its own transformation matrix (orientation, location, dimension) and its own characteristics (except mesh).

Irrlicht: Game Engine Open Source cross-platform using OpenGL and DirectX, with a physics engine, particles management system, 3D sounds, etc. Coppercube is a development Kit proprietary for games, based on Irrlicht and allowing to export the game into WebGL, Flash, on Mac OS, Windows or Android.

Inverse kinematics, IK: to describe a hand movement, we don't describe the movement of shoulder, elbow and hand. We can deduct the other movements from inverse kinematics calculations.

Joystick: device to control a character or a vehicle by moving the handle in a direction or pressing the buttons.

Kinect: device originally designed for Xbox, and made by cameras and sensors to replace the joystick. The system uses Motion Capture.

Lens Flare: light scattered in lens systems through generally unwanted image formation mechanisms, such as internal reflection and scattering from material inhomogeneities in the lens That's create orbs and halos when the camera is pointed at an intense light source like the sun.

Level Design: model everything needed for the game level. Make the map, collect illustrations and models, define possibles actions, events, etc.

Lightmap: texture with all the light received by a surface (statics lights), eventually with the ambient occlusion, the indirect lighting and sometimes the shadows. Lightmaps are baked from the Blender rendering system to be available in the Game Engine. They are stored in a texture added to the statics objects materials of the scene.

Level of Detail (LoD): LoD according to the distance between the object and the camera. When an object is far away, it's less detailed. This technique optimizes large landscapes management.

Logic layer: Layer from the «Logic Editor» to manage some «logic states» like in a Finite State Machine (FSM).

Lowpoly: modeling for realtime (game for example). When an object has a complex geometry (number of vertex and faces) the graphic card needs more time to display it. So, use simple models. The movie «Sintel» uses an Highpoly model, while the game uses Lowpoly model.

LUA: Interpreted programing language used to write scripts for applications and video games (World of Warcraft). Lua is used in the Sony PlayStation Portable too. Faster than Python.

Making of: Presentation in which developers explain their game creation, with technical and artistic details.

Material: the material define the properties and physical characteristics of the light returned by the object (diffuse, specular, etc.). A material can be made of several textures.

Maya: Animation, rendering and 3D modeling software, like 3DS Max.

Mesh: 3D geometry of an object. Named models also because objects are made with a modeler (3D modeling tool).

Mist (Fog): used to give the impression of depth on screen. To create fog, Blender mixes the background color with the visible object colors: when an object is far away, the part of the background color is important. Technique used with the clipping to improve the render performances. So the objects don't suddenly appear and disappear.

Modding: abbreviation of «modification». Modding is the modification of a video game by a hobbyist, who add some objects, create new maps, etc. Several modders became famous and sell theirs creations.

Motion blur: The motion blur is a graphic effect to blur the image while it moves. It magnifies the impression of speed.

Motion capture: method of animating some 3D characters by using real models, filmed with HD cameras or using motion sensors. When the actor moves its arm, the 3D model receives all the spatial information corresponding to the movement in space and reproduce it. Motion capture can be used on everything in movement.

Multiplayer: video game playable with other players simultaneously (Internet, LAN or split screen).

Normal map: like Bump map but with more details (**recipe VII.3**).

Occlusion Culling: Consists in eliminating hidden faces. For example, when we look at a sphere, we only see half of it – we don't have to render all faces of the hidden part (excepted for a transparent object).

Oculus Rift: virtual reality headset to play with 3D games with a real depth feeling and with head motion capture to modify the point of view.

Ogre 3D: 3D engine cross-platform (Linux, Win32, OSX, IOS, Android and Windows Phone 8) deemed for its speed and its source code quality. It's an additional abstraction layer above the API Direct3D and OpenGL, and with enhanced functions like objects loading in several formats, or the Scenegraph optimization.

OpenAL: open source library with functions to manage the sound card and with functions to manage 3D sounds.

OpenGL: functions of 2D or 3D images calculation library by Silicon Graphics to use the functions of the graphic cards (like Direct 3D). Mesa 3D is the open source implementation of OpenGL.

Open source: program with an available and modifiable source code. The source code is set of text files with all the instructions to be compiled or interpreted by a computer. It's compiled into machine language (binary code), or transformed by another program. An Open Source program is not necessarily free (like Unreal Engine)

OSL (Open Shading Language): Specific to Blender, it's a shading language used by Cycle.

Overlay: Scene at the forefront to display a menu, a text or another information (like HUD).

Panda 3D: Open Source and free game engine working on Windows, Linux and OSX. Its API is in C and Python so this engine is very easy to use. It has the same A.I. functions as BGE for the characters movements. It's used by Disney Online.

Path finding: A.I. technique used by a character to find a way from a given point to another in a virtual world, avoiding obstacles and respecting constraints. common algorithm: A* (ASTAR).

Path follow: technique used by a character to follow a path (curve or set of nodes).

Pegi: Evaluation system (2003 – E.U.), based on the player's age, to inform that some elements of the game can offend some sensitivities. Pegi 16: the game is not for the young under 16 years old. United States: ESRB. Japan: CERO.

Persistent world: virtual world which never stops (like MMO). Even if the player is not connected, others players are online and the world evolves. The player disconnected can be replaced by a NPC.

Physics engine: system to simulate the physical interaction between different bodies, like gravity, speed, forces and collisions. Physics engines bring realism to 3D video games. Examples: ODE, Bullet, PhysX, Havok.

Pixel: the smallest graphic unit of an image. It's a color point in a Bitmap image. Its depth determine the number of nuances of possible colors (ex: 8 bits = 256 col, 16 bits = 65536 col) and its transparency capacity (alpha). An image with size 200x100 contains 20.000 pixels.

PNG (Portable Network Graphic): image in open format, created to replace the GIF format. It uses a lossless compression, unlike JPG. It allows the images transparency thanks to the alpha channel.

NPC (Non player character): characters controlled by the A.I. and not by the player.

Post-mortem: report by a development team at the end of the video game creation: difficulties, the general feeling on the product, the number of sales, etc.

Procedural Texture: Texture generated from an algorithm to produce natural elements and realistic representation (wood, marble, metal or stone). The natural aspect of the result is obtained by the use of fractal noise and turbulence functions. These functions are used to reproduce the apparent randomness of Nature. Procedural textures are not yet supported by BGE, you must bake them.

Python: programming language with a hard dynamic typing, an automatic management of the memory by garbage collector and an exception management system; similar to Perl, Ruby, Scheme, Smalltalk and Tcl. Python is free license and works on most platforms: Windows, Linux, Mac OS, Android, iOS. It allows to optimize the programers productivity with high-level tools and an easy to use syntax. Python can be compiled with a C/C++ interpreter too (Cython).

Virtual reality: Technology to make an interactive simulation in realtime of the reality. It requires a large immersion: a virtual reality headset (Oculus rift or Morpheus) and other instruments to improve the interactions between the user and the virtual world. In the movie "The Lawnmower Man", we have a good introduction to this technology.

Recipe: modus operandi. Based on «how» instead of «why», and without "blah, blah, blah"!

3D Rendering (by rasterization): transformation of a scene made by "vectorial" objects into an image made by pixels. Actual graphic cards use the objects like a set of triangles with a material and transform them in images via complex calculations.

Resolution (object): level of details, i.e. number of faces used to represent it. There are Lowpoly and Highpoly. (LoD).

Resolution (screen): number of horizontal and vertical pixels of a screen. The higher the resolution is, the higher the quality is, but the render time is also higher. TV HD 1080p show 1920x1080 pixels.

Scenegraph: Scene hierarchy to store all the objects and with the object dependencies. Most of the optimization concern the scenegraph management (octree, etc.)

Script: program used by a video game to execute instructions in realtime. It's written in an interpreted language and allows to do quickly modifications on the game with a simple text editor.

Scrolling: horizontal/vertical of screen often used in 2D platform games or beat them all. When it's done in the 2 directions, it's a multidirectional scrolling. When it's made of several plans moving at different speeds to simulate a depth effect, it's a differential scrolling.

Shader: program compiled and sent directly to the graphic card to benefit from the graphic processor capacities

(GPU) and to reduce the central processor effort (sheet #8).

Shadowmap: a sort of shadowbuffer linked to the lamps. It's used, unlike to Lightmaps, for dynamics objects and lights. They are Z-buffers from the point of view of the light and are used to create shadows. To each point, we verify if the light is seen directly or not.

Shape key: animation key which stores the object geometry, i.e. its mesh. So, we can modify the object mesh and do a morphing between 2 shape keys per positions interpolation of each object vertex.

Skydome / skybox: A skybox is a textured cube with an image of landscape in front of the interior. So, we have a 3D View at 360° on the landscape. But from a face to the other, there's a visual deformation.
A skydome doesn't have this problem by using a sphere or half sphere (180°). This method allows to give more realism to an exterior scene and doesn't need a lot resources.

Slow motion: technique like «Bullet Time» – to slow down time to bring to light an effect.

Socket: communication channel – 2 computers can exchange data on a network.

Source Engine: game engine developed by Valve, used by games like Half-life or CounterStrike. The physics engine is Havok.

Specular (color): color returned by the object when it's touched directly by the light. It's the shiny or glossy appearance of a material.

Sprite: bitmap image, animated or not, in 2 dimensions. The Billboard is a kind of 3D sprite.

Realtime: 3d applications in which each image result of a calculation done just before its display. To obtain an animation, it's necessary to calculate between 25 and 60 images (frames) per second. The common technique used is the rasterization (but there is also the voxelization). The **ray tracing** more precise, but too slow to be used in realtime. The **ray marching** is an alternative technique to do a simplified ray tracing and which can be executed in realtime with good results.

Tessellation: Decomposition of polygons into smaller elements. Like the «subdivide» modifier of Blender. Creating smaller elements, we refine the object by applying smooths more efficient. If we add the «displacement mapping», we obtain realistic models from «**Lowpoly**» models.

Texel: smallest element of a texture applied to a surface. «texture element».

Texture: image applied on an object to give the impression of detail. For example, a texture «grass» can be applied on a plane to represent a vegetated surface. Textures must be correctly mapped, i.e. with an adapted UV-Mapping. Numerous parameters are linked to the texture: transparency, colors, geometric deformation (like bump map, but more elaborate deforming the object in its geometry), etc. We can apply several levels of texturing and manage the way of the textures are mixed. Examples: ambient occlusion textures and lightmaps.

UE4 (Unreal Engine 4) = successor of UDK (Unreal Development Kit): kit based on Unreal Engine with a scripting system C++ (replacing UnrealScript), a visual programing tool (Blueprints). It proposes an impressive 3D rendering engine, a level editor, physics, cinematic (Matinee/Level Sequencer) and other tools. Since March 2015, UE4 is free, the license costs 5% of sales if good results. It's probably the best game engine, for AAA and indies. It works with Windows, Linux, OSX, iOS, Android, PS4, Xbox One, and HTML5/WebGL.

Unity: games development kit to create games for Windows, OSX, iOS, Android, Wii, PS4, Xbox One, Windows Phone, Web (HTML5/WebGL). A good game engine and a large assets library. Before the prices modifications for UE4, it was the most common tool used by indies and mobile platforms.

UV Mapping: A textured object has a UV coordinates map to adjust the texture to the object.

Vertex: point in 3D space of an object geometry, like edges and faces.

Widget: graphic element of a GUI (window, title, button check box).

XNA: Microsoft framework to help game developers on Windows and Xbox, based on DirectX. This project was abandoned by Microsoft.

SHEET #2: VIDEO GAMES GENRES

A video game genre is a set of video games with a similar Gameplay. It's a kind of classification.

Advergame: «*advertising game*». It's an advertising video game created at the request of a mark.

Adventures: often named «*Point & Click*», characterized by missions to recover objects, assemble them (crafting), resolve enigma and talk to NPC. The player clicks with its mouse on a point where the character must move.
Examples: «*Zak McCracken*», «*Monkey Island*», «*Ankh*».

Beat Them All: Fight game with progression. The player must fight numerous enemies divided into different categories, in several levels opened with increasingly difficult, and often a Level Boss. Cooperation is frequent, each player controls its own character.
Examples: «*Double Dragon*» or «*Golden Axe*».

Casual game: Casual games derive their name from their ease of accessibility, simple to understand gameplay and quick to grasp rule sets. Additionally, casual games frequently support the ability to jump in and out of play on demand. Casual games as a format existed long before the term was coined and include video games such as Solitaire or Minesweeper.

Fighting game: Game in an arena. There's no scenario and the game is a fight between 2 characters.
Examples: « *Street Fighter* » or « *Soul Calibur* »

FPS (First-Person Shooter): or Doom-Like, shooting game based on fight in subjective sight. The player sees what the character sees. Opposed to third-person action game in which we see the back of the character.
Examples: «*Duke Nukem*» or «*Quake*».

Hack'n slash: Concept of the old role game («*Dungeons & Dragons*»). The representation is often in 3D-Isometric (I.e., top view and side view). The game is made of big dungeons or labyrinths with monsters to kill, objects to collect, competences to develop and doors.
Examples: «*Gauntlet*» or «*Diablo*».

MMO (Massively Multiplayers Online Games): Game often in a persistent world on line (via internet). The term «Massively» implies several hundreds or thousands players. Most of these games need a subscription. A **MMORPG** is RPG with MMO type.
Examples: «*World of Warcraft*» or «*Ultima Online*».

Platform games: Action games in which the player controls a character moving through levels. The player must control jumps from a platform to another, avoid obstacles, traps and enemies.
Examples: «*Mario Bross*» or «*Rick Dangerous*»

Puzzle game: smart game in which the player must assemble pieces or explore complexes places (labyrinth).
Examples: «*Tetris*» or «*Puzzle Bobble*»

RPG: Role-Playing Game with action. The character can evolve, gain skills with experience points, intelligence, agility, endurance, force, chance, etc.
Examples: «*Final Fantasy*» or «*The Elder Scrolls*»

Serious game: combine education and game. They are used for on-the-job training and simulation. The principal purpose is not the game but the training.
Examples: «*Adibou*» or «*America's Army*».

Shoot Them Up: Action game in which the player controls a vehicles or a character to kill enemies with weapons more and more powerful.
Examples: «*Space Invader*» or «*Xenon 2*»

Simulation (economic, management): manage a town, hospital, zoo, …
Examples: «*Sim city*», «*Railroad Tycoon*», «*Creatures*» or «*Sims*».

Simulation (vehicle simulation): realistic reproduction of car, plane, tank, train controls. With physics and vehicle parameters. Racing games too.
Examples: «*Flight Simulator*», «*Panzer Elite*» or «*Need for Speed*».

Smart game: Resolve puzzle, brainteaser, enigmas, labyrinths, etc. These games need strategic consideration.
Examples: chess, «*sokoban*», «*Lemmings*» or «*The Lost Vikings*».

RTS (*realtime Strategy*): In RTS, as in other wargames, the participants position and maneuver units and structures under their control to secure areas of the map and/or destroy their opponents assets. This is generally limited by a requirement to expend accumulated resources. These resources are in turn garnered by controlling special points on the map and/or possessing certain types of units and structures devoted to this purpose.
2 types of management: macro and micro control.
Examples: «*Dune 2*», «*Warcraft 3*» or «*Age of the Empire*».

Turn-based strategy game: the player must wait its turn to do actions like moving or fighting. A **Wargame** is a game based on historical event.
Example: «*Heroes of Might and Magic*» or «*King Bounty*»

Survival-horror: in a menacing universe, the player must survive. These games use traditional elements of horror movies with monsters (vampires, zombies, dinosaurs...), atmospherics perturbations and others morbid elements.
Examples: «*Alone in the Dark*» or «*Resident Evil*»

TPS (Third-Person Shooter): shooting game in which we see the back of the character.

SHEET #3: GAME & LEVEL DESIGN

Game Design

Playing to video game is a funny activity with rules. When there are too many rules, the game is too difficult. But the rules hold the player's interest. «Game Designer» define rules and progressively explain them.

The game quality is based on a **learning process**: «The video game rules are generally simple, but the difficulty comes from the fact they are not known by players. The handbook, rarely consulted, is a schematic description of the universe. The Player finds enemies, traps and strategies in a learning process controlled to give a self-surpassing feeling essential for the interest of the game. The player becomes stronger, understand more and more the hostile universe and wins with monsters bigger and bigger and resolves enigmas more and more complex. But, All this is a huge bluff: the game designer hides the rules and modifies them dynamically according to the player progress. If the player often loses, the game give it some help. When he wins with all monsters, the game sends him monsters resistant to its principal strategy» (Stéphane Natkin).

So, Chris Crawford, author of «The Art of Computer Game Design», one of the first books on this subject, and the creator of the Game Developers Conference says: «A video game designer can hide the rules to the player» - and must do it!

The **difficulty management** is an important point of Game Design and can be directly managed by the Level Designer. The publishers choose simpler and simpler rules to make it available to mass audience. This learning process is the key to the success of the difficulty system. To calibrate the difficulty evolution, use the learning curve. If we stay closed to this curve, the game will be not easy and not difficult. We can add some difficulties at some points too (example: boss at the end of the level). Difficult is optimal when there's a balance between the challenge and the player competences. It's the «flow» or the optimal experience of Mihály Csíkszentmihályi.

The best way is to adapt the difficulty to the player performances. However, this approach is criticized because it penalizes the good players.

The difficulty needs to be rewarded with a scenario increasingly rich with new weapons or points of experience. Difficulty must be the result of a process, and not the inadvertent resultant of a bad gameplay.
Thereupon, Level designer is responsible of the gameplay. **John Romero** (Doom), defines the levels as the places where the game occurs.

Level Design

The Level Designer is the one who thinks, imagines, conceives the level. He is the architect and not necessarily the builder (work of the «Level Builder»).

The first interaction between the player and the level is the **navigation**. The player needs to orient himself in the levels excepted in labyrinths or when it's needed. Making the navigation pleasant is very important. The implementation of objects easily recognizable in the landscape must be done at first. «Mirror Edge» from Dice is an example: stark colors and contrasts are used to identify anything we can use. In adventure games such as «click & play», the objects that the player can collect or use are often highlighted. It's important to help the player to know where to go.

The purpose of Level designer is to link the player with the mechanisms developed by the Game designer. He stages -   in terms of both story telling, graphic and sound scripting. Alternate narrows and open spaces, modify the lighting or the scripted events are the level designer tools. The purpose is «the player forget the computer and time».

Research phase:

1. **Define the level environment** (period, place, etc.)
2. **Collect information,** the basis of the inspiration: books, movies, other video games, architecture,

art and history. Collect elements (images, texts, movies).

3. **Define the story and the purposes:** scenario for the level. History for a map. Who is the character? Why the character is here? The scenario is given as one goes along.

4. Set up a set of sketches (Illustration 204): principal buildings and objects, general map of places. It's possible to use the **Silhouette Practice** (Illustration 205: draw only the outline of the object and fill with a uniform color). That can be done semi-automatically from photos with software, then retouched (*iWarp* for Gimp, *Liquify* for Photoshop). That allows to focus on the form, without thinking to perspective and colors. Used for characters, objects, landscapes. The superimposition of several silhouettes allows to obtain new images more creatives.

5. Define the **graphic style**: from silhouette to modeling, the more realistic with worked materials. The import of external models must respect the style.

Illustration 204: Example of sketch to represent a map

Illustration 205: characters silhouette examples

Creation phase:

1. **Floor plan:** with Blender, create a plane and subdivide it to obtain a fine grid to receive the map. Each «box» can be raised or lowered by extrusion. Define the characters moving zones while reserving a place for buildings and objects. (Illustration 206). It's possible to use the Heightmaps method for exteriors environments.
2. Depending on the game genre, modify the camera behavior for shooting.
3. Insert the objects (meshes and fakes like objects silhouettes) to test the Gameplay.
4. Program **the game logic** (interaction between characters and environment) and **physics** (mass, size, dynamical behavior, etc...).
5. **Model** the principal objects of the game (replace fakes), refine the landscape, without using materials. We can use the method of «generic bricks» (3D Tileset) to save modeling time. Model the landscape elements used many times like doors, windows, stairs, etc.
6. Set up the principal **textures**, design the **materials** and apply them.
7. Add the lights, create the **lightmap** and the **shadowmap**, apply. Test to set the lightning. Modify the shadows and the lights to create an atmosphere (ex: a forest is scarier in the night, etc).
8. Add **imperfections**, deformations. In reality, a wall is never uniform, there are holes, marks, etc. It's the time to differentiate the generic bricks.
9. Add logic elements to give **realism** to the game (fog, wind in trees, things in movement, etc.). It's time to use particles (smoke, fire, etc.) and other special effects (Lens flare, Volumetric lights, Glow and Bloom effects, etc.), set up the water effects (a lake, a river), rain, etc.
10. Add sounds, musics, videos and cinematics
11. Add the scripted elements (ex: object or monster apparition after a while) to give the impression of a living world.

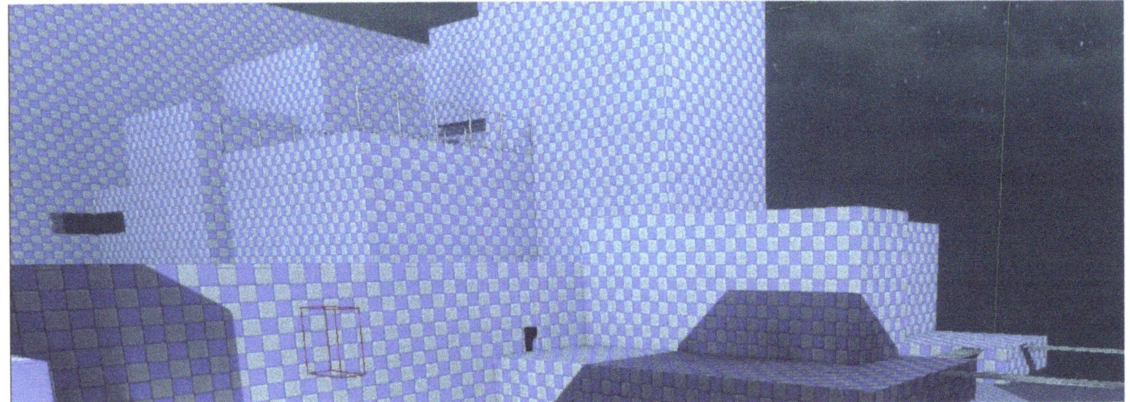

Illustration 206: Modeling from a grid

Phase Test:

1. Evaluate the dynamic **of the game, the difficulty** of several corridors (the game must be played by mid-level players) and refine. According to the skill of the player, we can add some events to help him (an advice, 1 object, 1 life, etc). The place to reborn (spawn points) are different under the circumstances. Set up the A.I (via script) of NPC, the bonuses to collect, the life elements, the ammos, depending on the level of difficulty selected.

2. **Ask other people to test the game** (alpha or beta version), study the incomprehension, the blocked situations. Modify the level or add some help. Assess the pleasure given by the game, the different **learning** to improve the next levels.

«loots» are the bonuses given by the enemy when he dies or objects left in a chest by a player. They are «relieve the boredom» or «Skinner boxes». **Skinner box** is an experimental system invented by B. F. Skinner early 1930s to simplify the study of conditioning mechanisms. It's based on the Pavlov's experiments, adding a randomly event. If we condition a pigeon to push a button when it's hungry to obtain its food, the pigeon will quickly learn. When it's not hungry, it doesn't push on the button. However, if there's random in the button answer, the pigeon pushes evenly. It works with humans too for money and social recognition. In game world, the player looks for rares and powerful objects to have a superiority in its quest, so the player opens all boxes, tombs and breaks all the objects he can (Diablo).

SHEET #4: MODELING WITH BLENDER

Blender Interface

Blender development is continuously in progress. The menu elements change very quickly! So it's why we prefer not to use too many screenshots. Blender is one of the most complex tools, it works on vast and varied domains.

In the menu bar, at the top of the screen, there's a check box with «Blender Render», «Blender Game» and «Cycles Render». We often use the second in this book, except to «bake» several textures or physics behaviors. We don't create an animated film as we create a video game, but there is a lot of common tools.

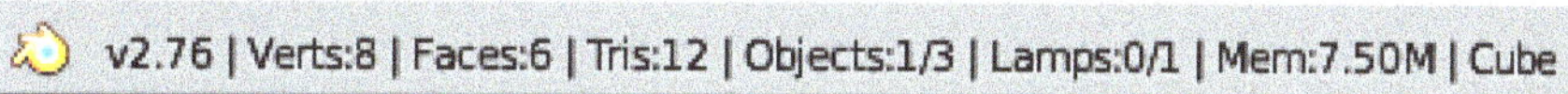

Illustration 207: Example of display in «Edit Mode». At the top of the screen, we can read the Blender version, VE: the number of points, ED: lines and FA: Faces in the current scene (Selection/Total). Near, the memory size used and the name of the selection (here: Cube)

We have a window containing several other windows.

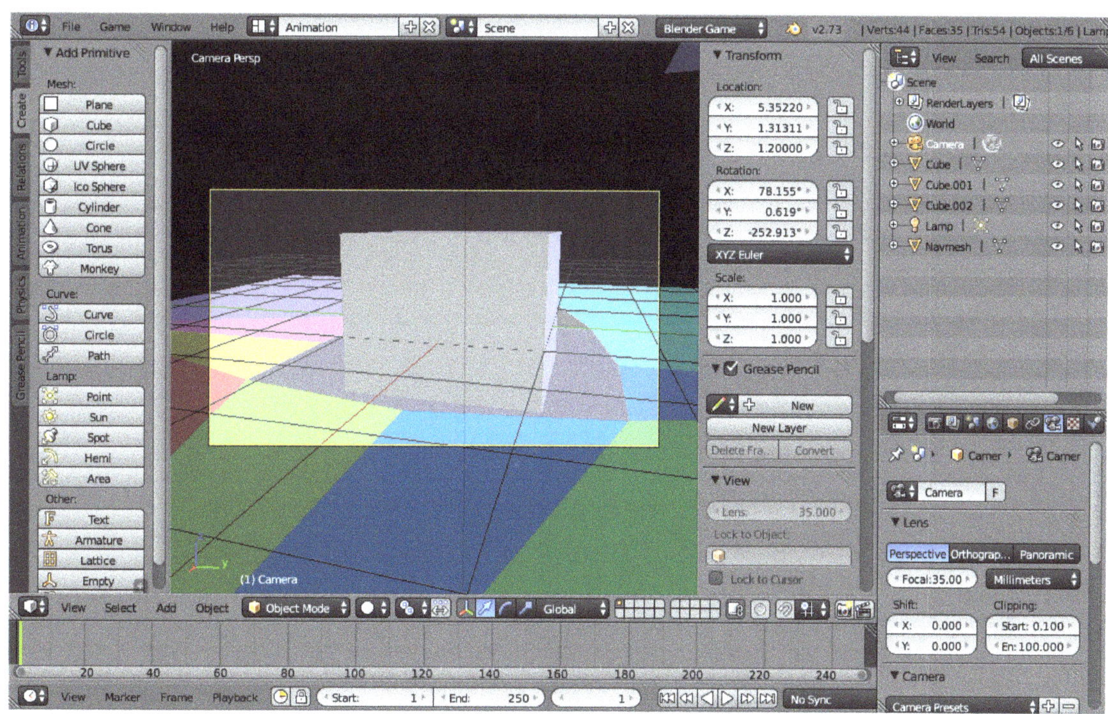

Illustration 208: Example of the display for modeling with Blender 2.7

The Illustration 208 shows 5 windows:

- **«info»: principal menu** (File, etc.). It allows the navigation from a scene to the other or the change of the views display with several models (Animation, Compositing, game logic, etc...).
- **«3D View»**: display of the cube. In this window, we have 2 menus:
    - **menu «Tool Shelf»** at left (Translate, Rotate, etc.) reorganized in the version 2.70.
    - **menu «Properties»** at right (Transform, Grease Pencil, etc.).

    It's the principal window used for the geometric modeling of objects. This window can be divided into 4 windows to have a simultaneously view: in front, from sides, from the top and via the active camera (button «Toggle Quad View» from the «Properties» menu, «Display» Panel).

- The **«Properties»** window (not the menu of the «3D View») has a Tab with several panels: «Render», «Render Layers», «Scene», «World», «Object», etc. These panels are contextual: for example, the texture panel is linked to «Material» being edited. It's often difficult to access for a beginner. It's probably the more often used window for modeling.
- The **«Outliner»** window displays the hierarchy of the different scenes while respecting the parent links between the objects. We can rapidly select an object, hide it or prevent its selection in the «3D View». The magnifying glass is used for researches and to use numerous objects.
- The «Timeline» Window allows to manage the different «frames» up to the animation. There's another window to setup an animation, but the «Timeline» is a general view of the progress.

You can substitute a window by another by clicking on the selecting box at the top left of the window. You can too resize a window by catching the corner at the top left and by dragging it. You can too divide the window in 2 by clicking with the left button of the mouse on the edges of the window («Split Area»). You can link 2 windows too («Link Area»).

The other windows used in this book are:
- **«Logic Editor»**: we link the different bricks corresponding to the game logic. It's a way to «program» the game, without write a code line.
- **«Python console»**: run python orders which are executed directly on Blender. If these orders return a result, the result is displayed in the window.
- **«Text Editor»**: used to write the scripts pythons called in the «Logic Editor». It allows to open any text file too.
- **«UV/image Editor»**: to modify images (mode «Paint»), most often, it's used to link UV coordinates with textures.
- **«NLA Editor» «Dope sheet» and «Graph Editor»** are used to setup animations. With Blender, animations are grouped in actions, they are visible in the window of the «Dope Sheet» and the «Graph Editor» channels with their editable key images. NLA Editor (Non linear Animation) allows to manipulate these actions blocks, to mix, accelerate, multiply and regroup them. It's a kind of editing studio for animations. Blender proposes an editing video software available through the windows **«Movie Clip Editor»** and **«Video Sequence Editor»**.
- **«Node Editor»** is used for the rendering in image synthesis, and for the materials adjustments. The process uses «nodes» to setup something.

The «3D View» window

- Complex and important window.
- **There are several layers** as in a design software. We can display simultaneously 1 or more layers, to move an object on other layer («M»), to separate the ground from the vegetation and houses. There are 20 layers available in the «3D View».
- It's possible to **modify the way of displaying the scene,** in the selection box «viewport Shading». We can display in mode:
  - **«Bounding Box»**: each object is represented by a box with the size of this object,
  - **«Wireframe»**: represent only the vertex and the edges,
  - **«solide»**: with faces, but without material and texture,
  - **«Textured»**: rendering near the «Game Engine»,
    «Rendered»: slow, rendering in ray tracing, not available in «Game Engine» mode

When we model an object, we often need to access to the elements of this object: vertex, edges and faces.

So, we can add a cube (Shift+A → «Mesh» → «Cube») and move the edges (in «**Edit Mode**») to create another form. We can to subdivide it («W» → «Subdivide») to create more complex forms, or add some new edges on the fly (Ctrl+LMB). We can extrude a face («E») to create new forms, etc.

«**Object Mode**»: to work directly on the object: to move it, to scale it, etc. The menus «Tool Shelf» and «Properties» are different from a mode to another. If you add a cube, go to «Edit Mode» and add a new cube, you don't add a new object (excepted with a special config in the users preferences). The first object called «cube» will be composed by a geometry (mesh) corresponding to 2 cubes. So always verify the mode before adding new elements.

«**Sculpt mode**»: to use brushes as in drawing software but not to color the object ! It's to modify the geometry. If you apply that on a cube, nothing appears (excepted if «Dynamic Topology» is activated). If the cube is subdivided, the Sculpt mode allows to model the object like «dough». To date, It's not very used to model for a game because we need models «Lowpoly». But this is quickly changing. However, we can use this mode with a complex object (Highpoly) and do an automatic simplification of the object at the end.

«**Vertex Paint**»: airbrush to assign colors to different points of an object, to do gradations. It's not used for game, the objects are textured.

«**Weight Paint**»: assign to a part of the object, a rate to a deformation, or a movement. Example: an animation with «armature» using an internal bone to deform a mesh and giving to it a liberty of movement. The leg of the character is composed of 2 bones: 1 for the upper leg and another for the lower leg. The first bone deform at 100% the upper leg, and the 2nd at 100% the lower leg. But what happened at the level of the knee: a division is done: 50% for one and 50% for the other.

Illustration 209: Set up «Fly/Walk» in «users preferences»

«**Texture Paint**»: we paint directly an object with brushes corresponding to textures. We take a landscape and we use a brush for the grass, a brush for the stones, a brush for the sand, etc. We can work directly in the 3D View and the result is visible automatically in the «UV/Image Editor» window corresponding to the texture of this object.

The «3D View» window has a large menu changing with the using context.

In the version 2.7: the camera mode «**Walk**». To activate it, open the users preferences (Ctrl+Alt+U), «Input» panel, check «Walk» Illustration 209). Check too «Gravity».

To use it, go to «3D View», activate the principal camera (0) and press «Shift+F»: the camera «fall» to the ground and it's possible to:

- move with the key arrows («Shift» pressed to go faster or «Alt» to go slower). The mouse directs the view like in a FPS (**recipe V.2**).
- pass over the obstacles by climbing over it automatically,
- jump with the key «V»,
- teleport behind an object or to go faster with the key «Space»,
- pass from the mode «gravity» to «free» with the key «Tab»,
- change the speed with the mouse wheel.

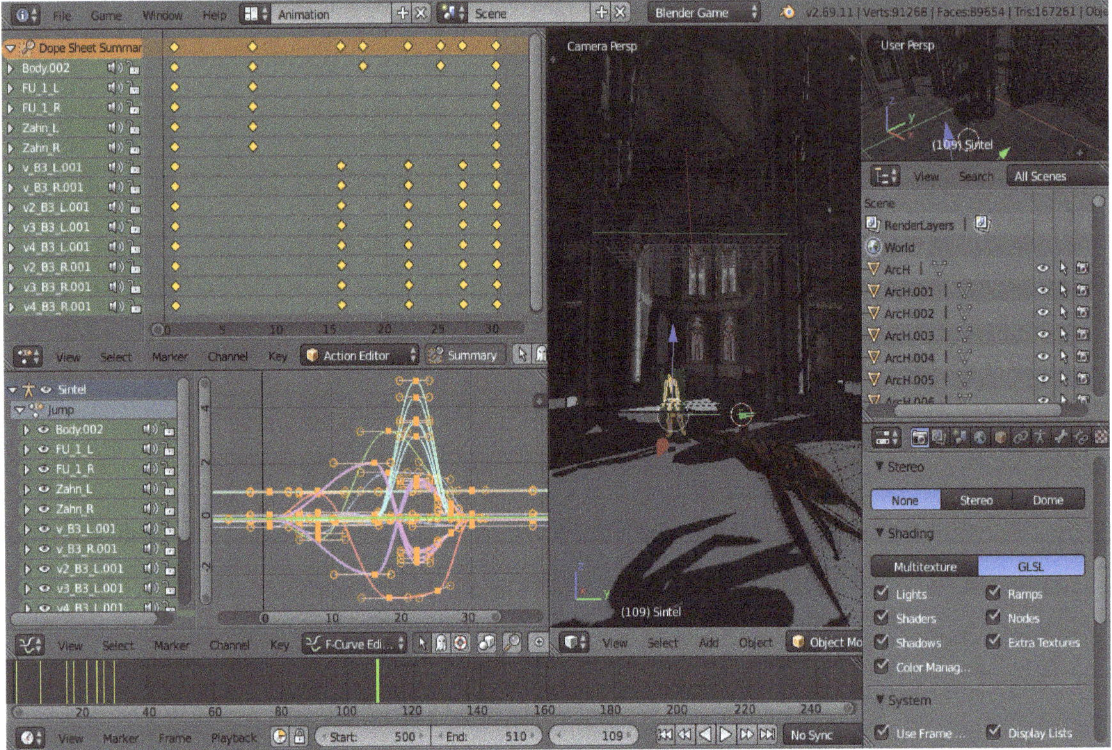

Illustration 210: Example of the display for the animation work

The shortcuts

The most useful shortcuts for «3D View»:

View management:
- **1**(Front side),
- **3**(Right side),
- **7**(Top),
- **[8;2]** to change the view,
- **[4;6]** to pivot Left-Right
- **0**(Camera defined)
- **[+;-]** zoom – **[/]** the selection is centered in the view and a zoom «to fit»,.(zoom on selection).

  Ctrl +↑: Zoom on the activated window, Ctrl +↓: mode multi windows

In any view (excepted for the camera view), we can choose between 2 types of projection:
- in perspective (the more realistic view: when you are way out, the objects seem little)
- or in orthonormal (to flatten the objects, to easily model forms).

From the perspective view to the orthonormal view (and vice versa): «**5**».

The transformation operations (Rotate, Scale, etc.) are realized through a **pivot** (symbolized by 3 color axes). By default, it's the median point of the selection.

Other possible pivots:
- «Active Element»: it's the point, line, face selected
- «Individual Origins»: when several objects are selected, each object uses its own rotation center
- «3D cursor»: it's the point moved with the mouse click («LMB»)
- «Bounding Box center»: the center is calculated by taking the center of the box including the selection

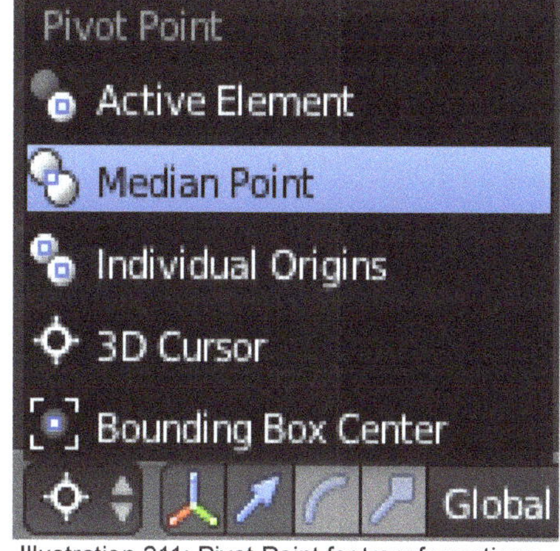

Illustration 211: Pivot Point for transformations

Mouse moving:
- Button central: view rotation
- Burton central+⇧ Shift: view moving

Common shortcuts:
- **Space:** access to any command with a key word!
- Ctrl+Z: Undo,
- ⇧ Shift+Ctrl+Z: redo
- Z: from mode Wireframe to full mode
   - Alt+Z go to mode GLSL
- A (All): select all (or nothing) – depends on the mode (point, line, faces, objects)
- ✎: select 1 element – depends on the mode (point, line, faces, objects)
   ⇧ Shift+✎: select an additional element (or remove one)
- **LMB:** Position of the cursor in space. Need to pass from a view to another to move it
- ⇧ Shift+S (snap): open a panel to move the cursor at the center of the object, the grid, etc.
- B: select a set of elements by catching them with lasso (selection rectangle). To select the invisible points, go to wireframe (Z).
   - ⇧ Shift+B: Zoom on a selection rectangle.
- C: select by using a selection circle like a brush (the mouse whee manage the size). Several clicks to select several elements. Scale the circle with the wheel (or + and – num keypad)
   - ⇧ Shift+C: global view
- G (Grab): move the object selected – if X,Y or Z is entered, the displacement is limited to the axis.
- S (Scale): Resize the selection – if X,Y or Z is entered, the scale is limited to the axis. Enter the value with keyboard.
   - If we want only X and Z: ⇧ Shift+ Z
- Alt+S to do a scale in relation to the center of the object (inflation effect)
- R (Rotate): by default, the rotation point is at the center of the object: Median Point. Choose 3D Cursor to choose any else rotation center
- Alt+S (Shrink/Flattent): near Scale and the extrusion
- X: remove the selected element
- T: display the Tools bar (different by mode)
- N: display the Properties bar (different by mode)
- F: connect some points to create lines, some lines to do faces
- E: extrude a face

- **W**→**Subdivide**: subdivide an object, a face, or a segment
- **Ctrl**+**J**: join some elements (2 elements are merged into 1 and the display is not changed)
- **Shift**+**F**: In camera view mode, to manipulate the camera until the next click and to make the modifications permanent
- **H**: hide,
  - **Alt**+**H** to display everything
  - **Shift**+**H**: to hide everything excepted that's selected
- **Ctrl**+**S**: Save the scene

Shortcuts «Object Mode»:

- **M**: Move to Layer → to go to the layer window. If the object is selected, do LMB on the layer needed then «ok»
- **Ctrl**+**G**: add to a group. Precise the name of the group in the dialogue box
  - **Ctrl**+**Shift**+**G** to add to a group existing
  - **Shift**+**G** to do operations on the group, as a selection.
- **Shift**+**D**: Duplicate an object
  - **Alt**+**D**: Duplicate with link (modify the geometry for one do a modification on the other)
- **Ctrl**+**P**: Select the first object, then all that we want to parent to the first
  - **Alt**+**P**: unparent or disconnect
- **Alt**+🖰: select an object hidden by another (via a contextual menu)
- Manips on the cursor:
  - **Shift**+**S**: reposition the cursor (cursor to center for example) or position an object on the cursor
  - **Shift**+**C**: Cursor original
  - **Shift**+**Ctrl**+**Alt**+**C**: Select the object origin: geometry to origin (move the object at the origin), origin to geometry (inverse), to cursor (move the origin towards the cursor) (= mode object/Tools/Origin)
- **Shift**+**A**: add an object
- **Ctrl**+**L**: link 2 objects while accounting for a characteristic, for example «Material». Select 2 objects then **Ctrl**+**L**→ «Material» and the first takes the Material of the second. Allows to copy an object from a scene to the other too.

Shortcuts «Edit Mode»:

These 3 icons allow to change the selection mode. We can work in point mode (vertex), line mode (edge) or face mode. The shortcuts have different behaviors.

- **W**: special menu (subdivision, fusion (merge)
- **Ctrl**+LMB: create a new vertex in point mode
- **P**: Separate entities – on a selection, a «Material» type, or separated objects (that have been joined for example)

- **Ctrl**+**R**: (add Edges Loop) cut the object along a plane. The wheel allows to do several edges loop at once.
- **Ctrl**+**B** (Bevel): add edges
- **J** (connect): connect 2 points with a line, a face with 2 lines, or several points, etc.
- **Ctrl**+**Tab**: to go from a selection mode (vertex, line, face) to another
- **K**: (knife tool) select the object visible faces to divide in 2, like with a knife. To cut in depth, use K, then Z
- **Ctrl**+**+**: Select the adjacent points, lines or faces, can be done several times
  - **Ctrl**+**−** reverse
- **I** (inset faces): by selecting faces, insert a frame in these faces, and eventually a relief (setting via the menu «Tools»→Inset Faces: Depth and Tickness of frame)
- **Alt**+**P** (Poke faces): by selecting faces, divide the into 4 triangles with a vertex at the center of the face
- **V**: separate a vertex in 2 by creating a new point from the first.

Shortcuts «Sculpt Mode»:

- **F**: dynamically resize the Brush (radius)
  - **Shift**+**F**: resize the texture (to do a cache and use only a part a the texture)
- **Ctrl**+**LMB**: remove instead of to add

Use the GLSL display with Blender

To see the true game render, activate the GLSL display in the «3D View». The mode «Multitextures» doesn't give the same result, we can be surprised. The principal reason is: some levels of textures and the illumination calculation are not treated in the same way («per-pixel» vs «per-vertex» for example).

To activate the GLSL display with Blender, open a «view 3D» window, press «N», in «Shading», select «GLSL» instead of «Multitextures». The modifications appears in realtime.

To use the shaders GLSL (filters and special effects), the graphic card driver must support an OpenGL version, to each OpenGL version, correspond a GLSL version.

Illustration 212: GLSL Display uses OpenGL

SHEET #5: LOGIC EDITOR

The logic bricks and the Python scripts are essential in the game logic. To display the logic bricks, open a new window with «Logic Editor» editor.

Illustration 213: Example of use of «Logic Editor»: The key « Arrow upward » is associated to a movement (motion) of Z: +1

«Logic Editor» defines the sensors and actions linked with an object:
- A **Sensor** detect an input or an event. That can be a key, a joypad, a proximity sensor, a modification on a variable or… random !
- An **Actuator** runs an action in the game, like moving an object, playing an animation or a sound
- A **Controller** link 1 or several sensors with 1 or several actuators. It allows complex controls on the interactions between the actuators and the sensors, connections conditions, etc. It's the place where we launch scripts !

There's a check-box (in red on the illustration) : to deactivate the processing.

Trick: the logic bricks are associated with an object. It's not possible to «copy- paste» brick after brick, but we can copy all the bricks from an object to another from the «3D View» (menu «Object» → «Game» → «Copy Logic Bricks»).

Game Properties

Properties are variables assigned to an object from the graphic interface. Sensors, controllers, actuators and scripts can use them.
In «Logic Editor», we can display or hide them by pressing «N».

Several types:
- «String»: characters string. To store words or phrases.
- «Float»: real numbers (with point)
- «Integer»: {..., -3, -2, -1, 0, 1, 2, 3, ...}
- «Boolean»: boolean values («True / 1»or «False / 0»)
- «Timer»: chronometer that increments with time (seconds).

The values can be read or modified with python:

```
own = cont.owner # Current Object, cont the controller
own['Life'] = 100
```

We can dynamically create properties too, and store complex objects (rays, other objects, etc.), but these properties are not visible in the editor.

Sensors

The common sensors options are presented on the Illustration 214:

- **The first «...»** (Activate True Level Triggering): if selected, the connected controllers are activated as long as the state of the sensor is positive
- **Le second «...»** (Activate False Level Triggering): if selected, the connected controllers are activated as long as the state of the sensor is negative. Be careful, they return «False»! However, a script can be launched (there's activation). It's not very used
- **Freq:** this parameter define the delay between the repeated activations, measured in images
- **Level** (Level Detector): Activate the connected sensors when the state «state» active is modified
- **Tap** (Trigger controller only for an instant): modify the sensor from the positive state to the negative state at each activation, activates the controller each time.
- **Invert:** if the sensor is positive, it's treated like negative and "vice et versa". That's invert the condition

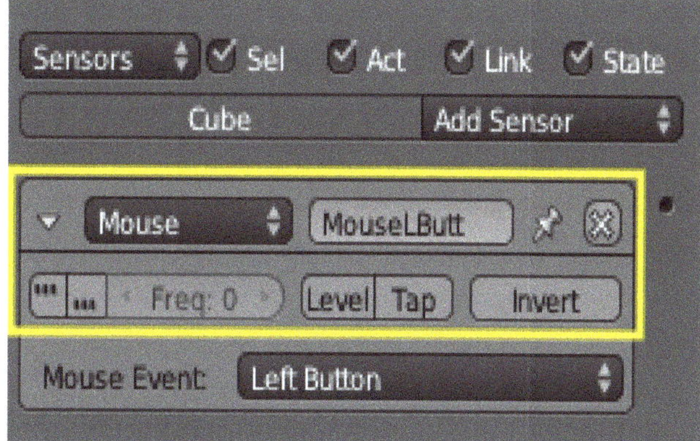

Illustration 214: Common Options to different sensors

To understand the differences, see the Illustration 215: a character is near a sensor. The zone in which the sensor locates the character is symbolized by a circle. Lower, each point represent a displayed image. If the frame speed is set up at 60 images per second, the space between a point and the nearest point represents 1/60ième of second.

On the left, there are different configurations to see the differences.

«Actuator» Sensor

Use: in «invert» mode, to activate an action when the actuator is activated.

«Always» Sensor

Use: to launch actions
- to each logic cycle by checking «Activate On True Level Triggering»
- every "x" cycles (with a parameter «freq»)
- once, at launch

«Delay» Sensor

Use: to wait for several seconds before activate, the end of another action or to be a «timer» event.

Configuration:

«Delay»: number of cycles in the course of which the sensor wait before to send a positive impulsion.

«Duration»: Duration of waiting for the sensor (after activation) before to send a negative impulsion.

«Repeat»: starts again when the delay is finished.

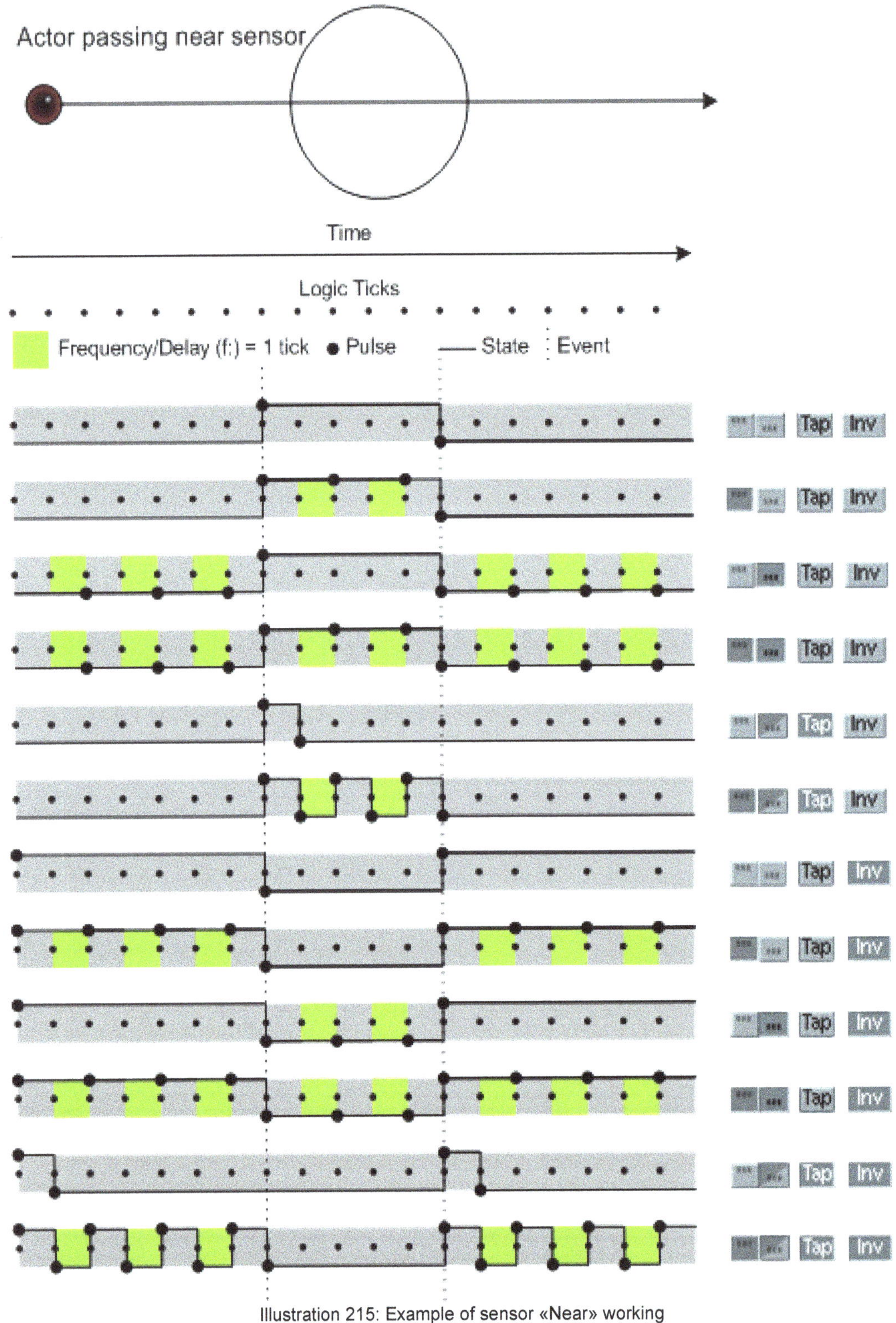

Illustration 215: Example of sensor «Near» working
Source: http://gameblender.wikia.com/wiki/Sensors

«Collision» Sensor

Use: activated when the object collides another object. A filter can be used: only the objects with a certain property or material generate a positive impulsion at the collision.

Configuration:
«M/P»: choose between the filtering by material or by property. If the field is empty, the collision is detected with any object (excepted «ghosts» and «no collision»).

«Pulse»: generate other collisions with the same type (same material or property) at the same time. If «pulse» is not checked, only one collision is detected, the next will be possible only when the first is finished.

A «python» controller allows to reference the object of the collision:

```python
sen = cont.sensors["sensor"] # cont, the controller
obj = sen.hitObject
```

We can reference the list of the objects in collision with hitObjectList, or the collision location with hitPosition.

«Joystick» Sensor

Use: trigered when we push a Joystick button or when a movement is detected in a particular direction (left/right, up/down, etc).

Configuration:
«Index»: to manage several Joysticks (0: first, 1: second, etc)

«Event Type»:
- «Axis»: Detect a movement on an axis.
    - «Axis Number» (1-8) specify the axis. Example:
        - #1 = lead angle Joystick (Right Axis/Left Axis/Up Axis/Down Axis),
        - #2 = Joystick «Twist» (the throttle lever with several joysticks) (Up Axis/Down Axis), Axis Number

        Depending on your model (handle Xbox 360, etc.), you have to test the options to collect all specificities
    - «Axis Threshold» (0-32768): specifies the precision and the sensibility by creating a «dead-zone» around the central la position. 0: «no dead-zone» and 32768: «everything in in dead-zone»
    - «Axis Direction» specifies the direction: left, right, up, down
    - «All events»: to use every axes
- «Single Axis»: idem with one axis
- «Hat»: Use a numerous for a specific Hat. A Hat is an additional button on joystick
    - «Hat Direction» specifies the direction: left, right, up, down, up right, …..
    - «All events»: to use every directions
- «Button»: Button Number to manage the number of the button
    - «All events»: to use every buttons

«Keyboard» Sensor

Use: Detect a pressed key – it can record the pressed keys in a String property too.

Configuration:
«Key»: only one key pressed. By clicking on the button near, then pressing this key, the key is assigned.
«All keys»: any key pressed

«Modifiers» allow the shortcut key, example: ⬆ Shift + Alt +etc.

«LogToggle» gives the Boolean property that determines if the key pressed is recorded in the String property (right) or not (false).

«Target» indicates the String property in which recording the pressed keys.

Python:
To test the key pressed in a python script:

```
Keyboard = bge.logic.keyboard
W_key = bge.logic.KX_INPUT_ACTIVE == Keyboard.events[bge.events.WKEY]
```

The keys complete list: http://tinyurl.com/lttseob
Test the keys via a python script is slower than use the logic bricks. However, it's the only way to do a key mapping which allow the player to choose its own keys.

«Message» Sensor

Use: triggered when the message indicated in «Subject» field is detected. The messages can be sent by scripts or by the actuator with the same name.

«Mouse» Sensor

Use: to detect mouse events (click, movement).

Configuration:
«Mouse Event»:
- «Left button»
- «Middle button»
- «Right button»
- «Wheel Up»
- «Wheel Down»
- «Movement»: any mouse movement
- «Mouse Over»: detects if the mouse is above the object
- «Mouse Over Any»: detects if the mouse is above any object. The sensor will be triggered only if the mouse is not yet above another object, excepted if «pulse» is activated.
  - «Pulse»: Each new object generates a new « pulse »
  - «X-Ray»: Get through objects, generate several events if several objects are superimposed.
  - «Property /Material»: filter on the objects with a property or a material.

«Near» Sensor

Use: detects the objects near. It can filter the objects with a property, like the sensor Collision.

Configuration:
«Property»: limit the sensor with the objects with this property.

«Distance» (in Blender units): corresponds to the limit of detection for the objects, it's the distance at which the object is detected.

«Reset»: distance at which the objects must be to reinitialize the sensor (send a negative impulsion), i.e. when the detected object goes away from this distance.

«Property» Sensor

Use: detect the objects properties modifications.

Configuration:
This sensor has 4 modes:
- «Equal» activate a positive impulsion when the property value correspond to the one of the sensor.
- «Not Equal» the opposite
- «Interval» activate if the value is between the Min and Max values of the sensor. Some «properties» can be used in Min and Max for comparison purposes.
- «Changed» activate a positive impulsion when the property value changes.

«Radar» Sensor

Use: work a sensor «Near», but only in a cone aligned with one of the axes, which has his vertex at the center of the object, and the base at a certain distance along the chosen axis.

Configuration:
«Property»: Restrict the sensor to the objects having this property.

«Axis»: determine the radar viewing cone direction.

«Angle»: determine the cone opening.

«Distance»: determine the length of the cone.

This sensor is used to give to the NPC a limited view (in front, for example). This «radar» see through the others objects. Combine it with a «ray» without «X-Ray mode».

«Random» Sensor

Use: Generate some pseudo random impulses. Launch some actions at random.

Configuration:
«Seed»: specify the generator seed (from this seed, chance is always the same) – actuator «random» for more information.

«Ray» Sensor

Use: launch a ray in the axis direction, and trigger a positive impulsion when it collides something. It can be filtered, to detect only the objects with a certain material or property. It has a lot common controls with the sensor «Radar».

Configuration:
«Property/Material»: to change the filtering mode.

«Axis»: to define the axis and the direction to use to launch the ray

«Range»: maximal distance for the ray. It's the limit of detection.

«X-Ray Mode»: to see though the objects which have not the property or the material specified in the filter field.

Controllers

The different Controllers:
- **AND**: all the connected sensors must be positive to send a positive impulsion.
- **OR**: 1 or more of the sensors must be positive.
- **XOR** (OR exclusive): only 1 must be positive
- **NAND** (NO AND): inverted and Controller.
- **NOR** (NO OR): inverted OR Controller
- **XNOR** (NO OR exclusive) - Controller XOR inverted.
- **Expression:** to use you own expression. Very useful!
- **Python:** to use a script or a python module

«Expression» Controller

Sometimes, we need to use complex conditions. For example, we want that a character jumps when:
- the sensor «keyboard» named «jump» is positive
- the sensor «ray» named «rayGround» is positive (we need a ground like support under the character)
- the sensor «ray» named «rayForward» is negative (there's nothing in front of the character)

To do that, use a controller with «expression» type and enter into value: *«jump AND rayGround AND NOT rayForward»*
It's also possible to use some properties like: *«(life > 0) AND(coins > 10)»*
We can mix all that by using sensors and properties names.
In every cases, the controller activates all the actuators if the condition is satisfied and sends a deactivation as soon as it's not satisfied yet.

To control, use:
«if(expression, pulse_if_expression_is_true, pulse_if_expression_is_false)»
Example of expression: «if ((coins > 10 and life > 0), False, True)»
This example sends:
- an activation signal if the condition is not satisfied
- a deactivation signal in other case

«Python» Controller

The «controller» python can be used in 2 ways: In «Script» mode and in «Module» mode. The second has several advantages: it's pre-compiled at first call (so, it's fester at second call), it has several entry points. The script is available by default but we recommend to use only modules.

Add some global code to a module (i.e. outside a function), allows to execute only once, even if several objects share the same module.
To create a compatible module with BGE, you must define several specific to BGE entry points. Example:

```python
def printControllerName(controller):
    print("I'm a BGE callable function of", controller.name)
```

To use it:
1. create a scene with a plane for example,
2. open a new text file named «MyModule.py» and insert the following code,
3. add an «Always» sensor,
4. add a «Python» controller by selecting «Module» and in the free field: MyModule.printControllerName (don't add '.py' as for a script call)

5. Test (P)

Actuators

«2D Filters» Actuator

Use: Filter for special effects like color «sepia» or «blur». The effects can be applied to all the elements of the scene, not only to the objects upon which they are applied.

Configuration:

«Remove Filter»: remove the filter connected to «Pass Number»

«Disable Filter»: deactivate the filter connected to «Pass Number», without remove it

«Enable Filter»: reactivate the filter connected to «Pass Number», previously deactivated

«Custom Filter»: activate a customized filter by using a script. See the **recipe VII.13** to use a HDR script (High Dynamic Range).

«Pass Number»: pass number of the effect to combine several effects and manage the executing order.

See filters details in the **recipe VII.9**.

«Action» Actuator

Use: To launch an action (an animation in Blender language).

Configuration:

We can select several «play-back» types:
- «Flipper»: when it receives a positive impulse, it launches the animation and stops it when it's at the end. When it receives a negative impulse, it launches the animation from the end and stops it at the beginning.
- «Loop end»: launches the animation in a loop from the beginning to the end.
- «Loop stop»: idem, but stops when it receives a negative impulse. If «continue» is checked, it'll restart at the frame where it has stopped.
- «Ping pong»: Like Flipper, but always begins from the beginning or the end as the impulsion, Flipper restarts where it has stopped.
- «Play»: launches the animation from the beginning or the end, then stops.
- «Property»: use a property as frame number to display

«add»: add the different transformations to the existing ones. If the action is to move a character from the origin to another position and if we apply it without «add», the character will always go away from the origin.

«force»: to transform the position modifications into linear forces and the rotations into «torque» (see «motion»). If «L» is checked, the force is applied along the object axis (so, with the rotations), else, the force use the global axis. The animation is launched from «Start Frame» to «End Frame».

«Blending»: determinate the number of frames used to interpolate the animation during an action change. Animation more fluid.

«Priority» (max: 100): The actions with a lower «priority» value are launched first, on the same layer. If, for example, the walk receives preference over the head, so the walk must have a lower priority.

«Layer» (0 to 7) is the animation layer. To have 2 actions launched simultaneously (ex: walk and shoot), use 2 different layers. If the 2 actions use common elements (ex: the same bone), use «Layer Weight» to mix both (mode «blend»).

«Layer weight»: percentage of use of the precedent layer. The mode «Add» combine the 2 actions without to mix them.

«Frame Property»: Select a property in which we'll store the animation frame numerous.
The actuator «action» is explained in the game project #7.

«Camera» Actuator

Use: To follow an object in a fluid manner. Created for cameras, but works with any object.

Configuration:
«Camera Object»: the object to follow.

«Height» (0-20): height (Z axis) on which you must position the object in relation to the followed object.

«Axis» (-X,+X,-Y,+Y): chosen axis to position the object in relation to the followed object.

«Min» and «Max» correspond to the minimal and the maximal distance on the chosen axis between the selected object and the followed object.

«Damping» (0-10): to create a delay between the «constraint» position and the real position.

If it's a camera, use to the actuator «Edit object»: «Track To» to orientate the camera.

«Constraint» Actuator

Use: The constraints are used to limit the position, the distance or the rotation. Used to control the physique since the game. When we apply them, they are permanents excepted if «time» is used.

Configuration:
«Constraints Mode»:
- «Location Constraint»: to force on 1 axis the object position with a minimal and a maximal value
- «Distance Constraint»: Distance to a surface along an axis and a direction.
    - If «L» is activated, we use the local axis, else, we use the global axis
    - If «N» is activated, the object is oriented relatively to the normal to the surface
    - «Range» the maximal distance of the radius used to apply the constraint. The distance is from the object center
- «Orientation Constraint»: to force the object orientation relative to the global axes. «Reference Direction» is given in cosine between the global axis and the local axis. «Min angle» and «Max angle» are the constraint interval in degrees: no correction is done in this interval.
- «Force Field Constraint»: to create an axial force field (like gravity) attractive or repulsive.
    - «Distance»: maximal distance beyond which the field has no effect
    - «Direction Axis»: a ray is launched from the object center in this direction. If it touches the corresponding property or material, the force field is activated.
    - «Force»: force on the object Negative, it attracts, positive, it rejects. If «N» is checked, the force will have the same orientation as the normal to the object face touched by the ray.
    - «M/P»: from «Material» mode to «Property» mode and conversely. The object can be attracted by another object with a certain property or material.
    - «PER»: if the actuator is activated with a sensor «Always» without «Activate on True Level Triggering», the ray will be launched only once and if the property and the material is not find, the force field will never activated. To have a persistent activator, check «PER».
    - «RotFh»: Align the object rotation axis to make it being parallel to the normal to the object face touched by the ray.
    - «RotDamp»: Use a different damping for the rotation

«Damping» (0-100) corresponds to the number of necessary frames to achieve the constraint (smoothing).

«Time» limits the constraint in the time (in number of frames) excepted for «Location».
To apply it on several axes, define several actuators.

«Edit Object» Actuator

Use: to modify the object geometry (and to do a new calculation for collides if necessary), to add an object or to destruct it.

Configuration:
Several modes:
- «Add Object»: add a new object at the place of the object. To control exactly the position, use an Empty as «generator». It's the base of BGE particles system.
  - «Object»: the object to add in the current scene (from an invisible layer)
  - «Time»: object lifetime, in number of frames. If «0» there's no time limit
  - «Linear Velocity»: check «L» to add this speed to the one of the object
  - «Angular Velocity»: Idem for «L»

- «End Object»: destroy the object on which the actuator is applied.

- «Replace Mesh»: by another. Modify the object display keeping the same logic controls. Examples: substitute the character by another if «Gfx» is activated or use a simplified geometry to do simpler collision calculations (so faster) if «Phys» is activated.
  - «Mesh»: the new object geometry
  - «Gfx»: if checked, the display is modified, but not necessarily the collision mesh
  - «Phys»: if checked, the used mesh for physic calculations is modify, but not necessarily the displayed geometry. It works only with the «Triangle Mesh» (see the «Physics» Tab in the «Properties» window, «Collision Bounds» panel)

- «Track To»: to orient the object towards another object. Very useful for a camera to follow an object.
  - «Object»: the object to track
  - «Time»: lifetime, in number of Frames, of tracking
  - «3D»: to do a 3D tracking
  - «Up Axis»: by default «Z-Axis»
  - «Track Axis»: the axis toward the object (by default «Y-Axis»)

- «Dynamics»: several operation types:
  - «set Mass»: to modify the object mass
  - «Disable Rigid Body»: if the object has a «Rigid Body» type, it'll be in «Dynamic».
  - «Enable Rigid Body»: if the object has a «Dynamic» type, it'll be in «Rigid Body».
  - «Suspend Dynamics»: stop the object dynamic management, but keep the collision management.
- «Restore Dynamics»: restart the dynamics management stopped by the precedent option.

«Game» Actuator

Use: Game basic events like restart, quit, save and load.

Configuration:
«Load bge.logic.globalDict»: load globalDict from a file with the extension «.bgeconf» and with a file name identical to the current Blend file.
  To input value in globalDict, with python:

```
bge.logic.globalDict["life"] = 100
```

  Only the values with type «int/string/bool/float/tuples/lists» can be saved, not the GameObjects.

«Save bge.logic.globalDict»: Save.

«Quit Game»: the blender player quit the game.

«Restart Game»: restart the game (load from the file).

«Start Game From File»: start another file .blend selected in «File».

«Message» Actuator

Use: Send messages to other objects to activate functions.

Configuration:
«To»: Recipient object.
> Left empty to send to all objects.
> Works between 2 scenes simultaneously actives.

«Subject»: It's the field that allows to filter the messages upon receipt.
«Body»: It can only be used by Python. Use a textual field with «Text» or send the property value with «Property».

«Motion» Actuator

Use: Apply a movement to the object, by applying a force or by moving directly the object. Rotation is one of these movements.

Configuration:
The setting proposes different option depending on whether the object is static or dynamic («Physics» Tab in the «Properties» window).

«Motion Types»:
- «Simple motion»:
    - «Loc» (X,Y,Z): Teleport the object from its position (a,b,c) to (a+X,b+Y,c+Z)
    - «Rot» (X,Y,Z): Do a series of rotations along the axes X,Y and Z
    - «Force» (X,Y,Z): Apply a linear force along the axes X,Y and Z. The result is based upon the object mass.
    - «Torque» (X,Y,Z): Apply an angular force along the axes X,Y and Z.
    - «Linear Velocity»: Apply the linear force necessary to obtain a linear speed along the axes X,Y and Z. If «Add» is checked, the speed is added for each call.
    - «Angular velocity»: idem for the rotation.
    - «Damping Frames»: number of frames to obtain the velocity. However, to each cycle there are gravity and friction forces. If the value is too high, the speed will never reached.

- «Character Motion»: If the object is with «Physics» type:«Character», we can move the character in the respect of the constraints defined in the «Physics» Tab, particularly the maximal height of the stairs or obstacles that the character can pass.

- «Servo Control»: use a PID regulator to allow the movement (info: http://tinyurl.com/5ux24or). Allow to apply a force with a value which is high when the difference between the speed needed and the actual speed fluctuates rapidly, i.e. when the derivative of the difference from the time is high. It's the principe of the speed regulator on a car.
    - «Reference Object»: add the other object speed. Used to keep a character on a plate-form.
    - «Linear Velocity»: apply the necessary linear force to obtain a linear speed along the X,Y and Z axes.
    - «X,Y,Z» (max,min): add a constraint of maximal and minimal force. To simulate the working of an engine, there's a minimal force below which no movement can be done, and a maximal force based on the engine supply and capacity.
    - «Proportional Coefficient» (0-200): It's the P in PID, the proportional coefficient. When the value is high, the answer is fast, but if it's too high, a divergence may appear (oscillations damping, Laplace).
    - «Integral Coefficient» (0-3): It's the I in PID, the integral coefficient. During a simple proportional control, there's a static error. When the system approaches its order, the error is not enough high to allow the engine to work. The term integral compensate the static error and gives a more stable system in steady state. When the coefficient is high, the static error is corrected.

- «Derivative Coefficient» (-100 to 100): it's the D in PID, the derivative coefficient. To limit the over order.

Use: to hide or to show the mouse, or to create a management mode for the camera with «mouse look» type.

Configuration:
«Mode»: to go from the settings of the visibility management of the mouse to the «mouse look» mode.
- «Visibility»: Uncheck «visible» to set the cursor invisible
- «Look»: to get control on the camera or the object on which the actuator is applied. It's used with the sensor «Mouse» and «Mouse Event»:«Movement». To activate or deactivate the axes management X («Use X-Axis») and Y («Use Y-Axis») of the mouse.
    - «Sensitivity»: to manage the sensibility of the servo control.
    - «Threshold»: to remove the spurious movements, this parameter allows to manage the movement rate before an action. At «0.5», it needs an important movement of the mouse to generate a movement of the object. At «0.0», any movement starts a reaction.
    - «Min» and «Max»: to add a constraint with an angle max along the axis.
    - «Local»: if activated, there are rotations along the object axes, else, use the world axis.
    - «Reset»: to refocus on X and/or Y the cursor position after calculations.

Use: parent the object to another or un-parent it

Configuration:
«Remove parent»: remove the links.

«Set Parent» design this object as current parent.
- «Parent Object» name of the parent object
- «Compound»: Include this object in the parent object collision box (only if the parent has a collision box)
- «Ghost» transform this object into ghost object (no collision) when it has a parent

Used to past an object to another (like a magnet) and to liberate it next. If in the beginning we parent a «Rigid body» to a «Static», via Blender, «Remove parent» doesn't restore the dynamic of the object «Rigid Body». However, if we parent it with «Set Parent», it works.

Use: Modify the objects properties values: assign, add or paste.

Configuration:
«Mode»:
- «Level»: the value changes according to the value of the input «level». For example, if we apply a sensor with«Keyboard» type, and we apply on a property with«int» type. The value of this property will be 0, excepted when the keyboard key is pressed. Works only on the properties with «bool/int/float/timer» type.
- «Assign»: the Property becomes equal to Value
- «Add»: add Value to the Property value (a negative value to subtract). For boolean, a value superior to 0 is seen as TRUE
- «Copy»: copy another object property value in the object property with the actuator when it's active.
- «Toggle»: commutator between 0 and 1 (if 1 then becomes 0, if 0 becomes 1). Any other number

than 0 becomes 0 if it's activated. Used to create switches ON/OFF.

«Property»: property that the actuator must modify.

«Value»: value used to modify the property.

«Random» Actuator

Use: To generate pseudo-random values stored in the properties.

Configuration:
«seed» (0-300000): value from which the pseudo-random numbers generator is initialized. We launch the scene and ask 3 numbers, these numbers seems to be random. But if we quit and launch again, we'll have the same sequence. To avoid that, change «seed». The advantage: in the «Minecraft» game, the world is randomly generated from a phrase with «seed» type. So, if 2 players use the same phrase, they will have the same world!

«Distribution»:
- «Bool Bernoulli»: Return «True» in «chance» (reel 0-1)% of cases, according to the Bernoulli's law.
- «Bool Constant»: Always return «False» if «Always True» is not checked. Else, always return «True»
- «Bool Uniform»: Return «True» in 50% of cases, «False» in the other cases.
- «Float Constant»: Return the value of real type contained in «Value» (0-1)
- «Float Neg Exp»: drawing lots are done according to an exponential distribution law with the «half-life time».
- «Float Normal»: drawing lots are done according to a normal distribution law. **The normal law** is one of the probability laws the more adapted for modeling natural phenomenons from several random events. «Mean» is the average value of the total draws.
- «Float Uniform»: drawing lots of real numbers are uniform between «min» and «max» (the standard).
- «Int Constant»: Return the integer of «Value»
- «Int Poisson»: drawing lots are done according to a Poisson distribution law with an average value «mean». Used to model the rare cases, some accidents, or mutations in biology, meteorology, finance, etc.
- «Int Uniform»: drawing lots of integers are uniform between «min» and «max» (standard).

«Scene» Actuator

Use: Manage the scenes of the file *.blend, useful to create user levels or interfaces (in Overlay).

Configuration:
8 modes:
- «Restart»: restart the current scene. Everything is reset.
- «Set Scene»: exchange the scene with the one selected
- «Set Camera»: change the camera used
- «Add Overlay Scene»: add another scene, and display it over the current scene. Useful to do a HUD interface, install a life bar, a munition or speed counter
- «Add Background Scene»: the opposite of an «Overlay Scene», this scene is displayed under current scene
- «Remove Scene»: remove the scene in parameters
- «Suspend Scene»: pause the active scene
- «Resume Scene»: restart the scene in parameters and which was in pause.

«Sound» Actuator

Use: to launch a sound or a music, with or without 3D position management of it (reduction of the sound with the distance of the camera and other stuff).

Configuration:
«Open» import a sound file (wav, mp3, ogg, mid or mod). We can check «cache» to have a sound unpacked and stored in memory at the time of loading – use it only for little sounds which are very often used (footsteps, shoots, etc.).

«Mono» convert the sound into «mono» for a better use in 3D mode.

When the sound is selected, other configurations are possible:

«Play mode»:
- «Play Stop»: launch the son only once from the beginning to the end, but stop when the actuator receives a negative impulse.
- «Play End»: launch the son only once from the beginning to the end
- «Loop Stop»: launch the sound in a loop from the beginning to the end, but stop when the actuator receives a negative impulse..
- «Loop End»: launch the sound in a loop from the beginning to the end
- «Loop Bidirectional»: launch the sound in a way, then, at the end, in the other and restart in a loop.
- «Loop Bidirectional stop»: idem, but stop when the actuator receives a negative impulse.

«Volume» (0-2): general volume control for sound (if the 3D mode is activated, the distance will modify this factor too).

«Pitch»: modify the speed of sound reading. Superior to 0, the sound seems to be shrill (rapid). Inferior to 0, the sound seems to be deep.

«3D Sound»: The sound volume is modified by the distance between the object and the active camera:
- «Minimum Gain»: minimal volume to have a sound by the farthest objects
- «Maximum Gain»: maximal volume so that the nearest objects are not deafening
- «Reference Distance»: maximal distance to which the sound is at its volume maximal
- «Maximum Distance»: maximal distance to which we don't hear the sound
- «Rolloff» (0-5): to obtain a non-linearity of the volume loss according to the distance, by modifying the coefficient of volume reduction
- «Cone Outer Gain»: Volume in the «Outer Cone»
- «Cone Outer Angle» (external cone: 0-360): angle around the -Z axis. In this cone, the volume will be an interpolation between the value of «Cone Outer Gain» and 100%, according to the distance to the internal cone
- «Cone Inner Angle» (internal cone: 0-360): angle around the -Z axis. In this cone, the volume will be at 100%

«State» Actuator

Use: To manage game «states» (logic layers) like Finite state machines. The states are logic layers accessible when we click on the button «+» near the object name in the «Controller» zone of the «Logic Editor». An example of layers use is given in the game project #3.

Configuration:
«Change State»: exchange the current state with another.

«Remove State»: deactivate a state

«Add State»: activate a state, without deactivate the others.

«Set State»: activate a state and deactivate all the others.

«Steering» Actuator

Use: add a «behavior» to the object: escape, following another object, with algorithms for shortest-path.

Configuration:
3 types of behavior:
- «seek»: to reach another object without using shortest-path function (the object can be uptight).
- «flee»: to flee from another object.
- «path following»: like «seek», but using shortest-path function (algorithm in A*). «Update period»: number of frames between each new calculation of the shortest-path (optimization).

«Target Object»: object to follow or to avoid.

«Navigation Mesh Object»: navigation mesh only used by «path following». See **recipe V.13**.

«Distance»: distance between the 2 objects.
- mode «seek», the object stops after reached this distance.
- mode «Flee», the object stops when it's at this distance from the other.

«Velocity»: speed used to follow or to avoid this object.

«Turn speed»: idem, but for the angular speed.

«Acceleration»: maximal acceleration that the object can take to follow or avoid the object.

«Facing»: determinate the axis to use to be in front of the object.

«N»: Use the normal vector to the navigation mesh to align the «Up» (Z) vector of the object, to follow the relief of the ground.

«Self terminated»: if checked, so when the distance reached, the behavior is deactivated.

«Visualize»: show the calculated path to reach the objective. Work only in «path following» mode.

«Visibility» Actuator

Use: Modify the object visibility.

Configuration:
«Visible»: choose visible or invisible.

«Occlusion»: activate/deactivate the occlusion. Initialize in the «Physics» Tab.

«Children»: activate/deactivate the recursion of the options – for the visibility and occlusion states of all the children objects, and children of the children (recursively)

Notes: Use the visibility actuator to save rendering time. There's no impact on the physique management: it's limited to make a level of details (LoD). Since the version 2.7, there's an integrated version of the LoD.

SHEET #6: BULLET PHYSICS ENGINE

«Bullet» is the only game engine available in BGE, but other engines could be added in the next versions.

The configuration is done from the World menu («Physics» Tab) for the general characteristics, and in the «Physics» Tab of the «Properties» window.

The «physics» types:
- An object with «**No collision**» is not managed by the physics engine, the other objects can pass trough them. Useful for an «Overlay» or any other element which doesn't need collision management.
- All the objects are «**Static**» **by default** : they are not subject to gravity but can collide (even if «Collision Bounds» is not checked)
- An object with «**Dynamic**» type can fall and move, but doesn't rotate like a ball. To do that, configure it in «**Rigid Body**» like most of the objects in movement
- A «**Soft Body**» is a deformable object (it its mesh allows that), it's too the object type which need the more resources by the game engine to manage it
- An «**Occluder**» optimizes the display management. The objects behind it (from the camera) are removed of the display and the physique management is stopped, to gain resources
- A «**sensor**» is invisible, it's a «ghost». It's parented to an object **to detect collisions**. We can know if a car approaches of the road edges by using a sensor on each side, at several inches of the car. Combined to a «collision» in the «Logic Editor», it's faster than a «radar» or a «near».
- A «**character**» is an object with «Dynamic» type and with additional configuration elements:
  - «step height» (the height of the obstacles that the character can cross without jumping,
  - «jump force» (the force needed for the jump)
  - «Fall Speed Max».
  - A specific actuator «Motion» allows too to do a jump thanks to a button «Jump». This type is not easy to configure now.
- A «**navigation mesh**»: manage the navigation meshes. It provides access to an interface to remove data and restart a calculation. Then, the object can be used as «Navigation Mesh» in the actuator «steering».

Important:
- «Ghost» means that the other objects (or the character) CANNOT collide with this object.
- «Actor» allows to be detected by the «near» and «radar» sensors
- When an object is not subject yet to collisions, or at the balance point (gravity), it passes to «sleeping» mode and stands still, to gain resources. However, if we check «No sleeping», the engine constantly search for the balance point, the object seems to shake.
- Mass is expressed in Kg and the physic engine always manages a distance Blender unit as 1 meter.
- In the «World» Tab, «Physics» panel, «Logic Step» allows to configure the number of game engine passes (by default: 5) for this object. By lowering it, the management is faster but more approximative.

Summary table of the different physique management types:

Type	Collision	Movement	Rotation	Deformation
No Collision	□	□	□	□
Static	■	□	□	□
Dynamic	■	■	□	□
Rigid Body	■	■	■	□
Soft Body	■	■	■	■

□ unsupported / ■ Supported

SHEET #7: BASIS OF PYTHON SCRIPTING WITH BLENDER

It's a summary of Python language and of the functions needed to write scripts for Blender. To increase your knowledge, read a book dedicated to Python.

You can try the following examples in the Blender Python interactive console.

Basis of language

The interpreter uses «PEDMAS» order («Parentheses, Exponents, Division, Multiplication, Addition, Subtraction»). If you ask: var = (5+7)*6**2+3*9/3, it'll do: var = 12x36+3x3 = 432+9 = 441.

IF:

```
if <condition>:
    <code>
elif <condition>:
else:
    <code>
```

Unlike other languages, spaces and tabulations are important. They define an execution level, like «Begin» / «End» in algorithmic or «{ /}» en C. Tab is different of spaces, and 1 space is different of 2 spaces, etc.

Example:

```
if condition1:
        if condition2:
                print ("condition2 is True")
        print ("condition1 is True")
```

The second print is at the same level than the second if. So it's executed when the condition1 is true.
But if it's at the same level than the first if, it's executed in all cases.

WHILE:

```
while <condition>:
    <code>
```

«break» to exit the loop.
«continue» to go to the next line.

FOR:

```
for elt in liste:
    <code>
```

«break» to exit the loop.
«continue» to go to the next line.
See the tuples and the directive range(x1,x2,inc) for emulating the for x=x1 to x2 step inc

Several operators

- Calculation: // (integer division), Modulo: <number>%<number> - ex: 17 % 3 = 2, Power: <number>**<power> - ex: 5**2 = 25
- comparison: ==(equal), !=(Different),>,<,>=,<=, is or is not
- binaries: &(and), |(Or), !(No),^(XOR), <<(L-SHIFT), <<(R-SHIFT)
- True, False

Data types

- type(variable) returns the type of variable
- dir(variable) returns
  - the list of properties ans methods if it's a class,
  - the list of functions if it's a module,
  - the list of functions accessible by an integer

Integers, floats:

- Conversion into string: **str**(nb)
- **complex**(real [, imag]): return a complex number
- **bit_length**(): number of bit to code the associated value

String/char:

- Size: len(string),
- Access the nth character: string[n] or from the end string[-n]
- Extraction: string[x1:x2] extract from x1 (include) to x2 (not include). string[:n] the n first, and string[n:] that's after the n first characters.
- string.**split**(): convert a string into a list of sub-string. We can choose the separator character by giving it as argument (by default: space). **Splitlines**() for complete lines. **join**(list) does the opposite. To add a space (or other), we do a string=" ".join(list).
- string.**find**(sch): to look for the position of a sub-string sch in the string. **index**(car[,n]): find the index of the first character car occurrence in the string (from n).
- string.**count**(sch): count the number of sub-strings sch in the string
- string.**strip**(): remove the spaces before and after, **lstrip**() before, **rstrip**() after
- Conversion: **int**(string), **float**(string), **long**(string),
- Concatenation: string=string1+string2
- Repetition: string = "word !"*4
- string.**ord**(ch): returns the ASCII code of the character ch, **chr**(num): returns the character of the ascii num code
- string.**lower**(), **upper**(): conversion minuscule/capital - **title**() the first letter of each word in capitals, **capitalize**() only the first letter in capitals, **swapcase**() from capitals to minuscules and vice versa.
- string.**replace**(c1, c2): replace all the c1 characters by c2 characters in the string
- Formatting: Insert {} in the string as field, then they are completed with: finalstring = string.-**format**(field1, field2,...).
  - we can precise the format like {:8.2f} for a float converted into 8 characters (2 decimals). We can use the scientific notation: {:6.2e} for example.
  - We can convert too: {:x} for hexadecimal, {:b} for binary, {:d} for decimal, {:o} for octal.
- string.**center**(width[, fillchar]): returns a string «centered» on a certain width, with a certain pad character. Str.**ljust**(width[, fillchar]): idem, but justified at left and its opposite **rjust**()
- string..**expandtabs**([tabsize]): replace the TAB by some spaces (def:8)
- string.**isalnum**() (numeric), **isalpha**(), **islower**(), **isupper**(), **isspace**(), **istitle**(): True, False

Lists:

- Mix of authorized types: list = ['monday', 'Tuesday', 'Wednesday', 1800, 20.357, 'Thursday', 'Friday']. A list can too contain some elements with list type!
- Access the element n: list[n]- or from the end list[-n]
- Number of elements: **len**(list) – list,**count**('element') returns the number of 'element' occurrences
- list.index(elt): returns the element in the list index
- Remove the elementt n: **del**(list[n]), del can be done on an interval: del list[x1:x2]. We can too use the notation: list[x1:x2] = []. list.**remove**(elt) looks fro the first element elt and remove it. list.**pop**() remove the last element.
- Add an element: list.**append**('saturday') –to add to a precise position: list.insert(position, 'element')
- To add a list: list.**extend**(list2).

- Transform a string into a list: list = **list**(string)
- Put into a list a suite of numbers separated by a coma: list = **list**(**eval**(ch))
- Extraction: list[x1:x2] extract x1 (included) to x2 (not included). list[:n] the n firsts, and list[n:] that's after the n first elements.
- list.**sort**(): to classify the list elements (numeric at first, then the string in alphabetical order, etc.). We can add as parameter the name of a function: "def size_sort(e1, e2): if len(e1) > len(e2): return 1; if len(e1) < len(e2): return -1; return 0"
- list.**reverse**(): inverse all list elements
- **Concatenation**: list=list1**+**list2
- **Union**: list=list1.union(list2) / **Intersection**: list=list1.intersection(list2) (or list = list1 & list2) / inter-section Inverse: list = list1. symmetric_difference(list2) (or list = list1 ^list2)
- **Repetition**: list = ["abc","bcd"]*2 --> ["abc","bcd","abc","bcd"]. The operator * is very useful to create a list with n identical elements
- to know if an element is in the list: if elt **in** list
- **min**(list), **max**(list)
- **zip** and **unzip**: zip(['a', 'b', 'c'], ['d', 'e', 'f']) => [('a', 'd'), ('b', 'e'), ('c', 'f')] and unzip do the opposite. Work with n lists.
- **map**(function, list): executes the function on each element of the list. We can use the directive lambda to not define the function. Ex: map(**lambda e: e + 1**, elements) add 1 to each element of elements.

Tuples:

Rather like the lists. A tuple is a collection of elements separated by comma, but with brackets and not with square brackets like for lists. Tuples need less system resources (less memory and treated faster by the interpretor). They are best to lists when we want to be confident of the transmitted data are not modified by mistake in a program.

- **range**([deb,]x[,inc]): make a tuple of 0,1,2,3,...,(x-1) or from deb if specified, and with an increment of inc if specified. Ex: range(3,17,4) --> 3,7,11,15
- obtain a list: list = **list**(tuple)
- **min**(tuple), **max**(tuple)

Set:

Instead of doing a list like [1, 2, 3], we can classify it with an index with a set([1, 2, 3]). During an insertion (in) for example, the complexity comes from n² to n. The methods are the same as for the lists.
To convert into a list: set = list(set1)
A **Frozenset** is an unchanging list: methods like add or remove can't be applied. Ex: fs = frozenset(['a','b'])

Dictionaries:

Like lists but we can access to any of dictionary with a specific index called a key, it can be alphabetic, numeric, or a composite type with certain conditions. Surrounded by curly brackets and not square brackets like for lists.
Dictionaries are a useful tool to do histograms.

Example:

```
dico = {}
dico['computer'] = 'ordinateur'
dico['mouse'] = 'souris'
dico['keyboard'] = 'clavier'
```

- to list the dictionary: print(dico) produces {'computer', 'keyboard', 'mouse'}
- to remove an element: **del** dico[key] – ex: del dico['mouse']. dico.**popitem**() returns the last tuple (key, value) and remove it from the dictionary.
- Size: dico.**len**()
- To list the keys: dico.**keys**() – to list the values: dico.**values**()
- To copy a dictionary (and not its reference): dico2 = dico.**copy**(). We can update with dico.**up-date**(dico2).
- **To run one's eye over the dictionary**: for key in dico: print(key, dico[key]) is less efficient than: for key, value in dico.items(). We can use dico.**get**(key,default) – it returns the key value, or default if

- the key is not found. **pop**(key,default) do the same thing, but removing at the same time.
- To know if the key is in the dictionary: dico.**has_key**(cle) – returns a boolean
- dico.**items**() returns a dico turples list (key, value), dico. **keys**() returns a key list and dico.**values**() the values. dico.**iteritems**() returns the first tuples couple (key,value) and dico.**next**() the next, and recursively. Works too with **iterkeys**() and **itervalues**().
- Generate a new dico: dico.fromkeys([1, 2, 3], 0) produces {1: 0, 2: 0, 3: 0}

Functions table:

```
dico = {'iron':fonctionA,
'wood':fonctionC,
'copper':fonctionB,
'stone':fonctionD,
... etc...}
dico[material]()
```

Special types (modules import)

Dates:

The date class represent a date: it's instantiated with a day, a month and a year.

```
from datetime import date
my_date = date(2004, 12, 3)
my_date.year
>>>2004
my_date.month
>>>12
my_date.day
>>>3
```

Methods:
- **today**(): returns a date object for the current date
- **fromtimestamp**(seconds): return a date object for the date corresponding to the number of passed seconds since Epoch
- **fromordinal**(ordinal): return a date object for the date corresponding to the number of passed days since the smallest date possible

Functions to apply to this object:
- **__str__**(): return a representation in the form of a characters string, calculated by isoformat()
- **ctime**(): similar to date.ctime() for the date
- **isoweekday**(): return the week number, with Monday in reference
- **isocalendar**(): return a tuple (year, week number, day number)
- **isoformat**(): return the date in the ISO 8601 format
- **replace**(year, month, day): return a date instance, by applying at first values modification
- **strftime**(format): call the function time.strftime() for the date
- **timetuple**(): return the date to the UTC format
- **toordinal**(): convert the date in passed days number since the minimal date
- **weekday**(): return the day of the week, with Monday = 0

Arrays:

The module <u>array</u> defines a data structure equivalent to lists but for elements with the same type. The elements are converted and placed in a container C, so, some manipulations are faster than with a list.

array(typecode[,initializer]): typecode determine the type of stored elements and correspond to the types:
- c/C: string of length 1 stored in a char
- u: unicode of lenght 1
- b/B: integer stored in a signed/(capital=unsigned) char
- h/H: integer stored in a short int
- i/I: integer stored in a signed int
- l: long integer stored in a signed long
- f: real stored in a float
- d: real stored in a double

initializer is a sequence containing some elements to place in the container.

<u>Methods</u>:
- **count**(x): return the number of occurrences of the element X in the table.
- **extend**(array or iterable): add the array or of the passed sequence elements.
- **index**(x): return the index of the first X occurrence in the table.
- **insert**(i, x): add the element X before the position element i.
- **pop**([i]): return the index element i and remove it from the table. If i is not given, it's the last element which is returned.
- **remove**(x): remove the first X occurrence from the table.
- **Reverse**(): return the inverted table.

<u>Conversion methods</u>:
- **tofile**(f): serialize the table in the object with type file or similar f
- **fromfile**(f, n): read n objects elements of the file type (not the similar)
- **tolist**(): convert the table into list object
- **fromlist**(list): add the list elements at the end of the table
- **tostring**(): convert the table into string object
- **tounicode**(): equivalent to tostring() but returns an unicode object and works only an array with u type
- **fromstring**(s): add the string elements at the end of the table
- **fromunicode**(s): equivalent to fromstring(), but add some unicode characters. The table must be with u type

Objects:

```
class object:
    def __init__(self,param1,...):
        <code constructor>
        self.variable1 =
        self.variable1 =
    def fonction1(self,param1,...):
            <code fonction1>
```

- By convention, the first function parameter is always **self**. It's the object passed in parameter to the function
- class object (parent): allows to **derive** the parent class object. If there are several parents, pass the parents separated by comas.
- To instantiate **it**: monobject = object()
- variable1 and variable2 are the class **properties**, but we can instantiate at any place
- The derivative class constructor must activate the parent class constructor, by transmitting the instance reference as first argument. Ex: in the code __init__(self) of Ion (children of Atome), we can call Atome.__init__(self). The **destroyer** (__del__) exists, but don't use it to avoid mistakes
- For the attributes protection, it's possible to define some private attributes to the class by adding the prefix to the name with 2 underline spaces. Example: __var1
- All methods and attributes can be **overloaded**

Exceptions Management

```
try:
    #code
except:
    #code if error(s) raised in bloc above
else:
    #code if no error raised
finally:
    #code executed whatever if error raised or not
```

To raise manually an exception:

```
def avg(numbers):
```

```
if not numbers:
    raise ValueError("Please enter at least one element")
return sum(numbers)/len(numbers)
```

sys.**exc_info**(): return some information about the exception

Functions, modules and packets

To define a function:

```
def name_function(param_1, param_2=value_default, ..., param_n):
    #code
    return value_1, value_2, ..., value_n
```

return: returns a list of values
To call it: list_value = name_function(param_1, param_2, ..., param_n)
or directly: value_1,value_2,value_3 = name_function(...)
We can call it too by **naming the parameters**: name_function(param3=value_3, param2=...) to pass **not explicit parameters** like def function(**param): «param» is a dictionary containing all the arguments. If we use only a *, it's a **tuple** and these are **arbitrary parameters**.

Modules:

import namefile.py allows to import all an external Python file functions and classes (a module) – **reload** allows to reload if there was some modifications.

```
if __name__ == "__main__":
```

This code determine if the program is executed like an import or like a principal program.

To import only several functions:

```
from module import namefunction1,...
```

To rename (**alias**):

```
from module import function as newname
```

If we do **import** [module], we must call the functions by [module].namefunction
If we do **from** [module] **import** *, we don't have to precise.

We we use external libraries, we must verify if they are here

```
try:
    import wx
except ImportError:
    raise ImportError,"The wxPython module is required to run this program."
```

Packets:

Modules can be organized into a directory tree called packet.
The character «.»is a separator, to locate a module in the directory tree. Ex:

```
from clientfile.core import application
```

In the directory clientfile, there's a directory core, and in this directory, a module. Each directory is a part of the packet and has a file __init__.py (empty or not).

Tricks:

- **Exchange 2** values: a, b = b, a
- Python allows to string several **comparisons**: if a<b<c<d is possible
- We can add a commentary on a function (**docstrings**) by adding """function description """. We can read the commentary with print(function.__doc__) or help(function).

Libraries

Basis functions:

- To display some text on the console: **print**("The square of", nn, "is", nn**2)
- To ask a key in: first name = **input**("Enter you first name: ")
- **sum**(...) takes lists, tuples, all sequences, even if mixed and gives a sum
- To evaluate an arithmetic expression: number = **eval** ("(5+6)*9")

Module Os:

- Name of the OS: **name()** → nt, posix

Files:

- **ifile**(file): return the file name
- **remove**(file): remove the file
- **rename**(file): rename the file,
- we can to move o file from a directory to another

Directories:

- Change of directory: **chdir**(dir)
- Current directory: **getcwd**()
- **mkdir**(dir): create a directory, **makedirs** creates them recursively
- **listdir**(way): lists the directories
- **rmdir**(dir) and its recursive **removedirs**(dir) (If a directory is not empty, removedirs stops)
- **idir**(file): returns the directory
- **stat**(chemin): returns an object stat_result with attributes containing way information:
    - st_mode: permissions
    - st_ino: inode numerous
    - st_dev: device
    - st_nlink: link number if direct link
    - st_uid: owner ID
    - st_gid: group ID
    - st_size: file size in octets
    - st_atime: last access date
    - st_mtime: last modification date
    - st_ctime: creation date on MS-Windows and last modification date of the metadata on Unix

Paths:

- **path.join**(path1,path2,...): concatenate elements to create a directory
- **path.split**(path): returns a tuple (dir,file)
  / path.splitext(path) returns a tuple (dir+file_without_ext,ext).
- **exists**(path): Boolean
- **walk**(top[, topdown=True[, onerror=None]]): recursively see the directories tree, by using the top way as root. walk() returns an iterator with each entry is a tuple made from 3 elements: (directory way, sub-directories list with os.listdir(), files list)

Module Platform:

- **architecture**(executable=sys.executable, bits='', linkage=''): returns the tuple (bits, linkage) containing 16,32, or 64 bits, and the linkage type (ELF,etc.)
- **machine**(): returns i386, i586, Amd64; etc.
- **node**(): computer network name
- **platform**(aliased=False, terse=False): recovers and concatenate system information. Not parsable with code (ex: «*Windows-7-6.1.7601-SP1*»)
- **processor**(): Returns the processor name. (ex: «*AMD64 Family 16 Model 5 Stepping 3, Authenti-*

cAMD»)
- **python_build**(), **python_compiler**() and **python_version**(): return the Python interpreter information, the number and the date of build, the used compiler, the version
- **release**(): release number of the system. **system**(): system name. **version**(): release version
- **uname**(): returns a complete tuple ('Windows', 'SuperBlenderPC', '7', '6.1.7601', 'AMD64', 'AMD64 Family 16 Model 5 Stepping 3, AuthenticAMD'). We can write: system, node, release, version, machine, processor = uname()

Threads Management:

To launch a function in parallel and to offer all synchronization mechanism.

```python
from threading import Thread
thread = Thread(target=visiteur)
thread.start()
while thread.isAlive():
    ...
```

class **Thread**(group=None, target=None, name=None, args=(), kwargs={})

Parameters:
- group: not implemented
- target: function name to call
- name: thread name, can be read by the **getname**() method
- args, kwargs: arguments in the function

Methods:
- **start**(): only once, start() launches a new thread and to execute the method run()
- **run**(): the thread is alive as soon as the method is called. When run() is over, at the end of the execution or by an exception raise, the thread is dead
- **join**([timeout]): wait the end of the thread. If timeout is given, a real determine in seconds the maximal waiting time. After this period, the thread is released.
- **IsAlive**(): returns True if the method run() is running.

We can too directly derive the class Thread and overload the method run:

```python
class engineer(Thread):
    def __init__(self, results):
        Thread.__init__(self)
        self._results = results
    def run(self):
        ...
```

The **Locks management** (for the critical sections protection) uses Lock and Rlock:

```python
from threading import Lock
locker = Lock()
locker.acquire()
#called in a Thread, protect the access to a shared variable for example
locker.release()
```

The class Rlock is the same but allows to the thread with the lock to call the method **acquire**() without causing deadlock

To synchronize threads, we use the **Event**():

```python
from threading import Event
env = Event()
env.set() #The event is positioned
...
env.wait(50) #Wait a env.set() from another thread or 50s
```

Other methods:
- isSet(): true(set)/false(clear)
- clear(): the state becomes false

Module Math:

- Constants: **pi, e** (Euler constant).
- square root: **sqrt**(number)
- Trigo: **sin**(angle), **cos**(angle), tan(angle), acos, asin, atan and the hyperbolic functions cosh, sinh and tanh. **degrees**(radians): Convert into degrees an angle expressed in radians, and its opposite **radians**(degrees). **hypot**(x, y): returns sqrt(x*x + y*y) the euclidean norm.
- **ceil**(x): returns in real number, the first integer value superior to the real x. The inferior value with **floor**(x)
- **exp**(x): returns e**x. e is the constant of value rounded
- **fabs**(x): returns the x absolute value in real. Equivalent of **abs**(x) for integers.
- **fmod**(x, y): returns x modulo y. To use at the place of x%y for reals because it's malfunctioning with python.
- **frexp**(x) -> Decompose x into (m, e), with x = m * (2**e). **ldexp**(m, e) do the opposite. M is a real.
- **log**(x[, base]), **log10**(x)
- **modf**(x): Decompose the real into its parts fractional and integer, in the form of a tuple of 2 reals.

Network Sockets:

The sockets management allows the communication through the network. From an IP address to another through a source port and a destination port.

Example of simple server:

```python
import socket, sys
HOST = '192.168.1.168'
PORT = 50000
counter =0 # activated connections counter

mySocket = socket.socket(socket.AF_INET, socket.SOCK_STREAM)
try:
   mySocket.bind((HOST, PORT))
except socket.error:
   print("The socket link at the chosen address has failed.")
   sys.exit

while 1:
   print("Server readyt, waiting for requests...")
   mySocket.listen(2)
   connection, addressee = mySocket.accept()
   counter +=1
   print("Client connected, IP address %s,port %s"%(address[0], address[1]))
   msgServeur ="You are connected to Marcel's server. Send your messages."
   connection.send(msgServeur.encode("Utf8"))
   msgClient = connection.recv(1024).decode("Utf8")
   while 1:
      print("C>", msgClient)
      if msgClient.upper() == "FIN" or msgClient =="":
         break
      msgServeur = input("S> ")
      connection.send(msgServeur.encode("Utf8"))
      msgClient = connection.recv(1024).decode("Utf8")

   connection.send("fin".encode("Utf8"))
   print("Stopped Connection.")
   connection.close()

   ch = input("<R>estar <F>inish ? ")
   if ch.upper() =='T':
      break
```

Example of simple client:

```python
import socket, sys
HOST = '192.168.1.168'
PORT = 50000

mySocket = socket.socket(socket.AF_INET, socket.SOCK_STREAM)
try:
   mySocket.connect((HOST, PORT))
except socket.error:
   print("connection failed.")
   sys.exit()

print("Connection established with the server")
msgServer = mySocket.recv(1024).decode("Utf8")
while 1:
   if msgServer.upper() == "FIN" or msgServer =="":
      break
   print("S>", msgServeur)
   msgClient = input("C> ")
   mySocket.send(msgClient.encode("Utf8"))
   msgServeur = mySocket.recv(1024).decode("Utf8")
print("Connection interrupted.")
mySocket.close()
```

Ftp:

The <u>ftplib</u> module gives a class FTP implements a complete client ftp.
class **FTP**([host[, user[, passwd[, acct]]]])

The principal methods are:
-   **abort**(): Stop a current uploading (success not guaranteed).
-   **close**(): Close a connection without sending a command QUIT to the server.
-   **connect**(host[, port]): Try a connection of the object to the server host and returns the received answer in the form of a string. Once call is necessary at the beginning of the session. Port is by default at 21
-   **cwd**(pathname): Change the current directory on the server and displays the operation result
-   **delete**(filename): delete the file
-   **dir**(argument[, …]): list the current directory with the command LIST. Additional arguments can be given, and are concatenated to the command sent to the server (like the sub-directory name to list)
-   **login**([user[, passwd[, acct]]]): connect to the FTP server by using the parameters user and passwd if they are given. If user is not given, anonymous/anonymous@
-   **mkd**(pathname): create a new directory on the server and returns its entire path.
-   **nlst**(argument[, …]): Equivalent to dir(), but returns the files in the form of a list
-   **pwd**(): return the current path on the server
-   **quit**(): send the signal QUIT to the server, and closes the connection. Then, close() must be called
-   **rename**(ex_name, new_name): Rename the file
-   **retrbinary**(command, callback[, maxblocksize[, rest]]): recover a file in binary mode, via the command, in the form «RETR file name».
    -   callback is a function named at each bloc of received data,
    -   maxblocksize to define the maximal size of the blocks in octets.
    -   rest is an optional characters string used in parameter in the command RESTART by the server if the uploading is stopped. It's a marker which determine the position where restart the loading.
    -   retrlines(command [, callback]): idem in text lines. If callback is not given, the line is printed via ftplib.print_line()
-   **rmd**(dirname): remove the directory dirname.
-   **storbinary**(command, file[, blocksize]): send a file pointed by a file object opened in reading. command is in the form of «STOR file name», blocksize determines the size of the buffer (8192 by default). The file is sent in binary mode. **storlines**(command, file): Equivalent to storbinary for the text files. Sends the content of the file line by line.

Example:

```
ftp = ftplib.FTP('localhost')
ftp.getwelcome()
ftp.login('tziade', 'xxx')
ftp.dir()
ftp.quit()
```

Text and binary files:

- To open: obFile = **open**('file','a')
    - (a=append, r=read, W=write, b=binary): to open in reading a binary file, we precise "rb" for example.
    - encoding ="Latin-1", "utf8", etc. to read some encoded files directly without encode or decode.
- To write: nbchar=obFile.**write**(string) / nbchar contains the number of written octets
- To read: string = obFile.**read**() or read(n) with n the number of octets to read. **readline**() to read line by line. **readlines**() transfer all the remaining lines in a string list. The end of the file is reached when string == ""
- To close: obFile.**close**()
- Conversion of a string bytes into string: ch_car = octets.**decode**("utf8"), the opposite with **encode**()

With:

```
with open(x,'U') as fh:
  name = fh.readline()[1:-1]
```

Files compression:

Module gzip: one file

- To compress:

```
compressed = gzopen(filename+'.gz', mode='wb')
try:
  for line in original.readlines():
    compressed.write(line)
finally:
  compressed.close()
```

- To uncompress:

```
try:
  archive = gzopen(filename)
  uncompressed = open(resultfile, mode='W')
  for line in archive.readlines():
    uncompressed.write(line)
  finally:
    uncompressed.close()
finally:
  archive.close()
```

Objects serialization with Pickle, Shelve or JSON:

JSON (JavaScript Object Notation) is a textual and generic data format, derived from the notation of the language objects ECMAScript. We can represent structured information. The Pickle and JSON modules serialize classes permitting their recording on the disk or a data base and the deserialization (inverse operation).

cPickle gives 2 types of functions to serialize the objects: **dump**() and **load**(), for a direct writing and reading in an object with file type; **dumps**() and **loads**(), to recover and give the flux in the form of string.

Example:

```
import cPickle
class MyClass:
value_1 = '1'
```

```python
value_2 = 5
# object creation
example = MyClass()
example.value_1= u'i am modified'
# save
with open('MyClass.sav', 'wb') as file_:
cPickle.dump(example, file_, 1)
# reloading
with open('MyClass.sav', 'rb') as file_:
new_example = cPickle.load(file_)
# values verification
print(new_example.value_1)
print(new_example.value_2)
```

cPickle is the older brother of the module pickle: implemented in C, it's faster.

The shelve module is based on cPickle to give a persistent dictionary system. This dictionary is used like any other dictionary in the program and can contain any pickable object. Data are saved in a database stored in the file system.

SQLite:

SQLlite is a database which doesn't need a server module installation. Everything is managed in the form of local files, but the requests are in SQL mode to use other database type MySQL or PostgreSQL. Python gives in its standard library an access to SQLite, but it must be installed.

To use the functions SQLite:
```python
import sqlite3
```
The packet is installed by default under Python.

To connect to a database and launch a request:
```python
fileData ="bd_test.sq3"
conn =sqlite3.connect(fileData)
cur =conn.cursor()

cur.execute("select * from clients")
conn.commit()

cur.close()
conn.close()
```

If fileData = ":memory:" **everything is in memory**. If the file doesn't exist, it's created.
Commit validates the base modifications, else everything is done in memory.
After the request executing, cur contains a serial of tuples, each tuple representing 1 of the results of the request.

To insert a list data:
```python
data =[(17,"Durand",1.74),(22,"Berger",1.71),(20,"Werber",1.65)]
for you in data:
    cur.execute("INSERT INTO members(age,name,size) VALUES(?,?,?)", you)
conn.commit()
```

Random:
- **random**(): returns a random number between 0 and 1
- **randrange** ([deb,]nb[,inc]): returns a random number between 0 (or deb) and nb, with a step of inc if defined. randrange(3, 13, 3) returns 1 of the numbers from the serial 3, 6, 9, 12

To access the scripting, open a «python console» window.

Import the Blender Python Mapper:

```python
import bpy
```

Don't use that in a game loop where you must import only BGE (otherwise there will be multiple calls of the same sensors and controllers).

The objects access

All objects are available thought the module **bpy.data**.{objet}[index]. Example, to access the material #2 in the scene: bpy.data.materials[1]

The objects in this scene: bpy.data.objects

To access the object via its name: bpy.data.objects['bed']

To explore the objects, use the Outliners/Datablocks window. Moving the mouse over the properties, we access the **name of the property python.**

Create a new element by doing for example: bpy.data.materials.new("MyMaterial")

To access the **selection**, we use the module context:

```python
# return selection like: bpy.data.objects['Cube']
bpy.context.object

#return all selected objects like:
#bpy.data.objects['Cube'], bpy.data.objects['Camera']]
bpy.context.selected_objects
bpy.context.object
bpy.context.selected_objects
bpy.context.visible_bones
```

To modify directly a mesh (in «Edit Mode»):

```python
#Flip normals of selected object
bpy.ops.mesh.flip_normals()

#Hide selected elements of object
bpy.ops.mesh.hide(unselected=False)

#To Apply Modifications like scale
bpy.ops.object.scale_apply()
```


Don't use the module «bpy» because it adds numerous logic cycles and it's not available via the **blender-player**. You must use the module «BGE». Unfortunately, they are not the same objects.

A module «python», is precompiled, and very fast, but slower than logic bricks (written in C). So, use, as often as possible, **logic bricks when you need repeated actions**. Avoid for example a key management via python, or writing a sensor «Near» for example.

We access the object information from a scene thanks to **GameObjects** (type KX_GameObjects with python).

<u>Launch an action</u>

If a «Python» controller is interfaced between a sensor and an actuator, the controller trigger or not the actuator. It's used to add some complexes conditions to the trigger action.

To do that, recover the associated actuator and activate it:

Example:

```
if (condition...):
    act = cont.actuators["ActionFire"] #cont, the controller
        cont.activate(act)
```

It can send a deactivation signal too: cont.**desactivate**(act).
It works also like an actuator, i.e. it can apply some changes in the game without using another actuator.

Access to the object informations

The object associated to the controller is accessible via: cont.**owner**
Be careful: it's a «game object» and not a «blender» object as accessible via the console module (bpy). For the moment, the access to these elements diverges in the way of access in control mode. So, consult the API (Application Programming Interface) of BGE to know the properties and functions usable in the «game object»: http://tinyurl.com/oyusy5r
Subsequently, BGE will be totally integrated. Maybe, the modules bpy and bge will be merged.

The controller «python» can execute any type of code written in python. We can import any external library, like SciPy (scientific), pyGame (game), openCL(parallelism) or OpenCV(webcam, recognition).

The sensors and actuators joined to a controller are accessible via:
  * cont.**sensors** (ex: cont.sensors['KeyJump'] to access the sensor ' KeyJump', or cont.sensors[0] to access the first)
  * cont.**actuators**

The script is launched 2 times?

The controller is launched whatever the sensor state (positive or not), I.e., when the sensor is active, then when it's deactivated. It's important to verify the sensor state at the controller launching. To test it, execute the following code:

```
def printFirstSensorStatus(cont):
    firstSensor = cont.sensors[0]
    if firstSensor.positive:
      print ("The status of the first sensor is True")
    else:
      print ("The status of the first sensor is False")
```

To verify a condition, write:

```
for sensor in cont.sensors:
        if not sensor.positive:
                return False
```

To list all detected objects by a sensor near:

```
def printSensedObjects(cont):
        sensor = cont.sensors[0]
        sensedObjects = sensor.hitObjectList
        if not sensedObjects:
                print ("no objects sensed")
                return
        print ("The sensed objects are", sensedObjects)
```

Access to «Properties»

obj['direction'] to access the object «obj» property «direction».
We can add and remove some properties dynamically. In that case, they are «internal properties». These last are not seen by the sensors «property».

By testing a property value which doesn't exist with an obj['property'], we create it. To avoid creating a new property by error (error in the name for example), we use the form obj.**get**('property'). If the property doesn't exist, it returns «None».

Messages system

The objects in the actives scenes can communicate with each other. They can be programed via the logic bricks system, or directly via python. Several messages can be received at the same time.

A message contains:
- a characters string containing the «subject» to filter to differentiate different types of messages
- a message «body» containing another character string or a «property»

Neither the recipient (in the actuator), nor the sender (in the sensor) are precised.

There are 2 ways to send a message with python:
- from the module «logic»: the 3 last parameters are optional, but it's possible to specify the recipient and the sender

```
bge.logic.sendMessage(subject, body, to, message_from)
```

- From an object:

```
obj.sendMessage(subject, body, to)
```

Compatibility of old scripts (2.49 and previous)

- Replace the modules import:
  - **GameLogic** by bge.logic,
  - **Rasterizer** by bge.render,
  - **GameKeys** by bge.events,
  - **PhysicsConstraints** by bge.constraints,
  - **GameTypes** by bge.types,
  - **VideoTexture** by bge.textures
- Replace **getOwner**() by owner
- Replace «if **hasattr**(obj, 'foo'):» (does the *property 'foo' exist in the object obj?*) by «if 'foo' in obj:»
- The print "blabla" by **print** ("blabla") (python 3.x).
- The operator **division** «/» on 2 integers returns a floating. In that case, replace it by «//» to obtain the previous result.

The most common errors

- To put in a global variable the access to a current scene or to the controller. In that case, the variables are initialized at the first use of the script an if the call is done from another controller, that returns every time the first. The controller is accessible via a first parameter in the call of the function if it's a module.
- Don't test the sensors states in a controller
- Use bpy

Example of use of script: do a screen capture

1. «text» Window → add a new python script: «screenshot.py»
2. copy the following lines
3. «Logic Editor» Window
4. Add a «Keyboard» sensor. Choose the key to use
5. Add a «python» controller and select the script «screenshot.py»
6. Link the sensor with the controller

Script screenshot.py:

```
import Rasterizer
Rasterizer.makeScreenshot("screenshot")
```

The format use for saving is the one of the current scene. We can change the color of the background just before by adding:

```
Rasterizer.setBackgroundColor([1.0, 0.0, 0.0, 1.0])
```

Here, the background is red (Red, Blue, Green) = (1.0, 0.0, 0.0)

Functions useful for the rendering

To pass in «Fullscreen»:

```
bge.render.setFullScreen(True)
```

«False» to come back in window mode.
We can recover the screen resolution with **getWindowWidth**() and **getWindowHeight**().

To draw a line, drawLine(start, end, color):

```
bge.render.drawLine([0,0,0],[100,100,0],[1,1,1])
```

KX_GameObject: useful variables and functions

- **applyForce**(force, local=False): apply a linear force local or global on the object. The force has the form [lx,ly,lz]
- **applyTorque**(force, local=False): apply an angular force local or global on the object. The force has the form [ax,ay,az]
- **getDistanceTo**(obj): returns the distance between the object and «obj»
- **getVectTo**(obj): returns the vector and the distance from «obj», a value in the form of: (distance, globalVector(3), localVector(3))
- **localPosition**: local position of the object in the form of [x,y,z]
- **parent**: parent parent or None
- **rayCast**(to, from, dist, prop, face, xray, poly): send a ray from an object «from» (or a position [x,y,z]) to another object «to» (or a position [x,y,z]) with a distance max «dist» by filtering with the property «prop». If «xray» = 1 then the mode «X-ray» is activated (get through the objects which no correspond to the filter). Returns the first object corresponding, the contact point and:
  - the normal to this contact point if «face»=1
  - the normal pointing at the object center if «face»=0
  - polygon if «poly» = 1
- **rayCastTo**(obj, dist, prop): send a ray to the «obj» center, with distance max «dist» by filtering on the property «prop» and returns the first object or None.
- **rotate_axis**(axis, angle): do a rotation relative to the axis ('X', 'Y', 'Z') with radians «angle»
- **scene**: Object scene
- **worldPosition**: global position of the object in the form of [x,y,z]

Create a thread or a process in background

2 modules can be used to create an action in background:

- the module «**threading**» to launch a thread
- The module «**multiprocessing**» to launch a process

A thread shares a memory space with the program that has launched it.

A process launches another program, clone of the first (fork) and with the same variables, but in another memory space.

After creation, the variables are not synchronized yet between the principal program and the generated process.

The module «multiprocessing» has functions to create a shared memory or to use some «pipes» (communication canal). The module «multiprocessing» create new Blender instances (using lot of memory) and is more difficult to use.

The use of several threads don't help you save time (even if there are several processors) because BGE is not «multithread». For more information, consult the GIL documentation (Global Interpreter Lock).

When we create a thread with Blender, it's not executed in parallel of Blender, because it's active only during the time given to Python **scripts**. It's executed in parallel of other Python scripts. If no python controller is biased, the thread will be frozen until any controller python is activated, and only during the run time of this script. So, the use of Thread is limited. To execute a **script in parallel of Blender, use the process**.

The more difficult point to work in parallel, is the **concurrent access to resources.** A global variable can be modified at the same time by 2 threads creating unexpected effects. Verify that the data is not blocked and if necessary block the access to the data (lock), modify it, then release it. There can be «deadlocks» if the program is not entirely secured. The **semaphores** are used to do that and are managed by the module «threading». **The rule is: don't modify any BGE elements (GameObjects) in a Thread:** to change an object position, use a global variable for the position and with a controller, copy the content of this variable in the corresponding object. We don't have all the functions to manage the competing access between the BGE and the thread executed in parallel, so, don't create this situation.

Simple example of thread:

```python
import threading
from time import sleep

def task(i):
   for n in range(0,i):
      print ("Hello ",n)
      sleep(1)

thread = threading.Thread(target=task,args=(10,))
thread.start()
```

Test this script in a controller (with an «Always» sensor, but used only once) to verify that the thread is frozen until BGE stop.

Illustration 216: If you want more information on Python programming: https://www.python.org/doc/

SHEET #8: GLSL SHADERS

Created by **Pixar** for its own video animations, shaders appear in video games and are now inescapable. They allow to **program directly the graphic card contrary to Blender**.

The graphic card processor (GPU) can't be programed in assembler. It's a high level language: the GLSL, linked to OpenGL, the only shader language supported by Blender. This language has commons points with the C: they have a syntax almost identical.

There are 3 types of shaders:
- A **vertex shader** is executed **for each vertex**. The vertex processing involves applying it some matrix transformations to obtain the data for the definitive vertex.
- A **fragment shader** (or **pixel shader**) is executed **for each pixel draw**. The fragment shader receives interpolated data of color and other attributes processed in the vertex shader.
- A **geometry shader** allows to modify each polygon geometry and create some new polygons. They are executed between the vertex shader and the fragment shader.

With BGE, we can execute directly a fragment shader thanks to the actuator brick **Filter2D** (**recipe VII.9**). We can put some **«variables» to these scripts automatically through an object «Property»**.

For example, to put a value with type Float:
- add to the object launching the script a property with «float» type, for example «x».
- in the script, add a declaration line: uniform float x;

The **recipe VII.21** use this process. The property with «Timer» type can often help you.

To use a vertex shader, use a python script that compile the shaders before executing them.

Example:

```python
import bge
cont = bge.logic.getCurrentController()
VertexShader = """
  void main(){
    gl_Position = gl_ModelViewProjectionMatrix * gl_Vertex;
  }
"""
FragmentShader = """
  void main() {
    gl_FragColor = vec4(1.0, 0.0, 0.0, 1.0);
  }
"""
mesh = cont.owner.meshes[0]
for mat in mesh.materials:
  shader = mat.getShader()
  if shader != None:
    if not shader.isValid():
      shader.setSource(VertexShader, FragmentShader, 1)
```

The **language used is python and not GLSL.** The script GLSL is contained into 2 strings: VertexShader and FragmentShader. These shaders are compiled and executed by the python script including the methods **getShader**() and **setSource**().

This vertex shader don't do anything itself: it recovers only the coordinates (x,y,z) used by Blender.

We could specify:

```
gl_Position = gl_ModelViewProjectionMatrix *
        (vec4(1.0, 0.1, 1.0, 1.0)* gl_Vertex);
```

In this case, all the coordinates are multiplied by 0.1. It's a scale operation.

The fragment shader doesn't use the color information available, it only transform it into an opaque red: vec4(red,green,blue,opacity).

To exploit this shader:
1. Go to the «Text» window and create a new file
2. Paste the precedent script (the script, not only the modification)
3. Select 1 of the objects of the scene and go to the «Logic Editor» Window
4. Add an «Always» sensor
5. Add a «Python» controller, select the script. Then, link the sensor with the controller

Geometry Shader

Geometry shaders officially appeared in the versions 10 of DirectX and 3.2 of OpenGL (or OpenGL 1.1 by using the extension EXT_geometry_shader4).
They are used after the Vertex Shaders and before the Fragment Shaders. They receive as input the primitive geometry. They are used for Tesselation (ex: the subdivide «Catmull-clark»b realtime by the GPU), shadow volumes, particles with «Point-Sprite» type (ex: effect «snow»).

The simplest Geometry Shader is:

```
void main(){
  for(int i=0; i<gl_VerticesIn; ++i) {
    gl_Position = gl_PositionIn[i];
    EmitVertex();
  }
}
```

It does nothing. It takes as input the position of each primitive point and returns it without modification.
Now, Blender has not yet setSource() to use a Geometry Shader. Here, we could find a modification project of the Blender source code: http://tinyurl.com/ks9xa3e.

The purpose of this book is not to teach you how to create your own shaders because it's too vast. However, you have now the bases to use shaders written by others and to adapt them for Blender. Some shaders can't work on your computer, according to your graphic card and the driver installed. Shaders are probably the **best source of extensions** to exceed the BGE's limits.

And the BGL?

It's possible to access directly to the OpenGL functions thanks to the module bgl.
Example of script which can be called by a BGE controller and draw directly in OpenGL:

```
import bgl,bge
sce = bge.logic.getCurrentScene()

def TheList():
  bgl.glBegin(bgl.GL_TRIANGLES)
  bgl.glVertex2f(-1,-1)
  bgl.glVertex2f(1,-1)
  bgl.glVertex2f(-1,1)
  bgl.glEnd()

sce.post_draw = [TheList]
```

SHEET #9: HOW TO PUBLISH

A standalone version of the game (executable)

How to create a version of the game to give or to sell, to play it without installing Blender ?

Activate the addon: «User Preferences» Window (`Ctrl`+`Alt`+`U`), «Addon» Tab → «Game Engine» → «Save As Game Engine Runtime»: check to activate.

A new option appears: «info» window, «File» → «Export» → «Save As Game Engine Runtime».

Don't forget to integrate the textures and other useful files in the blend: «info» window, «File» → «External Data» → «**Pack all into blend**».

An **executable** file is generated without the blend file and with several libraries useful for the Game Engine. With Windows, it's a file «exe», with Linux, a file «Elf» and with OSX, a bundle «.app».

The view is automatically the one of the camera, not the modeling mode camera.

It's possible to setup the scene in the «Properties» window, «Scene» panel in the «Game Engine».

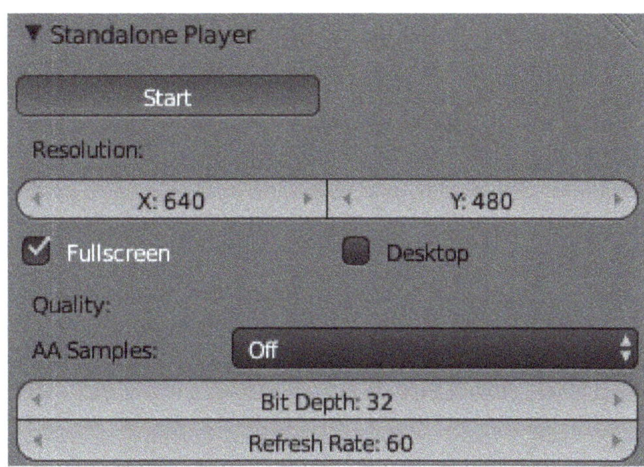

Illustration 217: Standalone player configuration

To publish on the web

It's possible to publish directly on the web thanks to a plugin, Burster, working with the navigators Firefox, Opera, Internet Explorer and Chrome (**Windows and Linux**). The files can be protected (encrypted) and it's possible to obtain a certificate, but you need to buy it.

Install the plugin: http://geta3d.com/

To publish the file, upload it on a website and use the following embedder in the HTML calling the file:

```
<OBJECT classid="CLSID:8318DE8B-B213-426b-B1B6-0A2589859898" width="800"
height="600">
<PARAM name="type" value="application/x-burster"/>
<PARAM name="src" value="yourfile.blend" />
<embed type="application/x-burster" src = "yourfile.blend"
width = "800" height = "600"> </embed>
</OBJECT>
```

We can add the following parameters:
- pluginbg value="#FF2233"- background color
- progressbg value="#4455EF"- background color of the progress bar
- progressfill value="#FBFF00"- color of the bar

Install and use Blend4Web

To install:

1. Download the development kit (SDK) and the plugign for Blender from the offcial Web Site (section Downloads): http://blend4web.com

2. Unpack and install the SDK

3. Unpack and install the plugin in the directory « scripts\addons » of Blender

4. Launch Blender and open the users preferences (Ctrl+Alt+U). Select « Community » and activate « Blend4web » in the category « Import-Export », after specify the installation directory of the SDK of Blend4Web.

5. Click on « Save User Settings ». It's done.

To test the examples:

1. Launch Blender

2. In the « Properties » window, « render » Tab, « Blend4web » panel, click on the button « Start ».

3. 2 new buttons appears: click on « Open SDK ». A navigator window is opened and shows several examples to test.

If your navigator supports WebGL, you have the following message:

Blend4Web SDK Free 15.02

WebGL: supported

Please make sure you are accessing this web page by using a web server. Alternatively, your browser must be set up for loading local resources.

For more info about your WebGL implementation see WebGL Report.

Otherwise, go to http://get.webgl.org and « visit the support site for your browser ».

There are tutorials to learn SDK.

SHEET #10: RESOURCES TO CREATE A GAME

To create a game with Blender, there is **no royalty** to remit to the Blender Foundation. However, if your game encounters success, you can make a gift to the foundation to help it improving this wonderful tool.

The license used by BGE is the GNU Lesser General Public License (**LGPL**).

The LGPL allows to link the program to non LGPL code. It's possible to distribute BGE with the game and to choose the license for the game.

When you use external contents, textures, sounds, you must verify their origin.

Here there's several free licenses (Creative Commons) you can see and choose for your creation:

 **Attribution**: Licensees may copy, distribute, display and perform the work and make derivative works based on it only if they give the author or licensor the credits in the manner specified by these.

 **No commercial use**: Licensees may copy, distribute, display, and perform the work and make derivative works based on it only for non-commercial purposes.

 **Share on equal terms**: Licensees may distribute derivative works only under a license identical to the license that governs the original work. (See also copyleft.)

 **No modification**: Licensees may copy, distribute, display and perform only verbatim copies of the work, not derivative works based on it.

These 4 options can be mixed to create 6 different licenses. To publish your game with one of these licenses, specify it by adding to the Blend file a file «licence.txt» containing this choice.

You can find these licenses on blendswap.com and models for games.

There are other licenses: copyright and another free licenses (Apache, BSD, GNU, Mozilla, etc.).

A marketplace for Blender

If you look for model or other resources for your games, or if you want to sell your creations, you can use the Blender Market, by **CG Cookie**.

The purpose is to create some help for the community, at any level.

Official Web Site: http://blendermarket.com

Illustrations, design arts

- **Has Graphics:** Sprites and textures in the public domain to create 2D games or billboards
  http://hasgraphics.com
- **The blueprints:** characters, vehicles, buildings, etc models.
  http://the-blueprints.com
- **Game Icons:** icons for games, for inventories and different overlays (menu, dialogues, etc.)
  http://game-icons.net

3D models

- **Blend Swap**: one of the best sources, all models are in format BLENDER. Depending on the model license, you can use it and name or not its author.
  www.blendswap.com

- **Yobi3D**: search engine for 3D objects. By key words, format, resolution and license. We can select the format « Blend ».
  Site : www.yobi3d.com

- **The Free 3D Models**: Numerous objects from video games. However, be careful to the licenses if you want to share your creation
  http://tf3dm.com

- **The Model Resource**: Ripped models of consoles, to use for your family games, be careful to the licenses to share it.
  www.models-resource.com

- **Goggle Trimble**: Major databank for 3D objects in the format .skp (archive zip). Be carreful to the licenses
  https://3dwarehouse.sketchup.com/

- **Turbosquid:** 3D model to buy. Several models cost 250$, but a creation by a graphic designer is much more expensive
  www.turbosquid.com

Textures

- **Gtextures**: textures for game creators.
  www.cgtextures.com
- **Texturemate**: more than 3000 textures by type
  www.texturemate.com
- **Game Textures**: A library pro. Monthly price
  http://gametextures.com

Sounds

- **FreeSFX**: more than 450.000 sounds – no rights
  www.freesfx.co.uk
- **FreeSound**: sounds bank. You can search and listen in line before to download the sounds.
  http://freesound.org
- **Sound Library**: more than 22 Go of free sounds

www.stephanschutze.com/sound-library.html
- **The Sound Bible Encyclopedia**: public domain sounds
  www.pdsounds.org
- **Sample Swap**: Approximately 10To of sounds and musics, several free. For 40$, it's possible to download all the sounds and musics or to receive a CD.
  http://sampleswap.org

Musics

- **Jewel Beat**: More than 4000 musics and sounds effects, free

  jewelbeat.com/free
- **CCMixter**: musics for films and video games

  http://dig.ccmixter.org/#/free
- **IndieGameMusic:** musics made for video games. Several are free, other to buy.

  www.indiegamemusic.com
- **Free Music Archive:** Free musics and songs, by genre
  http://freemusicarchive.org
- **Jamendo**: Songs, musics,
  Site: www.jamendo.com/fr
- **Incompetech**:

  http://incompetech.com

To train

- **Tutorials For Blender 3D:** site with numerous tutorials for BGE. The tutorials use some screen shot with ex versions of blender, but it's possible to navigate
  www.tutorialsforblender3d.com
- **Blender Art Mag (BAM)**: Blender webzine. Free with a good level

  http://blenderart.org

Other sites:

- **OpenGameArt:** you find all that you want to create a game.

  http://opengameart.org
- **Pixel Prospector:** resources for game creation.
  www.pixelprospector.com/indie-resources

3D models RIP

We can interrogate the memory of 3D graphic cards in running to recover objects, textures and shaders, during the game.

The software «3D Ripper DX» works with DirectX 6.x, 8.x and 9.x applications. OpenGL, and other versions of DirectX are not supported.
www.deep-shadows.com/hax/3DRipperDX.htm

For OpenGL, there's «OpenGL Extractor», but its recovers only the geometry. There are other tools like HijackGL or OGLe.
http://sourceforge.net/projects/ogle/

IX - INDEX

TO GO FURTHER

There's a resource packs on USB Key - **16Go**.

It contains about **100 game projects** (and source code) using Blender Game Engine, more than **250 3D models** (characters, decors, objects, etc.), approximately **3000 characters animations**, **300 textures**, **300 fonts**, **600 sounds** effects and **musics**, **videos**, useful documents, **magazines**, and all the sources and resources of this book. It's an ideal companion to help you in your video game projects.

For more information:
www.graziel.com

There is also a downloadable version.

Author's blog : www.benicourt.com on video game creation.

To help us to improve this book, you can send your comments at the following address:

Editions Graziel

9, chemin des Barroutiers 81300 Graulhet

FRANCE

Tel: 09 52 05 40 15 / Fax: 09 57 05 40 15
RCS: Castres B 801 370 800

mail: editions@graziel.com

site web: www.graziel.com

This book was written by Grégory Gossellin De Bénicourt. Most of the scripts and illustrations was made by him. You can contact the author at: blender@benicourt.com

Copyright Graziel Press – Legal depot: december 2015
ISBN: 979-10-93846-01-9

9 791093 846019